CW01022743

German Immigrants in Britain during the Nineteenth Century, 1815–1914

German Immigrants in Britain during the Nineteenth Century, 1815–1914

Panikos Panayi

BERG

Oxford • Washington D.C.

First published in 1995 by
Berg Publishers Limited
Editorial offices:
150 Cowley Road, Oxford, OX4 1JJ, UK
13590 Park Center Road, Herndon, VA2201, USA

Library of Congress Cataloging-in-Publication Data
A catalogue record for this book is available from the Library of Congress

British Library Cataloguing in Publication Data
A catalogue record for this book is available from the British Library

ISBN 1 85973 092 2

Printed in the United Kingdom by WBC Bookmanufacturers, Mid-Glamorgan

Contents

List of Tables

List of Abbreviations

BA	*Bundesarchiv*
BLPES	British Library of Political and Economic Science
CAB	Cabinet
HLRO	House of Lords Record Office
HO	Home Office
MEPO	Metropolitan Police Office
PP	Parliamentary Papers
PRO	Public Record Office
WO	War Office

Acknowledgements

I would like first to express my gratitude to the organisations which provided funding for this project. I am deeply grateful to the Alexander von Humboldt Foundation, which granted me a one-year award which allowed me to complete the German research for the project, as well as providing me with teaching-free time to complete the project in peace. I am also indebted to De Montfort University for allowing me to take up the award and for a grant which helped with the publication of this book. Financial assistance was also provided by the Twenty-Seven Foundation and the Department of History at the University of Keele, where I held a temporary post in 1989–90, both of which provided funding for research in England.

Of libraries and librarians I would particularly like to thank the inter-library loan staff at De Montfort University and the University of Osnabrück who provided me with numerous sources. I am also grateful to Chris Lloyd of Tower Hamlets Local History Collection and Howard Bloch, who looks after Newham's Local History Archive, both of whom shared their knowledge of East London sources with me.

Of individuals, I am especially grateful to Klaus Bade, who accepted me as a Humboldt Fellow at his *Institut für Migrationsforschung und Interkulturelle Studien* (IMIS) at the University of Osnabrück, and offered me facilities and much encouragement as well as reading through my entire manuscript. Also at Osnabrück, Renate Vollmer and Dieter Steinert helped my project, while Patrick Wuster and his AISEC colleagues in the University assisted by speaking to me about subjects other than Germans in nineteenth-century Britain. I would also like to mention Peter Marschalck, who looked at the second chapter of this study as well as offering much hospitality during my time in Bremen. Of individuals in England who helped in various ways, I would like to mention Samantha Carty, Kate Nicholls, Tony Kushner and Colin Holmes. Lucio Sponza, whose book on Italians in nineteenth-century Britain acted as something of a model for the present study, offered helpful comments for the improvement of the book. I am also very grateful to my family, especially my sister Roda who offered much moral support, and my father who provided me with everything I needed from England.

Introduction

In the classic statement on immigration history, Oscar Handlin wrote in 1951, 'Once I thought to write a history of the immigrants in America. Then I discovered that the immigrants *were* American history.'[1] Because of the truth of this statement, the study of race, immigrants and minorities has since the 1950s formed a core area of historical scholarship in the USA, although we should not deny that the study of immigrants had begun before Handlin, especially under the influence of Marcus Lee Hansen.[2] In the postwar period, apart from the regular appearance of histories of immigration to the USA,[3] historians have also passed through a series of methodological stages in the study of immigrants and minorities.[4] A number of books about the history of individual national and racial groupings within the country as a whole or even within individual cities have been published.[5]

If we turn to Europe, the study of immigration and minorities compares pitifully. In Germany, for instance, the study of non-Jewish groups has increased in the past two decades, under the influence

1. Oscar Handlin, *The Uprooted: The Epic History of the Great Migrations that Made the American People*, 2nd edn, London, 1979, p. 3.

2 See for instance Hansen's *The Atlantic Migration, 1607–1860*, Cambridge, Massachusetts, 1940; 'Immigration as a Field for Historical Research', *American Historical Review*, vol. 32, 1927, pp. 500–18; and *The Immigrant in American History*, Cambridge, Massachusetts, 1940.

3. See for instance Maldwyn Jones, *American Immigration*, Chicago, 1960; Leonard Dinnerstein, Roger L. Nichols, and David M. Reimers, *Natives and Strangers: Blacks, Indians, and Immigrants in America*, New York, 1979; and, most recently, Roger Daniels, *Coming to America: A History of Immigration and Ethnicity in American Life*, New York, 1990.

4. The methodological changes in American immigration history are well summarised by Frederick C. Luebke, 'Turnerism, Social History, and the Historiography of European Ethnic Groups in the United States', in Luebke, *Germans in the New World: Essays in the History of Immigration*, Urbana and Chicago, 1990, pp. 138–56.

5. For studies on Germans alone see for example Luebke, *Bonds of Loyalty: German Americans and World War I*, De Kalb, Illinois, 1974; Stanley Nadel, *Little Germany: Ethnicity, Religion, and Class in New York City, 1845–80*, Urbana and Chicago, 1990; Kathleen Neils Conzen, *Immigrant Milwaukee, 1836–1860: Accommodation and Community in a Frontier City*, London, 1976; and Walter D. Kamphoefner, *The Westfalians: From Germany to Missouri*, Princeton, 1987.

Introduction

especially of Klaus J. Bade,[6] but also of several other scholars including Ulrich Herbert[7] and Christoph Klessmann.[8] Nevertheless, it will take decades before the study of immigration in Germany can approach its equivalent in the USA, primarily because of the political refusal to recognise the country as one of immigration until very recently. This is despite the constant movement of peoples into Germany during its history.[9]

In Britain the study of minorities has, particularly during the last two decades, begun to move towards the centre of historical study, although it has a long way to go before it reaches that point and perhaps never will. There are at least two reasons for this. First, immigration has not played the fundamental role in the development of Britain during the nineteenth and twentieth centuries which it has in the USA and other countries which were built in a large part on the arrival of peoples from other parts of the world. British industrial development utilised its own growing population rather than, as in the case of the USA, the population of other countries; Britain has remained a country of emigration during the last two centuries.[10]

Nevertheless, one cannot deny the importance of immigration in the history of Britain. While the history of Britain may not consist of the history of immigration, newcomers have played an important part in the development of the country. During the nineteenth century the Irish and east European influxes changed the face of many British cities, while the entry of middle-class Germans, especially of Jewish origin, played a significant role in the development of specific industries. In the postwar period, immigrants have changed the nature of Britain in a way in which perhaps no other development in postwar British history has done.

Industry, eating habits and sport are just three areas in which newcomers have transformed Britain. Cities such as London, Leicester and Bradford depend fundamentally upon immigrant entrepreneurship

6. The most recent major study he has produced in this area is the collection of essays entitled *Deutsche im Ausland: Fremde in Deutschland: Migration in Geschichte und Gegenwart*, Munich, 1992.
7. Ulrich Herbert, *A History of Foreign Labour in Germany, 1880–1980: Seasonal Workers/Forced Labourers/Guest Workers*, Ann Arbor, 1990.
8. See, for instance, 'Long-Distance Migration, Integration and Segregation of an Ethnic Minority in Industrial Germany: The Case of the "Ruhr Poles"', in Klaus J. Bade (ed.), *Population, Labour and Migration in 19th- and 20th-Century Germany*, Leamington Spa, 1987, pp. 101–14.
9. This is tackled in Klaus J. Bade, *Vom Auswanderungsland zum Einwanderungsland? Deutschland 1880–1980*, Berlin, 1983.
10. Colin Holmes, *John Bull's Island: Immigration and British Society, 1871–1971*, London, 1988.

Introduction

and immigrant labour. Every British high street has several Indian restaurants. The English football team and, more especially, the British athletics team, depend on their black contingents. Yet, amazingly, one of the most recent histories of postwar Britain has devoted no more than a few pages to minorities within the country.[11] Tony Kushner and Kenneth Lunn have explained this state of affairs by suggesting that it represents 'a measure of the scope and tenacity of British xenophobia'.[12]

In addition we can also give a third reason for the lack of study of immigration history, the ethnic composition of the historical profession in Britain, which is overwhelmingly English. The only minorities which have made any impact consist of Jews and, less so, the Irish. It is unfortunate but true that a significant percentage of scholars of minorities themselves originate from an ethnic background[13] and it is doubtful if the study of immigration will reach centre stage in British historical studies until people of Caribbean, Asian and other Commonwealth origins begin to secure history posts in British universities.

Nevertheless, we should view developments in the study of the history of immigration within Britain with optimism. If we turn our attention to the pre-1945 period, we can see that several groups have received attention, including especially the Irish[14] but also late nineteenth-century eastern European Jewish immigrants,[15] blacks and Asians[16] and, more recently, Germans and Italians.[17] In addition,

11. Kenneth O. Morgan, *The People's Peace*, Oxford, 1990, contains 516 pages of analysis and script, yet no more than 6 of these concern race. Out of a select bibliography of over 250 books not a single one concerns immigration.
    12. Tony Kushner and Kenneth Lunn, 'Editors' Introduction', in Kushner and Lunn (eds.), *The Politics of Marginality: Race, the Radical Right and Minorities in Twentieth Century Britain*, London, 1990.
    13. The study of Jewish history has, with some notable exceptions including Colin Holmes and Kenneth Lunn, been dominated by Jewish scholars, from Cecil Roth through to V. D. Lipman and, most recently, Geoffrey Alderman, Tony Kushner, David Cesarani and Bryan Cheyette.
    14. See, for instance, J. A. Jackson, *The Irish in Britain*, London, 1963; L. H. Lees, *Exiles of Erin: Irish Immigrants in Victorian London*, Manchester, 1979.
    15. Bernard Gainer, The Alien Invasion, London, 1972; Lloyd P. Gartner, *The Jewish Immigrant in England 1870–1914*, London, 1960; John A. Garrard, *The English and Immigration 1880–1910*, London, 1971.
    16. Peter Fryer, *Staying Power: The History of Black People in Britain*, London, 1984; Rosina Visram, *Ayahs, Lascars and Princes: Indians in Britain 1700–1947*, London, 1986. James Walvin has written several books on black people in Britain, including *Black and White: The Negro in English Society 1555–1945*, London, 1973.
    17. For Italians see Lucio Sponza, *Italian Immigrants in Nineteenth Century Britain: Realities and Images*, Leicester, 1988; Terri Colpi, *The Italian Factor: The Italian Community in Great Britain*, Edinburgh, 1991. For Germans see Rosemary Ashton, *Little Germany: Exile and Asylum in Victorian England*, Oxford, 1986; and Panikos Panayi, *The Enemy in Our Midst: Germans in Britain during the First World War*, Oxford, 1991.

Introduction

several books and collections of essays have appeared which deal with the history of minorities.

However, several major gaps exist. In the first place there has been a lack of attention focused upon the process and mechanics of immigration. There are a few exceptions in this context, notably on the Irish movement to Britain during the mid-nineteenth century.[18] Second, the history of ethnicity, of the lives of the immigrants, their social institutions, churches and clubs, has tended to be ignored, although this does not represent as large a gap as that concerning the immigration process. We can point for instance to the work of Lees on the Irish, Gartner on the Jews, and Berghahn on German Jewish immigrants.[19] Much work has also focused upon the study of political exiles in Britain, despite their relatively small numbers.[20]

The main theme in the history of minorities in Britain has concentrated upon newcomers as victims. This applies especially to the work of Colin Holmes,[21] but we can further point to the large numbers of books on, for instance, the internment episode during the Second World War.[22] My own previous work has also focused upon immigrants as victims. [23] We must continue to welcome the appearance of further similar studies because they form part of a re-interpretation of British history which questions Britain's liberal traditions, which one scholar has described as a process of historiographical revision.[24] But while every immigrant grouping in British history has faced hostility, the history of immigrant groups is more complex than simply the negative reactions of British society towards them. In some cases

18. See for instance Brenda Collins, 'Proto-industrialization and Pre-famine Emigration', *Social History*, vol. 7, 1982, pp. 127–46; and the opening chapters of Lees, *Exiles of Erin*.

19. Lees, *Exiles of Erin*, pp. 182–241; Gartner, *Jewish Immigrant*; Marion Berghahn, *Continental Britons: German-Jewish Refugees from Nazi Germany*, Oxford, 1988.

20. Most notably Ashton, *Little Germany*; Bernard Porter, *The Refugee Question in Mid-Victorian Politics*, Cambridge, 1979; Hermia Oliver, *The International Anarchist Movement in Late Victorian London*, London, 1983; and William J. Fishman, *East End Jewish Radicals*, London, 1975.

21. See his *Anti-Semitism in British Society 1876–1939*, London, 1979, and *A Tolerant Country? Immigrants, Refugees and Minorities in Britain*, London, 1991.

22. Tony Kushner, *The Persistence of Prejudice: Anti-Semitism in British Society during the Second World War*, Manchester, 1989; Francois Lafitte, *The Internment of Aliens*, 2nd edn, London, 1988; Peter and Leni Gillman, *'Collar the Lot': How Britain Interned and Expelled Its Wartime Refugees*, London, 1980; David Cesarani and Tony Kushner (eds), *The Internment of Aliens in Twentieth Century Britain*, London, 1993.

23. See Panayi, *Enemy*; and Panayi (ed.), *Racial Violence in Britain, 1840–1950*, Leicester, 1993.

24. Frederick M. Schweitzer, reviewing Kushner's *Persistence of Prejudice*, *American Historical Review*, vol. 96, 1991, p. 521.

Introduction

feelings towards newcomers have had positive manifestations, as the present study recognises, although it admits that various forms of hostility have also existed. Nevertheless, minorities can develop their own institutions despite the hostile reactions of British society, as this volume demonstrates.

A final gap in the history of immigrants within Britain is the lack of studies which trace the development of communitiesä on a national scale over any period of time. With regard to the history of Jews in Britain, impressive studies of the late nineteenth century have appeared, as well as that of Manchester Jewry by Bill Williams.[25] Yet no nationwide study of the nineteenth and twentieth centuries appeared until 1992, when Geoffrey Alderman's *Modern British Jewry* was published. Before that, the best work available was V. D. Lipman's unacademic *History of the Jews in Britain Since 1858*,[26] and a collection of essays edited by David Cesarani.[27] We can make similar comments about the history of the Irish in Britain. Here there have been numerous metropolitan studies over varying periods of time,[28] but until the appearance of Graham Davis's superficial study, the closest to a national history was the two outstanding volumes edited by Roger Swift and Sheridan Gilley. Only Jackson's dated study previously filled this gap.[29]

The number of more recent nationwide histories remains few, except in the history of black and Asian peoples where Fryer, Walvin and Visram have taken a national and wider chronological perspective. In the history of pre-1945 European minorities, one immigrant grouping which has received its fair share of national attention over any length of time is the Italians, where two books by Terri Colpi and Lucio Sponza have been published.

The present study offers a history of the German community in Britain as a whole during the years 1815–1914, a period which we might describe as the 'long nineteenth century' from the end of the

25. Bill Williams, *The Making of Manchester Jewry 1740–1875*, Manchester, 1985 reprint.
26. Geoffrey Alderman, *Modern British Jewry*, Oxford, 1992; V. D. Lipman, *A History of the Jews in Britain Since 1858*, Leicester, 1990.
27. David Cesarani, (ed.), *The Making of Modern Anglo-Jewry*, Oxford, 1990.
28. See for instance W. J. Lowe, *The Irish in Mid-Victorian Lancashire*, New York, 1989; Frances Finnegan, *Poverty and Prejudice: A Study of Irish Immigrants in York, 1840–1875*, Cork, 1982; Frank Neal, *Sectarian Violence: The Liverpool Experience 1819–1914*, Manchester, 1988; Lees, *Exiles of Erin*.
29. Graham Davis, *The Irish in Britain, 1815–1914*, Dublin, 1991; Roger Swift and Sheridan Gilley (eds), *The Irish in the Victorian City*, London, 1985; and *The Irish in Britain 1815–1939*, London, 1989.

Napoleonic Wars until the beginning of the First World War. However, because of the availability of evidence, it mainly focuses upon the period 1851–1914. The historiography of Germans in Britain begins essentially with Karl Heinrich Schaible's *Geschichte der Deutschen in England*, published in 1885,[30] which still represents the most comprehensive history of Germans in Britain before the nineteenth-century. The works of the next two authors to approach the subject of Germans in Britain, Ian Colvin[31] and C. R. Hennings,[32] are unreliable because in both cases the First World War colours the perspectives of the authors. Only from the 1970s has the history of Germans in Britain begun to attract significant amounts of attention, focusing primarily upon refugees from Nazism but also, in more recent years, concentrating on the nineteenth and early twentieth centuries.[33]

The nature of this study is that of an introductory history, which is all that can be undertaken given the lack of prior research on German immigrants in nineteenth-century Britain. It would be impossible to produce a purely primary source-based study of an immigrant community over such a long time scale without the help of numerous research assistants. The present book, with its mixture of primary and secondary sources, therefore resembles some of the major histories of communities over a lengthy period of time including those by Alderman on Anglo-Jewry, Lees on the Irish and Sponza on the nineteenth-century Italians.

As the bibliography indicates, the book uses virtually all of the secondary material available on Germans in nineteenth-century Britain. In addition, it utilises a wide range of primary material in archives in both Britain and Germany. Its major primary sources consist of the papers of German cultural and religious organisations, used in Chapter 3 and, more especially, Chapter 4. The book also utilises a wide range of contemporary printed material in both German and English. German newspapers are simply sampled, given the impracticability of going through print runs of more than forty years as well as the fact that sufficient information can also be obtained from other sources.

The present volume divides in the following way. The opening chapter, on 'The Pre-Nineteenth Century Background', traces the

30. Karl Heinrich Schaible, *Geschichte der Deutschen in England*, Strasbourg, 1885.
31. Ian Colvin, *The Germans in England 1066–1598*, London, 1915.
32. C. R. Hennings, *Deutsche in England*, Stuttgart, 1923.
33. For refugees from Nazism see Gerhard Hirschfeld (ed.), *Exile in Great Britain: Refugees from Hitler's Germany*, Leamington Spa, 1984. See also the recent outstanding collection of essays, W. E. Mosse et al. (eds), *Second Chance: Two Centuries of German-speaking Jews in the United Kingdom*, Tübingen, 1991.

immigration of Germans to Britain before 1815. These pre-1815 settlers consisted of Dark Age Anglo-Saxons, the medieval Hansa merchants, religious refugees and economic immigrants in the early modern period, and a larger influx in the eighteenth-century. The chapter argues that the growth of immigration in the nineteenth century owed much to the migration of the pre-1815 settlers, especially in the development of ethnic institutions and particularly churches, which began to be established from the end of the seventeenth-century. We can also point to the fact that much of the nineteenth-century influx has its origins in the period before 1815, including the movement of refugees, businessmen, trans-migrants and more straightforward immigrants.

The second chapter, 'German Migration to Britain during the Nineteenth Century', attempts to establish the reasons why Germans made their way to Britain during the course of the nineteenth century so that, until 1891, they formed the largest immigrant group within England and Wales after the Irish. Any attempt to explain the reasons for migration must be complex and requires a theoretical basis. This chapter deals with push, enabling, and pull factors in turn, and also tackles the concepts of underlying, short-term and personal reasons for movement. It further recognises economic, political, religious and even cultural migration. Thus we can point to the underlying economic push factors, rooted in the large population growth within nineteenth-century Germany but also connected with other factors such as changing patterns of land ownership. We can also establish underlying pull factors, which focus upon the greater industrial development of Britain. This advanced economic growth pulled thousands of German immigrants into the country, but could not bring in the millions which the much larger-scale industrial development of the USA could do; although in many cases German immigrants moved to North America with a dream of owning a small family farm, a dream which often, however, never became reality. Short-term factors also proved fundamental in movement, such as harvest failures and booms in the American economy, while personal factors, such as the presence of relatives already within England led to a process of chain migration. The chapter argues that those people who made their way to England came from the same areas as those who went to the USA, as is revealed by correlating the places of birth of Germans within Britain with emigration statistics of individual German states.

At this stage an important factor is introduced into the argument, which played a major role in the development of all immigrant

Introduction

groupings within nineteenth-century Britain. Here we refer to enabling factors, the growth of shipping routes from the continent to the USA which passed through Britain. A wide range of contemporary evidence suggests that both the German and Jewish communities in nineteenth-century Britain developed through transmigrants who decided to remain within Britain.

At the same time, we have to recognise different strands of economic immigrants, a subject which is also tackled in Chapter 3. Immigrants, transmigrants and middle-class businessmen, as well as people who intended to make their way to Britain for a short period of time in order to improve their financial position or skills, represent different strands of movement fairly independent of each other.

But in addition to economic immigrants there also existed refugees, a distinct if small component in nineteenth-century communities in British cities. Here again we have to consider underlying and short-term push and pull factors. In the former case we need to point to the traditions of intolerance within German society and Britain's continental reputation as a liberal state during the course of the nineteenth century. However, virtually all refugees who moved to Britain did so as a consequence of short-term political crises in the 1830s, late 1840s and late 1870s. Chapter 2 also asks whether religious persecution had a role to play in the movement of Germans, especially Jews, to nineteenth-century Britain, but suggests this was of minimal importance. In short, the chapter suggests that German migration to Britain was a complex process which can only be understood if we recognise the different levels of causation and the different types of migration involved.

Chapter 3, on 'Residential, Age and Gender, and Occupational Distribution', devotes most of its attention to the first and last aspects of the title. In terms of distribution, the most obvious point involved the concentration of the Germans upon London, which meant that about fifty per cent of all German immigrants in nineteenth-century Britain lived within the capital. Outside London, while settlements which could sustain a social life did develop, they remained miniscule by the standards of immigrant communities in North American cities. Within London major areas of settlement developed, focusing upon the East End throughout the period 1815–1914, the West End towards the end of the nineteenth century and, to a lesser extent, Soho and suburban south-west London. Settlement patterns, like much else about Germans in Victorian and Edwardian Britain, reveal a division along class lines.

Introduction

Age and gender distribution display a lack of family migration and a relative over-representation of males, in comparison with more general migration from Germany to the USA. Occupational patterns again demonstrate the class divisions within German immigrant society in London. In the first place there was an underclass, which consisted of thieves, swindlers, the homeless, pimps and prostitutes. Above this group there existed the German poor and working classes; these consisted of those who had difficulty in making a living, working in industries in which they faced serious exploitation, usually from their own countrymen, in areas such as sugar-baking and tailoring. Still further up the social scale we can identify a petty bourgeoisie, made up of shopkeepers in the baking, hairdressing and meat trades; these also involved the exploitation of German labour. The petty bourgeoisie also includes clerks who had an impact on the British labour market in this area, despite their small numbers. However, clerks can also fit into the group of more solidly middle-class German occupations within Britain, which also includes orchestral musicians, teachers, governesses, university lecturers as well as businessmen, who in many cases established large-scale businesses.

The fourth chapter, on 'Ethnic Organisations', fundamentally confirms the different strands within German immigrant life in nineteenth-century Britain. Throughout Chapter 4 the concept of ethnicity is used, and this needs some definition here. Abner Cohen has pointed out that the term has an enormous variety of meanings according to 'the discipline, field experience, and interest of the investigators'.[34] The best recent definition for our purposes comes from a study of Greek Cypriots in postwar Britain by Floya Anthias, who recognises that 'ethnic groups are premised on the development of solidary bonds and consciousness and an imaginary origin (often called a myth of origin) which may be located in diverse ways, historically, culturally or territorially.' Anthias also recognises the existence of class divisions within ethnic groups.[35] The main purpose of Chapter 4 is to demonstrate one of the fundamental ways in which ethnicity, 'the myth of origin', is maintained through the development of official and unofficial institutions amongst the Germans in nineteenth-century Britain.

34. Abner Cohen, 'The Lessons of Ethnicity', in Cohen (ed.), *Urban Ethnicity*, London, 1974, p. ix.
35. Floya Anthias, *Ethnicity, Class, Gender and Migration: Greek Cypriots in Britain*, Aldershot, 1992, pp. 11–12.

These bodies revolved around religion, philanthropy, culture and politics. In religion, the most important gelling agent amongst the Germans in Britain, we can identify Lutherans and Evangelicals, Catholics and Jews, in that order of numerical importance. Virtually every British city with any German population of any size had a Protestant Church, which in most cases had attached to it a series of educational and philanthropic bodies. Within London itself, Protestant places of worship existed in every significant area of settlement. In addition the capital also had a German Catholic congregation, the only one which existed within the country. The only Jewish congregations established by German immigrants were in Bradford and Dundee; both were much smaller than the London Catholic congregation.

Cultural activities developed fundamentally along class lines, as revealed by the activities of the mainly middle class *Vereine*, about which considerable information has survived. Significantly, these also counted English members, indicating connections between middle-class British and German society; a picture confirmed by the financing of German church buildings in the nineteenth century, which came from German, Anglo-German and purely British sources.

On political and trade union lines, the German immigrants divided even further. In the case of the former they firstly formed themselves into groupings within the same occupation, although in hairdressing and waiting several groups existed at any one time. In political terms, the refugees divided in numerous ways. In the first place there existed liberal and more left-wing groupings, which in the case of the latter consisted of Communists in the mid-nineteenth century and anarchists from the 1870s, reflecting the political affiliations of the refugees who made their way to Britain during these two periods.

Chapters 3 and 4 taken together present one of the book's fundamental arguments; any concept of a single-strand German ethnicity does not hold together because the Germans were divided in numerous ways, above all along class lines. A poor East End immigrant would have virtually no contact and little in common with a wealthier German who lived in Sydenham. They worshipped in their own churches, nearly all of which had their own priests, and worked in their completely different occupations. The only thing they had in common lay in their nationality, which could not keep them together in nineteenth-century industrial Britain. One of the few ways in which Germans of different classes had any contact, although not on a personal basis, lay in the German philanthropic bodies which developed; but these simply confirmed rather than broke down class barriers, with richer Germans giving money to support their poorer countrymen whom they did not see. This does not prove enough to represent a single ethnicity.

Chapter 4 does not deal with the issue of assimilation for several reasons. First, the book as a whole is about first-generation immigrants and their institutions. While assimilation may begin to take place amongst the newcomers themselves, it is usually their children who move into English society. The purpose of Chapter 4 is to demonstrate the extent to which the first-generation newcomers remained German. It is also difficult to find sources for measuring assimilation.

The final chapter, 'British Attitudes Towards Germany, Germans and German Immigrants', argues firstly that until the beginning of twentieth century there existed an underlying positive image of Germany and Germans which focused on the German countryside, German learning and culture, and racial affiliations. These underlying images help to explain the relative lack of hostility towards German communities in nineteenth-century Britain.

However, animosity did exist, although until the Edwardian years it was on a much smaller scale than that directed against the Irish in the mid-nineteenth century and Russian Jews from the 1880s. The varieties of pre-1900 hostility towards Germans were many, but revolved essentially around socio-economic factors, especially competition for jobs. From about 1900 animosity against German immigrants became more widespread, so that there developed what can best be described as Germanophobia, a fear of Germany, Germans and their representatives within Britain, which manifested itself in increased hostility towards German immigrants in printed sources as well as in the introduction of measures to combat the perceived German threat. However, we can only understand the increasingly Germanophobic atmosphere of the Edwardian period if we place it within the perspective of the deteriorating image of Germany within Britain, which had changed from one of admiration for German culture and learning to one where 'Prussian Militarism' became a catch word, and against the background of the increasing German diplomatic, military and imperial strength which began to threaten British interests from the 1890s.

The present study therefore offers an introduction to the history of Germans in nineteenth- and early twentieth-century Britain, covering a wide range of aspects of their lives. It does not follow much of the previous research on immigrants in Britain, which has concentrated upon hostility. Neither does it look simply at ethnicity. Instead, the book represents the first study of all aspects of the life of German immigrants in nineteenth-century Britain. It focuses mainly upon economic newcomers but does not ignore refugees, using all the secondary sources and a wide range of primary material in both Germany and England. It deals with first-generation German newcomers rather than their descendants, which means that it does not fundamentally tackle issues such as assimilation. It provides a starting point for the largest continental grouping in Britain for much of the nineteenth century. The scope for further studies on this minority remains endless, with possible focuses upon each theme described in the individual chapters.

The Pre-Nineteenth Century Background

Although the nineteenth and twentieth centuries have seen migration on
an unprecedented scale[1] and the development of ethnic communities in
every part of the world, movement of peoples has taken place in all periods. Few modern day ethnic communities have developed suddenly,
without an already established base; almost invariably, there has already
been a stream of migration from one country to another. In the case of
modern groups in Britain, for instance, the Cypriot community experienced its main expansion during the late 1950s and early 1960s, but
migration from Cyprus to Britain had begun during the inter-war years.
The origins of black and Asian communities within Britain date back
centuries, rather than decades.[2]

The history of German communities abroad reveals a similar pattern,
where growth during the nineteenth century had a basis in longer-term
migration. North America provides the best example, where the mass
movement of the years after 1800, involving over five million people,
had its origins in the seventeenth century and in a combination of religious, political and economic factors, and continued to grow during the
1700s so that by the end of the eighteenth century as many as 200,000
Germans may have already made their way to America.[3]

Such traditional migration patterns prove important as they can
establish migratory routes and develop transport networks, as well as
providing an established ethnic group to receive a large influx of newcomers. While this traditional grouping may be small, it provides the
roots from which a large community can develop. An example is the
case of Jewish migration to Britain where 'the overall effect of the

1. A recent study, Dudley Baines, *Emigration from Europe 1815–1930*, London,
1991, pp. 1–3, states that over fifty million people left Europe from 1815–1930.
2. For Cypriots see Robin Oakley, *Changing Patterns of Distribution of Cypriot
Settlement*, Coventry, 1987. The pre-War history of Black and Asian groups in Britain can
be traced in Peter Fryer, *Staying Power: The History of Black People in Britain*, London,
1984, and Rosina Visram, *Ayahs, Lascars and Princes: Indians in Britain 1700–1947*,
London, 1986.
3. Peter Marschalck, *Deutsche Überseewanderung im 19. Jahrhundert*, Stuttgart,
1973, pp. 30–51; Wolfgang Köllmann and Peter Marschalk, 'German Emigration to the
United States', *Perspectives in American History*, vol. 7, 1973, pp. 509–16.

migrations' of the late nineteenth century 'was to consolidate Jewish life in the growing urban centres' of Britain.[4]

Similarly the German communities in Britain during the nineteenth century did not appear out of nowhere but expanded on previous settlements which involved the economic participation of German migrants in particular activities and the establishment of churches in many parts of Britain, especially London. While this process began to take shape during the late seventeenth and eighteenth centuries, its origins lay as far back as the Roman period if not before. In fact, we can trace four flexible and overlapping periods in the 'pre-history' of the Germans in Britain which will form the focus of this chapter. First, there were early movements before the year 1000, which receive only passing attention. Second, there was the migration of tradesmen and craftsmen during the High and Late Middle Ages. Third, there were religious refugees, travellers, scholars and economic newcomers who arrived in the period 1500–1700. Fourth, there were the economic immigrants and businessmen, Hanoverian court officials and travellers who moved to Britain during the eighteenth century.

The concept of a 'German' before 1871 creates problems because of the lack of existence of a unified German state. In the discussion which follows the term is used widely to cover people who originated within the present geographical boundaries of Germany, as well as to refer to people who spoke German or were otherwise 'culturally' Germans.

Dark Age and Medieval Settlers

'The first German had actually trod on North American soil...in the exploratory voyage of the Viking Lief in AD 1000.'[5] An attempt to establish when the first German set foot in England would prove impossible because, as one source points out, 'From its earliest history, Britain has been inhabited by sporadic settlements of Germanic peoples.' This author refers to the ' "Beaker Folk" from the Rhineland' who 'arrived in 1900 to about 1000 BC'.[6]

The most authoritative account of the history of pre-nineteenth-century German migration to Britain claims that Germans already inhabited many parts of the British Isles by the time of the Roman invasion in the

---

4. The quotes are based on Bill Williams, *The Making of Manchester Jewry: 1740–1875*, Manchester, 1985 reprint, pp. 268–9, but this book as a whole provides an excellent example of expansion.

5. Köllmann and Marschalck, 'German Emigration', p. 509.

6. Maureen Neumann, 'An Account of the German Hospital in London from 1845 to 1948', unpublished B.Ed thesis, University of London, 1971, p. 7.

first century BC. He identifies the ·Kauken', from Saxony, who settled
in Ireland, and German-Belgians in southern England. German soldiers
entered the country with the Romans and there exists evidence of their
presence in Scotland from the first century AD. German migration
increased in the last two centuries of the Roman occupation and then
took place on a large scale following the withdrawal of the Romans
between 402 and 420.

During the second half of the fifth century and into the sixth century
Angles and Saxons began to make their way to southern and eastern
England. These came from north Germany and for several centuries
played a role in shaping England. The number of Anglo-Saxons in
England may have reached 50,000–100,000, meaning that they made up
as much as ten per cent of the population.[7]

By the tenth century, when England had become an independent
state, most German visitors to England consisted of people involved in
trade together with their artisans, book-keepers, 'warriors' and sailors.
A 'Corporation of German Merchants', before the Hansa, almost certainly existed on the banks of the Thames during the tenth century.[8]
Merchants became fundamentally important in the history of the
Germans in Britain, especially during the remainder of the Middle Ages
but also even down to the nineteenth century. An explanation for this
probably lies in the geographical proximity of the two nations, which
facilitated both trade and travel.

By the end of the eleventh century, merchants from the north German
port of Bremen had made their way to England and within a hundred
years the number of foreign, especially German, merchants, had
increased on the Thames.[9] The first important German merchant community in England consisted of wine traders from Cologne during the
twelfth century, who by the end of that century had organised themselves into a guild and received trading benefits from Richard I which

7. Lloyd and Jennifer Laing, *Anglo-Saxon England*, London, 1979, pp. 19–43; Gustav
Schönberger, 'Geschichte der Deutschen in England', in Schönberger (ed.), *Festschrift
zum 70. Geburtstag von Freiherrn Bruno von Schröder*, London, 1937, pp. 14–15; F. M.
Stenton, *Anglo-Saxon England*, 2nd edn, Oxford, 1947, pp. 1–31; Karl Heinrich Schaible,
Geschichte der Deutschen in England, Strasbourg, 1885, pp. 1–19.

8. Tony Dyson and John Schofield, 'Saxon London', in Jeremy Haslam (ed.),
Anglo-Saxon Towns in Southern England, Chichester, 1984, p. 302; Schaible, *Geschichte
der Deutschen*, pp. 20–1.

9. Schönberger, 'Geschichte der Deutschen in England', p. 18; Bremer Staatsarchiv,
C. 4 h. 1, Friedrich Preusser, 'Bremer Kaufleute in England'. T. H. Lloyd, *Alien
Merchants in England in the High Middle Ages*, Brighton, 1982, p. 10, points out that merchants from 'Tiel, Bremen and Antwerp had to remain below London Bridge, unless they
were willing to be ruled by the law of the city.' See also Elenora M. Carus-Wilson, 'Die
Hanse in England', in Kölnisches Stadtmuseum (ed.), *Hanse in Europa: Brücke zwischen
den Märkten 12.-17. Jahrhundert*, Cologne, 1973, p. 87.

were confirmed by successive English kings. They could travel throughout the country and trade wherever they wished within it. These benefits also extended to Westfalians.[10]

During the early thirteenth century merchants from the north German coastal ports, initially Lübeck, began to make their way to Britain where they faced hostility from the already established traders from Cologne. 'In August 1238, however, Henry III extended to Lübeck certain rights already enjoyed by some other German merchants,' though 'not as wide as the privileges enjoyed by Cologne'. Hamburg merchants obtained protection in 1252,[11] and: 'In 1266 the merchants from Hamburg, and in the following year those from Lübeck were given the privilege of forming a Hansa of their own on the model of the merchants of Cologne. It is in these two documents that we find for the first time the word "hansa" applied to groups of merchants from north Germany.'[12]

As 'German immigration to England is a theme which has been for a long time linked with the history of the Hansa',[13] we need to pause here and provide some details about it, as the Hansa has been the subject of more research than perhaps any other alien group in High and Late Medieval England[14] and remained an important force until the end of the sixteenth century. We can trace the main contours of its development, providing at the same time details about organisation and settlement.

As we have seen, by the second half of the thirteenth century three different trading organisations of German merchants, from Cologne, Lübeck and Hamburg existed within Britain. These groups eventually joined together in 1281, recognizing that conflicts between the individual groups were proving harmful, and 'it can be said that 1281 saw the

10. Lloyd, *Alien Merchants*, pp. 128–30; Phillipe Dollinger, *The German Hansa*, London, 1970, p. 39; Herman Kellenbenz, 'German Immigrants in England', in Colin Holmes (ed.), *Immigrants and Minorities in British Society*, London, 1978, p. 63; C. R. Hennings, *Deutsche in England*, Stuttgart, 1923, pp. 20–1; Emil Stargardt, *Handbuch der Deutschen in England*, Heilbronn, 1889, p. 1; Arthur Shadwell, 'The German Colony in London', *National Review*, Vol. 26, pp. 798–9; Schaible, *Geschichte der Deutschen*, p. 40; J. W. Archer, 'The Steelyard', *Once A Week*, vol. 5, 1861, p. 52.
11. Lloyd, *Alien Merchants*, pp. 130–1.
12. Dollinger, *German Hansa*, pp. 39–40.
13. Kellenbenz, 'German Immigrants', p. 63.
14. Apart from the sources quoted in notes 9 and 10 see also, for instance, Friedrich Schulze, *Die Hanse und England: Von Eduards III. bis auf Heinrichs VIII. Zeit*, Berlin, 1911, Stuttgart, 1978; E. Dänell, *Die Blütezeit der Deutschen Hanse: Hansische Geschichte von der Zweiten Hälfte des XIV. Jahrhunderts bis zum Letzten Viertel des XV. Jahrhunderts*, 2 Vols, Berlin, 1905–6, 1973; Inge-Maren Peters, *Hansekaufleute als Gläubiger der Englischen Krone (1294–1350)*, Cologne, 1978. All of these sources concern themeselves in depth with political issues.

foundation of the Hanseatic Kontor in London.' It 'lay under the authority of an alderman, elected by the merchants and confirmed in his office by the city.'[15] During the course of the fourteenth century the trading privileges of the Hansa within England expanded and its financial power grew to such an extent that it played a part in political developments, as Edward III became heavily dependent upon its members for loans.[16]

Membership of the Hansa 'must surely have stemmed from citizenship of certain German towns', although disagreement exists as to which ones. T. H. Lloyd lists Cologne, Dortmund, Münster, Soest, Osnabrück, Recklinghausen, Hamburg, Lübeck, Greifswald and Gotland during the early thirteenth century, but suggests that merchants from Rostock, Stralsund, Deventer, Stavesen and Attendom may also have become part of the organisation. For the fifteenth century, Dollinger gives a quite different list which includes Riga, Krakow and Königsberg. All of these towns were in northern Europe, focused upon Germany, and the Hansa was a Germanic trading organisation with interests throughout Europe, London being only one major centre.[17]

In fourteenth-century England, outside London, there also existed 'branches' of the Hansa in other east coast ports. Dollinger lists 'Hanseatic settlements' in Ipswich, Yarmouth, Hull, York and Newcastle, which from the fourteenth century sent delegates to London 'to co-operate in working out a common policy'. Carus-Wilson speaks with more confidence of the existence of provincial centres, providing much detail on their trade, as does Lloyd, who focuses upon Lynn, Hull and Boston in particular. Initially, the provincial centres proved attractive to merchants from the east, from 'Hamburg, Lübeck, and the Prussian towns', but these then also began to concentrate in London, which had originally acted as the focus for trade with the Rhine. The Hanseatic merchants also ventured inland to sell their goods at fairs in Norwich, York, Stanford, Lincoln, Westminster, Canterbury and Winchester, and settled in and traded with Scottish towns such as Dunbar, Glasgow and Aberdeen. The main commodities imported and exported by German

15. Dollinger, *German Hansa*, p. 40.
16. Ibid., pp. 55–8; Schulz, *Hanse in England*, pp. 5–10; Peters, *Hansekaufleute*.
17. Lloyd, *Alien Merchants*, pp. 140–1; Lloyd, *England and the German Hansa 1157–1611: A Study in Their Trade and Commercial Diplomacy*, Cambridge, 1991, pp. 35–6; Dollinger, *German Hansa*, map, p.86, which states that the other three of the 'four great Kontore' lay in Bruges, Bergen and Novogrod. See also Gustav Luntowski, *Dortmunder Kaufleute in England im 13. and 14. Jahrhundert: Ein Quellennachweis*, Dortmund, 1970.

merchants in England and Scotland included wool, cloth, herrings, wine, grain, furs and wax.[18] From the late fourteenth to the end of the sixteenth century the history of the Hansa in Britain involved the gaining and losing of favours depending on the prevailing political and economic conditions. During much of the fifteenth century the Wars of the Roses (1414–72) meant that the Hansa merchants could obtain benefits due to 'the discorded state of the kingdom', although they also faced hostility from native merchants, a situation which existed throughout their time of influence in England.[19] However, under the Tudor dynasty, the Hansa's position in England began to decline until it eventually faced expulsion and the confiscation of its property in London in 1598 (property which was returned in 1605). Queen Elizabeth supported a rival English organisation, the Merchant Adventurers, which had begun to develop from the mid-thirteenth century.[20] We might view the action of Elizabeth as the most potent example of hostility towards Germans in Britain during the years before 1600, and we can draw a link between the hostility of the late medieval period and the end of the nineteenth century when, in both cases, German economic power caused a development in negative feeling.[21]

As well as the merchants of the Hansa, other Germans made their way to Britain during the Middle Ages. In 1436 over 400 Germans swore fealty to the king during a diplomatic crisis after the Duke of Burgundy switched from an alliance with England to one with France. The same crisis and subsequent rise of xenophobia meant that many Germans moved out of the city of London and into Southwark. A list of sixteenth-century 'Alien Members of the Book Trade' consists primarily of people of French and Dutch origin but there are also a number from Germany. Earlier, at the end of the thirteenth century, Richard of Cornwall, the brother of Henry III, imported miners from central Germany to work in tin and copper mines in Cornwall. During the sixteenth century, more German miners and metal-workers entered Britain;

18. Lloyd, *England and the German Hansa*, pp. 82–94; Dollinger, *German Hansa*, pp. 56–7, 105–6, 243–4, 246; Schulz, *Hanse in England*, pp. 11, 13; Peters, *Hansekaufleute*, pp. 99–104; Carus-Wilson, 'Hanse in England', pp. 91, 92, 94, 96, 98–101. For details of the Norfolk 'outpost' see Donovan Purcell, 'Der hansische "Steelyards" in Kings Lynn, Norfolk, England', in Kölnisches Stadtmuseum, *Hanse in Europa*, pp. 109–12.
19. Dollinger, ibid., p. 284; Archer, 'Steelyard', p. 54.
20. Dollinger, ibid., pp. 315–16, 341–3; Georg Syamken, 'Englandfahrer und Merchant Adventurers', *Hamburger-Wirtschafts-Chronik*, vol. 5, 1975, pp. 17–28; W. E. Lingelbach, *The Merchant Adventurers of England: Their Laws and Ordinances with Other Documents* (Philadelphia, 1902), pp. xv–xxxi.
21. Schulz, *Hanse in England*, Dänall, *Blutezeit*, and Lloyd, *England and the German Hansa*, deal substantially with Anglo-Hanseatic relations.

these included Joachim Hochstetter from Augsburg, whom Henry VIII appointed 'principal surveyor and master of all mines in England and Ireland' in 1528. Shortly afterwards more Germans entered the country in order to work at the Mint and to serve as miners, and in 1563 a German mining company was floated. Several hundred Germans moved to Cumberland to mine copper. Further mining experts entered the country including Joachim Gundelfinger, Burchard Kranich and Daniel Hochstetter. Others worth mentioning include craftsmen from Augsburg, Cologne, Innsbruck and Nuremberg involved in the manufacture of armour.[22]

German pilgrims also made their way to England during the Middle Ages to visit the tomb of Thomas à Becket in Canterbury, while soldiers entered the country in the service of either the Hansa or the English monarchy. German students attended English and Scottish universities. The painter Hans Holbein was one of the most famous Germans in early sixteenth-century London, where he lived and worked from 1526–43.[23]

The Sixteenth and Seventeenth Centuries

From the middle of the sixteenth century[24] a new and distinct group of Germans began to enter London, consisting of Protestant refugees from religious persecution fleeing as a result of the changes and instability caused by the Reformation. This group has attracted much attention from previous researchers, and we can devote some attention to them. We can see these German refugees as the first in a stream coming to England, which continued into the first half of the twentieth century.

During the reign of Edward VI (1547–53), foreign Protestant refugees from more than one European country entered England. In 1548 Calvinist services took place in Canterbury, and by 1550 foreign congregations existed in London and other parts of southern England. The largest and most important of the centred on the Austin Friars

22. E. J. Worman, *Alien Members of the Book-Trade during the Tudor Period*, London, 1906; Sylvia L. Thrupp, 'Aliens in and Around London in the Fifteenth Century', in A. E. J. Hollaender and William Kellaway (eds), *Studies in London History Presented to Philip Edward Jones*, London, 1969, pp. 255–6, 259; Schaible, *Geschichte der Deutschen*, p. 35; W. Cunningham, *Alien Immigrants to England*, London, second edition, 1969, pp. 116, 122–3; W. H. G. Armytage, *The German Influence on English Education*, London, 1969, p. 10.
23. Schaible, *Geschichte der Deutschen*, pp. 50–7, 106–8; Hennings, *Deutsche in England*, p. 32; Edgar Stern-Rubarth, 'Ihnen wurde England zur Heimat', *Europa*, vol. 13, 1962, p. 51.
24. Cunningham, *Alien Immigrants*, p. 140, writes that 'In the reign of Henry VIII, religious motives probably co-operated with other influences to cause a stream of immigrants to flow to this country.'

Church in the capital; it received its charter in 1550. Johannes A. Lasco, a Polish nobleman, acted as its superintendent and spiritual leader. As indicated above, the congregation had no specific character, as 'French, Walloon and Flemish people were united by the common faith', together with Germans; however, these groups worshipped separately 'in their own language and according to their own customs', and the Germans even had their own Sunday school. The members of the German congregation consisted of 'Niederdeutschen' from the Netherlands and Westphalia. Karl Heinrich Schaible claims that Germans used another church in London but does not provide its name. Outside London, a German religious community also existed in Norwich.

Following the accession to the throne of Queen Mary in 1553, a Catholic reaction took place forcing foreign Protestants to leave the country together with newly-created English refugees. Important destinations included Emden and, particularly, Frankfurt, where the Protestants re-established their communities. When the Protestant Queen Elizabeth ascended the throne in 1558, many of the refugees returned and again focused on the Austin Friars Church, which now came under the supervision of the Bishop of London as Lasco died in Poland in 1560. The Austin Friars Church subsequently acted as a focus for Germans who found themselves in London, and the congregation became wealthy over time; members contributed £20,000 to a loan for James I in 1617.[25]

We can pause here in order to attempt to establish the number of Germans in Britain up to the mid-sixteenth century. For the medieval period this is difficult, but estimates do exist for various dates between 1500 and 1600. For instance Carl Schöll, writing in 1852, claims that the Austin Friars congregation in the early 1550s counted 3,000 members, while Schaible quotes an Italian resident in London in 1548, Bernadinus Ochinus, who believed that more than 5,000 Germans lived in the capital. C. R. Hennings claims that a return of foreigners during the reign of Elizabeth included 3,838 Germans in London, but a more scholarly study by C. W. Chitty expresses doubts about sixteenth-century estimates, claiming that: 'The local officials of Elizabeth's reign could not have been particularly skilful in compiling such returns, and some may possibly have had a vested interest in exaggerating the number of

---

25. Ibid., pp. 147–8; C. W. Chitty, 'Aliens in England during the Sixteenth Century', *Race*, vol. 8, 1966, p. 139; Schaible, *Geschichte der Deutschen*, pp. 130–8; J. Rieger, 'The British Crown and the German Churches in England', in F. Hildebrandt (ed.), *And Other Pastors of the Flock*, Cambridge, 1942, pp. 101–2; Carl Schöll, *Geschichte der Deutschen Evangelischen Kirchen in England*, Stuttgart, 1852, pp. 1–6; Friedeborg L. Müller, *The History of German Lutheran Congregations in England, 1900–1950*, Frankfurt, 1987, p. 15; Gustav Adolf Besser, *Geschichte der Frankfurter Flüchtlings-Gemeinden 1554–1558*, Halle, 1906.

strangers in their parish.'[26] In short, before the censuses from the mid-nineteenth century which counted aliens, we can only guess at the numbers of Germans within Britain.

Another group which began to appear in England during the sixteenth century consisted of travellers from Germany.[27] In addition German scholars and students continued to enter Britain.[28] The best-known of these included several chemists such as Peter Stahl, who taught at the University of Oxford, and Gottfried Hanckwitz, a phosphorous producer. Several Germans resident in seventeenth-century London played a role in the foundation of the Royal Society in 1660; these included Samuel Hartlib from Elbing, Heinrich Oldenberg of Bremen, Prince Rupert of the Palatinate, and Theodore Hawk from Neuhausen, near Worms. In addition numerous literary scholars and theologians resided in London during the seventeenth century, as well as many artists.[29]

German businessmen and craftsmen also continued to enter Britain during the late sixteenth and seventeenth centuries. Amongst these we can include Sir John Spielman, who established a paper mill in Dartford in 1588, and Gottfried Box who set up a machine to make brass wire and copper plates in 1590. Other German immigrants played a part in metal industries such as cutlery, steel and needle-making. A sword factory in Hounslow during the reign of Charles II had German owners and German workers. Also during the seventeenth century, German miners worked in Staffordshire.[30]

Significant developments took place in the history of Germans in London during the seventeenth century, so that by 1800 four German churches existed within the capital. Schöll mentions Hamburg businessmen and sugar refiners who may have formed the basis of a German community. The sugar refiners may also have laid the foundations for the later domination of this trade by Germans during the eighteenth and nineteenth centuries. Schöll estimates the German population of London in the late seventeenth century at under 2,000. If this is accurate, the size of the London German community did not play a decisive role in the establishment of the German churches.[31]

26. Schöll, *Geschichte der Kirchen*, p. 7; Schaible, *Geschichte der Deutschen*, p. 130; Hennings, *Deutsche in England*, p. 33; Chitty, 'Aliens', pp. 139–40.
27. W. D. Robson-Scott, *German Travellers in England 1400–1800*, Oxford, 1953.
28. Schaible, *Geschichte der Deutschen*, pp. 171–82.
29. Ibid., pp. 205–51; Kellenbenz, 'German Immigrants', pp. 69–70.
30. Schaible, *Geschichte der Deutschen*, p. 183; Kellenbenz, 'German Immigrants', pp. 65–6, 68; John F Hayward, 'English Swords 1600–1650', in Robert Held (ed.), *Arms and Armour Annual*, vol. 1, Northfield, Illinois, 1973, pp. 158–60; Cunningham, *Alien Immigrants*, p. 215.
31. Schöll, *Geschichte der Kirchen*, pp. 15–16.

The foundation of the first of these, the Hamburg Lutheran Church in the City, stemmed from the aftermath of the Fire of London in 1666. Before that time German merchants had participated in Lutheran services held at All Hallows the Great, but the fire had destroyed this place of worship. German craftsmen, together with German and Swedish businessmen as well as the Swedish Ambassador, appealed to Charles II to allow the construction of a new Church. He issued a Royal Charter in 1669 and services began to take place there from 1673, although the congregation had met from as early as 1668. Initially the congregation consisted of Lutherans of other nations as well as Germans, but this situation changed by 1710 when the Danish and Swedish members founded their own churches. The church served a thriving German community, indicating that Schöll may have underestimated the number of Germans in London: 'In the years from 1686–1713, 300 baptisms are entered in the records of the Hamburg Church. This means that, each year, an average of eleven children were baptised, a number which has never been reached since that time.'[32]

By 1700 three more German churches had come into existence. The passage of the Toleration Act in 1689 proved important here, as this allowed foreign congregations to worship in Britain without the grant of a royal charter. The first of these was established in 1692 when a group of thirty-four Germans, living west of the City of London and denied voting rights at the Hamburg Lutheran Church, formed themselves into a congregation. They applied to William III in 1693 through the Duke of Braunschweig-Celle for permission to worship in the Savoy Palace, receiving permission in the following year. This church had the name of St Mary's in the Savoy. Soldiers and court officials belonged to the congregation and the first pastor, Frenaus Crusius, 1694–1705, presided over 168 baptisms and 67 marriages. Georg Ruperti succeeded Crusius in 1706, and between 1709 and 1731 he carried out 13 baptisms and 37 weddings, though many of the latter included Palatine refugees passing through the country from 1708–12, who are discussed below. Ruperti also established a school in 1708 and acted as its first teacher.[33]

In 1697 emigrants from the Palatine in the Rhineland, fleeing from Roman Catholic persecution, established St Paul's Evangelical Reformed Church, also in the Savoy Palace. The first two pastors, Samuel König and Johann Eckins, each remained for less than a year but

32. Walter Ramge, 'Focal Points in the History of the Hamburg Lutheran Church', in *Hamburg Lutheran Church, London 1669–1969*, Hamburg and Berlin, 1969, pp. 81–7; Rieger, 'British Crown', pp. 102–3.
33. BA, Potsdam, AA 38989, 'Geschichte der deutschen evangelischen St. Marien Schule'; Schöll, *Geschichte der Kirchen*, pp. 34–6; Ramge, 'Focal Points', pp. 86–7.

the third, Johann Jacob Ceaser, stayed until 1719.[34] The final German church established in London at this time, in 1700, owed its existence to Prince Georg of Denmark whom Queen Anne (1702–14) had married in 1683. He brought with him his own German Lutheran chaplain, Mecke, who held regular services in St James's Palace attended only by members of the royal family and its household. Mecke actually resigned and A. W. Bohme succeeded him.[35] In addition a congregation also came into existence in Dublin in 1698, based on an original group of just 24 with Marcus Lichtenstein, the preacher to a German regiment in Ireland, as its pastor. Services took place in German, Danish, and Swedish; in 1723, a church and vicarage were built.[36]

By the end of the seventeenth century the first synagogue for German Jews existed in London. The congregation were primarily Sephardic Jews from Holland, the West Indies and the Iberian Peninsula, who had begun to enter Britain following the decision to re-admit Jews to the country in 1656.[37] However, Ashkenazi Jews from Poland, Germany and Holland also moved to England in increasing numbers, so that by 1690 an organized Ashkenazi community had come into existence with 300 members by 1700. In 1692 the London Ashkenazi community established its first synagogue in Duke's Place.[38]

The Eighteenth Century

The late seventeenth century is an important stage in the history of Germans in Britain because from this point we can trace clear links down to the early twentieth century. The religious establishments set up during these years formed the basis of the communal life of Germans in Britain and continued to exist into the twentieth century, although their geographical location changed as the German communities moved out of the

34. Greater London Record Office, Acc 1767, 'A Short History of the German Evangelical Reformed Church'; Heinrich Deicke, *A Short History of the German Evangelical Reformed St Paul's Church* (London, 1907), p. 1; Rieger, 'British Crown', p. 103; BA, Coblenz, R57 neu, 1064/42, 'Kurze Geschichte der evangelischen reformierten St Paulsgemeinde'.

35. Rieger, 'British Crown', pp. 104–5. For details about Mencke, see Rieger, 'Der Erste Deutsche Hofprediger in London', *Evangelische Diaspora*, vol. 31, pp. 84–92.

36. Schöll, *Geschichte der Kirchen*, p. 51.

37. V. D. Lipman, *A History of the Jews in Britain since 1858*, Leicester, 1990, pp. 1–3; David S. Katz, *Philo-Semitism and the Readmission of the Jews to England 1603–1655*, Oxford, 1982.

38. Lipman, *History of the Jews*, p. 4; Cecil Roth, *The Great London Synagogue 1690–1940*, London, 1950, pp. 1, 13, 22, 23; J. Mills, *The British Jews*, London, 1853; Moses Margoliouth, *A History of the Jews in Great Britain*, 3 vols, London, 1851, vol. 2, pp. 51–2.

City of London and Westminster and into east London. During the eighteenth century a series of new groups entered the country, some of whom remained permanently while others stayed only temporarily. For both short-term and long-term visitors, increased documentation provides more details than the Germans who have so far received attention.

The Palatines represent a group which has received much attention from both British and German scholars. Although most of these immigrants did not remain permanently, they were one of the largest pre-nineteenth century influxes of Germans into Britain. They did not originate only in the Palatinate, which was a region divided in two with the Lower Palatinate centering on the Rhine around Worms and the Upper Palatinate stretching eastward from Nuremberg. Instead, their area of origin extended from Coblenz to Basle in a north-south direction and from Thuringia to Lorraine along an east-west axis.[39]

The reasons for movement out of the area, the push factors, are at least threefold and probably overlap. First there were political factors, as the area faced attack from French armies on at least three occasions between 1674 and 1709.[40] A series of economic factors, both short-term and long-term, also proved important. The former focused on the breaking-up of land into small plots, due to population growth which meant that each child's inheritance shrank.[41] Heavy taxation also caused discontent. A severe winter in 1708–9, which destroyed fruit trees and vines, acted as a precipitating factor;[42] the vast majority of those who made their way to Britain consisted of 'husbandsmen' and 'vinedressers', an indication both of the rural origins of the immigrants and of the fact that frosts had played a role in the destruction of their vines and fruit trees.[43] The importance of religious persecution for this emigration has caused much controversy. Those who put this factor forward claim that Protestants wanted to leave the Palatinate in order to find religious tolerance as the area had a Catholic ruler, although the Peace of Westphalia, which had brought the Thirty Years War to an end in 1648, recognised Catholicism, Lutheranism and Calvinism in the state.[44]

39. Walter Allen Knittle, *Early Eighteenth Century Palatine Emigration*, Baltimore, 1979 reprint, p. 2; Köllmann and Marschalck, 'German Emigration', p. 513.

40. Knittle, *Palatine Emigration*, pp. 2–5.

41. Köllmann and Marschalk, 'German Emigration', pp. 513–4.

42. Knittle, *Palatine Emigration*, pp. 4–5.

43. John Tribbeko and Georg Ruperti, *Lists of Germans from the Palatine Who Came to England in 1709*, Baltimore, 1965 reprint.

44. Those who mention religious persecution as a factor include Rüdiger Renzig, *Pfälzer in Irland: Studien zur Geschichte deutscher Auswandererkolonien des fruehen 18. Jahrhunderts*, Karlsruhe, 1989, p. 27; and Richard Hayes, 'The German Colony in County Limerick', *North Munster Antiquarian Journal*, vol. 1, 1937, pp. 45–6. Knittle, *Palatine Emigration*, pp. 6–11, disagrees.

The migrants came to England after encouragement by advertising agents and the British Government, which wanted emigrants for the British colony in Carolina.[45] However, the Government could not have expected the numbers which eventually arrived during 1709, which vary according to differing sources from 13,000 to 15,000.[46] The large numbers of newcomers created problems of housing and negative reaction from both public and Government. The migrants had to live in makeshift accommodation throughout London; thousands lived in unhygienic conditions in camps in Blackheath in Greenwich and in Whitechapel Fields, as well as in barns, cheap houses and warehouses. The death rate may have reached as high as twenty per cent.

Public and private charity supported them with a collection of approximately £20,000.[47] Nevertheless, hostility developed towards the newcomers of a type prevalent in more recent British history, when public opinion has united to oppose newcomers in a variety of ways. For instance, leaflets spoke of their lack of hygiene and their being a drain on public funds. One leaflet claimed that the government had spent £300,000 on them. They also faced hostility for apparently undercutting English workmen by accepting employment for lower wages. They became victims of racial violence; in one instance migrants were attacked by people armed with axes, and milder attacks took place on other occasions.[48]

Under these circumstances, the Government acted to disperse the Palatines. About 250 families remained in England; some weavers went to Bolton and others found employment with the Liverpool corporation. By January 1710 over 3,000 had made their way to Ireland, but about half of them subsequently left. The majority of those who remained moved to the estate of Sir Thomas Southwell in County Limerick. Of the rest, about 3,000 went to New York and 600 to North

---

45. Knittle, *Palatine Emigration*, pp. 12–31; H. T. Dickinson, 'The Poor Palatines and the Parties', *English Historical Review*, vol. 82, 1967, pp. 465–6.

46. The figure of between 13,000 and 15,000 fits into the estimates provided by Wilhelm Mönckmeier, *Die deutsche überseeische Auswanderung*, Jena, 1912, p. 9; Renzig, *Pfälzer*, p. 12, who gives a wide range of possible figures; and Knittle, *Palatine Emigration*, p. 65. E. Heufer, *Pennsylvanien im 17. Jahrhundert und die Ausgewanderten Pfälzer in England*, Neustadt an der Hardt, 1910, pp. 73–6, provides far higher figures, implying that over 30,000 Palatines found themselves in London.

47. *East London Observer*, 23 March 1912; Knittle, *Palatine Emigration*, pp. 67–9; Walter Beasant, *East London*, London, 1903, p. 188; Hans Fenske, 'International Migration in the Eighteenth Century', *Central European History*, vol. 13, p. 337; Dickinson, 'Poor Palatines', p. 469.

48. Hayes, 'German Colony', p. 46; Knittle, *Palatine Emigration*, pp. 71–2; Renzig, *Pfälzer*, pp. 38–41; Dickinson, ibid., pp. 473–4, 485.

Carolina, while nearly 4,000 Catholics faced repatriation to the Continent.[49]

Another interesting German group in eighteenth-century Britain are the Brethren. Their establishment has its origins in a group of emigrants who moved from Moravia to find refuge in Upper Silesia on the estate of Count Zinzendorf. About fifty of them then moved to east London in the late 1730s where they initially developed connections with the Wesleyans, which, however, quickly dissolved. Despite initial hostility, including physical attacks, numbers increased to about 1,200 and the group spread to other parts of the country, including Fulneck, near Leeds, Hampstead, Oxford, Bradford and Basingstoke. In 1744 the Brethren aroused suspicion as 'Papists' because they spoke a foreign language. Consequently they made declarations of loyalty and in 1750 'the Brethren's congregations in England were by the laws of the realm recognised as belonging to an ancient Protestant and Episcopal Church.' They subsequently spread to other parts of the country including Bedford, Northampton, Bath, Bristol and Plymouth.[50]

Various developments during the eighteenth century meant an increase in the movement of Germans into Britain, though it is difficult to measure the importance of these factors in relation to each other. In the first place we can point to a growth in German emigration from areas of *Realteilung* (equal inheritance) in the south-west, including the Palatine, Württemberg and Baden. Major destinations apart from North America, included Hungary, Russia and Poland. Peaks in emigration occurred regularly, especially between 1748 and 1754.[51]

As during the nineteenth century, much of the Atlantic emigration during the eighteenth century occurred via England, as we have seen with regard to the Palatines in 1708–12.[52] One source, an account from a German visitor to England, described an incident of a sort which also occurred many times after 1800, involving the arrival of destitute German immigrants in London, abandoned by the person who had promised to ship them to North America:

49. Hayes, 'German Colony', p. 47; Renzig, *Pfälzer*, pp. 46, 52, 55, 57, 61, 68, 86; Fenske, 'International Migration', pp. 336–7; Mönckmeier, *Auswanderung*, p. 9; Cunningham, *Alien Immigrants*, pp. 252–3.

50. See G. A. Wauer, *The Beginnings of the Brethren's Church ('Moravians') in England,* Baildon, 1901; and F. A. Wenderborn, *A View of England Towards the Close of the Eighteenth Century,* 2 vols, London, 1791, vol. 2, pp. 461–6. Rieger, 'British Crown', pp. 113–14, provides different details. For more general information on this group, although with virtually no coverage of England, see Roy Coad, *A History of the Brethren Movement,* Exeter, 1968.

51. Fenske, 'International Migration', pp. 337–42; Marschalck, *Deutsche übersewaderung,* pp. 30–1; Köllmann and Marschalck, 'German Emigration', p. 514.

52. Rolf Engelsing, *Bremen als Auswandererhafen 1683–1880,* Bremen, 1961, pp. 14–15.

In the year 1765 he went to London, at the head of eight hundred emigrants, consisting of men, women, and children, whom he had collected in the Palatinate, in Franconia, and in Swabia, by persuading them that they would find a more comfortable subsistence in the British colonies. Upon their arrival in London, this singular man disappeared, and was never heard of more. Destitute and forsaken, the unfortunate beings found themselves lost in that immense city, without knowing a word of the language, and without the acquaintance of a single person in it; the greater part of them were covered only with a few rags; they had no shelter, not even bread to give their own children who were crying for want, and they knew not whom to address.

They camped in Goodman's Fields in east London but eventually a fund, launched by the pastor of one of the German churches in London, collected enough money to support them in London for five months and then to allow them to proceed to North America.[53]

Sources on Germans who entered Britain on a more permanent basis during the eighteenth century do not indicate the countries of origin of the newcomers so that, as with the period after 1815, we have difficulties in establishing whether the German community in England consisted of the same groups that formed the larger migration to the USA.[54] Many authorities, however, point to the specific attractions of England for Germans from 1714 onward and focus upon the cultural, political and economic climate of England during the eighteenth century after the accession of the Hanoverian Kings to the English throne.

To deal with the first point, our concern lies particularly with visitors, whose numbers increased during the course of the eighteenth century. Three factors contributed to the attractions of England. First, by the mid-eighteenth century, 'England had at last been fully "discovered", and had definitely begun to take the place of France as the cultural ideal of intelligent Germans and as the country most worth visiting for the serious student of human affairs.'[55] At the same time, British interest in Germany and its culture began to take shape from the late seventeenth century, as evidenced by the appearance of an early German grammar book in 1680. Subsequently knowledge of German literature, especially of Goethe, also developed.[56]

53. Johann Wilhelm von Archenholtz, *A Picture of England*, London, 1797, pp. 52–6.
54. Ramge, 'Focal Points', p. 87, claims, with some exaggeration and inaccuracy, that 'The stream of immigrants to America in the 18th and 19th century, all passed through London. And many a one, irked by the political or religious restrictions of his home country, and seeking a life of greater freedom on the other side of the Atlantic, stayed after all in London, where there was a wider scope of possibilities for industrious and open-minded people.'
55. Robson-Scott, *German Travellers*, p. 135.
56. Friedrich Althaus, 'Beiträge zur Geschichte der deutschen Colonie in England. II', *Unsere Zeit*, vol. 9, 1873, pp. 534–9.

England's attraction also lay in its political freedom, as perceived by Germans. In fact, German travellers to Paris and Rome as well as London sought to 'experience' freedom. In the last of these, they found it in political life, the theatres, parks and coffee houses, and the anarchy of the streets. Some Germans regarded England as 'the home of liberty, the land of free thought and of a free constitution', possessing a 'constitutional monarchy and parliamentary institutions'.[57] Here we can draw a link with the exiles from Germany during the nineteenth century.

Some of the most famous 'visitors' to England during the eighteenth century kept records and have received attention from literary scholars. We can mention some of them here, such as the Göttingen University physics professor George Lichtenberg (1742–90), who visited the country in 1770 and 1774, when he met royalty, politicians, academics and businessmen.[58] Carl Philip Moritz (1759–93) visited England in 1782 when he was a schoolteacher; he subsequently obtained a chair in Berlin. He published his impressions in *Reisen eines Deutschen in England im Jahr 1782*.[59] G. F. A. Wenderborn (1742–1795) actually served as a German pastor in London and has received attention from several literary scholars because of his published accounts of England. Finally, there was Johann Wilhelm von Archenholz (1741–1812), a Hanoverian soldier who had fought in the Seven Years War and spent a total of six years in England.[60]

The economic situation in England acted as a more important attraction for German travellers than did cultural and intellectual factors, especially towards the end of the eighteenth century when Britain began to experience the fundamental economic changes known as the Industrial Revolution. Leaving aside representatives of companies who remained within the country, who receive attention below, Germans visited England for numerous reasons, often after much preparation in the

57. Johann Gottlieb Burckhardt, *Kirchen-Geschichte der Deutschen Gemeinden in London*, Tübingen, 1798, p. 10; Conrad Widemann, '"Supplement seines Daseins"? Zu den kultur- und identitätsgeschichtlichen Voraussetzungen deutscher Schriftstellerreisen nach Rom-Paris-London seit Winckelmann', in Burckhardt (ed.), *Rom-Paris-London: Erfahrung und Selbsterfahrung deutscher Schriftsteller und Künstler in den Fremden Metropolen*, Stuttgart, 1988, pp. 13–14. The quotes come from Robson-Scott, *German Travellers*, p. 136.

58. Margaret L. Mare and W. H. Quarrel (eds), *Lichtenberg's Visits to England*, Oxford, 1938; Wolfgang Promies, 'Lichtenberg's London', in Widemann, *Rom-Paris-London*, pp.560–70.

59. P. E. Matheson, *German Visitors to England 1770–1795 and Their Impressions*, Oxford, 1930, pp. 3, 7; Manfred Beller, 'Typologia reciproca: Über die Erhellung des deutschen Nationalcharakters durch Reisen', in Widemann, *Rom-Paris-London*, pp.36–9.

60. Matheson, *German Visitors*, pp. 3, 9, 17–19; Robert Elsasser, *Über die politischen Bildungsreisen der Deutschen nach England*, pp. 24, 31–4; Wendeborn, *View of England*, vols. 1 and 2; Archenholtz, *Picture of England*.

customs and language of the country. This preparation involved reading travel books, of which a supply had already developed, as well as contacting people who had already spent time in England. Among visitors, we can identify scientists who made research trips to one of the many institutions which existed in Britain by the eighteenth century, such as Barthold Georg Niebuhr, who visited the Royal Society in 1798. There were also many young businessmen who travelled to various European cities as part of their apprenticeship, often involving visits to factories until legislation came into existence at the end of the eighteenth century forbidding foreigners visiting English factories. German 'mediators', including Lichtenberg, often acted in England for German firms. English industries which received attention included copper and iron production, machine construction, coal mining (in Derbyshire, for instance) and porcelain. During the eighteenth century representatives of the Prussian King, Frederick II, made their way to England in order to learn about both agriculture and industry.[61]

Some Germans who visited England for economic reasons remained within the country and developed companies which, in some cases, would become leaders in British banking, commerce or industry, a process which occurred to a greater extent during the course of the nineteenth century. In other instances, representatives of larger firms entered the country and opened major concerns within Britain; this also continued after 1800.

Although many businessmen moved to Britain at the end of the eighteenth century, particularly during the Napoleonic Wars (1793–1815), some migration had taken place previously. Individuals we can identify include Samuel Levi, who settled in Haverfordwest and established banks in that town and in Milford Haven.[62] By the mid-eighteenth century, several hundred merchants in London were of non-British origin, though it is not clear how many originated from Germany.[63]

A number of the newcomers came from Bremen, such as Andreas Grote who entered Britain in the mid-eighteenth century; originally an agent, he founded a banking house in the City of London in 1776. The financial house of Baring also originated in Bremen; John Baring, the

---

61. This paragraph is based upon Werner Kroker, *Wege zur Verbreitung technologischer Kenntnisse zwischen England and Deutschland in der zweiten Hälfte des 18. Jahrhunderts,* Berlin, 1971; and Martin Schumacher, *Auslandsreisen deutscher Unternehmer 1750–1851 unter besonderer Berücksichtigung von Rheinland und Westfalen,* Cologne, 1968, pp. 46, 64–84.

62. Harold Pollins, *Economic History of the Jews in England,* London, 1982, pp. 84–5.

63. See Stanley D. Chapman, 'The International Houses: The Continental Contribution to British Commerce, 1800–1860', *Journal of European Economic History,* vol. 6, 1977, pp. 6–7, 10.

son of a cloth merchant, moved to Britain in 1717 and settled in Larkbear near Exeter as the West Country provided an important source of trade in wool for north Germany. Baring became apprenticed to the Exeter merchant Edmund Cock, traded with merchants from Bremen and eventually established a business as a wool merchant himself. In 1723 Baring became a British citizen and subsequently married an English woman, Elizabeth Vowler. By the time he died in 1748 he had accumulated considerable amounts of capital and land. Another Bremen merchant, John Duntze, followed him to Exeter; yet another native of Bremen, Johann Heinrich Albers, an indigo merchant, entered England during the late eighteenth century, but returned in 1816.[64]

The migration of businessmen during the second part of the eighteenth century resulted partially from a change in trading practices, whereby German fairs decreased in importance as German merchants entered Britain and carried out more direct business between British and German manufacturers, which cut out the need for the continental fair. Nathan Mayer Rothschild became the most famous of these traders. He entered Britain in 1798 as a representative of his father's Frankfurt-based firm, which traded in English textiles. He originally went to gain experience with the firms of L. B. Cohen and Levi Salomans in London before establishing an agency of his own in Manchester, where he began to purchase goods from local textile firms. Other German firms followed Rothschild to Manchester in order 'to tap the rich supply of cotton goods at source', including Oppenheimer and Liepmann of Berlin. The father of the poet Heinrich Heine, Samson Heine, also a cloth merchant, employed an agent in Liverpool and visited Britain himself on at least one occasion in 1809.[65]

More German businessmen entered the country as a result of the effects of the Napoleonic Wars. Napoleon's armies occupied Hamburg

---

64. Wilhelm Lührs, *Die Freie Hansestadt Bremen und England in der Zeit des deutschen Bundes (1815–1867)*, Bremen, 1958, pp. 160, 162; Schaible, *Geschichte der Deutschen*, p. 420; Percy Ernest Schramm, 'Die deutschen Überseekaufleute in Rahmen der Sozialgeschichte', *Bremisches Jahrbuch*, vol. 49, 1964, p. 40; Philip Ziegler, *The Sixth Great Power: A History of One of the Greatest of All Banking Families, The House of Barings, 1762–1929*, New York, 1988, pp. 14–15.

65. Chapman, 'International Houses', pp. 10–11; Chapman, 'The Foundation of the English Rothschilds: N. M. Rothschild as a Textile Merchant', *Textile History*, vol. 8, 1977, pp. 101–2; Williams, *Manchester Jewry*, pp. 17–19; S. S. Prawer, *Frankenstein's Island: England and the English in the Writings of Heinrich Heine*, Cambridge, 1986, pp. 3–4. See also Chapman, 'The Migration of Merchant Enterprise: German Merchant Houses in Britain in the Eighteenth and Nineteenth Centuries', *Bankhistorisches Archiv*, vol. 6, 1980, pp. 32–3, who mentions that 'Not all the German houses established in Britain were branches of established concerns in' Germany. He gives the example of William Uhde who 'came to Manchester in 1788 as a clerk in the employ of Taylor & Maxwell', a cotton firm, but then went into business on his own.

and Frankfurt from 1806–12 and the trade of these cities deteriorated due to the blockade. Consequently, more firms moved to or sent representatives to London. The most famous included Christian Mathias Schröder, a Hamburg merchant, who sent his sons Johann Frederick and Johann Heinrich to London. In 1809 Frederick Huth, another Hamburg merchant, moved to London from Spain where he had lived since 1797. With 4,000 thalers, which he had saved and taken with him, he became a commission-agent and initially dealt primarily in tea and silk. In addition, the Bremeners Wilhelm Heinrich Goschen and Heinrich Fruhling also established themselves in London at this time, and five German merchants moved to Manchester between 1812–14, at least three of whom were of Jewish descent.[66]

Another reason put forward for the more general immigration of Germans during this period is the Hanoverian succession, whereby the Kings of Hanover ascended to the British throne in 1714 and continued to rule until 1837. This affected the flow of immigration in the first place by acting as a factor in attracting travellers, especially academics, as the University of Göttingen within the Kingdom of Hanover became a major centre of learning.[67] At the same time, 'the personal entourage of King George I, from his body-servants upwards, consisted...entirely of Germans', although Germans obtained virtually no government positions despite the fact that the King continued to have German advisors.[68]

Furthermore, the connection with Hanover also meant the use of German troops in the service of England, especially during the American War of Independence, although soldiers from Germany did not appear in England until 1803 with the formation of The King's German Legion in Bexhill, which remained in existence until 1816. These troops fought against Napoleon and also helped to suppress a mutiny in Ely in 1811. The chaplain of the German court chapel acted as the spiritual guide for the troops. Germans also played a part in the instruction of British troops; Johann Müller and J Landmann, for instance, held chairs at the Royal Military Academy in Woolwich.[69]

66. Chapman, 'International Houses', pp. 11–12; Chapman, 'Migration', p. 29; Williams, *Manchester Jewry*, p. 22; Heinrich Gerdes, 'Ein Sohn Harsefelds als Grosskaufmann in London', *Stader Archiv*, vol. 14, 1924, p. 14; Lührs, *Freie Hansestadt Bremen*, p. 164.

67. Lichtenberg, for instance, was a professor of physics at Göttingen, for which see Mare and Quarrel, *Lichtenberg's Visits*, pp. xiii–xiv. See also Elsasser, *Politische Bildungsreisen*, p. 7.

68. Adolphus William Ward, *Great Britain and Hanover: Some Aspects of the Personal Union*, Oxford, 1899, pp. 48, 49, 67.

69. Charles P. Moritz, *Travels, Chiefly on Foot, Through Several Parts of England in 1782*, London, 1792, p. 91; Schaible, *Geschichte der Deutschen*, pp. 359–67; Karl Schneider, 'Deutsche Soldaten in englischem Dienst', *Deutsche Erde*, vol. 6, 1908, pp. 211–12; David Green, *Great Cobbett: The Noblest Agitator*, London, 1983, p. 345.

The 'Hanoverian Kings of Great Britain made London a mecca for composers, instrumentalists and singers from continetal Europe'.[70] Other factors also contributed to the migration of German musicians to England. By the beginning of the eighteenth century 'Germany was ripe for musical export. With increasing prosperity music had permeated every corner of the land and was actively encouraged by the small courts and wealthy municipalities.' At the same time, 'English music was at a low ebb. Since the death of Purcell in 1695 no great composer had arisen to succeed him.'[71]

Among the outstanding German musicians, George Friedrich Handel is the most famous. He first made his way to London in 1710 and died there 1759, although he left England on numerous occasions in between. During his stay in the country he produced many operas and oratorios, together with smaller pieces including works for the stage and for royal occasions. Other major composers who visited England during Handel's time included the opera composers Johann Adolf Hasse and Christoph Gluck. Following Handel's death Johann Christian Bach moved to London in 1762 and became music master to the Queen. Three years earlier Karl Friedrich Abel had made his way to England because of the Seven Years War, and the Queen appointed him as her chamber musician with a salary of £200 a year. Together with Bach, Abel established subscription concerts. In 1764 the eight-year-old Wolfgang Amadeus Mozart visited England with his father and sister; Joseph Haydn spent periods in England in the 1790s during which he composed his London Symphonies, and received an enthusiastic reception and wide publicity in the press.

Germans also formed a large proportion of orchestral players in England during this period. Music-playing was the only profession of this period 'dominated by foreigners'. The trend accelerated after 1750 when military bands entered the country following the Seven Years War. Not surprisingly, given their large numbers, Germans played a large part in the formation of the first benevolent fund for musicians in England. As well as German composers there were also makers of musical instruments, who worked in the country because of

70. Reginald Hatton, 'England and Hanover 1714–1837', in Adolf M. Birke and Kurt Kluxen (eds), *England and Hanover*, Munich 1986, p. 26.

71. Herma Fiedler, 'German Musicians in England and their Influence to the End of the Eighteenth Century', *German Life and Letters*, vol. 6, 1939, p. 6. See also pp. 1–5 for details on the smaller number of German musicians in Britain before 1700, which became a 'German invasion' after this date.

better pay, tools and materials, and these remained in significant numbers into the next century.[72]

A final group of Germans who entered England during the eighteenth century consisted of Jews, although we must immediately recognise here that immigrants from Germany were just one component of the Jewish community of Britain. We have already paid some attention to wealthy merchants; here we can mention more humble immigrants. Various authorities have speculated on the size of the Jewish community, although without official census statistics, all figures remain estimates. Cecil Roth wrote of a growth in the Jewish community in England from less than 1,000 in 1700 to 6,000 by mid-century and between 20,000 and 30,000 in 1815. Lipman estimates that the Jewish community numbered 2,000 Sephardim and 20,000 Ashkenazim in London by the end of the eighteenth century, while Israel Finestein has written that Anglo-Jewry numbered 22,000 in 1800, of which 'the Ashkenazim exceeded three-quarters'. A contemporary source mentioned 12,000 Jews in late eighteenth century England, 11,000 of whom lived in London and 4,000 of whom originated from Portugal, Spain, Italy, France, Barbary and the Levant.[73]

Although all of these remain estimates, all commentators agree that the Ashkenazi Jewish community increased during the course of the eighteenth century. A series of reasons have been put forward to explain the growth. In the first place, Roth mentions that the Ashkenazi community 'was recruited from abroad with great rapidity, the influx being yet further stimulated when the accession of George I brought England and Germany into a closer relationship'. Roth also mentions the effects of pogroms in the Ukraine and asserts that: 'All the communities in Germany were sending their youth to the land of toleration and of opportunity, where so many of their kinsmen had prospered.' Finestein provides similar explanations.

More recent accounts have also focused on a combination of social and economic factors. Lipman used a list of 58 Plymouth Jewish aliens to demonstrate that 43 of these came from Germany, of whom 26 orginated in a 'relatively narrow belt running eastwards from the Rhine

72. See Christopher Hogwood, *Handel*, London, 1984; Fiedler, 'German Musicians', pp. 6–14; Cyril Ehrlich, *The Music Profession in Britain Since the Eighteenth Century: A Social History*, Oxford, 1985, pp. 16–17; Wendeborn, *View of England*, vol. 2, pp. 240–1; Armytage, *German Influence*, p. 15; Reginald Nettel, *The Orchestra in England: A Social History*, London, 1946, pp. 76, 78, 84.

73. Cecil Roth, *A History of the Jews in England*, Oxford, 1941, p. 239; Roth, *Great London Synagogue*, p. 114; Lipman, *Jews in Britain*, pp. 4–5; Wendeborn, *View of England*, pp. 468–9; Finestein, *A Short History of Anglo-Jewry*, London, 1957, p. 67. For other estimates, see Todd M. Endelman, *The Jews of Georgian England 1714–1830*, p p. 172–3; and George, *London Life*, p. 134.

into Franconia', the same area from which more general emigration out of Germany took place during the eighteenth century. Lipman asserts that, 'Many of the small princely states followed the pattern of the Prussian General patent of 1750 which severely limited the right of Jews to transmit their property right to their children. In the smaller German communities Jews had to move because they could not live, nor earn a living, at home'. Until 1771, Jews, and presumably others, could travel free across the North Sea and English Channel on ships carrying mail.[74]

Having examined the reasons for eighteenth-century German immigration into England, we can now look at the economic and social condition of Germans within the country. It is is difficult to estimate the total numbers of Germans living in England. Schaible estimated the German population of London at 4,000–5,000 in mid-century, which increased to 6,000 by 1800, but this does not match the figures quoted above for the Jewish communities, which suggest that more German Jews than Gentiles lived within the country. This seems unlikely, however, because more German Christian than German Jewish places of worship existed. On the other hand, the figures given in studies of the German churches in London suggest that the Gentile community may have been larger than 5,000–10,000.[75]

Whatever the true figure, it seems clear that, although German communities existed in Edinburgh, Liverpool and Bristol, the majority of the Germans in eighteenth-century Britain lived in London. The fact that all the German churches in Britain, with the exception of the one in Dublin mentioned above, were in London provides the best indication of this. In addition to those churches established in the late seventeenth and early eighteenth centuries, two more came into existence during the middle of the eighteenth century. In 1763 a German sugar refiner called

74. Roth, *Jews in England*, pp. 198, 233; Roth, *Great London Synagogue*, p. 114; Finestein, *History of Anglo-Jewry*, p. 67; Lipman, 'The Plymouth Aliens List of 1798 and 1803', *Miscellanies of the Jewish Historical Society of England*, vol. 6, pp. 187–95; Lipman, 'The Origins of Provincial Anglo-Jewry' in Aubrey Newman (ed.), *Provincial Jewry in Victorian England*, London, 1975, pp. 5–6. See also Endelman, *Jews of Georgian England*, pp. 175–9.

75. Schaible, *Geschichte der Deutschen*, p. 368. The various estimates of the sizes of the church communities come from Greater London Record Office, Acc 1767, 'A Short History of the German Evangelical Reformed Church in Hooper Square, Leman Street', which states that by 1790, when the location of the church was in the Savoy, 'the congregation blossomed and the membership numbered 3–400.' Ramge, 'Focal Points', p. 87, states that 'The number of Germans in one of the Lutheran churches in 1700 increased to double that number in 1750, (from 2,000 to 4,000)' though he does not say which one and neither does he provide any sources. Georg Timpe, *Die Deutsche St. Bonifacius-Mission in London 1809–1909*, London, 1909, pp. 21, 24, states that the number of German Catholics alone in London was estimated at 4,000 in 1808 but he regards this as an exaggeration. Perhaps more accurate is the membership figure for St Bonifacius's Church of 262 in 1812.

Beckmann provided funding for the establishement of St George's Lutheran Church in Little Alie Street, Whitechapel, indicating that some movement of Germans out of the City of London had taken place. Seven years later, F. A. Wenderborn played a major role in the foundation of St John's Evengelical Church in Ludgate Hill, of which he remained pastor for the next twenty years. In 1809 the first German Catholic church came into existence in Great St Thomas Apostle Street in the City of London in 1809, although some German Catholics had previously used the chapel of the Austrian ambassador in London. The German Jewish community also remained concentrated upon London, although Lipman gives a list of over twenty provincial cities with Jewish communities by the end of the eighteenth century, including Birmingham, Liverpool, Norwich and Sunderland.[76]

Birmingham contained three German merchant houses by 1820, founded, according to Roth, 'when itinerant merchants from the capital (mainly Ashkenazim) began to perambulate the countryside, some of them settling as watchmakers and silversmiths in the more important market-towns and sea-ports, where they were reinforced by others who came direct from the Continent'. The number of merchant houses in Manchester had reached 28 by 1820, and migration of German merchants began to develop on a large scale from about this time. Manchester also had the foundations of its Jewish community by the end of the Napoleonic Wars, consisting of both German immigrants and settlers from other parts of Britain, notably Liverpool. As mentioned above, Nathan Mayer Rothschild was the best known German immigrant in Manchester. He played an important role in the local Jewish community. He became involved in banking in 1808, helping to finance the Government's campaign in Spain, and in 1810 he moved to London.[77]

We can establish the occupations of many of the Germans in eighteenth-century London. Musicians and merchants have already been mentioned. Sugar bakers were often Germans both in the eighteenth century and well into the nineteenth century. During this period, sugar entered the London docks from West Indian colonies in a 'raw' condition which meant that it faced boiling several times to turn it into a powder, after which it then underwent dilution. After that process, the sugar

76. Burckhardt, *Kirchen-Geschichte*, p. 14; Müller, *Lutheran Congregations*, pp. 16–17; Schaible, *Geschichte der Deutschen*, pp. 369–70; Matheson, *German Visitors*, p. 9; Timpe, *St. Bonifacius-Mission*, pp. 18, 22; Lipman, 'Origins', p. 4. Cecil Roth, *The Rise of Provincial Jewry: The Early History of the Jewish Communities in the English Countryside, 1740–1840*, London, 1950, pp. 25–6, states that no Jewish communities existed before 1740 but that during the next sixty years they developed in 22 provincial towns.

77. Chapman, 'International Houses', p. 19; Williams, *Manchester Jewry*, pp. 11–29.

went into an oven to be baked into a loaf and undergo further dilution. From as early as the mid-eighteenth century Germans played a significant part in this industry as 'boilers', earning between thirty and fifty pounds a year. By the time of the French Revolutionary and Napoleonic Wars, many second-generation German immigrants worked in the London industry. The wars, which resulted in a decline in the supply of British labour, meant that East London firms recruited sugar bakers from Hamburg and Bremen, though the number obtained does not seem to have been more than one hundred. In comparison with English workmen, the German employees remained docile, although those who had entered the country earlier during the century played a role in the Society of Sugar Refiners.[78] Germans also found themselves employed in a variety of other trades in London during this period including clockmaking, tailoring, shoemaking, baking and, higher on the social scale, as doctors.[79]

As we have seen, German Jews became involved in the hawking and peddling of goods both within London and the provinces. In the capital, many traded in Petticoat Lane. In the country as a whole they entered a trade which required little skill or capital and which they had practised on the continent. But many Jews in the provinces also became involved in the production of luxury goods such as jewellery and watches for which the growth of provincial cities provided a market.[80]

With regard to the social composition of the eighteenth-century immigrants, we have seen that this varied in both Jewish and Gentile communities from rich merchants to artisans. Much attention focused upon poverty amongst Ashkenazi Jews. Joshua van Oven wrote in 1802 that amongst Jewry in London, 'The class denominated German Jews...constitute the greatest body, and have comparatively the fewest rich, and the largest number of poor amongst them.'[81] Archenholtz wrote that 'We are astonished at the difference between the Portuguese and the German Jews established in this island. Dress, language, manners, cleanliness, politeness, everything distinguishes

78. R. Campbell, *The London Tradesman*, Newton Abbot, 1969 reprint, pp. 272–3; Thomas Fock, 'Über Londoner Zuckersiederein und deutsche Arbeitskräfte', *Zuckerindustrie*, vol. 3, 1985, p. 233; Peter Towey, 'German Sugar Bakers in the East End', *Anglo-German Family History Society Mitteilungsblatt*, vol. 5, 1988, pp. 3–5; Walter M. Stern, 'The London Sugar Refiners Around 1800', *Guildhall Miscellany*, no. 3, 1954, pp. 29–31.
79. Burckhardt, *Kirchen-Geschichte*, pp. 16–17, 19–21; Timpe, *St. Bonifacius-Mission*, p. 17.
80. Endelman, *Jews of Georgian England*, p. 179; Lipman, 'Origins', p. 6; 'Plymouth Aliens List', p. 189.
81. Joshua van Oven, *Letters on the Present State of the Jewish Poor in the Metropolis*, London, 1802, p. 8.

them, much to the advantage of the former.'[82] Wenderborn made similar comments.[83]

Poverty amongst the German Gentile community attracted less attention, but it clearly existed, as evidenced by the foundation of at least two primarily German charities during the eighteenth century. The first of these came into existence in 1712 and its only publication stated that 'not only Germans shall be received but also such of other Nations, as are thus far acquainted with the High-Dutch, that they may be present at, and improved by such Discourses as, at the beginning of every meeting, are made on Subjects tending to Piety and mutual edification.' Little information exists upon how long this body lasted. More material survives on the Society of Friends of Foreigners in Distress, which receives more detail below. One of its publications mentioned the fact that 'applications were often made for relief by Foreigners, not only to the Clergymen of their respective churches in this country, but to foreign merchants and others distinguished for their philanthropy, whose business rendered it difficult for them to ascertain the authenticity of testimonials, or the justice of the petitioners' claims'.[84]

To conclude this discussion on Germans in eighteenth-century Britain, we can examine the extent to which communities had developed. By the late nineteenth century Germans had developed into strong ethnic groups in major Britsh cities, especially Liverpool, Manchester, Bradford and several parts of London. The immigrants maintained their ethnicity through political activity, musical and sporting societies, and religion and education. During the eighteenth century only the last two had developed to any great extent, although we can identify German Freemasons lodges within England. But the more general absence of societies may reflect the absence of organised leisure within Britain as a whole[85], and also emphasises the importance of religion for the maintenance of German ethnicity. The churches served like rods of steel in the development of the German communities in Britain from the late seventeenth to the early twentieth centuries, as they represent institutions which existed throughout this whole period. We have previously mentioned that two new Protestant and one Catholic church came into exis-

---

82. Archenholtz, *Picture of England*, p. 177.

83. Wenderborn, *View of England*, vol. 2, p. 470.

84. *Rules and Ordinances for a Charitable Society Set Up By Some Germans at London in the Year MDCCXII*, London, 1713; Society of Friends of Foreigners in Distress, *Songs, Duets, &c. in the Grand Miscellaneous Concert at the King's Theatre, on Friday, June 3rd, 1814, for the Benefit of the Society of Friends of Foreigners in Distress*, London, 1814, p. 21.

85. Moritz, *Travels*, p. 32. See also Roy Porter, *English Society in the Eighteenth Century*, Harmondsworth, 1982, pp. 232–68; and George Rude, *Hanoverian London 1714–1808*, London, 1971, pp. 64–81.

tence in the eighteenth and early nineteenth centuries, and here we can provide a few more details about religious life amongst German Gentiles in London during the years 1715–1815.

St Mary's Lutheran Church in the Savoy experienced several important developments during the eighteenth century, including the receipt of an annual grant from the Crown in 1740, an indication of general support by the Hanoverian Kings for the German churches in London during the eighteenth century. In 1768 St Mary's moved out of the Savoy Palace into a newly built church in the vicinity. The construction also received support from the Royal Family.[86] St Paul's Reformed Church in the Savoy obtained financial assistance from the Prussian King Frederick I from 1701 but, when it moved from the Savoy Chapel to the dilapidated French Church in Dutchy Lane in 1771, renovation took place with a £500 grant from King George III as well as with support from senior British clerics.[87]

As mentioned above, St Mary's church had a school connected with it from 1708. In 1726, a grant of £400 from Princess Caroline, wife of the future George II, helped in the construction of a new building, 'for the keeping and maintaining of a Charity school for the Education of Children in the German tongue'. The school moved again in 1768 with the new church, and by the end of the century it offered instruction not only in English and German reading and writing but also in religion, mathematics, geography, history and natural history. A school constitution from 1782 described its purpose as the creation of good citizens and Christians and the keeping and extension of the congregation.[88]

The efforts of the pastor of St George's Church in Whitechapel, Christian Scwhabe, led to the foundation of St George's school in 1805. Finance came from contributions from members of the congregation, particularly Johann Holz, who gave £372 14s. The number of pupils initially totalled seventeen but within three months this figure had risen to forty, which became forty-five in the following year and seventy by 1812. At its height, in the late nineteenth century, the figure reached 400, but by that time the German community in east London had significantly expanded. The growth from 1805–12 suggests an enthusiastic response from German parents in the area, again illustrating the importance of the foundations of these years for the development of the

86. John Southernden Burn, *The History of the French, Walloon, Dutch, and Other Foreign Protestant Refugees Settled in England*, London, 1846, p. 239; Rieger, 'British Crown', pp. 112, 116.

87. Rieger, 'British Crown', p. 119; BA, Coblenz, R57 neu, 1064/42, 'Kurze Geschichte der deutschen evangelischen reformierten St. Paulsgemeinde'.

88. BA, Potsdam, AA, 38989, 'Geschichte der deutschen evangelischen St. Marien Schule'.

German community later in the nineteenth century.[89] The establishment of St George's school also demonstrates the importance of philanthropy from wealthy Germans in Britain in the support of the German institutions within the country. This support became widespread and fundamentally important for German ethnic institutions during the course of the nineteenth century.

The most important German philanthropic body before 1815 consisted of the Society of Friends of Foreigners in Distress, which continued to exist until the First World War. The Society differs from other bodies because it concerned itself not only with Germans. Its origins lay in the establishment of the Society of Universal Good Will in Norwich during the 1780s by foreign Protestant clergymen, but this group had limited funds and transformed itself into the Society of Friends of Foreigners in Distress at a meeting in London in 1806. The Society aimed 'to grant relief to indigent Foreigners here, without distinction of country or religion; especially to those who are not entitled to parochial aid: and to provide the means, to such as are desirous, to return to their own country'. A board of directors sat once a week in order to examine petitions for relief, 'selecting such as deserve protection, and preventing others becoming a burden to this country and a disgrace to their own'. By 1814 it had helped 1,200 persons, excluding their wives and families, and contributed small weekly pensions to support forty families. It received support from 'wealthy Foreigners settled in this Country' and its patrons included English nobles.[90]

As previously indicated, we can also identify the development of German Jewish communities by the late eighteenth century, although these create problems in the sense that they rarely consisted purely of German immigrants but also include newcomers from other countries together with 'English' Jews born in England. This situation developed in Manchester, for instance, which by 1815 had a synagogue and Jewish burial ground, being based on a settlement of 14–15 families in the 1780s.[91] In London, meanwhile, a series of Ashkenazi institutions had come into existence by the early nineteenth century. The most important of the synagogues which existed in London by 1800 was the Great Synagogue in Duke's Place, which was consecrated in 1726 and underwent enlargement and repair in 1767. Its rabbi also served as the Chief

89. Tower Hamlets Local History Collection, 'Jubiläums=Bericht der deutschen und englischen St. Georg's Schule, 1. Juli 1905'.

90. Society of Friends of Foreigners in Distress, *Songs Duets, &c.*, pp. 20–3; also *Account of the Society of Friends of Foreigners in Distress for the Year 1817*, London, 1817, pp. 8–10.

91. Williams, *Manchester Jewry*, pp. 14–15, 24–5; N. J. Laski, 'The History of Manchester Jewry', *Manchester Review*, vol. 7, 1956, pp. 366–7.

Rabbi of Ashkenazi Jews in Great Britain. Those who held this office during the eighteenth century and into the nineteenth often made their way from Germany; they include Judah Ephraim Anschel Cohen from Hamburg, who moved to Rotterdam in 1731, and David Cohen from Frankfurt, who took up the post of Chief Rabbi in 1764.

Perhaps the second most important Ashkenazi Synagogue consisted of the one in Fenchurch Street in the City, known as Hambro's Synagogue. Also in the City we can identify a synagogue in Leadenhall Street, as well as the Westminster Synagogue in the Strand, which had a branch in Covent Garden by 1815. Together with these religious institutions, there also existed, in early nineteenth-century London, the Jews Hospital (founded in 1807), the Ladies Benevolent Institution (1812), the Jews Free School (1816), and the Ladies Benevolent Society (1818) which provided clothing for young girls. In addition, the Board of Deputies of British Jews, had come into existence in 1760 at the instigation of Sephardic Jews, but also with the support of a committee to represent their German co-religionists.[92]

During the course of the nineteenth century, the purely German-Jewish ethnic group would weaken, in contrast to its Gentile counterpart and the Jewish community more generally. The main reason for this lies in the small scale immigration of German Jews to Britain after 1815, compared with the larger-scale influx of German Protestants and Ashkenazi Jews from Eastern Europe as the century progressed. Both these groups provided a dynamism as their members had a desire to remain tied to their past, in contrast to German-Jewish individuals born in England, and consequently they were formed by the norms of their land of birth.[93]

British attitudes towards Germany and Germans, both Gentiles and Jews, changed from ambivalence, a mixture of positive, negative and indifferent feeling in the nineteenth century into overwhelming hostility during the early twentieth century culminating in universal hostility during the First World War.[94] But we have also seen that animosity towards Germans in England surfaced during earlier periods; for instance towards the Hansa, culminating in their expulsion under Queen Elizabeth. However, attitudes before the eighteenth century were not simply negative. The connection between the two nations due to Anglo-Saxon immigration and a shared religion after the Reformation,

---

92. Margoliouth, *Jews of Great Britain*, vol. 2, pp. 70, 116, 117, 198, 199; Finestein, *History of Anglo-Jewry*, p. 73; Van Oven, *Letters*, pp. 8–9; Lipman, *Jews of Great Britain*, p. 6; Aubrey Newman, *The Board of Deputies of British Jews 1760–1985*, London, 1987, p. 4.
93. The question of numbers does not receive systematic treatment in Todd M. Endelman, *Radical Assimilation in English-Jewish History 1656–1945*, Bloomington, 1990. See for instance, Chapter 4, 'German Immigrants in the Victorian Age', pp. 114–43.
94. See Chapter 5 of the present study.

received attention, for instance; by the eighteenth century ideas of 'racial Anglo-Saxonism' also became more widespread, with a stress upon the alleged racial superiority of the English and German 'races' due to their common origins. These ideas date back to the eighth-century historian Bede, but had circulated throughout the intervening eleven centuries, especially in the work of historians.[95]

During the eighteenth century there were a series of strands of hostility towards Germans and Germany, which will be dealt with below. These had their roots in a more traditional stereotype of Germans, stretching back to at least the sixteenth century and focusing on two elements. The first of these, 'Faustianism', focused on mysticism, a strong religious spirit and 'Teutonic philosophy', the last of which survived into the nineteenth century. The second element was the 'Grobianisch', with commentators focusing on German 'barbarism' – from at least the High Middle Ages – dullness and, especially, drunkeness.

The last stereotype certainly existed during the eighteenth century, as indicated by Daniel Defoe's satirical poem on English xenophobia, *A True Born Englishman*, which has individual verses describing the English view of different nations. The stanza on Germany runs:

Drunkeness, the darling favourite of hell,
Chose Germany to rule; and rules so well,
No subjects more obsequiously do obey,
None please so well, or are so pleased as they.
The cunning artist manages so well,
He lets them bow to heaven, and drink to hell.
If but to wine and him they homage pay,
He cares not to what deity they pray,
What God they worship most, or in what way.
Whether by Luther, Calvin, or by Rome,
They fail the heavens, by wine he steers them home.[96]

95. Hugh A. MacDougall, *Racial Myth in English History: Trojans, Teutons, and Anglo-Saxons*, London, 1982, pp. 31–85; Reginald Horsman, 'Origins of Racial Anglo-Saxonism in Great Britain Before 1850', *Journal of the History of Ideas*, vol. 37, p. 392. Bernadotte Everly Schmitt, *England and Germany, 1740–1914*, Princeton, 1916, pp. 116–18, stresses the closeness of the two countries during the eighteenth century.

96. Daniel Defoe, *A True Born Englishman: A Satyr*, Philadelphia, 1778 edition. The best account of English views of Germans before 1800 is Willi Radczun, *Der englische Urteil über die Deutschen bis zur Mitte des 17. Jahrhunderts*, 30–40, 101–10, and passim. More recently, see Franz K. Stanzel, 'National Character as Literary Stereotype: An Analysis of the Image of the German in English Literature Before 1800', *Anglistik und Englischunterricht*, vols. 29–30, 1986, pp. 7–20. See also Theodor Kornder, *Der Deutsche im Spiegelbild der englischen Erzählungsliteratur des 19. Jahrhunderts*, Erlangen-Bruck, 1934, pp. 1–6; Fritz Schultz, *Der Deutsche in der englischen Literatur vom Beginn der Romantik bis zum Ausbruch des Weltkrieges*, Göttingen, 1939, pp. 1–6.

More specifically-focused hostility developed in connection with the Hanoverian succession and Hanoverian rule generally. Here animosity existed in all spheres of life, from Parliament to the populace. In 1713 Defoe listed a series of reasons put forward against the succession of the House of Hanover, all of which were fundamentally based on hostility to the fact that a non-English dynasty would provide the next English King. Defoe provided numerous reasons to oppose this, such as the fact that it would prove divisive and could lead to War with France, although he dismissed these assertions by stating that those who opposed the Hanoverian sucession and supported the Stuart claim, acted in a traitorous manner against Queen Anne. Following the actual succession of George I, hostility focused upon his poor command of the English language and the fact that he had German advisers. Much of the opposition had a more fundamental political foundation in animosity to the whole Hanoverian dynasty and support for the Jacobean claim,[97] but a recent essay on attitudes towards the early Hanoverians, while admitting the fundamental importance of the succession as a divisive issue in British politics, asserts that opposition did not necessarily mean a desire for a change in dynasty.[98]

The riots which broke out immediately after the accession of George I cannot be described as purely anti-German, unlike the disturbances which broke out against German residents in the late nineteenth century, because of their fundamental connection with mainstream political issues and socio-economic conditions in the country, and the fact that the victims were not Germans. The riots occurred in early August 1714, the spring of 1715, November 1715 and the spring and summer of 1716, and broke out on anniversaries connected either with the Hanoverian succession or dynasties which had proceeded it. These incidents became ritualised, involving different sets of youths.[99]

More obviously anti-German are printed attacks on the King's German Legion in the early nineteenth century, including a famous assault upon it by the radical publicist William Cobbett in his *Weekly Political Register*, following the suppression by a cavalry squadron from the Legion of a mutiny by conscripts in Ely in 1809. Here the author does stress German origins. Referring to the mutineers, he writes:

97. Daniel Defoe, *Reasons Against the Succession of the House of Hanover*, London, 1713; William Thomas Laprade, *Public Opinion and Politics in Eighteenth Century England to the Fall of Walpole*, pp. 205–28;

98. Graham C. Gibbs, 'English Attitudes towards Hanover and the Hanoverian Succession in the First Half of the Eighteenth Century', in Birke and Kluxen (eds), *England and Hanover*, p. 35.

99. Nicholas C Rogers, 'Popular Protest in Early Hanoverian London', *Past and Present*, vol. 79, 1978; Rude, *Hanoverian London*, pp. 206–8.

What, shall the rascals dare to mutiny, and that, too, when the German Legion is so near at hand! Lash them, lash them, lash them! They deserve it. O, yes; they merit a double-tailed cat. Base dogs! What, mutiny for the sake of the price of a knapsack! Lash them! flog them! Base rascals! Mutiny for the price of a goat's skin; and, then, upon the appearance of the German Soldiers, they take a flogging as quietly as so many trunks of trees![100]

Several authorities have commented upon the existence of more general hostility towards foreigners in eighteenth-century Britain. M. Dorothy George, for instance, wrote that 'All foreigners in London who had an outlandish look were liable to be roughly treated, or at least abused, by the mob.'[101] F. A. Wenderborn wrote that:

There are certain features in the character of the English, that are thought to be remarkable and striking, which I shall now relate. One of the first, which may be looked upon as general, is a national pride. All nations love their respective countries; but the English, I believe, show it in the highest...

From the high opinion they entertain of themselves, it may easily be supposed, that they look upon foreigners as much inferior. This fault in their national character was visible many centuries ago... When I, more than twenty years ago, was, for the first time, at Oxford, much kindness and civility were shown to me by several gentlemen at the university; but I was given to understand, that I was a foreigner; and a very worthy and learned professor, since deceased, who did me the honour to invite me, during my stay at Oxford, to his house, paid me once, after an agreeable conversation of several hours, the following complement: 'Sir, you look and think like an Englishman; it is a pity you were not born in this country.'[102]

Hostility also developed during the eighteenth century towards poor Jews. The German traveller Carl Philip Moritz wrote that 'antipathy and prejudice against the Jews, I have noticed to be far more common here, than it is even with us, who certainly are not partial to them.' Hostility focused particularly upon allegations that they played a large part in the peddling of stolen goods, which resulted in attacks upon them to the extent that 'Jew-baiting became a sport'. One German traveller wrote of 'the general discontent of the nation occasioned by the German Jews, a class of men, detested as the offscourings of humanity'.[103] A peak of hostility against Jews and other aliens,

100. *Cobbett's Weekly Political Register*, 1 July 1809. The context of these incidents receives attention in Green, *Great Cobbett*, pp. 344–7.
101. M. Dorothy George, *London Life in the Eighteenth Century*, Harmondsworth, 1966 edition, p. 137.
102. Wenderborn, *View of England*, vol. 1, pp. 369, 373.
103. Moritz, *Travels*, pp. 113–14; George, *London Life*, pp. 136–8; Williams, *Manchester Jewry*, pp. 8–9; Archenholtz, *Portrait of England*, p. 177.

affecting both high politics, journalism and 'public opinion' occurred in 1753 with the passage of the Jewish Naturalisation Bill, which, however, because of of the intensity of animosity towards it, was almost immediately repealed.

Xenophobia developed further during the French Revolutionary and Napoleonic Wars, and the Government introduced the Alien Act in 1793 which provided wide powers for the control of foreigners including possible deportation of those regarded as 'undesirable' aliens. In addition, enemy subjects faced internment. The main victims in this period, however, consisted of Frenchmen rather than Germans.[104]

There is a detectable pattern in hostility towards Germans in pre-nineteenth-century Britain, a pattern which can be seen in subsequent animosity. Hostility during the French Revolutionary and Napoleonic period repeated itself during the Crimean War and the Boer War, although on all three occasions the victims did not consist simply of Germans. This wartime hostility is common with the experiences of all countries in all periods of history, as animosity inevitably increases due to the insecurity caused by war.[105] The animosity towards the Hanoverian succession also repeated itself during the nineteenth century when Prince Albert attracted attention, both upon his marriage to Queen Victoria and during the Crimean War. There was also animosity due to large influxes of immigrants, particularly in 1709 but also during the second half of the eighteenth century, when German Jews received attention; this animosity would repeat itself again at the end of the nineteenth century when the main focus of attention was on Russian Jews but also included other groups such as Germans and Italians.

By about 1815 we can detect the main themes in the history of the German communities in Britain, which would develop fully during the course of the nineteenth century. The newcomers had entered Britain due to a combination of push factors from Germany, connected particularly with changing land patterns within the country, and pull factors, especially Britain's more advanced economic development. Groups of newcomers which stand out before 1815 include businessmen, who would continue to enter the country in large numbers, and economic immigrants, who formed the main bulk of the nineteenth century influx.

104. Thomas W. Perry, *Public Opinion, Propaganda, and Politics in Eighteenth Century England: A Study of the Jew Bill of 1753*, Cambridge, Massachusetts, 1962; Clive Emsley, *British Society and the French Wars 1793–1815*, London, 1979, pp. 20–1; Elizabeth Sparrow, 'The Aliens Office, 1792–1806', *Historical Journal*, vol. 33, 1990, pp. 361–84.

105. See Panikos Panayi, 'Dominant Societies and Minorities in the Two World Wars', in Panayi, (ed.), *Minorities in Wartime: National and Racial Groupings in Europe, North America and Australia during the Two World Wars*, Oxford, 1993, pp. 3–23.

With the exception of the mid-sixteenth century religious exiles, refugees prove less easy to detect before 1815 but they became an important group during the nineteenth century. Ethnicity only begins to develop during the eighteenth century and does not solidify until after 1850. Hostility, meanwhile, becomes particularly potent 'at times of important historical change',[106] although other factors such as sudden influxes also play a role.

106. Colin Holmes, *John Bull's Island: Immigration and British Society, 1871–1971*, London, 1988, p. 304.

–2–

German Migration to Britain During the Nineteenth Century

The number of Germans who entered Britain between 1815 and 1914 probably exceeded the entire total who had made their way to the country during the previous thousand years. While no comprehensive census statistics exist for the years before 1861, from this date until the outbreak of the First World War, the German population of Britain did not fall below 30,000, and at its peak it totalled over 60,000. German statistics, while again not comprehensive, demonstrate that migration to Britain took place throughout the nineteenth century, as do figures from various unofficial sources within Britain.[1] The main purpose of this chapter will be to establish the reasons for remigration from Germany to Britain. Furthermore, it also aims at ascertaining the regional origins of the emigrants and giving an indication of the numbers involved. It will examine the 'enabling factors' which made movement possible both out of the country and towards Britain, and the attractions offered by the latter. Finally, the chapter argues that while economic factors proved fundamental to immigration into Britain, religious and political motives cannot be discounted.

Wolfgang Köllmann and Peter Marschalck, in an important essay on German migration to the USA, have drawn up a typology of migration in which they deal with 'motivation', 'impetus', 'form' and 'goal'.[2] In this chapter these ideas are adapted in a more simplified form. Emphasis is placed on more straightforward push and pull factors and on the different levels of motivation which we can distin-

---

1. *Census of England and Wales for the Year 1861*, vol. 2, London, 1863, p. lxxv, shows a figure for the German and Prussian population of England and Wales of 28,654. By 1891 the total for all Germans, including Prussians, had reached 50,594, as indicated by *Census of England and Wales, 1891*, vol. 3, London, 1893, p. xxxvi, and by 1911 the figure totalled 65,261, as calculated in *Census of England and Wales, 1911: Summary Tables*, London, 1915, p. 372, although by this time the method of calculation had changed. For a thorough examination of the numbers of Germans in Britain see Chapter 3. German statistics for movement into Britain are presented in the present chapter.

2. Wolfgang Köllmann and Peter Marschalck, 'German Emigration to the United States', *Perspectives in American History*, vol. 7, 1973, p. 503.

guish as underlying, short-term and personal. There were economic, political, religious and even cultural reasons for movement, and for each type of movement the different levels of motivation played a role.

Other migration theories may be relevant. A Marxist interpretation would stress the attractions of higher wages to the populations of less-developed lands, an idea we cannot dismiss with regard to Germany in the nineteenth century. This argument was put forward by Lenin and has recently received forceful development by Dirk Hoerder, who argues that during the nineteenth century, 'The labour migrations to the American continent...do not constitute an...immigration, but form part of the transfer of labour toward capital (investment) in the Atlantic economies.'[3] While this concept may help to explain mass migrations on a fundamental level, it proves more difficult to apply to the smaller movement of Germans to nineteenth-century Britain, as will be seen.

As mentioned in Chapter 1, emigration out of Germany should be viewed as part of a more general population movement out of Europe, primarily from Britain, Ireland, Italy and Germany which, from 1841 until 1890, meant a population movement of 22.8 million[4] which becomes 51.7 million if we extend the time period to 1815–1930.[5] This colossal movement, which represents one of the most fundamentally important developments in recent history, took place against the background of overpopulation which began in Britain during the late eighteenth century and subsequently spread to the rest of Europe during the course of the following hundred years. Initially, immediately after the first stage of overpopulation, emigration offered the most straightforward way of relieving the problem; subsequently, industrialisation employed the surplus population.[6] More immediate factors such as harvest failures also played a part as migration went through peaks and troughs.[7]

3. W. I. Lenin, 'Kapitalismus und Arbeiterimmigration', in *Werke*, vol. 19, Berlin, 1971, pp. 447–50; Dirk Hoerder, 'An Introduction to Labor Migration in the Atlantic Economies, 1815–1914', in Hoerder (ed.), *Labor Migration in the Atlantic Economies: The European and North American Working Classes During the Period of Industrialization*, London, 1985, p. 8.
4. Charlotte Erickson (ed.), *Emigration from Europe 1815–1914*, London, 1976, p. 27.
5. Dudley Baines, *Emigration from Europe 1815–1930*, London, 1991, p. 9.
6. Peter Marschalck, 'Social and Economic conditions of European Emigration to South America in the 19th and 20th Centuries', in Richard Konetzke and Hermann Kellenbenz (eds.), *Jahrbuch für Geschichte von Staat, Wirtschaft und Gesellschaft Lateinamerikas*, 1976, pp. 11–12.
7. In Ireland, for instance, we can point to the effects of the late 1840s; for which see, for example, W. E. Carrothers, *Emigration from the British Isles*, London, 1965, pp. 186–206.

Germany provides a good example of this unevenness. Four peaks in emigration, of varying sizes and with differing immediate causes, occurred during the nineteenth century. These took place in the period immediately after the Napoleonic Wars; the years just before and just after the 1848 revolutions; 1864–73; and 1880–1893, although none of these periods have rigid dates.[8] In total, Germany lost 4.8 million people through emigration between 1815 and 1930, making it the fifth largest exporter of population from Europe during this period.[9] At the same time, movement of population took place more generally within Germany so that by 1871 nearly 38 per cent of Germans did not reside in the locality in which they were born, while by 1907 almost half of all Germans had moved from their place of birth.[10]

In order to assess the reasons for German emigration we need to discuss both the underlying socio-economic changes which led to the population movement, as well as the shorter-term factors which caused the various peaks mentioned above and affected different parts of the country at varying times. The most important long-term reasons for movement consisted of changes in population, lack of industrial opportunities and patterns of landownership, all of which are linked.

Nineteenth and early twentieth-century studies of German population movement recognised overpopulation as a fundamental cause of emigration. Between 1816 and 1910 the population of Germany, defined by the boundaries of 1910, increased from 24,831,000 to 64,568,000.[11] K. T. Eheberg, in a book published in 1885, counted this as an important factor in emigration, although he also stressed the economic attractions of North America.[12] Wilhelm Mönckmeier laid more stress on overpopulation as a major factor leading to emigration, beginning in the southwest of the country and then spreading to affect the rest of Germany during the course of the nineteenth century. As the country became more industrialised it could absorb its excess population, which consequently meant a decline in emigration, a point examined by Fritz Joseephy who focused upon emigration from Germany after 1871.[13]

---

8. The peaks 1846–57, 1864–73, and 1880–1893 are given in Klaus J. Bade, 'German Emigration to the United States and Continental Immigration to Germany in the Late Nineteenth and Early Twentieth Centuries', *Central European History*, vol. 13, 1980, p. 354.
9. Baines, *Emigration from Europe*, p. 9.
10. John E. Knodel, *The Decline of Fertility in Germany, 1871–1939*, Princeton, 1974, p. 192.
11. Ibid., p. 32.
12. K. T. Eheberg, *Die deutsche Auswanderung*, Heidelberg, 1885.
13. Wilhelm Mönckmeier, *Die deutsche Überseeische Auswanderung*, Jena, 1912, pp. 26–8; Fitz Joseephy, *Die deutsche Überseeische Auswanderung seit 1871*, Berlin, 1912, pp. 51–6.

Hilde Wander repeated much of what Mönckemier had to say in an article published in 1958.[14]

In recent years, from the mid-1970s, historians of German population movement and growth including Peter Marschalck, Wolfgang Köllmann and John E. Knodel have refined Mönckmeier's ideas for the development of emigration on a national scale, while numerous other historians have carried out more detailed studies on specific areas of the country.

Marschalck and Köllmann have published numerous works on the question of German population history and migration and, as we have seen, have developed theoretical ideas about migration based on empirical research. Like Klaus J. Bade, they do not simply stress overpopulation as the main factor causing population loss but link it with industrialisation, land policies, the attractions of America and immediate and local factors. With regard to population they have shown that in the eighteenth century Germany was a country which experienced high marital fertility but also high mortality, meaning a fairly stable population with an annual growth rate of about five per thousand. In the first half of the nineteenth century a relative population growth resulted in an overcrowding of, or unemployment in, specific trades and a pressure to move.

Population increase continued in the second half of the nineteenth century, particularly as a consequence of changes in life expectancy, as this period witnessed a decline in the German fertility rate. By this time, however, population growth became relatively less important as a factor in emigration, as John E. Knodel has demonstrated, because after 1870, 'areas with relatively large net migratory losses' did not correlate with those which had experienced a high rate of population increase.[15]

It is therefore necessary to look at other factors, such as patterns of land ownership, to explain nineteenth-century German emigration more fully. Wander points out that 'emigration started from the territories of south-western Germany, where estates are divided between the heirs of the deceased owner, and spread more into the region of the large estates in the east and in the north. Both forms of property made it difficult to absorb a growing population'.[16] Marschalck and Köllman, and Bade,

14. Hilde Wander, 'Migration and the German Economy', in Thomas Brindley (ed.), *Economics of International Migration*, London, 1958, p. 198
15. Peter Marschalck and Wolfgang Köllman, 'German Overseas Migration since 1815', in Commission Internationale d'Histoire des Mouvements Sociaux et des Structures Sociales, *Les Migrations Internationales de la Fin du XVIIIe Siecle a Nos Jours*, pp. 455–7; Marschalck, 'The Age of Demographic Transition: Mortality and Fertility', in Klaus J. Bade (ed.), *Population, Labour and Migration in 19th and 20th Century Germany*, Leamington Spa, 1987, pp. 15–28; Knodel, *Decline of Fertility*, p. 204.
16. Wander, 'Migration and the German Economy', p. 198.

have in recent studies taken an overview which suggests property ownership was a factor leading to emigration, while the older chronological accounts of Marcus Lee Hansen and Mack Walker stressed it as a fundamental factor. The latter wrote that land division amongst all heirs had existed for centuries which 'fragmented agricultural lands into a multitude of tiny holdings...which were ordinarily barely able, and often unable, to support the families which depended upon them.'[17] Hansen, meanwhile, wrote that 'fragmentation had reached a point that made it an important factor in emigration', because many farmers realized that if they had to divide their land between as many as six children, they would be 'doomed to the status of "potato earners"'.[18] In northeast Germany, meanwhile, Bade has more recently written of the inheritance system which gave land to the oldest son, which, in many cases meant that, for the rest of the sons, 'there was only one way of maintaining the social status and economic way of life: the exodus to the new world'.[19]

Bade, however, together with Marschalck and Köllmann and, especially, Walter D. Kamphoefner, has also stressed the importance of changes in the system of production. Still in the northeast, this factor became important during the late nineteenth century because of a decline in wheat prices, a move to machine harvesting, and an increase in root crops. During the summer there was an increased demand for seasonal workers but this declined in the winter, meaning that emigration represented an alternative for those who owned small pieces of land but could not sufficiently supplement their incomes through hiring out their labour.[20]

A different state of affairs developed in western Germany during the early nineteenth century, which has been studied by Kamphoefner and by Marschalck and Köllmann. The former has described the situation as one of 'proto-industry', which involved 'the decentralized, rural, labour-intensive production of goods for a distant market, usually supplemented by marginal agriculture'. Kamphoefner questions the claims of Hansen and Walker that the break-up of land holdings was fundamentally important during the early part of the nineteenth century; some areas of northwest Germany, including Minden and Osnabrück, experienced a population loss as heavy as that of Baden and Württemberg, traditionally recognised as areas of high population loss, and higher than some areas of the Rhineland which, with similar

17. Mack Walker, *Germany and the Emigration, 1816–1885*, Cambridge, Massachusetts, 1964, p. 3.
18. Marcus Lee Hansen, *The Atlantic Migration 1607–1860*, Cambridge, Massachusetts, 1941, p. 214.
19. Bade, 'German Emigration to the United States', pp. 360–1.
20. Ibid., p 361.

land inheritance, had undergone industrialisation. Kamphoefner believes that the existence of 'cottage industries' categorises the main areas of emigration during the early nineteenth century and 'their downfall is the predominant factor that must be superimposed upon inheritance systems to understand patterns of emigration.' This downfall came about in the early nineteenth century due to the economic effects of the Napoleonic Wars and competition from cheaper British goods due to mechanisation.[21]

Economic factors in general played an important role in emigration, particularly in its decline at the end of the nineteenth century. Mönckmeier's view that overpopulation became less of a stimulus to emigration during the late nineteenth century as Germany industrialised has been taken up by Bade. He links the decline in emigration with industrialisation, which meant that the eastern parts of the country which retained an emigration potential sent emigrants to the industrialised western area of the Rhineland and Westphalia. This movement became particularly important after 1880, although for much of the 1880s internal migration and emigration took place simultaneously. Bade plays down the idea put forward by Köllmann and Marschalck that the declaration in 1890 by the government of the USA, the main destination of nineteenth-century German emigrants, that free settlement on its land had come to an end also led to a decline in emigration; he stresses instead, 'the bust of the 1890s, especially the Panic of 1893 in America, and the simultaneous beginning of the prewar boom period in Germany'.[22]

Clearly, the underlying socio-economic push factors in nineteenth-century Germany, overpopulation, land inheritance and changes in the economy, have fundamental connections with each other, which scholars working in the area of German emigration have stressed to different degrees.[23] Having outlined these background causes of German population loss, we can now move on to give a chronological account of emigration from Germany during the nineteenth century including the areas affected, the immediate reasons for emigration, the composition of the emigrant group, numbers of immigrants, and their destinations.

21. Walter D. Kamphoefner, 'At the Crossroads of Economic Development: Background Factors Affecting Emigration from Nineteenth Century Germany', in Ira D. Glazier and Luigi De Rosa (eds), *Migration Across Time and Nations: Population Mobility in Historical Contexts*, New York, 1986, pp. 174–8.
22. Mönckmeier, *Überseeische Auswanderung*, pp. 27–8; Köllmann and Marschalck, 'German Overseas Migration', p. 457; Bade, 'German Emigration to the United States', pp. 362–5.
23. See David Luebke, 'German Exodus: Historical Perspectives on the Nineteenth-Century German Emigration', *Yearbook of German-American Studies*, vol. 20, 1985, pp. 1–17, for another survey of German emigration.

The previous chapter demonstrated that eighteenth-century emigration from Germany came mainly from the southwest of the country, an area which continued to lose population during the first half of the nineteenth century, as we can see from the first peak which occurred shortly after the end of the Napoleonic Wars in 1816–17.[24] This movement took place against a background of 'proto-industrialisation', 'population growth' and equal land distribution. However, the region had also suffered during the conflicts through destruction of property and plundering by troops. In 1816 there came 'the worst agricultural catastrophe anybody could remember' and the climax of a series of bad harvests and severe winters which had destroyed the vine crop. The affected areas included south Germany, Switzerland and Alsace. There followed an increase in wheat prices and consequent hunger, resulting in hopelessness and an almost spontaneous stream of families out of southwest Germany and to the USA. Between 1816 and 1819 about 25,000 people left Germany, including 17,500 from Württemberg alone during the years 1816–17.[25]

Following this first minor peak of emigration from Germany there was a relative lull, until the first major movement out of Germany between about 1845 and 1855. Emigration did take place in the intervening years, in some instances on a larger scale than in the years 1816–17. From 1820–9 22,500 people left Germany, a figure which increased to 145,100 in 1830–9 and 110,600 in 1840–4. [26] This decade also witnessed the first significant movement of Germans to Brazil, totalling between 7,000 and 10,000 from 1823–30.[27]

24. However, emigration had certainly taken place from Germany during the Napoleonic Wars. Württemberg alone had lost 17,500 people between 1800 and 1804, particularly to Russia. See Günter Moltmann (ed.), *Aufbruch nach Amerika: Friedrich List und die Auswanderung aus Baden und Württemberg 1816/17: Dokumentation einer Sozialen Bewegung*, Tübingen, 1979, p. 21. For movement towards Russia, see also Eugen von Philippovich, 'Auswanderung und Auswanderungspolitik im Grossherzogtum Baden', in Philippovich (ed.), *Auswanderung und Auswanderungs Politik in Deutschland*, Leipzig, 1892, pp. 103–8.

25. Moltmann, *Aufbruch nach Amerika*; Harold Focke, 'Friedrich List und die südwestdeutsche Amerikaauswanderung 1817–1846', in Moltmann (ed.), *Deutsche Amerikaauswanderung im 19. Jahrhundert*, Stuttgart, 1976, pp. 72–3; Wolfgang von Hippel, *Auswanderung aus Südwestdeutschland: Studien zur Württembergischen Auswanderung und Auswanderungspolitik im 18. und 19. Jahrhundert*, Stuttgart, 1984, p. 138; Marschalck, *Deutsche überseeische Auswanderung*, p. 35; Walker, *Germany and the Emigration*, pp. 4, 6, 7, 17, 29, 39; Philippovich, 'Auswanderung in Baden', pp. 109–16.

26. Köllmann and Marschalck, 'German Overseas Emigration', p. 453. Only 5,700 people went to the USA during the 1820s.

27. Frederick C. Luebke, *Germans in Brazil: A Comparative History of Cultural Conflict During World War I*, Baton Rouge and London, pp. 8–9; Walker, *Germany and the Emigration*, p. 39; Philippovich, 'Auswanderung in Baden', pp. 119–26.

Clearly, from the figures quoted above, there was an increase in emigration during the 1830s, especially to the USA. Improved transportation, together with a spread of migration from the southwest of the country northwards to Westaphalia, Hanover and Oldenburg, were partly responsible for this increase. Immigration continued from the traditional areas as well. For instance from Württemberg, where 56,000 people migrated between 1831 and 1846. There was also an increase in emigration from Bavaria during the years 1835–43.[28]

While emigration had continued to rise in the 1830s and early 1840s, the first peak recognised by Bade began in the year 1846 and lasted until 1857. According to figures provided by Mönckmeier, a total of 1,437,519 people left Germany via Hamburg and Bremen during these years. In 1854 alone Germany lost 251,931 emigrants.[29] The average annual migration rate rose from 173 per ten thousand in 1841–50 to 250 per ten thousand in the following decade,[30] in other words from 1.7 percent to 2.5 per cent. Clearly, this represents population loss on a massive scale.

Before looking at the details of this movement in more detail, we need to consider its causes. An overview might see it as part of a mid-nineteenth century social, political and economic crisis in Europe, sparked off by poor harvests but feeding on resentments caused by the early and exploitative stages of industrialisation. Germany was not the only country to endure a period of turmoil during these years; virtually every other European country was affected. In Ireland the reaction took the form of a mass migration, while in other countries the result was political upheaval. Germany, perhaps uniquely, experienced both phenomena.[31]

The crop failures of the mid-1840s represent a good starting point for understanding the mid-century migration from Germany, although once again these must be placed against the background of the underlying social and economic developments discussed above, especially

28. Walter D. Kamphoefner, *The Westfalians: From Germany to Missouri*, Princeton, 1987, pp. 15, 42; Walker, *Germany and the Emigration*, p. 47; Georg von Viebahn, *Statistik der Zollverein und Nördlichen Deutschlands*, vol. 2, Berlin, 1862, p. 244; Ministerialsekretär Fey, 'Die Entwicklung des Auswanderungswesens und Auswanderungsrechtes im Grossherzogtum Hessen', in Phillipovich, *Auswanderungspolitik*, p. 226; F. C. Huber, 'Auswanderung und Auswanderungspolitik im Königreich Württemberg', in Philippovich, *Auswanderungspolitik*, pp. 236–7.

29. Bade, 'German Emigration to the United States', p. 354; Mönckmeier, *Deutsche Überseeische Auswanderung*, p. 16.

30. Erickson, *Emigration from Europe*, p. 29.

31. For a broad coverage of economic, social and political developments during this period, see Eric Hobsbawm, *Europäische Revolutionen, 1789 bis 1848*, Zurich, 1962. For an introduction to the German situation see James J. Sheehan, *German History 1770–1866*, Oxford, 1989, pp. 453–504, 637–53.

the fragmentation of land ownership, which continued apace. The harvest disasters represent no more than a spark to fuel the general insecurities. The year 1845 had resulted in a below-average crop yield in many parts of Germany and in the following year there followed potato, rye, wheat, and fruit failures. During the early 1850s similar agricultural failures took place, affecting a wide variety of crops. Inevitably, widespread poverty became a major consequence of these developments.[32]

Nevertheless, neither the underlying socio-economic changes nor the immediate living conditions of the mid-nineteenth century can alone explain the mass migration of these years because, while crop failures had as we have seen led to population movements from Germany in the past, they had not caused the virtual exodus which developed now. Emigration had become a 'craze' which 'represented the cure for all ills, private and public'.[33] The emigration movement was in fact not dissimilar to the revolutionary movement which was developing in Germany almost simultaneously.[34] As democratic ideas became so widespread that they developed into the virtual obsession which led to the 1848 revolutionary outbreak, so in the same way the idea of emigration, which also offered an alternative to present conditions, became widespread before the years 1848–54.

Several factors helped spread the popularity of emigration. The first was the advertising activities of states which wished to attract immigrants, such as Russia during the 1820s and Brazil from as early as 1818, which offered free passage and free land to emigrants. Other states which began advertising from the 1840s included Chile, Canada and Australia. The agents of these countries often worked with those of shipping companies, providing an attractive image of the destination of the potential emigrants.[35] By the 1840s emigration had become a political question attracting the activities of publishers, resulting in countless newspaper articles, journal essays, brochures and books. Emigration societies developed, as did a series of newspapers devoted specifically

32. Marcus L. Hansen, 'The Revolutions of 1848 and German Emigration', *Journal of Economic and Business History*, vol. 2, 1929, pp. 648, 653–4; Hippel, *Auswanderung aus Südwestdeutschland*, p. 163.

33. Hansen, *Atlantic Migration*, p. 288.

34. The importance of the revolution for emigration receives attention subsequently in this chapter but Walker, *Germany and the Emigration*, pp.129–30, has perceptively compared emigration with the revolutions of 1848 as reactions against the prevailing social, political and economic situation in Germany.

35. Hermann von Freeden and Georg Smolka (eds), *Auswanderer: Bilder und Skizzen aus der Geschichte der deutschen Auswanderung*, Leipzig, 1937, pp. 49–51; Mönckmeier, *Deutsche überseeische Auswanderung*, pp. 31–2.

to the issue.[36] The extent of public interest helped force the issue of emigration onto the political agenda; the freedom to migrate became an important issue during the 1848 Revolution and the meeting of the Frankfurt Parliament, which accepted freedom of emigration. In Baden, meanwhile, emigrants actually received financial support from the state during the early 1850s.[37]

Also important was the availability of shipping, which receives more detailed attention below in the discussion on routes through Britain. Particularly important were the development of Bremen and Hamburg as ports of departure which began to take over from Le Havre, Antwerp and Rotterdam, which most German emigrants had used during the 1830s. Between 1846 and 1851 the numbers of people using non-German ports decreased from 56,523 to 56,477, while those using German ports grew from 38,058 to 56,070. Between 1846 and 1858, 550,000 out of 1,360,000 German emigrants left the country through Bremen. This increase resulted partly from actions taken by the governments of Hamburg and Bremen, including the establishment of offices to advise emigrants.[38] However, we also need to point to the development of the steam ship, which by the end of the 1860s had taken over the emigrant traffic from sailing vessels, and the growth of shipping lines for the transportation of trans-Atlantic travellers.[39]

Turning to the areas of origins of the emigrants Tables 2.1 and 2.2 show that migration from the east of Germany remained low so that East Prussia, West Prussia, and Berlin and Brandenburg actually showed an increase in population from 1851–60, although Pomerania and the Prussian Province of Saxony displayed a loss of significant numbers. Nevertheless, the areas with the largest proportion of emigrants consisted of the traditional southwestern areas of Baden and Württemberg,

36. Hans Fenske, 'Die deutsche Auswanderung in der Mitte des 19. Jahrhunderts', *Geschichte in Wissenschaft und Unterricht*, vol. 24, 1978, p. 222. Marschalck, *Deutsche überseewanderung*, pp. 19, 21, lists eight emigration newspapers from 1846–84, and twenty-seven societies at various times during the years 1833–1850.

37. Michael Kuckhoff, 'Die Auswanderungsdiskussion während der Revolution von 1848/49', in Moltmann (ed.), *Deutsche Amerikaauswanderung*, pp. 102–45; Philippovich, 'Auswanderung in Baden', pp. 131–42.

38. *Jahrbuch für Volkswirtschaft und Statistik*, Berlin, 1852, p. 264; Brigit Gelberg, *Auswanderung nach Übersee: Soziale Probleme der Auswandererbeförderung in Hamburg und Bremen von der Mitte des 19. Jahrhunderts bis zum ersten Weltkrieg*, Hamburg, 1973, pp. 7–15.

39. Peter Marschalk, 'Zur Geschichte der Auswanderung über Bremen: Entwicklungslinien und Forschungsprobleme', *Bremer Archiven*, vol. 53, 1986, p. 20; Rudolf Engelsing, *Bremen als Auswandererhafen 1683–1880*, Bremen, 1961, pp. 92–108; Philip Taylor, *The Distant Magnet: European Emigration to the USA*, London, 1971, pp. 131–66. Freeden and Smolka, *Auswanderer*, pp. 56–9, give details of the journey to America.

which lost 0.7 and 0.8 per cent of their population respectively between 1851 and 1860, and those which had begun to experience emigration during the 1830s, Hanover (which included Osnabrück)[40] and Hesse-Nassau, with an annual loss of almost 0.7 per cent from 1851–61.

Schleswig-Holstein also experienced an increase in emigration during these years, which Walker linked to a more general loss from other areas of north and east Germany caused by a depression of crafts and industry and the continued break-up of land ownership, as well as by the proletarianisation of peasants in the east due to a takeover of land by Prussian landowners. However, the spread of emigration fever to these areas may also have been responsible. In Mecklenberg, for example, emigration societies became active from 1850.[41]

Many statistical accounts provide us with details of the social, sex and age composition of the emigrant groups. With regard to the first of these, Mönckmeier demonstrated that for the years 1846–52, artisans and businessmen accounted for 60 per cent of emigrants who left Germany via Hamburg while the rest consisted of farmers and day labourers. His figures for age and sex ratio of emigrants do not begin until 1855. From then until 1857, the last of Bade's peak years, 75,104 people migrated through this port, of whom 41.6 per cent consisted of men and 20 per cent children under ten years of age,[42] indicating that families made up a substantial proportion of the emigrants. Destinations by this time were overwhelmingly in North America. Of those who left Germany via Bremen and Hamburg in 1856 and 1857, nearly 85 per cent went to the USA and 4 per cent to British North America, while 2.5 per cent made their way to Brazil and 2.7 per cent to Australia.[43]

Following the peak migration of the late 1840s and early 1850s there was a decline, which lasted until 1864. From 1858–63 a total of 269,400 people left Germany, and between 1861–3, the annual total fell to below 40,000.[44] Most commentators explain this reduction by the effects of the American Civil War which lasted from 1860–65. While push factors may have remained strong within Germany, the news of the conflict 'was generally interpreted so negatively that, although other American pull factors continued in full force, their effect was largely neutralised'. We can also point to 'the psychological frame of

40. For more detailed statistics of migration from this area during the mid-nineteenth century, see Kamphoefner, *Westfalians*, p. 15.

41. Walker, *Germany and the Emigration*, pp. 161–3; Lindig, 'Entwicklung und gegenwärtiger Zustand des Auswanderungswesens im Grosherzogtum Mecklenburg', in Philippovich, *Auswanderungspolitik*, pp. 296–8.

42. Mönckmeier, *Deutsche überseeische Wanderung*, p. 139.

43. *Jahrbuch für Volkwirtschaft und Statistik*, Berlin, 1861, p. 144.

44. Marschalck, *Deutsche überseewanderung*, p. 36.

German Immigrants in Britain

mind of the potential emigrant, which in one case is supportive of emigration and in another would suggest postponement or even acceptance of existing circumstances'.[45] The Civil War years also resulted in an increase of return migration, a phenomenon which developed throughout the nineteenth century. At the same time, population pressure within Germany declined and continuing industrialisation led to an economic upturn.[46]

While 'the statistical waves and peaks' of emigration may 'reflect a response to a multi-faceted combination of push factors (in the region of emigration) and pull factors (in the area of immigration)',[47] it seems that the Civil War did represent the main obstacle preventing people taking the decision to cross the Atlantic. Although population loss increased in the years 1864 and 1865 (to 60,700 and 88,700 respectively), only from 1865 onward did it begin to reach the sorts of levels which it had a decade earlier. On five occasions between 1866 and 1873, over 100,000 people left Germany, making a total of 1,404,000 for the years 1864–73.

There are several explanations for this second major wave of emigration. The main external factor was again the attractions of the USA. Most historians dealing with German migration have described this as the movement of people who had postponed their decision to leave Germany due to the American Civil War and who now decided to move, which resulted in the sudden surge.[48] At the same time, the American government passed the Act to Encourage Immigration in 1864;[49] the US economy was growing faster than the German one at this time, even though the latter was also entering a period of rapid expansion immediately before and after the creation of a unified German state in 1871.[50]

Push factors which led people to leave Germany at this time included the effects of the wars of 1864 against Denmark, in 1866 against

45. Reinhard R. Dörries, 'German Transatlantic Migration from the Early Nineteenth Century to the Outbreak of World War II', in Bade (ed.), Population, Labour and Migration, pp. 124–5.
46. Köllman and Marschalck, 'German Emigration to the United States', p. 531; Günter Moltmann, 'American-German Return Migration in the Nineteenth and Early Twentieth Centuries', Central European History, vol. 13, 1980, pp. 378–92.
47. Dörries, 'German Transatlantic Migration', p. 124.
48. See, for instance, F. Burgdörfer, 'Migration Across the Frontiers of Germany', in Walter F. Willcox, International Migrations, 2 vols, London, 1969 edition, vol. 2, p. 343.
49. Ingrid Schöberl, 'Emigration Policy in Germany and Immigration Policy in the United States', in Günter Moltmann (ed.), Germans in America: 300 Years of Immigration, 1683–1983, Stuttgart, 1982, p. 41; Charlotte Erickson, American Industry and the European Immigrant 1860–1885, New York, 1957.
50. Walker, German and the Emigration, pp. 181–3; Heinzpeter Thümmler, 'Zum Problem der Auswanderung aus dem Deutschen Reich zwischen 1871 und 1900', Jahrbuch für Wirtschaftsgeschichte, 1975, part 3, p. 74.

Austria, and in 1870–1 against France. According to Burgdörfer, 'Districts in which the inhabitants had suffered from war or were dissatisfied with the change in political conditions or with the introduction of compulsory military service, contributed largely to the new current'. Nevertheless, we should remain cautious about this factor.[51]

Other unmeasurable 'subjective' factors include those tackled by Joseephy, who wrote of 'physiological' and psychological motivations including the restlessness of some individuals and the desire for adventure. While we cannot dismiss these ideas, which probably play a part in the decision of every individual to move, we can suggest that the individual would not move without the presence of a larger mass migration created by economic developments. Tables 2.1 and 2.2 demonstrate that during the decade 1871–80 there was a significant increase in emigration from several eastern provinces, notably East and West Prussia, Posen and Silesia, together with a decline or levelling off of movement from southwest and western Germany, trends which continue into the following decades. These changes have previously received explanation with regard to the spread of industry to the southern and western areas and the changing land conditions in the east which left many agricultural labourers landless because of land division and the introduction of new farming techniques.[52]

51. Burgdörfer, 'Migration Across the Frontiers of Germany', p. 343. If this argument contains truth then we would expect migration to have increased from, for instance, Schleswig and Holstein, Saxony, Hanover, Hesse-Cassel, Alsace and Lorraine during the 1860s and early 1870s, as these lands faced the Prussian military. If we look at Tables 2.1 and 2.2, this argument receives some support from the dramatic increase of emigration from Schleswig-Holstein, as well as from an increase from Hanover, for instance. See also 'Die Einwanderung und Auswanderung der preussischen Staates in den Jahren 1862 bis 1871', in *Preussische Statistik*, vol. 26, 1874, pp. viii–ix, which demonstrates a dramatic increase in Prussian emigration during the years 1866–7 from 18,016 in the former to 40,543 during the latter, but, a decrease in 1870–1. These statistics suggest that the impact of the annexations of Schleswig-Holstein, Hanover, Hesse-Cassel, Frankfurt and Nassau in 1866 may have proved important, but we cannot come to any definite conclusions. See also A. E. Rosenkranz, *Geschichte der deutschen evangelischen Kirche zu Liverpool*, Stuttgart, 1921, p. 56 which mentions an influx of Hanoverians into Liverpool in 1866, the year of Prussian annexation. For an examination of the relationship between military service and emigration in Hesse during the nineteenth century see Kurt Günther, 'Beiträge zum Problem der kurhessischen Auswanderung im 18. und 19. Jahrhundert, insbesondere nach Nordamerika', *Zeitschrift des Vereins für hessische Geschichte und Landeskunde*, vol. 75–6, 1964–5, pp. 522–33, who regards escape from military service as a major reason for movement from this region. Brief details about the main developments in the wars of German unification can be found in William Carr, *A History of Germany 1815–1945*, London, 1981 reprint, pp. 87–124.

52. See above pp. 6–7. For physiological and psychological factors see Joseephy, *Deutsche überseeische Auswanderung seit 1871*, pp. 41–51. This author also stresses the role of 'propaganda' for emigration which continued to have the same importance as it had earlier in the century through the activities of the press and agents.

Table 2.1 Emigration from Germany, 1841–1900

Years	1841–50	1851–60	1861–70	1871–80	1881–90	1891–1900
Prussian Provinces						
East Prussia	− 23,066	+ 33,729	− 19,504	− 95,216	−210,837	−233,519
West Prussia	+ 11,811	+ 13,668	− 31,999	−108,455	−198,300	−137,151
Berlin & Brandenburg	+ 65,141	+ 7,065	+132,003	+184,450	+325,948	+367,156
Pomerania	− 4,320	− 29,424	−119,386	−130,707	−222,502	−109,439
Posen	− 9,188	− 11,987	− 90,247	−145,320	−233,100	−218,178
Silesia	− 5,944	− 19,011	− 45,967	−123,858	−219,852	−151,237
Saxony (Province)	− 17,040	− 54,973	− 69,403	− 85,563	− 60,950	−132,969
Schleswig-Holstein	− 12,348	− 33,233	− 58,189	− 60,920	− 48,215	− 22,704
Hanover	− 81,075	− 80,385	− 92,401	− 52,162	− 85,206	− 25,951
Westphalia	− 32,462	− 32,133	− 9,641	+ 9,331	+ 36,815	+212,193
Hesse-Nassau	− 47,465	− 84,902	− 23,581	+ 9,402	+ 45,732	+ 3,665
Rhineland	− 12,970	+ 3,659	+ 4,205	− 13,733	+ 30,303	+196,499
Prussia	−188,022	−361,298	−512,858	−467,835	−928,973	−256,318
Rest of Germany						
Bavaria	−116,460	− 87,594	−145,712	− 48,757	−159,664	− 72,631
Saxony (Kingdom)	+ 18,413	+ 19,612	+ 33,410	+ 74,552	+ 88,034	+105,444
Württemberg	− 71,911	−136,612	− 66,827	− 66,329	−138,025	− 94,198
Baden	− 72,180	− 92,622	− 39,350	− 55,263	− 65,246	+ 15,207
Alsace Lorraine	− 53,623	− 90,967	− 94,098	−116,776	− 68,516	− 26,147

Source: Charlotte Erickson (ed.), *Emigration from Europe 1815–1914*, London, 1976, p. 28.

Table 2.2 Emigration from Germany per 100,000 inhabitants, 1841–1900

Years	1841–50	1851–60	1861–70	1871–80	1881–90	1891–1900
Prussian Provinces						
East Prussia	−160	+220	−110	−490	−1,080	−1,180
West Prussia	+120	+120	−260	−780	+1,400	−920
Berlin & Brandenburg	+323	+31	+500	+614	+881	+795
Pomerania	−40	−250	−820	−830	−1,460	−700
Posen	−70	−90	−590	−830	−1,350	−1,180
Silesia	−30	−50	−130	−290	−510	−340
Saxony (Province)	−100	−290	−340	−330	−250	−490
Schleswig-Holstein	−140	−340	−570	−410	−420	−180
Hanover	−460	−440	−480	−230	−390	−110
Westphalia	−230	−210	−60	+80	+160	+630
Hesse-Nassau	−380	−670	−530	−60	−290	+20
Rhineland	−50	+10	+10	−10	+60	+390
Prussia	−82	−143	−228	−181	−326	−80
Rest of Germany						
Bavaria	−263	−259	−315	−97	−294	−124
Saxony (Kingdom)	+98	+115	+131	+271	+274	+276
Württemberg	−392	−803	−391	−351	−689	−450
Baden	−496	−708	−287	−366	−406	+87
Alsace Lorraine	−372	−558	−605	−754	−435	−158

Source: Charlotte Erickson (ed.), *Emigration from Europe 1815–1914*, London, 1976, p. 29.

The peak of the 1860s and early 1870s came to an end with the stock market crash of 1873 and the subsequent depression, so that the year 1875 displays the highest percentage of return migration relative to emigration from the USA to Germany. The trough which began in 1874 lasted until 1879; in each year less than 50,000 people migrated, for a total of less than 200,000. The final peak lasted from 1880–93, a period of economic upturn in the USA when 1,783,700 people left Germany; in two particularly high years, 1881 and 1882, over 200,000 people emigrated. Throughout the late nineteenth century the major destination remained the USA, although there was a slight increase in the numbers destined for Brazil.[53]

As to the sex and age composition of the migrants of the late nineteenth century, statistics compiled by Mönckmeier demonstrate that the proportion of males to females was similar to the situation earlier in the century, with women making up between 40 and 45 per cent from 1871–1910. The proportion of adults to children under ten years old also did not dramatically change until the decline in German migration after 1895, with less than 15 per cent of emigrants consisting of children. These figures are illustrated in Table 2.3.

An attempt to give definite figures about the social composition of German emigrants proves more difficult. We have seen that in the years between 1846 and 1852 just over 40 per cent of people leaving Germany consisted of farmers and labourers, while business people and artisans made up the remainder. As the century progressed the social composition of the emigrants consisted more of agricultural labourers and industrial workers, reflecting both the shift in focus to eastern agricultural districts and the continuing industrialisation process in Germany, which meant a decline in the number of artisans and a rise in the number of proletarians.[54]

Emigration certainly continued after the mid-1890s but, as we have seen, it became smaller in scale as Germany had industrialised sufficiently to absorb its surplus population. As Table 2.4 demonstrates, after

53. Freeden and Smolka, *Auswanderer*, p. 43; Wolfgang Helbich, W. D. Kamphoefner and Ulrike Sommer, *Briefe aus Amerika: Deutsche Schreiben aus der Neuen Welt, 1830–1930*, Munich, 1988, pp. 17, 18; Moltmann, 'American-German Return Migration', pp. 388–9. As Walker, *Germany and the Emigration*, pp. 181–2, points out, the 'most striking feature' of the peaks and troughs of the late nineteenth century 'is that emigration was heaviest just at times of high economic activity and business advance and low at times of economic retreat and stagnation', but we must remember the fact that the pull of the American economy remained stronger than that of the German one.

54. See Marschalck and Köllmann, 'German Emigration to the United States', pp. 536–41; Mönckmeier, *Deutsche überseeische Auswanderung*, pp. 162–7; Thümmler, 'Zum Problem der Auswanderung', pp. 90–1.

Table 2.3 Emigration of Germans according to Age and Sex

Years	Percentage of Males	Percentage of Females	Percentage under 10 years of age
1855–9	58.25	41.75	20.66
1860–4	59.99	40.01	20.32
1865–9	60.05	39.95	20.76
1871–4	58.00	42.00	21.70
1875–9	58.20	41.80	18.50
1880–4	57.50	42.50	22.70
1885–9	54.80	45.20	19.00
1890–4	54.70	45.30	18.00
1895–9	55.10	44.90	11.70
1900–4	57.20	42.80	14.50
1905–9	58.00	42.00	13.40
1855–1909	57.40	42.60	18.30

Source: Wilhelm Mönckmeier, *Die deutsche überseeische Auswanderung*, Jena, 1912, pp. 140, 144, 146.

1894 emigration never totalled more than 40,000 in any one year. Burgdörfer describes 'a sort of temporary emigration made up of trained industrial labourers, technical labourers, foremen, engineers and tradespeople, who removed overseas for a long period rather than for life, to profit from the favourable economic conditions'.[55] Consequently, between 1815 and 1900 Germany changed from a country of mass emigration to one which, after the mid 1890s, even experienced a gain in population due to an influx of workers from the east.[56] The movement out of the country changed from one consisting primarily of artisans and small business people in the first half of the century to one made up mostly of proletarians and agricultural labourers from about the 1870s onwards, and finally, when emigration had declined, to one consisting of temporary emigrants.

We have outlined the major economic push factors, but in the case of the mass migration, we have also seen that the attractions of the USA proved as important as any socio-economic factor which led people to leave Germany. Thus, as Table 2.5 illustrates, the main concentration of Germans abroad by the First World War was in the USA, where the

55. Burgdörfer, 'Migration Across the Frontiers of Germany', p. 344. See also Joseephy, *Deutsche überseeische Auswanderung seit 1871*, p. 83, who lists the occupations of middle-class emigrants from 1907–11.

56. See Table 120 in Burgdörfer, 'Migration Across the Frontiers of Germany', p. 316, which demonstrates that there was an excess of immigration over emigration for the first time in the years 1901–10.

Table 2.4   German Emigration in Thousands, 1816–1914

Year	Emigration	Year	Emigration	Year	Emigration
1816–19	25.0	1851	78.8	1883	173.6
1820	3.0	1852	176.4	1884	149.1
1821	2.8	1853	150.7	1885	110.1
1822	1.1	1854	239.2	1886	183.2
1823	1.3	1855	83.8	1887	104.8
1824	1.6	1856	80.9	1888	104.0
1825	3.2	1857	103.1	1889	96.1
1826	1.4	1858	56.8	1890	97.1
1827	1.2	1859	47.4	1891	120.1
1828	5.2	1860	57.9	1892	116.3
1829	1.7	1861	36.1	1893	87.7
1830	5.5	1862	31.4	1894	41.0
1831	7.2	1863	39.0	1895	37.5
1832	11.2	1864	60.7	1896	37.5
1833	7.7	1865	88.7	1897	24.6
1834	19.5	1866	120.4	1898	22.2
1835	9.1	1867	138.4	1899	24.3
1836	22.8	1868	59.0	1900	22.3
1837	26.1	1869	136.2	1901	22.1
1838	12.9	1870	122.2	1902	32.1
1839	23.1	1871	76.2	1903	36.3
1840	32.7	1872	128.2	1904	28.0
1841	16.8	1873	110.4	1905	28.1
1842	22.4	1874	47.6	1906	31.1
1843	15.9	1875	32.3	1907	31.7
1844	22.9	1876	26.6	1908	19.9
1845	37.8	1877	22.9	1909	24.9
1846	63.3	1878	25.6	1910	25.5
1847	80.3	1879	35.9	1911	22.7
1848	62.6	1880	117.1	1912	18.5
1849	64.2	1881	220.9	1913	25.8
1850	83.2	1882	203.6	1914	11.8

Source: Peter Marschalck, *Deutsche Ueberseewanderung im 19. Jahrhundert,* Stuttgart, 1973, pp. 35–7.

emigrant population numbered over 2,500,000. As was the case earlier in the century, the greater proportion of German emigrants preferred America.[57] Significantly, peaks of migration from Germany coincide with similar peaks in Britain and in Europe more generally, suggesting the fundamental importance of an underlying pull factor of a powerful US economy which attracted large-scale immigration from the whole of Europe when an economic upswing occurred.[58]

Table 2.5 shows that the German population in the British Isles was 56,000 in 1911, making up 0.1 per cent of the population. Having seen that there were economic push factors which caused people to leave Germany, we now need to establish which economic pull factors existed in Britain. First, however, it remains to be seen whether those Germans who entered Britain during the nineteenth and early twentieth centuries formed part of the same stream which flowed out of Germany during this period; in other words, did the German immigrants who came to Britain leave their homeland for the same reasons as those who left for other parts of the world? We can best attempt to answer this question comprehensively by seeking to establish the regions of origin of Germans in Britain. This will help to weigh up the relative importance of push and pull factors with regard to Britain as a destination. As we have seen, American pull factors proved fundamental for more general German emigration; it remains to be seen if the same was true of Britain.

There are no comprehensive statistics on the origin of Germans in Britain. Published British census figures simply give the country of birth.[59] Other primary sources available include first, accounts of the German community in Britain, or in a particular city within the country; second, incomplete German statistics; third, *Annual Reports* of the Society of Friends of Foreigners in Distress, which give the states of birth of Germans whom it assisted; and fourth, the marriage registers of St George's German Lutheran Church in Whitechapel, which recorded the places of birth of brides and grooms.

As for secondary sources, some information survives in publications concerned with religion or religious groups. For instance, C. C.

---

57. Burgdörfer's table excluded Brazil but see p. 355 of his 'Migration Across the Frontiers of Germany', where he asserts that, according to Brazilian statistics, 190,000 Germans entered the country between 1818 and 1926. For an earlier count of Germans abroad see 'Die Deutschen im Auslande und die Ausländer im deutschen Reich', in *Kacerliches Statistisches Amt, Monatshefte zur Statistik des Deutschen Reichs*, August 1884, p. 18.

58. Brinley Thomas, *Migration and Economic Growth: A Study of Great Britain and the Atlantic Economy*, Cambridge, 1954.

59. But see *Census of England for the Year 1861*, vol. 2, p. lxxv, which actually has figures for Germans and Prussians. However, these distinctions are too broad to offer us any assistance.

Table 2.5 Major Focuses of German Populations before the First World War

Country	Census Year	German Population (thousands)	Germans per 1000 inhabitants
Luxembourg	1910	22	81
Switzerland	1910	220	47
United States	1910	2,501	27
Denmark	1911	35	13
Australia	1911	33	7
Belgium	1910	57	7
Netherlands	1909	38	6
Austria	1910	126	4
Chile	1907	11	3
France	1901	90	2
British Isles	1911	56	1
Argentina	1914	27	0.3
Italy	1911	11	0.03

Source: F Burgdörfer, 'Migration Across the Frontiers of Germany', in Walter F Willcox (ed.), *International Migrations,* London, 1961 reprint, p. 382.

Aronsfeld claims that most German Jews who made their way to England 'hailed from northern Germany, Hamburg, Hanover and Cologne, also from Berlin and what was then the Grand Duchy of Posen (now western Poland). By contrast, Jewish emigrants from southern Germany, especially Bavaria, usually chose the USA, the watershed being the city of Frankfurt', from which 'proportionately as many' Jews went to Britain as to the USA. Nevertheless, Aronsfeld quotes no sources and, while not dismissing his assertions, we have to question their reliability.[60]

More reliance may be placed upon accounts of German Christian communities within Britain, as some descriptions make use of church records. For instance, a history of St Paul's Church in East London, written in 1907 by the pastor at the time, Heinrich Deicke, cites church registers during the service of Johann Tiarks as vicar (1822–58) showing that the congregation included people from the Rhineland, Westfalia, Hesse, Hanover and Friesland, among other areas. Subsequently under Theodor Kübler (1858–75), there followed an influx of Württembergers.[61]

60. C. C. Aronsfeld, 'German Jews in Victorian England', *Leo Baeck Yearbook*, vol. 7, 1962, p. 313. See the subsequent discussion in this chapter on the entry of German Jews into Britain.
61. BA, Coblenz, R57 neu, 10642/42, 'Kurze Geschichte der deutschen evangelischen reformierten St Paulsgemeinde'.

Table 2.6   Emigration from Prussia, 1862–7

Area of Origin	Total	Total to Great Britain	Percentage to Great Britain
Königsberg	529	56	10.6
Gumbinnen	53	1	1.9
Danzig	2,049	22	1.1
Marionwerder	3,153	3	0.1
Berlin	250	56	22.4
Potsdam	9,515	9	0.1
Frankfurt	6,234	14	0.2
Stettin	20,991	23	0.1
Köslin	10,393	2	0.02
Stralsund	9,764	4	0.04
Posen	1,923	80	4.4
Bromberg	7,037	65	0.9
Breslau	1,448	7	0.5
Liegnitz	988	9	0.9
Oppeln	1,739	6	0.3
Magdeburg	3,265	39	1.2
Merseburg	2,293	18	0.8
Erfurt	2,480	11	0.4
Schleswig	10,239	113	1.1
Hanover	5,724	40	0.7
Hildesheim	3,509	21	0.6
Lüneberg	5,083	19	0.4
Stade	8,186	152	1.9
Osnabrück	7,396	2	0.02
Aurich	7,166	9	0.1
Münster	5,728	22	0.4
Minden	10,349	45	0.4
Arnsberg	2,355	17	0.7
Cassel	12,679	140	1.1
Wiesbaden	3,520	302	8.6
Coblenz	6,760	250	3.7
Düsseldorf	2,401	110	4.5
Cologne	1,668	60	3.5
Trier	8,354	63	0.7
Aachen	1,032	12	1.2
Sigmaringen	358	1	0.3
Jadesgebiet	17	0	0.0
Prussia	186,408	1,803	1.9

Source: 'Die Einwanderung und Auswanderung des Preussischen Staates in den Jahren 1862 bis 1871', in *Preussische Statistik*, vol. 26, 1874, p. xi.

The massive history of the German church in Liverpool by A. E. Rosenkranz, who served as one of its vicars and who made wide use of records held by the church, provides useful information on the origins of the Liverpool community. He writes that during the early and middle part of the century the local German community consisted of immigrants with origins in the north of the country, from Bremen and Hanover; but that subsequently, from the mid-1860s, many Germans from the northern part of Württemberg settled in Liverpool.[62] The accounts by Deicke and Rosenkranz represent the most reliable secondary sources on the origins of Germans in Britain,[63] and tie in with other sources of information as indicated below.

As for German statistical information, there are difficulties because of its incompleteness. There are no detailed returns running for any length of time of German emigrants from particular states with details of their country of destination. Nevertheless, some information can be extracted, for instance from the *Statistisches Jahrbuch für das deutsche Reich*, which indicates country of destination but, unfortunately, not the area of Germany which the emigrants were leaving.[64] The most reliable published statistical source on the origins of German immigrants in Great Britain unfortunately covers only the years 1862–71, and refers only to Prussia. This information indicates that 1,803, out of 186,408, emigrants made their way to Britain during these years; 1.9 per cent of the total. Destinations broken down by region fit within this pattern, falling within 1.8 per cent of this figure, between 0.1 and 3.7 per cent. Exceptions include Königsberg (10.4), Berlin (22.4), Posen (4.4) and Düsseldorf (4.5), as well as Osnabrück (0.02), Köslin (0.02), Stralsund (0.04) and Jadesgebiet (0.0). With this data it is difficult to reach any specific conclusions about the importance of push factors because, with few exceptions, the migration of Germans to Britain follows a similar pattern to that of more general German emigration.

Another set of data, again incomplete, comes from a few surviving annual reports of the Society of Friends of Foreigners in Distress which

62. Rosenkranz, *Geschichte der Kirche zu Liverpool*, pp. 56–7.
63. Less reliable is Wilhelm Schuster, 'Unsere Schwaben in England', *Deutsch Evangelisch im Auslande*, vol. 7, 1907, pp. 191–2, who claimed that most Germans in England at the time of writing originated in Swabia and the most northern part of Germany. See also O. Zuckschwerdt, 'Auswanderernöte', *Der Deutsche Auswander*, vol. 11, 1913, pp. 29–33, who mentions the passage of German-Russians through Liverpool on their way to America, but does not indicate that any remained in the city.
64. As the title indicates, this publication appeared annually. The information it contains about numbers of German immigrants to Britain proves interesting in itself, although incomplete. The counting does not begin until 1899. However, from this date until 1912 we discover from *Statistisches Jahrbuch für das deutsche Reich*, Berlin, 1913, that 8,629 Germans moved to Britain.

give the areas of origins of Germans it assisted. The years for which reports survive are 1866, 1878 and 1883, and the results are indicated in Table 2.7. Again, there are difficulties in reaching any conclusions with this information. There is however a pattern in the decline in the number of people from Hanover and Hesse receiving relief (which ties in to some extent with a more general decrease in the number of Germans assisted) and also to an increase in the number of Prussians receiving assistance.

Finally, there are the marriage registers of people married in St George's Lutheran Church in Whitechapel. Comparing this data with the records of the Society of Friends of Foreigners in Distress, it can be seen that there was an over-representation of Hanoverians and people from Hesse, which remained fairly constant during the course of the nineteenth century. There were also a number of people from other states in the southwest, notably Württemberg,[65] which would tie in with information from Deicke and Rosenkranz. One other trend is a growth in the number of Rhinelanders as well as an increase in people from the northeast, particularly Pomerania, the part of the country which experienced the greatest emigration in the late nineteenth century. It seems therefore that the same push factors which sent people to America during the nineteenth century also forced them to Britain.[66] All surviving records point out that the Germans who settled in Britain came from areas of high emigration, as a glance at Tables 2.1 and 2.2 indicates.

Both Hesse-Nassau and Hanover suffered large losses of population; why they should be over-represented in Britain is difficult to ascertain. In the case of Hanover, there were traditional links with Britain through the unification of the two kingdoms during the eighteenth century, and if migration from that state had taken place during the eighteenth century we might speculate that a process of chain migration had continued; but

---

65. If we use figures for emigration from Württemberg from Hippel, *Auswanderung aus Südwestdeutschland*, p. 255, we can establish that 387 from 30,350 emigrants from this state made their way to Britain in the years 1866–1870. For migration from Hesse see Günther, 'Beiträge zur Geschichte der kurrhessischen Auswanderung', which does not deal with movement to England, although it thoroughly covers many other aspects of movement out of this state. Other studies covering Hesse generally but not focusing upon England as a destination include Peter Assion (ed.), *Von Hessen in die Neue Welt*, Frankfurt, 1987.

66. In this context see *Report of the Select Committee on Emigration and Immigration*, pp. v–vi, Parliamentary Papers, vol. 10, 1889, which mentions that some 'respectable' immigrants entered Britain from Scandinavia, but that 'Most of the remainder arrive from Hamburg, and consist of very poor Germans and Russian Poles. The great majority of these are also booked through to America, but a small percentage, variously estimated at six to ten, either remain in Hull or settle in Manchester, Leeds or Bradford.'

Table 2.7 Origins of Germans Assisted by the Society of Friends of
Foreigners in Distress for Selected Years

Area of Origin	Number and year in which Assisted		
	1865–6	1877–8	1883
Baden	44	38	19
Bavaria	81	71	32
Hanover	222	–	–
Hanse Cities	106	63	47
Hesse	440	327	24
Mecklenburg	12	9	–
Nassau	112	–	2
Oldenburg	2	1	–
Prussia	703	1,569	454
Saxony	42	16	47
Württemberg	33	55	28
Other States	76	2	–

Source: Society of Friends of Foreigners in Distress, *An Account of the Society of Friends of Foreigners in Distress for the Year 1866*, London, 1866, p. 33; Bremer Staatsarchiv, 2T 6t 4d, 'An Account of the Society of Friends of Foreigners in Distress for the Year 1878'; *Londoner Courier*, 6 February 1884.

in this case, migration would have continued for a long period.[67] Another possible and perhaps more plausible explanation lies in the residence of people from the same states in the same areas, a fact common to all immigrant groups. In a study of Germans in New York, for instance, Stanley Nadel has demonstrated that Hanoverians, Bavarians and Prussians tended to reside in different parts of the city.[68] We might speculate that Hanoverians concentrated in Whitechapel, the location of St George's church, a conclusion which would tie in with their small number recorded in the *Preussische Statistik* in 1874. This may also help to explain the over-representation of people from Hesse in this area.

67. For information on emigration from Hanover see Hans Linde, 'Das Königreich Hanover an der Schwelle des Industriezeitalters', *Neues Archiv für Niedersachsen*, vol. 5, 1951, pp. 425–8. Chain migration is discussed in Kamphoefner, *Westfalians*, pp. 3–9. A suggestion that chain migration may have taken place with regard to German movement to Britain is provided by E. Armfelt, 'German London', in George R. Sims (ed.), *Living London*, 3 vols, London, 1903, vol. 3, p. 104, who, writing of the arrival of German passenger ships in London, states that 'We see an eager, expectant crowd of friends – well-dressed and prosperous looking – waving handkerchiefs and shouting greetings to the new-comers.'
68. Stanley Nadel, *Little Germany: Ethnicity, Religion, and Class in New York City*, Urbana and Chicago, 1990, pp. 37–9.

Table 2.8 Birthplaces of Germans Recorded in Marriage Registers of St George's Church Lutheran Church, Whitechapel

Area of Origin	Number and years in which Married					
	1843–53	1853–6	1856–62	1862–9	1869–82	1883–96
Prussia	13	5	8	16	13	22
Pomerania	–	2	2	1	7	19
Mecklenburg	–	1	2	1	2	–
Silesia	–	1	–	–	1	2
Saxony	3	3	4	–	–	9
Hanse Cities	4	2	2	4	1	7
Schleswig-Holstein	1	9	2	4	1	6
Hanover	23	19	21	29	25	24
Oldenburg	1	1	3	3	3	2
Rhineland	7	3	2	1	4	19
Westfalia	–	1	2	5	–	3
Baden	2	1	2	2	2	5
Hesse-Nassau	50	34	48	41	41	36
Württemberg	5	4	3	9	21	15
Bavaria	–	10	2	7	4	10
Smaller German States	11	5	8	3	7	25
Britons	9	5	3	3	14	25
Other States	3	2	2	1	4	21
Total	132	108	114	128	150	230

Source: Tower Hamlets Local History Collection, TH/8371/13, St Georges German Lutheran Church, Whitechapel, Marriage Register, 1843–53, years 1843–52; TH/8371/14, St Georges German Lutheran Church, Whitechapel, Marriage Register, 1853–56, years, 1853; TH/8371/15, St Georges German Lutheran Church, Whitechapel, Marriage Register, 1856–62, years, 1859; TH/8371/16, St Georges German Lutheran Church, Whitechapel, Marriage Register, 1862–9, years, 1864; TH/8371/17, St Georges German Lutheran Church, Whitechapel, Marriage Register, 1869–82, years, 1869, 1870, 1877; TH/8371/18, St Georges German Lutheran Church, Whitechapel, Marriage Register, 1883–96, years, 1883, 1891, 1896.

The second fact which emerges from both the article in the *Preussische Statistik* and from information in St George's marriage registers is the relative under-representation of East Prussians, rather than those with Prussian nationality but belonging to Prussian provinces in central or western Germany.[69] We might again speculate about residence patterns in this context, suggesting that east Prussians may have lived in other localities in London or Britain. Two further points need to be made. In the first place, the records of the Society of Friends of Foreigners in Distress[70] show a larger number of Prussians than either the marriage registers from St George's Church or the article from *Preussische Statistik*. This may be because the Society did not record the German states of origin in its statistics. At the same time, the marriage registers from St George's Church, as mentioned above, show an increasing number of East Prussians as the century progresses. Furthermore, as Table 2.9 indicates, the majority of those who received

Table 2.9   Origins of Germans Assisted by the Liverpool Branch of the Society of Friends of Foreigners in Distress for the Year 1864–5

Area of Origin	Number of Applications		
	Granted	Refused	Total
Prussia	283	80	363
Hesse	85	8	93
Minor States	63	21	83
Hanover	65	17	82
Württemberg	60	3	63
Baden	50	2	55
Bavaria	43	12	55
Nassau	40	7	47
Free Cities	38	9	47
Saxony	36	9	45

Source: Bremer Staatsarchiv, 2T 6t 4c, 'Thirteenth Annual Report of the Society of Friends of Foreigners in Distress, November, 1865'.

69. One other source which makes use of the St George's marriage registers, as well as those of St Paul's, also in Whitechapel, is Jerome Farrell, 'The German Community in Nineteenth Century East London', *East London Record*, vol. 13, 1990, pp. 3–4. His sample consists of 1,402 names from 1860–9 and he has similar results to my own.
70. See also Society of Friends of Foreigners in Distress, *An Account of the Society of Friends of Foreigners in Distress for the Year 1892*, London, 1892, which, although it does not contain details of people it assisted in the previous year, carries details of the people who received pensions in 1892. The most numerous in this case consist of Prussians (46), people from Hesse-Nassau (34), and Hanoverians (14).

assistance in Liverpool from the local branch of the Society of Friends of Foreigners in Distress in 1864–5 came from Prussia, while the numbers from Hesse and Hanover remained much smaller, supporting the idea that London, especially East London, was a particular destination for natives of these two states.

As well as these push factors there were also pull factors which attracted Germans to Britain. In fact, we might begin by considering an 'enabling factor', the availability of shipping. In a recent study of Jewish migration to Britain during the nineteenth century, Harold Pollins has written:

> One sometimes gets the impression that the Anglo-Jewish community was built up of those who did not get to America – the standard folklore tales are of those who got to Britain but were cheated out of their money and could not proceed; or thought they were already in New York; or, travelling by train westwards to Liverpool from Hull, alighted at Leeds or Sheffield, or Manchester, and stayed in the Jewish quarter near the railway station. Why they should have got off is not very clear.[71]

An examination of evidence concerning Germans in nineteenth-century Britain suggests that a proportion of the settlers remained in Britain for similar reasons.

In the first place one needs to realise the overall importance of transport to European as well as German emigration in the nineteenth century. During the nineteenth century the journey across the Atlantic became quicker, cheaper and safer, while the development of railways, canals, and improvement in river routes also meant that potential emigrants could reach their port of embarkation more easily. Bremen, for instance, increased in importance during the 1830s partly due to the fact that people could reach it more easily by sailing along the Weser, the river on which it lies, while railway companies subsequently ran special trains from a variety of German cities direct to Bremen with reduced prices. As has been seen, efforts by the city government also played a part in attracting emigrant traffic.[72]

As mentioned above, from the 1840s onward the German ports of Hamburg and Bremen became the main places of embarkation for German emigrants, so that by 1859 three-quarters of those leaving Germany sailed from there.[73] During the eighteenth century, Germans

71. Harold Pollins, *Hopeful Travellers: Jewish Migrants and Settlers in Nineteenth Century Britain*, London, 1991 reprint, pp. 25–6.
72. Hansen, *Atlantic Migration*, pp. 191–2; Ehlers, 'Bremen als Auswandererhafen', pp. 133–6.
73. *Jahrbuch für Volkswirtschaft und Statistik*, Berlin, 1861, p. 143.

crossing to North America sailed via Britain; during the 1820s and 1830s most ships from Bremen continued to pass through Britain or Holland, but during the course of the nineteenth century direct routes developed from Bremen and Hamburg to North American cities which eliminated the need for using ports in Britain as a staging post. This need became even less with the development of steamships.[74]

Nevertheless, indirect routes, sailing to east coast British ports and then by rail to Liverpool, remained important in Britain throughout the nineteenth century, not just for German emigrants but for those from other European states. Liverpool had developed as an emigration port both for Europeans and for people sailing to North America from Britain and Ireland. A pamphlet on Liverpool in 1859 pointed out that 483,035 emigrants had sailed out of the port between 1855 and 1858, reaching a peak of 155,647 in 1857. The document suggested that 'The rate of increase of the Anglo-Saxon and Anglo-Celtic races is not likely to diminish; and the tide of German emigration now flows strongly through England, and especially through Liverpool, which presents advantages for emigrants, even when compared with such flourishing ports as Hamburg and Bremen.' [75]

With regard to the development of the indirect route we see that, although Britain had always played a role as a staging post between continental Europe to North America, its importance increased during the mid-nineteenth century, as is suggested by the above quotation. The major study on the importance of Britain in the trans-Atlantic emigrant trade dates the growth of German travel through England to the late 1830s and ascribes this growth particularly to the role of both British and German agents and merchants, who saw the business potential of transporting German emigrants across the Atlantic. Initially during the 1840s, London was the port into which the immigrants sailed and then departed; Liverpool became more important during the course of the 1850s. Throughout both decades shipping agents had attracted potential customers using advertisements in many parts of Germany, including the Rhineland, Hesse, Württemberg and Bavaria,[76] leading to

74. Engelsing, *Bremen als Auswandererhafen, 1683–1880*, pp. 85–108; Ehlers, 'Bremen als Auswandererhafen'; E. Baasch, 'Gesetzgebung und Einrichtung im Interesse des Auswanderungswesens', in Philippovich, *Auswanderung und Auswanderungspolitik*, pp. 389–413.
75. Thomas Baines, *Liverpool in 1859*, London, 1859, pp. 21–2.
76. M. A. Jones, 'The Role of the United Kingdom in the Transatlantic Emigrant Trade, 1815–1875' (unpublished D. Phil. thesis, University of Oxford, 1955), pp. 162–4, 320–36. Walker, *Germany and the Emigration*, p.168, mentions that the Union Steamship Line of Liverpool and Philadelphia had twenty-one agents in Württemberg alone during the early 1850s. See also the extract from the *Morning Chronicle*, 15 July 1850, in Erickson, *Emigration from Europe*, pp. 247–8.

hostile comment in some German newspapers on the nature of their activities.[77]

Clearly, crossing the Atlantic via England meant a short stop in the country, and this led to the construction of accommodation to house the emigrants. An article from April 1852 in *The Times* commented that 'Several large boarding houses have been formed in Liverpool for the accommodation of the German emigrants during their brief sojourn in that town, and for the last week or two they have all been crowded.' Frederick Sabell, a London commission merchant, owned one of them, having established it at the end of 1849 with a licence to hold 300 emigrants. He claimed that it had reached its capacity in 1850 and told the Select Committee on the Passenger's Act that he had opened his house to prevent the emigrants from facing exploitation by the lodging-house keepers who had previously accommodated them.[78]

While most Germans arrived in Britain on regular passages to the USA, others did not. In October 1833, for instance, eighty German emigrants 'under delusive promises to be assisted here were induced to come over from Bremen on their voyage to the United States and were in the utmost distress' but a collection of £150 payed for their fare to New York. In the following July a similar group arrived from Hesse. Having failed to meet their ship in Bremen 'they fell in with the Captain of a Prussian ship on the point of sailing, with whom they entered into a negotiation to convey them to England... with an understanding at the same time that he would, on his arrival in the port of London, procure passages for them all to America' for £2 each. However, he failed to do this and they found temporary accommodation in a warehouse provided by a Mr Schnerer, 'a ship biscuit-maker, on Millwall'. One eye-witness stated that 'a majority of them were labouring under illness, and were entirely destitute of everything.' The emigrants eventually sailed to the USA.[79] According to a letter from the Society of Friends of Foreigners in Distress, hundreds of other emigrants who made their way to London during the 1830s in the hope of securing a ship to the USA found themselves stranded for several years.[80]

77. See, for instance, *Bremer Handelsblatt*, 1 May 1852.
78. *Report of the Select Committee on the Passengers Act*, PP, vol. XIX, questions 3715–22, 3731; *Deutsche Allgemeine Zeitung*, 24 April 1852; *The Times*, 17 April 1852. See also Rosenkranz, *Geschichte der Kirche zu Liverpool*, p. 49, who mentions that emigrants attended services at the German church in Liverpool reaching a peak of 4,000 in 1852. In Hull, meanwhile, another group of visitors passing through who attended German church services there during the 1840s consisted of German sailors for which see Deutsches Kirchen Verein, *Bericht des deutschen Kirchen-Vereins in Hull*, Hull, 1845.
79. Bremer Staatsarchiv, 2-P.8.B.a, Bd. 2, Nr. 242.
80. Bremer Staatsarchiv, 2-P.8.B.a, Bd. 2, Nr. 327.

Cases of German emigrants finding themselves unexpectedly spending time in Britain continued until later in the century. In January 1866, the Hamburg ship *Hertha* sailed from her home port to Leith and then to Portsmouth. The ship carried emigrants suffering from serious diseases. On the journey to Leith two children died of diphtheria, while in Leith one adult 'died of natural causes by old age' and diphtheria claimed the lives of eight more children. From Leith to Portsmouth, two adults perished from smallpox, four children died from diphtheria, and three were 'dead born'. Twelve more children died in Portsmouth, while forty-two people were discovered to have smallpox. Nevertheless, the emigrants sailed to New York on 21 February, 'with the exception of six or seven suffering from typhus who are left on board the Quarantine Hulk'.[81]

Four months later, in June 1866, R. G. C. Hamilton wrote to *The Times* about 'the wreck of the German emigrant ship *Lessing* which occurred on' 23 May near the Shetland Islands. Although nobody died, 'the emigrants and the crew, numbering 480, were thrown, in an utterly destitute condition, on the hospitality of the islanders'. However, the emigrants did not remain there long because the owners of the ship, 'acting with great promptness, had despatched a steamer and removed the emigrants from Shetland'.[82]

As well as Germans who unexpectedly found themselves in Britain on their way to North America, some of whom clearly remained for some time, others continued to enter the country as part of a planned stop. This process lasted as long as German emigration to America continued. The emigrants entered the country through a variety of east coast ports, primarily Hull and London but also through ports such as Hartlepool and Grimsby,[83] and then sailed almost invariably through Liverpool.[84] The decline of German trans-Atlantic emigration at the end of the century also meant a consequent decrease in the number of Germans passing through the country,[85] although by this time a large

81. Hamburg Staatsarchiv, 132–5/7 London, Hanseatische Residentur London, 17, Nr. 19.
82. *The Times*, 9, 20 June 1866.
83. *Dr Theodore Thomson's Report to the Local Government Board on the Methods Adopted at Certain Ports for Dealing with Alien Immigrants*, PP, vol. LXVII, 1896.
84. See also Ruhr-Universität Bochum, Arbeitsgruppe Geschichte Nordamerikas, Archive, letter of Karl Uterhart to his mother, 31 December 1862, who sailed from Cardiff after meeting a German captain in London who offered him a journey to New York on his ship carrying coal.
85. With the decline of migration from Germany the emigration business turned its attention to transporting members of other nationalities who wished to sail across the Atlantic, with Britain retaining its role as a staging post. See *Standard*, 10 January 1905; *Dr Theodore Thomson's Report to the Local Government Board on the Methods Adopted at Certain Ports for Dealing with Alien Immigrants*, PP, vol. LXVII, 1896; *Report of the Select Committee on Emigration and Immigration*, PP, vol. X, 1889; Marschalck, 'Geschichte der Auswanderung über Bremen', pp. 23–5.

number of routes existed for travelling to England for a variety of prices.[86]

It seems likely that some of the transmigrants settled in England. In Liverpool for instance, some emigrants who found work in the city, particularly before it became a city of mass emigration, decided to remain rather than to sail on to Australia or North America.[87] Opportunities for employment for transmigrants continued to exist throughout the century. Karl Uterhart, who passed through Britain in 1862, received an offer to act as a German tutor to a family in London, but he refused despite his fears of travelling further, as he had 'firmly decided to go to New York'. Karoline Ihls, who passed through England later in the century, did not remain so determined to sail to the USA; she secured employment as 'a nanny or children's maid in the Richmond or Kenton areas of London and Middlesex', before eventually marrying a German baker in south London.[88] There were numerous and regular advertisements by trans-Atlantic shipping lines in the German newspapers in London, offering passages to those in transit who may have decided to spend a spell in the capital.[89] Furthermore, as late as 1910 the German Society of Benevolence mentioned the presence in London of many German emigrants who had made their way to Britain as part of the journey to the USA but found that they did not have sufficient funds to proceed to North America, and consequently remained in London.[90]

While some passengers in transit did decide to stay in Britain, it is impossible to ascertain what percentage of the German population of Britain consisted of those who had originally intended to sail to America. Many emigrants, however, chose to move to Britain in particular, either permanently or temporarily. In the previous chapter we mentioned that the industrialisation of Britain drew Germans to the country during the eighteenth century, while this chapter has shown that American industry acted as a fundamental attraction for both German and other immigrants in the nineteenth century. It is time to consider whether these same pull factors existed in nineteenth-century Britain.

First, it is necessary to point out that Germans represented just one group which made its way to Britain during this period. Ireland was the source for the largest immigrant group during much of the nineteenth

86. See A. Reusch, *Ein Studienaufenthalt in England: Ein Führer für Studierende, Lehrer und Lehrerinnen*, Marburg, 1902, pp. 17–19.

87. Rosenkranz, *Geschichte der Kirche zu Liverpool*, p. 49.

88. Ruhr-Universität Bochum, Arbeitsgruppe Geschichte Nordamerikas, Archive, letter of Karl Uterhart to his mother, 31 December 1862; Roy Bernard, *My German Family in England*, Cookham, 1991, p. 5.

89. *Londoner Courier*, 28 January, 12 March 1884.

90. BA, Coblenz, R57 neu, 1065/3, 'Jahresbericht der Deutschen Wohltätigsgesellschaft in London 1910–11'.

century,[91] while towards the end of the period hundreds of thousands of newcomers made their way to Britain from eastern Europe, primarily from Russia and its Polish territories.[92] Small minorities from other European countries, notably France and Italy, also made their way to Britain during this period.[93] In all these cases, the migrations represented a movement from a poorer to a richer country, from an agrarian to an industrialised nation which, by mid-century, employed virtually eighty per cent of its population outside agriculture.[94] In the case of the Irish, for instance, a major wave of immigration occurred following the famine but further numbers entered the country later in the century, finding employment in a variety of occupations. East European Jews also moved from a poorer to a richer country, but it would be difficult to suggest that they simply migrated because of the attractions of an industrialised land; in many cases they continued the trade they had practised in their homeland.[95] Similar comments apply to Italian immigrants.

Great Britain certainly did not have the kind of centripetal pulling power of the USA, which sucked in countless millions of immigrants when an economic upturn took place; in fact, Britain acted as a net exporter of population for much of the nineteenth century.[96] Nevertheless, the country did attract large numbers of immigrants and there were economic factors which attracted them to the country.

When trying to understand these factors, the most obvious starting point is the opinions of the emigrants themselves. For instance, the catalogue of emigrants from the Osnabrück area during the nineteenth century, which survives in the city archives,[97] lists 27,000 names but less than fifty were people who made their way to England. Of these, only

91. See for instance J. A. Jackson, *The Irish in Britain*, London, 1963; L. H. Lees, *Exiles of Erin: Irish Migrants in Victorian London*, Manchester, 1979; Brenda Collins, 'Proto-Industrialization and Pre-Famine Emigration', *Social History*, vol. 7, 1982, pp. 124–46; J. H. Clapham, 'Irish Emigration into Great Britain', *Bulletin of the International Committee of Historical Sciences*, vol. 5, 1933, pp. 596–604; D. Fitzpatrick, 'Irish Emigration in the Later Nineteenth Century', *Irish Historical Studies*, vol. 22, 1980, pp. 129–30.
92. Bernard Gainer, *The Alien Invasion*, London, 1972; Lloyd P. Gartner, *The Jewish Immigrant in England 1870–1914*, London, 1960; Pollins, *Hopeful Travellers*.
93. Lucio Sponza, *Italian Immigrants in Nineteenth Century Britain*, Leicester, 1988.
94. E. J. Hobsbawm, *Industry and Empire: From 1750 to the Present Day*, Harmondsworth, 1969 edition, p. 327.
95. Joseph Buckman, *Immigrants and the Class Struggle: The Jewish Immigrant in Leeds 1880–1914*, Manchester, 1983, p. 3.
96. Colin Holmes, *John Bull's Island: Immigration and British Society, 1871–1971*, London, 1988, pp. 14–15, 36–9.
97. Niedersächsisches Staatsarchiv, Osnabrück, Verzeichnis der Auswanderungsknosense. This source is discussed in M. Brockel, 'Auswandererverzeichnis im Staatsarchiv Osnabrück', *Archive in Niedersachsen*, vol. 9, 1990, pp. 26–7.

eight give a reason for moving to the country. Some of these names prove interesting because they suggest possible further lines of enquiry. There is some evidence for chain migration, which was discussed previously. For instance, Anton Friedrich Schröder from Quackenbrück, who emigrated in 1866, simply stated that his reason for moving lay in the residence of a brother-in-law in London. Johann Thies, who left in 1866, mentioned that his uncle lived in London.[98] Albertus Hiltermann stated that his reason for going to Liverpool lay in the fact that two of his father's cousins had businesses in Rotterdam, Amsterdam and Liverpool.[99]

There is also evidence about economic opportunities; a Mr Meyer left the country in 1862 in order to undergo business training in London.[100] Numerous businessmen, or potential businessmen, made their way to Britain from Germany, a fundamental economic pull factor examined below. One important economic attraction, mentioned in several accounts during the nineteenth century and connected with greater industrialisation, is the fact that the migrants felt that they could achieve a better standard of living in Britain; the most fundamental pull factor in all economic migrations. A letter to *The Times* in 1869 explained the attraction of England for Germans rather dramatically:

> Not very long ago a poor German lady came travelling third-class to London from a distant town in Germany. She had come away from her home in the vague, desperate hope of finding means to collect a certain sum of money. It was not very much – about 150l [*sic*]. The poor lady did not know where to go, only somehow, somewhere, she had to get the money to save her home, and her husband and her children from utter ruin, and she came to London as the most likely place to find it.[101]

Other contemporary accounts also speak of the perceived opportunity to earn a living more easily. A book on the German colony in London by Heinrich Dorgeel describes the perception of 'rich England, where money lies on the street'. Dorgeel believed that London sometimes represented a temporary staging post. If immigrants failed to succeed there,

98. Niedersächsisches Staatsarchiv, Osnabrück, Verzeichnis der Auswanderungskonsense, Nos. 2136, 5150.

99. Niedersächsisches Staatsarchiv, Osnabrück, Verzeichnis der Auswanderungskonsense, No. 20090.

100. Niedersächsisches Staatsarchiv, Osnabrück, Verzeichnis der Auswanderungskonsense, No. 1660.

101. *The Times*, 12, 17 June 1869. See also W. Fischer and A. Behrens, *Amely Bolte: Briefe aus England an Varnhagen von Ense (1844–1858)*, Düsseldorf, 1955, p.1, who write that Bolte's decision to leave Germany for England in 1839 was not unusual as many German women hoped to 'earn their bread more easily in the rich land than they could in their homeland'. Governesses receive detailed attention in Chapter 3.

they would then sail on to America. But Dorgeel also provided one of the most accurate pictures of German migration to London, writing of newcomers who arrived 'with little money, without references' and 'little knowledge of the English language', who after several days in hotels found a more permanent home, after which they began to look for employment.[102]

Leopold Katscher believed that 'the hope of improving their personal condition or of some lucky stroke of fortune' induced 'annually many thousands of Germans to wend their way to London without introduction and scantily provided with money'.[103] A study of immigrant poverty in London during the 1860s stated that 'the Hamburg immigrant' entered England in order to improve the condition of his children. One interviewee for the book stated: 'I may suffer poverty and die myself, but they will have a chance for better things, and will probably escape from the misery I have myself endured.'[104] An article from the *London City Mission Magazine*, referring to immigrants from 'Russia, Poland, and North Germany', stated that 'most arrive penniless, and to obtain the common necessaries of life, they generally join themselves to a countryman who has been longer here, who takes the new arrival with him on his rounds, and teaches him his own trade of itinerant glaziering.'[105] All of the above claims prove useful if connected with push factors.

Dorgeel also described another phenomenon, temporary migration. We have already seen that 'return migration' took place from America during the nineteenth century. The opportunities for remaining temporarily in Britain were greater because of the smaller distances and transport costs involved, although no statistics exist of people who returned from Britain to Germany. Temporary migration had been taking place from the northwestern German provinces to Holland for centuries, but this involved agricultural work and consequently differed from any movement to Britain.[106] However, many contemporary sources did comment on temporary migration of Germans to nineteenth-century Britain. The following quotation offers a colourful interpretation of this movement:

102. Heinrich Dorgeel, *Die deutsche Colonie in London*, London, 1881, pp. 17, 19–21.

103. Leopold Katscher, 'German Life in London', *Nineteenth Century*, vol. 21, 1887, p. 732.

104. J. H. Stallard, *London Pauperism Amongst Jews and Christians*, London, 1867, p. 7.

105. *London City Mission Magazine*, February 1874.

106. Wilhelm Kleeberg, 'Hollandgänger und Heringfänger', *Neues Archiv für Landes- und Volkskunde von Niedersachsen*, vol. 2, 1948, pp. 193–216.

An old German custom which has been the subject of discussion in England is that of the *Wanderschaft*, or wandership of young Teutons, which has frequently, and erroneously, been described as *Auswanderung* or emigration. A hundred years ago the Teuton would be seen carrying his knapsack through the villages and towns of his native land in search of work, which would increase his skill and knowledge. To-day we see him in Continental capitals and London learning all that can be learnt. It is the apprenticeship, or the training in some technical school, which makes the Teuton – even when he has no aptitude – a thorough hard worker. There are technical schools for all professions, even waiters. If his father is well off, the young Teuton will be trained for the military career or finance, commerce, or what not; if he is poor, he will be apprenticed to a trade. And the Prussian kings have sealed with their example the training, the apprenticeship and the *Wanderschaft*. It does not deprive the Fatherland of its sons, and it makes them cleverer men. After a stay of three or four years in England all the young fellows we see will be called home for military service; others will take their places; and the chances are that we will see them no more.[107]

Although containing elements of elaboration, Armfelt's comments do touch on some fundamentally important points which need to be considered in more detail.

First, there is Armfelt's idea of *Wanderschaft*, or travelling from one locality to another in search of employment as part of an apprenticeship, which he claims had moved to encompass non-German cities by the time he wrote in the early twentieth century. In fact the process he describes reached its height during the period before large-scale industrialisation, when the economy worked upon a system of production in which artisans rather than proletarians played a large part.[108] Nevertheless, sources other than Armfelt also refer to a temporary migration of male workers. An article from 1918, for instance, claimed that the early twentieth-century movement to Britain contained few women and children and consisted of men who wished 'to spend a year or more abroad to become acquainted with a land and its people and to learn a language, before returning to Germany.' They would only remain in England if they married an Englishwoman.

The author believed that by this period few 'unskilled workers' would travel to London.[109] He pointed particularly to waiters, and there is much evidence from the late nineteenth century to suggest that this

107. Armfelt, 'German London', p. 58.
108. Klaus J. Bade, 'Altes Handwerk, Wanderzwang und Gute Policy: Gesellenwanderung zwischen Zunfökonomie und Gewerbereform', *Vierteljahrschrift für Sozial und Wirtschaftsgeschichte*, vol. 69, 1982, p. 10.
109. Johann Sassen Bach, 'Deutsche Arbeiter in England', *Auslandsdeutsche*, vol. 1, 1918–19, p. 6.

group entered the country with a view to remaining only temporarily. The desire to learn English acted as an important motivation as there existed 'a great demand abroad for waiters who can speak' it.[110] An article in the *London Hotel and Restaurant Employees Gazette* claimed that:

...in Switzerland and Germany the owners of hotels, after giving their sons a liberal education, send them to foreign countries to pick up as many languages as possible and to learn their profession from the very lowest rungs of the social ladder. The 'roughing' may not be pleasant, but the experience gained is great... After spending a year or two in London and Paris, they return home and assist in their parents' establishments. They have acquired a certain knowledge of both French and English...and they have also become acquainted with the wants of hotel visitors and the foibles of their fellow workers, which knowledge is valuable when they, in their turn, become hotel proprietors or occupy responsible positions.[111]

Another article in the same journal painted a far less optimistic picture of prospects for German waiters who travelled across Europe, but this article also accepted that an eventual return to Germany would take place.[112] Another source, however, claimed that 'a great many stay here, preferring the greater freedom of this country.'[113]

German clerks also made their way to London on a temporary basis at the end of the nineteenth century. 'Many of the better-to-do young Germans consider a couple of years in a foreign country merely a stepstone in life, and are quite prepared to lose, say a pound a week, for the privilege of getting an insight into the routine of English business, and perfecting their knowledge of the language.' In many cases they received assistance from Mercantile Unions as part of a formal apprenticeship to a merchant and were 'frequently the very best', usually from north Germany. In other instances they consisted of the sons of German customers of English firms.[114]

There was even a seasonal migration of German brass bands to England, as the following press extract indicates with regard to one group:

110. BLPES, Manuscripts Section, Booth Collection, Group B, vol. 159, p. 43.
111. *London Hotel and Restaurant Employees Gazette*, 6 September 1890.
112. Ibid., 28 February 1891.
113. BLPES, Manuscripts Section, Booth Collection, Group B, vol. 159, p. 43.
114. *Clerks Journal*, 1 March 1889; *Report on the Early Training of the German Clerk*, PP, vol. LXXVII, 1889; *National Review*, March 1910, pp. 84–6. Clerks receive more attention in Chapters 3 and 5.

The band always came from one village in the Black Forest – it was a supe-rior kind of German band. One man, called the captain, organised the band, was responsible for remuneration, and pledged his land near the village so as to secure this payment. The band practised through the winter. In the spring they came across to Hull, and tramped through the country, playing at the various towns on their way. This would take several weeks, and would land them at their destination in time for the summer season. When the engage-ment was over, they went straight home.[115]

This represents one type of movement, because, as will be seen in Chapter 3, some musicians remained in Britain on a longer-term basis.

Many middle-class immigrants entered the country during the nine-teenth century because of its more advanced development. This process was examined in the last chapter, and the entry of merchants and repre-sentatives of companies was a continuation of the middle-class migra-tion begun during Britain's industrialisation in the eighteenth century. The push and pull factors remained the same. Underlying the movement there existed an image within Germany, during the first half of the nine-teenth century at least, which saw Britain's economy as well as her cul-ture and political system as a model. Britain was the major industrial and trading power in the world and therefore to be emulated, although as such Britain also aroused some hostility as a threat to the more limited German industry. But Germany's industrialisation depended to a con-siderable extent upon the importation of British machinery, from textile machines to steam engines. The established trading links, including those between the Hansa cities and Britain continued.[116]

This was the background against which representatives of German firms made their way to London during the nineteenth century. Stanley Chapman, who has carried out the most important research on this topic, has explained this migration in various ways. There was the desire to open branches of existing companies in England, often by sending over a younger son; there was also the impetus provided by the continued decline of the international fairs, meaning that mer-chants wanted to be 'on the spot' in Lancashire and Yorkshire, the major textile manufacturing areas. Chapman has also identified a

115. *Musical Herald*, 1 December 1899.
116. Martin Schumacher, *Auslandsreisen Deutscher Unternehmer 1750–1851 Unter Besonderer Berücksichtigung von Rheinland und Westfalen*, Cologne, 1968, p. 132; Percy Ernest Schramm, 'Die deutsche Wirtschaft und England um 1840', *Mitteilungen des Instituts für Österreichische Geschichtsforschung*, vol. 62, 1954, pp. 517–37; Paul M. Kennedy, *The Rise of the Anglo-German Antagonism 1860–1914*, London, 1990 reprint, p. 41; Bremer Staatsarchiv, C.4.h.1, Friedrich Preusser, 'Bremer Kaufleute in England'; Karl Friedrich Schinkel, *Reise nach und durch England, Schottland und Paris im Jahre 1826*, Berlin, 1986, pp. 7–11.

movement of Jewish bankers from Frankfurt to the City of London during the 1880s and 1890s, as a result of the fact that Berlin had replaced Frankfurt as the banking capital of Germany. This resulted in financial difficulties for the older banks, some of which went into liquidation while others moved to other European cities. For example, Samuel Japhet transferred his business from Frankfurt to Berlin and then London during the course of the 1890s. There was also a movement of individuals who began as clerks and then became involved in business on their own account.[117] German industrial expansion into the international arena during the late nineteenth and early twentieth centuries depended upon the securing of new markets, which meant the sending of commercial travellers abroad with the support of bodies such as the Commerce Defence League. German businessmen and traders were found all over the world by the late nineteenth century as the country's economy grew.[118]

These processes can be illustrated by providing brief details of individual examples with the motivations which the emigrants or their biographers see as the reasons for movement to Britain. There are several examples of representatives of family firms. In Schröder's banking house, for instance, several sons of the dynasty entered England at the start of the nineteenth century. One of these, John Henry Schröder, established J. Henry Schröder in London as a branch of the German company in 1818; his son John Henry William Schröder became a partner in 1849 and moved to London the following year. In 1888, Bruno Schröder transferred to London from Hamburg as part of his commercial training; in 1893 he returned to become a partner.[119] Similarly, the international banking house of Speyer and Co. opened its London house of Speyer Brothers in 1861, subsequently directed by Edgar Speyer,[120] while that of Schusters sent different generations to London, notably in 1808 and following Prussian annexation of Frankfurt in

117. Stanley D. Chapman, 'The International Houses: The Continental Contribution to British Commerce, 1800–1860', *Journal of European Economic History*, vol. 19, 1977, pp. 15, 19, 21–3; Chapman, *The Rise of Merchant Banking*, London, 1984, pp. 50–1; Saemy Japhet, *Recollections of My Business Life*, London, 1931, pp. 51, 57, 62. Outside banking another person who entered Britain earlier in the century, in 1851, because his firm faced financial difficulties, was Julius Reuter. See Graham Storey, *Reuters Century 1851–1951*, London, 1951, pp. 5–7, 12; Paul H. Emden, 'Baron Paul Julius de Reuter', *Transactions of the Jewish Historical Society of England*, vol. 17, 1953, pp. 215–18.
118. D. H. Aldcroft, 'The Entrepreneur and the British Economy, 1870–1914', *Economic History Review*, vol. 17, 1964, pp. 125–6; Joseephy, *Deutsche überseeische Auswanderung seit 1871*, pp. 81–2.
119. Richard Roberts, *Schroders: Merchants and Bankers*, London, 1992, pp. 26–151; Chapman, 'International Houses', pp. 15–16.
120. Paul H. Emden, *Jews of Britain*, London, 1943, p. 344.

1866, when the business moved to Manchester under Francis Joseph Schuster.[121]

Earlier in the century several representatives of German firms involved in textiles entered Britain, notably Jacob Behrens and, most well-known of all, Frederick Engels. Behrens took over his father's firm, which traded in textiles, in 1826 and began to travel in search of new markets. In 1832 he moved from Hamburg to Hull, on a 'paddle steamer', and then went on to Leeds where he 'took a liking for England, especially because it presented a picture totally different from that I had known in the dismembered and retrogressive Germany... Not only did I feel myself a man amongst men, but the times were great.' Behrens intended to persuade his 'supplier of merinos, Thomas Clapham (who would not answer letters on the subject) to adopt a different finish for the goods supplied, and to pack them in smaller bales'. Having failed to achieve his aims after a visit in 1833, he returned in 1834 and launched the company of Jacob Behrens which produced and exported the cloth as he wished. He remained in Britain, and his two brothers Louis and Rudolf followed him in 1837.[122]

One of the most famous Germans in nineteenth-century Britain, Frederick Engels, made his first trip to Britain in 1842 partly for business reasons to work in the Manchester branch of the firm in which his father was a partner, Ermen and Engels; the visit was also important for his political development. He remained in the city for twenty months, working as a clerk in the Manchester branch of Ermen and Engels and completing his commercial training, like so many other German businessmen in nineteenth-century Britain. We cannot see Engels in quite the same light as the other representatives of firms described here because his own personal reason for entering Britain lay in the desire to see the effects of industrialisation at first hand. However, while he may have returned to London in 1849 for political reasons, escaping from potential arrest because of his part in revolutionary activities in Baden and the Palatine, financial motives, centering on the availability of a secure income, dictated his decision to move back to Manchester in the following year as a clerk in the firm of Ermen and Engels. The motivations of Engels prove particularly interesting if only because they illustrate the complexity of causation involved in the move to England. Engels would probably have migrated to England for political reasons in any case, along with other German revolutionaries, but his father's firm

121. Ibid., p. 347; G. C. Simpson, 'Sir Arthur Schuster 1851–1934', *Obituary Notices of Fellows of the Royal Society*, vol. 1, 1932, p. 409.

122. Sir Jacob Behrens, *Sir Jacob Behrens, 1806–1889*, London, 1925, pp. 19, 25, 29–33; D. T. Jenkins, 'Sir Jacob Behrens', in *Dictionary of Business Biography*, vol. 1, London, 1984, p. 251.

acted as an enabling factor, providing him with the financial opportunity to make the move certainly in 1842.[123]

We should not see the complexity of Engels' decision to move as unique in the migration of German 'businessmen' to England. For instance, a biographical sketch of Henry Simon, an engineering equipment contractor, shows that the death of his uncle, a revolutionary liberal, in 1860 sparked his decision to move from a machinery firm in Magdeburg to Manchester. Nevertheless, this event was only a spark, because the underlying structural factor, the existence of a more industrially-advanced country offering greater opportunity, remained.[124] Similarly, Sir Ernest Cassel initially migrated to Liverpool in 1869 at the age of sixteen and took up a position as a clerk with a firm of German grain merchants, Blessing, Braun and Co. After a year he moved to Paris to work for the Anglo-Egyptian Bank, but returned to London on the outbreak of the Franco-Prussian War where he began working for Bischoffsheim and Goldschmidt.[125]

There are also more straightforward examples of individuals involved in banking and industry who migrated to Britain for primarily economic reasons, particularly in connection with the textile industry. For instance, Ludwig Knoop originally moved from a cotton-trading firm in Bremen in 1838 to spend a year in a similar company, De Jersey, in Manchester.[126] Bradford attracted numerous Germans involved in cloth production and export during the nineteenth century, including Julius Delius, the father of the composer, who moved to the city in order to establish a branch of his brother's wool company which the latter had set up following his migration to Manchester earlier in the century.[127] Georg Weerth, the revolutionary and writer, initially moved to Bradford before becoming fully politically conscious, unlike Engels, in

123. W. O. Henderson, 'Friedrich Engels in Manchester', *Memoirs and Proceedings of the Manchester Literary and Philosophical Society*, vol. 98, 1956–7, pp. 14–19; Mick Jenkins, *Frederick Engels in Manchester*, Manchester, 1951, pp. 5, 9–10; Harry Schmitdgall, *Friedrich Engels Manchester Aufenthalt 1842–1844*, Trier, 1981, pp. 9–10 and passim; Norman Levine, 'Engels, England and the Working Class', in Gottfried Niedhart (ed.), *Grossbritannien als Gast und Exilland für Deutsche im 19. und 20. Jahrhundert*, Bochum, 1985, pp. 58–89.

124. Geoffrey Tweedale, 'Henry Simon', *Dictionary of Business Biography*, vol. 5, p. 174.

125. Kurt Grunwald, '"Windsor-Cassel" – The Last Court Jew: Prolegomena to a Biography of Sir Ernest Cassel', *Leo Baeck Yearbook*, vol. 14, 1969, p. 123.

126. A. Charles, *International Business in the Nineteenth Century: The Rise and Fall of a Cosmopolitan Bourgeoisie*, Brighton, 1987, p. 149; Stuart Thompstone, 'The Arkwright of Russia', *Textile History*, vol. 15, 1984, p. 47–8.

127. Bradford Heritage Recording Unit, *Destination Bradford: A Century of Immigration*, Bradford, 1987, pp. 10, 12; Lionel Carley, *Delius: A Life in Letters*, vol. 1, London, 1983, p. 1.

November 1843, having made a previous journey to London two months earlier in an unsuccessful attempt to secure a position with a German firm there. He took up employment as a clerk with the German wool firm of Ph. Passavant and Co., which had its headquarters in Manchester.[128] The movement of Germans to Dundee, in connection with linen, and to Nottingham, where they dealt in lace, should also be mentioned.[129]

In addition to the attractions of business opportunities and possibilities, other Germans entered the country because of its technological opportunities. The two attractions relate fundamentally to each other and both revolve around Britain's earlier industrialisation, as illustrated by the Great Exhibition of 1851 which attracted 11,929 Germans to London, including businessmen, industrialists and engineers.[130] Technological entrepreneurs entered Britain on a more permanent basis throughout the nineteenth century. Ludwig Mond is probably the most famous of these; born in Cassel in 1839, the son of a Jewish silk merchant, he studied at the University of Marburg in 1855 and then went to Heidelberg in the following year, which he left in 1858 without a degree, feeling he had gathered enough knowledge. In 1860 he went to work as an apprentice in a factory in Mainz which produced acetic acid. He subsequently went to Utrecht in Holland, by which time he had patented a process for producing soda. His decision to move to England in 1862 came about both because of the greater opportunities for his process there and because of the greater tolerance of the country towards Jews.[131]

Another technological entrepreneur was Carl Wilhelm Siemens who originally entered England in 1843 for the purpose of marketing a 'thermo-electric battery'. He subsequently established a branch of the Siemens Brothers Electrical Company in Woolwich, in south London. In 1867 another member of the family, Alexander, moved to London to

128. Uwe Zemke, 'A Biography of George Weerth (1822–1856)' (unpublished Ph.D thesis, University of Cambridge, 1976), pp. 39–41; Zemke, 'Georg Weerth in Bradford', in Bernd Füllner (ed.), *Georg Weerth: Neue Studien*, Bielefeld, 1988, pp. 125–8; Rosemary Ashton, *Little Germany: Exile and Asylum in Victorian England*, Oxford, 1988, pp. 71–2.

129. C. C. Aronsfeld, 'German Jews in Dundee', *Jewish Chronicle*, 20 November 1953, p. 15; Aronsfeld, 'Nottingham's Lace Pioneers: Part 2', *Guardian Journal*, 20 April 1954; R. A. Church, *Economic and Social Change in a Midland Town: Victorian Nottingham, 1815–1900*, London, 1966, pp. 76–7.

130. See Schumacher, *Auslandreisen Deutscher Unternehmer*, pp. 45–6, 132–43, 175–93; E. F. Melzer, *Nach London! Zur unterhaltenden und nützlichen Vorbereitung auf die Reise zur Welt-Austellung*, Breslau, 1851.

131. W. J. Reader, *Imperial Chemical Industries, A History*, 2 vols, vol. 1, London, 1970, pp. 37–9; Jean Goodman, *The Mond Legacy*, London, 1982, pp. 7, 15, 20–1; Hector Bolitho, *Alfred Mond: First Lord Melchett*, London, 1933, p. 15.

play a part in the operation of the works.[132] Several Germans entered Sheffield because of the attractions of the city's steel industry during the nineteenth century, including Sir Joseph Jonas who moved to the city in 1867 after an apprenticeship in a German firm, beginning as a commercial traveller before moving on to found a steel firm with Robert Culver. Carl Wilhelm Kayser made his way to the city in 1860 originally in order to study the Sheffield cutlery and steel trades before returning to Solingen, but he eventually remained in Sheffield and followed a similar career path to Jonas; as did Paul Kühnreich, who began as a clerk in Marsh Brothers, a steel manufacturer.[133] People who moved to Britain for purely technological reasons included scientists such as Carl Schorlemmer, who became a Professor of Chemistry at Owens College, Manchester.[134]

Having examined the reasons for middle-class migration to Britain we can conclude this section on the economic causes of movement to Britain by briefly mentioning what we might describe as 'forced migration', although not in the sense of the transportation of criminals which took place to the USA during this period.[135] In particular this group includes prostitutes, who in some cases entered the country under force, while in others they came under the deception of securing a post of another nature in Britain. In other cases still, some women fell into this occupation after entering the country.[136] This group also includes people forced to move to Britain because of trouble with the German police or military authorities; these include deserters from military service and thieves. Among the latter was nineteen-year-old Gustav Adolf Fiedler, who had stolen 715 marks from his principal in Halle.[137]

It is difficult to reach any conclusions on economic motivations for German migration to Britain. Apart from the fact that non-economic causes often also contributed to the decision to move, the relative importance of push and pull factors also proves difficult to establish. We have already accepted that all German economic migrants to Britain left

132. William Pole, *The Life of Sir William Siemens*, London, 1888, p. 44; Geoffrey Tweedale, 'Alexander Siemens', *Dictionary of Business Biography*, vol. 5, p. 155.

133. Geoffrey Tweedale, 'The Razor Blade King of Sheffield: The Forgotten Career of Paul Kühnreich', *Transactions of the Hunter Archaeological Society*, vol. 16, 1991, pp. 39–51; 'Kayser, Ellison & Co. Ltd., Makers of High Grade Special Steels', *Histories of Famous Firms*, vol. 18, no. 6, 1958, p. 4.

134. Robert H. Kargon, *Science in Victorian Manchester: Enterprise and Culture*, Manchester, 1977, pp. 195–6.

135. Moltmann, 'Die Transportation von Sträflingen im Rahmen der deutschen Amerikaauswanderung des 19. Jahrhunderts', in Moltmann, *Deutsche Amerikaauswanderung*, pp. 147–96.

136. See pp. 116–8 for more details.

137. Hamburg Staatsarchiv, 132–6, Hamburgischer Konsulat in Liverpool, 6, 2814.

against the background of the push factors which sent Germans to other parts of the world; the reasons why they entered Britain varied according to any number of factors including their class, their area of origin, and their route across the Atlantic. While in some cases the move had been planned in advance, in others people decided to remain in Britain and either not proceed to America or not return home because an opportunity arose within the country.

The underlying pull factor remained Britain's more advanced industrial development. The fact that its economy did not expand to the same extent as did the US economy, and the fact that its own surplus population provided the industrial proletariat, meant that Britain did not have a need for foreign labour in the same way as the US economy or in the way that the British economy needed immigrant manpower after the Second World War, which resulted in the importation of refugees and then immigrants from the Commonwealth.[138] At the same time while Britain's more advanced economy may have acted as the basic pull factor for a large proportion of the German newcomers, in other cases, such as waiters, there were more specific attractions such as the fact that England provided an opportunity to learn the main international language used in their employment. The same point could be made about clerks. However, within the overall hierarchy of factors, the non-economic reasons for German migration to Britain also need to be examined.

Political factors and motivations are as complex as economic ones in the sense that there are both push and pull factors, together with underlying determinants and sparks. In the section dealing with economic reasons for movement, we identified the underlying push factors of overpopulation and proto-industrialisation, together with the fundamental pull factor of a more advanced economic development within Britain. Any attempt to provide underlying political motivations, however, is difficult and revolves around the idea of the existence of an intolerant illiberal Germany during the nineteenth century, which contrasted with a freer England, Switzerland, France, or America, the destinations of many political refugees. But the use of the word 'refugee' suggests a reaction against a particular event: when we deal with political motivations for movement, our concern lies essentially with reaction against specific developments more than with economic factors; although we have already seen that short-term factors such as agricultural conditions immediately after the Napoleonic Wars or during the late 1840s or the growth in the US economy during

138. Panikos Panayi, 'Refugees in Twentieth Century Britain: A Brief History', in Vaughan Bevan (ed.), *The International Refugee Crisis in the Twentieth Century: British and Canadian Responses*, London, 1993, pp. 95–112.

the 1880s, proved fundamentally important in causing a rise in the number of emigrants. Therefore political motivations for movement can best be approached by concentrating on the main waves of political emigrants rather than underlying factors. These occurred in the 1830s, which was a time of political repression, the years following the 1848 revolutions, and the years immediately after the passage of the Anti-Socialist Laws of 1878.

We must begin by briefly examining whether the idea of underlying political factors has any validity. The undemocratic German political system during the nineteenth century may have served as an underlying push factor, and some individuals gave rather vague reasons such as the existence of 'Prussian militarism' in combination with other motivations for leaving the country.[139] Perhaps more important, however, is the fact that in the progression towards becoming a liberal democracy, which it did not ultimately achieve until 1948, Germany had to go through a series of traumatic crises (which Britain had faced in the seventeenth century), notably 1848 and 1933, which forced countless thousands of refugees out of the country.[140]

Several scholars on the study of refugees in nineteenth century Britain have looked at underlying pull factors, particularly Bernard Porter, Rosemary Ashton and Gottfried Niedhart. Porter has illustrated these factors most eloquently:

> From time to time during the nineteenth century, whenever for some reason or other the bubbling cauldron of continental European politics could no longer contain them, little bands of political exiles were found crossing the channel or the North Sea to Britain, to rest and recuperate – or maybe to continue their struggles – in an environment which was politically more tranquil, and more safe.

Furthermore, while Britain 'was not unique in offering asylum' to refugees during the nineteenth century, 'Britain took in anyone', including autocrats, liberals and socialists. Most importantly of all, 'from 1826 until 1848, and again from 1850 to 1905, there was nothing on the statute book to enable the executive to prevent aliens from coming and staying in Britain as they liked... This freedom of entry applied to all

---

139. Robin Craig and Michael Robson, 'Sir Robert Ropner', *Dictionary of Business Biography*, vol. 4, London, 1985, mention 'a dislike of Prussian militarism' as one of the possible reasons why this middle-class migrant made his way to Britain.

140. Much work has been carried out on German refugees to Britain after 1933, a lot of it summarised in contributions to Gerhard Hirschfeld (ed.), *Exile in Great Britain: Refugees from Hitler's Germany*, Leamington Spa, 1984.

foreigners, whether refugees or not, and for whatever reason they desired entry.'[141] Rosemary Ashton has listed what she describes as 'the vaunted freedoms enjoyed by Britons and denied to Germans in their own country', which included 'the freedom to set foot in the country of their choice and stay there without fear of expulsion' and 'freedom of speech, of the press, and of association'. Nevertheless, Ashton devotes much attention to the negative aspects of nineteenth-century British liberal democracy as seen by the German newcomers; the image of Britain may be viewed simply as a pre-conception or model, which did not live up to reality.[142]

Britain proved in many cases to be the last choice of asylum for refugees, a fact recognised by Porter, Ashton and Niedhardt.[143] Nevertheless, the opposite preconception survived until the end of the century, so that in 1890 an article in a newspaper for German waiters in England could declare that, 'For a long period of time England has been viewed as the land of freedom and world trade, and all foreigners unhappy with their political situation have looked towards the country. And understandably so.'[144]

All of the above remain underlying factors. Virtually all Germans who entered Britain for political reasons during the nineteenth century did so in response to a political crisis or following a period of repression. For instance, during the 1830s we can identify an entry of what might be described as representatives of the German workers movement, who consisted of at least three strands. First, there was the expulsion from Germany of the members of the liberal Young Germany movement during the 1830s, who initially made their way to Switzerland but left in 1836 when the Swiss Government expelled them and all other refugees under pressure from the German Confederation, a quasi-governmental organisation which united the German states.[145] The second strand consists, according to several sources, of German apprentices who made their way to London because of a crisis for artisans during the 1830s as a result of the initial effects of industrialisation, which forced many apprentices to look for work in France, Switzerland

141. Bernard Porter, *The Refugee Question in Mid-Victorian Politics*, Cambridge, 1979, pp. 1, 2, 3.

142. Ashton, *Little Germany*, pp. 38, 44, and *passim*.

143. Ibid., p. 30; Porter, *Refugee Question*, p. 2. See also Niedhart, 'Einleitung', in Niedhart, *Grossbritannien als Gast- und Exilland*, pp. 7–11.

144. *London Hotel and Restaurant Employees Gazette*, 6 September 1890.

145. Werner Brettschneider, *Entwicklung und Bedeutung des deutschen Frühsozialismus in London*, Bottrop, 1936, p. 19. August Jäger, *Der Deutsche in London*, 2 vols, vol. 1, London, 1839, pp. 1–2, claims that one hundred refugees were expelled from Switzerland, of whom sixty made their way to England.

and England.[146] Thirdly, there was the entry into Britain in 1839 of 'three important exiles', Karl Schapper, Heinrich Bauer, and Joseph Moll, following the failure of an uprising in Paris which had acted as a gathering point for refugees during this period, together with Wilhelm Weitling, who entered Britain in 1844 after release from a jail sentence for his political activities within Germany. These movements into the country formed the basis for the German Workers Educational Association.[147]

Many of the German exiles in London returned home during the revolutions of 1848 but, following their failure, re-entered Britain together with many newcomers. The importance of the 1848 revolutions for German emigration can be examined. As has been seen above, the fundamental reasons for German emigration during the nineteenth century remained economic; any movement which took place out of Germany for political reasons was minimal in size, as several historians have stressed. Peter Marschalck for instance has dismissed the political motivation by stating that the emigration of these years had its concrete origins in the economic crisis of the mid-1840s.[148] Marcus Lee Hansen made similar observations in an earlier article in which he set out to disprove the importance of political events, as did Theodore Hamerow subsequently.[149] While the observations of these scholars contain truth, there was also a small emigration which was purely political.

An indication of the size of this emigration is suggested by a London Metropolitan Police file of 1852 which claimed that 150 German refugees lived in the capital out of a total German population of 10,237; in other words over eleven per cent of the population were refugees, although the method of working out who constituted a refugee is not indicated so the figure may contain some exaggeration.[150] The Prussian Ambassador in London, Christian von Bunsen, provided a much small-

146. Alexander Brandenburg, 'Der Kommunistische Arbeiterbildungsverein in London: Ein Beitrag zu den Anfängen der deutschen Arbeiterbildungsbewegung (1840–47)', *International Review of Social History*, 1979, vol. 14, p. 342; Jacques Grandjonc, 'Die deutsche Binnenwanderung in Europa 1830 bis 1848', in Otto Büsch, et al (eds), *Die frühsozialistischen Bünde in der Geschichte der deutschen Arbeiterbewegung*, Berlin, 1975, pp. 4–5.

147. Carl Wittke, *The Utopian Communist: A Biography of Wilhelm Weitling, Nineteenth Century Reformer*, Baton Rouge, 1950, pp. 90–7; Henry Weisser, *British Working Class Movements and Europe 1815–48*, Manchester, 1975, pp. 125–6; Brandenburg, 'Arbeiterbildungsverein', p. 344.

148. Marschalck, *Deutsche Überseewanderung*, p. 39.

149. Hansen, 'Revolutions of 1848 and German Emigration'; Theodore S. Hamerow, 'The Two Worlds of the Forty-Eighters', in Charlotte L. Brancaforte (ed.), *The German Forty-Eighters in the United States*, New York, 1989, pp. 19–35.

150. PRO MEPO 43; *Census of Great Britain, 1851, Population Tables, II*, vol. 1, London, 1854, p. 36.

er figure of 300 for the number of German members of democratic clubs in London in 1851, which may come closer to the truth although it excludes 'non-democratic' exiles.[151]

Whatever the true size of the community, emigration followed the repression of the liberal revolutions which had broken out throughout Germany in 1848 and culminated in the formation of the unsuccessful and impotent Frankfurt Parliament opposed both by the equally weak working-class reform movement and the Prussian state. Faced with the threat of prison sentences, which in some cases materialised, many of the failed revolutionaries left Germany and made their way to American or European destinations. Some eventually found themselves in Britain following short periods in other continental states, including Switzerland and France. The former again expelled all its political refugees under pressure from neighbouring states in 1850.[152]

For those who did make their way to Britain, the underlying pull factors were those outlined above, including 'the most free political system in Europe' and its liberal asylum laws. At the same time, for political exiles from the failed 1848 revolutions in all European countries, London remained a centre from which they could continue their political activities in the hope of influencing reform movements on the continent and eventually returning to their lands of origin.[153]

The ideological beliefs of the refugees ranged from 'liberal' to 'communist', although even within these groups there were numerous sub-divisions. Of the liberals, the most famous included Arnold Ruge and Gottfried Kinkel; others include the doctor, Karl Heinrich Schaible, together with other doctors, artists and teachers. Kinkel actually escaped from Spandau prison and then rode to Rostock, from where he sailed to Leith, although his wife and children progressed to the country along the more conventional route of steamer from Holland to London.[154] Karl Heinrich Schaible, who had taken part in revolutionary activity in Baden, eventually reached England in 1853 via Strasbourg, Paris and Basel;[155] the musician Charles Halle, who

151. See Julius H. Schöps, '"Der Kosmos": Ein Wochenblatt der Bürgerlich-Demokratischen Emigration in London im Frühjahr 1851', *Jahrbuch des Instituts für Deutsche Geschichte*, vol. 5, 1976, pp. 211–12.

152. Robert Richter, *Studien zur London Emigration von 1850–1860*, Berlin, 1966, p. 34.

153. Christine Lattek, 'Die Emigration der deutschen Achtundvierziger in England: Eine reine "school of scandal and of meanness"?', in Niedhardt (ed.), *Grossbritannien als Gast-und Exilland*, pp. 23–4.

154. J. F. Schulte (ed.), *Johanna Kinkel: Nach ihren Briefen und Errinerungs-Blättern*, Münster, 1908, pp. 90–1; Ashton, *Little Germany*, pp. 153–4.

155. Karl Heinrich Schaible, *Siebenunddreissig Jahre aus dem Leben eines Exilierten*, London, 1895, pp. 1–63.

had been working in Paris, entered England after the French revolution of 1848 although his reasons for moving also revolved around the possibility of securing a position in the country.[156] At least one exile, the father of the artist Hubert von Herkommer, moved to England after a stay in America.[157] Karl Marx was perhaps the most famous of all the exiles who entered Britain after the failure of the 1848 revolutions, arriving in London in August 1849. At the same time, many members of the workers movement who had left Britain to participate in the revolutionary uprisings on the continent returned to Britain after the failure of those revolutions.[158]

A further influx of politically-motivated refugees from Germany occurred towards the end of the century following the passage of the Anti-Socialist Law in October 1878, in response to two assassination attempts on the Kaiser which Bismarck and the German right blamed on the socialists. This legislation gave the police and authorities the power to suppress socialist organisations, meetings and newspapers. Socialists reacted in a variety of ways. Some remained in the country to reorganise, although many faced imprisonment. Several hundred left the country over the following decade, often making their way to London, while others actually faced expulsion.[159] Those forced to leave included Johann, most who went from Berlin to Hamburg, having received twenty-four hours notice to leave the former city after release from prison and then proceeded to London.[160] Subsequently in 1888 Edward Bernstein made his way to the capital together with the *Sozialdemokrat* newspaper, following, like many exiles earlier in the century, his banishment from Switzerland where he had spent ten years.[161] In 1895 Rudolf Rocker, the anarchist, made his way to London following anti-anar-

156. C. E. and Marie Halle, *Life and Letters of Sir Charles Halle: Being an Autobiography with Correspondence and Diaries*, London, 1896, pp. 92–7.

157. Sir Hubert von Herkommer, *The Herkommers*, London, 1910, pp. 16–30.

158. David McLellan, *Karl Marx: His Life and Thought*, London, 1973, p. 226; Asa Briggs, *Marx in London: An Illustrated Guide*, London, 1982, pp. 33–4; Werner Brettschneider, *Entwicklung und Bedeutung des deutschen Frühsozialismus*, p. 55.

159. John Quail, *The Slow Burning Fuse: The Lost History of British Anarchists*, London, 1978, pp. 10–11; Heinzpeter Thümmler, 'Zur Sozialen Struktur der Ausgewiesenen unter dem Sozialisten Gesetz (1878 bis 1890)', *Jahrbuch für Wirtschaftsgeschichte*, 1971, part 3, pp. 131–40; Gordon A. Craig, *Germany 1866–1945*, Oxford, 1981 reprint, pp. 145–7; Vernon L. Lidtke, *The Outlawed Party: Social Democracy in Germany, 1878–1890*, Princeton, 1966, pp. 70–82; Ignaz Auer, *Nach Zehn Jahren: Material und Glassen zur Geschichte der Sozialistengesetzes*, Nuremberg, 1913.

160. Quail, *Slow Burning Fuse*, p. 11; Rudolf Emil Martin, *Der Anarchismus und Seine Träger*, Berlin, 1887, p. 19; Rudolf Rocker, *Johann Most: Das Leben eines Rebellen*, Glashütten im Taunus, 1973, pp. 59–63.

161. Eduard Bernstein, *My Years of Exile: Reminiscences of a Socialist*, London, 1921, pp. 150, 174.

chist pressure in Paris, where he lived. He initially enquired about the prospect of returning to Germany at the London embassy, but would have faced imprisonment if he did go and consequently decided to remain in London.[162]

Thus, in the complexity of factors involved in the decision to move to Great Britain, apart from the underlying push and pull factors, short-term political developments proved fundamental while personal motives played a part for different individuals. Two further observations should be made; the first concerns the importance of not only the German background but also the asylum policies of other European countries, especially Switzerland, from where many refugees made their way to London. At the same time, a fundamental pull factor from the 1830s onward was the existence of German political organisations in England, which clearly attracted newcomers almost in the way that chain migration worked.

Turning to the religious reasons for migration, we can again detect a similar pattern of underlying push and pull factors together with personal motivations, although medium-term factors seem more difficult to establish. For instance, it would be difficult to trace a peak of German-Jewish immigration to Britain similar to the Jewish immigration which flowed out of Russia partially as a reaction to the rise of anti-semitism in the late nineteenth century.

Before 1800 we have seen that Christian religious groups entered the country in the form of the Brethrens and the Palatines, although in the case of the latter a combination of religious, political and economic motives caused the migration. Christian groups also left the country during the nineteenth century in the form of, for example, the Swabian Pietists who moved to Russia just after 1800 and Old Lutherans, who migrated to North America and Australia.[163] But none of these groupings seem to have made their way to Britain.

However, German Jews certainly did come to Britain for various reasons. The most important article on this subject, by Abraham Barkai, has pointed out that 'at least until the 1870s', legal and social discrimination played a major role in forcing Jews to leave Germany. He points to the 'Matrikel-laws which denied many young Jews the right to remain in their birthplace and found a family' and also states that legal discrimination had 'economic aspects, like the limitation of freedom of movement, settlement and occupation.' Barry Supple made similar

---

162. William J. Fishman, *East End Jewish Radicals*, London, 1975, p. 234.
163. Köllman and Marschalck, 'German Emigration to the United States', p. 522; Hansen, *Atlantic Migration*, p. 135.

observations in a 1957 article on movement to the USA.[164] C. C. Aronsfeld has written, more directly, that 'anti-semitism was the major cause of the emigration' of Jews from Germany, although he also points to the 'strictly economic' motives for movement of, for instance, commercial agents, some of whom have received attention above. In fact, it seems difficult to distinguish much of Jewish from non-Jewish migration from Germany. The reason for the movement of Jews to Bradford throughout the nineteenth century remained the attractions of its textile industry.[165]

Elsewhere, Aronsfeld has written that German Jews emigrated in order to escape the 'indignities' and 'murderous ravings' of German anti-Semitism, and moved to England because 'they hoped to find freedom' there. For those individuals who emigrated, it seems that these motivations did play a role. For instance, when Ludwig Mond moved to Britain, his mother seems to have encouraged him to leave a country where 'not only army officers, but many influential people were anti-semites', which consequently meant that 'there were no long-term prospects for her son'.[166] Similarly after Sigmund Freud, an Austrian, visited his half-brother in Manchester he 'never ceased to envy' him 'for being able to live in England and bring up his children far from the daily persecution Jews were subject to in Austria', although he did not move to Britain until the Nazis seized power in Austria in 1938.[167] Nevertheless, we must be cautious about accepting such statements because of the existence of anti-Semitism in Britain which differed from its continental strains only in degree.[168] At the same time, we have to

164. Avraham Barkai, 'German-Jewish Migrations in the Nineteenth Century', *Leo Baeck Institute Year Book*, vol. 30, 1985, pp. 312–13; Barry E. Supple, 'A Business Elite', *Business History Review*, vol. 31, 1957, pp. 146–9. See also Rudolph Glanz, 'The German Jewish Mass Emigration: 1820–1880', *American Jewish Archives*, vol. 22, 1970, pp. 49–66.

165. C. C. Aronsfeld, 'They Settled in England: German Jewish Immigrants in the Nineteenth Century', *Association of Jewish Refugees Information*, May 1954, p. 6; M. R. Heilbron, 'Bradford', in Aubrey Newman (ed.), *Provincial Jewry in Victorian England*, London, 1975, p. 1; A. R. Rollin, 'The Jewish Contribution to the British Textile Industry: "Builders of Bradford"', *Transactions of the Jewish Historical Society of England*, vol. 17, 1951, pp. 45–51.

166. Aronsfeld, 'German Jews in Victorian England', pp. 313–14; Jean Goodman, *Mond Legacy*, p. 15; Bolitho, *Alfred Mond*, p. 15.

167. Ernest Jones, *The Life and Work of Sigmund Freud*, 2 vols, vol. 1, p. 26; Mitchell G. Ash, 'Central European Emigre Psychologists and Psychoanalysts in the United Kingdom', in W. E. Mosse, et al (eds), *Second Chance: Two Centuries of German-speaking Jews in the United Kingdom*, Tübingen, 1991, p. 111.

168. The most thorough investigation of anti-semitism in Britain is Colin Holmes, *Anti-Semitism in British Society, 1876–1939*, London, 1979. See also in this context Todd M. Endelman, *Radical Assimilation in English Jewish History, 1656–1945*, Bloomington and Indianapolis, 1990, p. 209, who contrasts English and continental anti-Semitism.

recognise once again the complexity of factors in the decision to move to Britain. Clearly, emigration took place against a background of official and unofficial anti-Semitism but for those who entered Britain the economic opportunities available within the country proved as attractive as they did to any Gentile German immigrant.

The numbers of German Jews who moved to Britain during the course of the nineteenth century cannot be established, as censuses did not record religious denomination. But there seems little doubt that the vast majority of German immigrants to Britain were Gentiles, as evidenced by the numbers of German churches in contrast to German synagogues. Any attempt to provide figures for Jews can only remain speculation, and Aronsfeld's claim that the number of German Jews who settled in nineteenth-century Britain 'never exceeded a very few thousand', remains the most likely guess.[169] Nevertheless some doubt must be cast on the research of scholars who suggest that middle-class migrants made up the bulk of those who moved. Evidence against this includes both the humble origins of many of the Jews in the more general Jewish emigration from Germany, and the existence of a German Jewish community in the poorer part of London in the East End from the mid-nineteenth century; although, once again, there is difficulty in providing any accurate figures.[170]

A final group of emigrants, which was small in number, consisted of what might be described as cultural migrants or visitors, many of whom spent just a short spell in the country. This process represents a continuation of a movement dating back centuries. In the nineteenth century we can identify the migration of novelists, musicians (although their motives were also fundamentally economic), artists and travellers or tourists. Again, underlying motives might be found in the cultural attractions of England; short-term developments such as the 1848 revolutions, which sent many artists, musicians and writers to London so that it experienced 'a kind of artistic invasion';[171] and, perhaps more

169. Aronsfeld, 'German Jews in Victorian England', p. 312.
170. Among earlier commentators to make this point we can include Aronsfeld, p. 312, 'German Jews in Victorian England', who asserted that 'the Anglo-German Jews of the Victorian age, were men of substance and of standing'. Lloyd P. Gartner, *The Jewish Immigrant in England*, London, 1960, p. 33, and Todd M. Endelman, 'German-Jewish Settlement in Victorian England', pp. 37–8, have made similar assertions. For an indication of the existence of a more humble German Jewish community in Victorian Britain, see Charles Booth, 'The Inhabitants of Tower Hamlets (School Board Division), their Condition and Occupations', *Journal of the Royal Statistical Society*, vol. 50, 1887, pp. 365–7. See also Bill Williams, *The Making of Manchester Jewry 1740–1875*, Manchester, 1985 reprint, p. 127, who writes that, of the German-Jewish immigrants into Manchester during the 1830s and 1840s, 'most arrived penniless, or nearly so'.
171. Wilhelm Kuhe, *My Musical Recollections*, London, 1896, pp. 104–5.

important for cultural than for any other type of movement, personal objectives.

These objectives could include a desire to sample freedom and to extend knowledge and experience.[172] For the poet Heinrich Heine, who visited London in 1827, his main wish was to be out of Germany when the second volume of his *Pictures of Travel* appeared.[173] For others, such as academics and musicians, career motives played a role and they moved in order to obtain a position. Among the latter, we can include Ignaz Moscheles, who settled in London as a piano teacher at the Royal Academy of Music and conductor of the Philharmonic Society. Similarly, Heinrich Ernst moved to London in 1855 because of the existence of a receptive audience for his composing and performing.[174] The creation of chairs in German at the new universities in the late nineteenth century attracted academics, although scholars in other fields had taken up posts within Britain throughout the course of the nineteenth century.[175] Finally, the existence of German tourism to Britain is revealed in the publication of travel guides from as early as 1851, the year of the Great Exhibition,[176] although it seems likely that the movement of 'tourists' was an extension of the visits of travellers in earlier centuries.

In fact, the motives for emigration by Germans to Britain during the period 1815–1914 were often similar to those which had developed in previous centuries. For instance the purely economic immigrants, moving from a poorer to a wealthier land, have their precursors in the Palatine immigrants of the eighteenth century; the middle-class immigrants into Britain during this period can be linked with the entry of Hanseatic merchants during the medieval period and certainly with the eighteenth-century merchant migrants, as the post-1815 emigration simply continued the process which began around 1720. The political refugees were a new phenomenon, although connections can be drawn with the sixteenth-century religious emigrant groups. The Jewish migra-

172. Conrad Wiedemann, 'Einführendes Referat', in Wiedemann (ed.), *Rom-Paris-London: Erfahrung und Selbsterfahrung deutscher Schriftsteller und Künstler in den fremden Metropolen*, Stuttgart, 1988, pp. 11–18.

173. S. S. Prawer, *Frankenstein's Island: England and the English in the Writing of Heinrich Heine*, Cambridge, 1986, p. 42; Gerhard Weiss, 'Heine's England Aufenthalt (1827)', *Heine Jahrbuch*, vol. 2, 1963, p. 4.

174. *New Grove Dictionary of Music*, vol. 6, 1980, p. 236, vol. 12, 1980, p. 599.

175. Ernst Leopold Stahl, 'Das erste deutsche Lektorat in England', *Die Neueren Sprachen*, vol. 18, 1911, pp. 33–35; Anglo-German Publishing Company, *Die Deutsche Kolonie in England*, London, 1913, pp. 36–9.

176. See *London in Jahre 1851*; Karl Baedeker, *London und Seine Umgebung*, Coblenz, 1862; R. Kron, *The Little Londoner*, Freiburg, 1908; A. Rutari, *Londoner Skizzenbuch*, Leipzig, 1906. The last two of these may be directed towards immigrants as well as travellers.

tion of the nineteenth century becomes more middle class, but we should recognise that there were middle-class Jewish immigrants before this period and poor Jews from Germany. Finally, as noted, the 'cultural' migrants also have their predecessors.

As well as distinguishing different strands of migration of Germans into Britain, this chapter has also focused upon the complexity of identifying different levels of causation. Concentrating upon underlying push and pull, short-term and personal factors, it has tried to apply these different levels of causation to each of the four strands of migration. This has proved easier with some strands than with others. At the same time, the four strands certainly do not clearly distinguish themselves from each other. Many individuals made their way to Britain for complex reasons; economic motivations clearly proved the most important, but even for many of those entering for political and religious reasons economic motives proved fundamental, as we have seen in the case of individuals such as Engels and Mond.

Dealing with the relative importance of push and pull factors we have seen that, with regard to economic immigrants, Britain did not possess the pulling power of the United States as its economy remained too small and could not expand at the same rate as the US economy. Those economic immigrants who moved to Britain did so for a variety of reasons, affecting both different groups and individuals. Often, in the case of transmigrants, the decision to remain was accidental. With political refugees, we see that the particular attractions of Britain were of more importance as the country offered a refuge to virtually all Europeans persecuted because of their political beliefs, although their welcome once in England varied from enthusiastic to hostile.[177] In short, as this chapter has demonstrated, we can only establish the reasons for movement to Britain by looking at groups and individuals, each of which had different motivations.

177. Porter, *Refugee Question.*

–3–

Residential, Age and Gender, and Occupational Distribution

Having outlined the pre-eighteenth-century background of German migration to Britain and demonstrated the combination of reasons which led Germans to make their way to Britain after 1815, this and the following chapter will attempt to deal with the life of the German community in its new environment. The present chapter contains three sections, covering the geographical distribution of the Germans throughout Britain and especially within London, where they concentrated; the age and gender composition of the community, about which detailed census statistics exist; and the occupations of the immigrants, which can be gleaned from a large number of unofficial documents which have survived.

Size and Geographical Distribution

An important point which must be made at the outset of this chapter concerns the size of the German community in nineteenth-century Britain, which has already been mentioned previously. Although forming the largest continental immigrant group until the end of the nineteenth century, its numbers in comparison with German communities in North American cities remain relatively small, as they do in comparison with those of the Irish in nineteenth-century Britain. In the USA in 1880 five cities had a German-born population of more than 50,000, and at least nine counted more than the 21,966 who lived in London according to the British census of 1881. In New York the German-born of the city made up between 14 and 16 per cent of the total population during the mid-nineteenth century, while the figure for Milwaukee fluctuated around 30 per cent.[1] An examination of the Irish in London and other British cities also reveals large numbers; in the capital between 1851

1. Stanley Nadel, *Little Germany: Ethnicity, Religion, and Class in New York City, 1845–80*, Urbana and Chicago, 1990, p. 22.

and 1881 the numbers of Irish varied between 75,000 and 109,000, although their population as a percentage of the total London population remained small in comparison to the American examples just mentioned, hovering between 2.1 and 4.6 per cent. Nevertheless in other British cities, notably Glasgow, Manchester and Salford, the Irish counted over ten and in some cases more than twenty per cent of the population for much of the nineteenth century.[2]

But there also existed communities in nineteenth-century Britain smaller even than the Germans. For instance there were the Italians, whose pre-First World War peak numbers 25,365 in 1911; 11,668 of these were in London.[3] In all of these cases the newcomers formed distinct communities; they lived in the same areas, became involved in the same occupations and indulged in the same social activities, although equally they did not remain a totally enclosed ethnic community without contact with the native population. The extent of this contact varied according to a wide variety of factors.

The first problem is to establish the size and distribution of the German communities in nineteenth-century Britain. This task only proves possible with any degree of accuracy from 1861, because only from that date did the census statistics record the date of birth of immigrants in Great Britain.[4] Any attempt to establish numbers before that date remains speculation, of the type also involved in discovering the total number of Germans who resided in Britain before the nineteenth century. Much of this speculation is rather wild, such as the claim of the London City Mission that 40,000–50,000 Germans resided in London in 1848 or, even more extreme, the assertion of a London German newspaper in 1859 that between 80,000 and 150,000 Germans lived in the capital.[5] Even after the publication of census statistics which counted the numbers of foreigners in the country, commentators on the German community in London still ignored official figures in favour of guesses. J. Rethwisch, for instance, writing in 1889, thought that 200,000 Germans lived in Britain, of whom between 40,000 and 180,000 resided in London. Heinrich Dorgeel provided the wildest guess of all, claiming

2. Lynn Hollen Lees, *Irish Immigrants in Victorian London*, Manchester, 1979, p. 47; Frank Neal, *Sectarian Violence: The Liverpool Experience 1819–1914*, Manchester, 1988, pp. 9–10.

3. Lucio Sponza, *Italian Immigrants in Nineteenth Century Britain: Realities and Images*, Leicester, 1988, p. 322; Terri Colpi, *The Italian Factor: The Italian Community in Great Britain*, Edinburgh, 1991, p. 48.

4. *Census of Great Britain, 1851, Population Tables*, II, vol. 1, London, 1854, p. ci, actually listed the total number of foreigners, but not their land of birth. The number of foreigners in Britain amounted to 72,637.

5. *The Thirteenth Annual Report of the London City Mission*, London, 1848, p. 35; *Hermann*, 15 January 1859.

in 1881, that no less than 250,000 Germans lived in London alone, together with 20,000 in Manchester and 10,000 in Liverpool. Emil Stargardt provided a similar overestimation in 1889.[6]

The reasons for these guesses seem unclear, except possibly that the authors who made them counted more than just the German-born population and included second and even third generation immigrants. Even then, however, the estimates seem wild. There seems no reason for distrusting the size of the German population of England and Wales based on census statistics and outlined in Table 3.1. These present the total number of Germans at 49,133 in 1901 and 53,324 in 1911, the peak in size of the German community in Britain. At the same time the census statistics for 1901 and 1911 present only the major areas of German settlement within the country. Thus for 1901 the data gives the following major areas of settlement: London, 27,427; Essex, 2,398; Lancashire, 4,314; Middlesex, 2,223; and Yorkshire, 2,515.[7]

The census statistics of 1911 prove more useful because they provide details of major metropolitan areas of settlement outside London. The major concentrations of German population according to the 1911 census statistics consist of London, 27,290; Middlesex, 3,762; Essex, 1,970; Liverpool, 1,326; and Manchester, 1,318. In addition, two cities in Yorkshire have a notable number of Germans: Bradford with 372, which increases to 474 if we add Germans who became naturalised, and Hull, which had 654 people of German nationality and 738 if the total includes naturalised British subjects.[8]

Several settlement patterns emerge from the census statistics. Before dealing with the obvious geographical patterns, it is important to realize that the German community until 1891 formed the largest foreign minority in the country. In 1861, for instance, the total number of Germans and Prussians within England and Wales amounted to 28,644, while the number of foreigners stood at 86,090, meaning that Germans constituted a third of all foreign-born residents within the country. This proportion remained stable until 1881, although by this time the number of Germans was growing no more quickly than that of Russians. A sig-

---

6. J. Rethwisch, *Die Deutschen im Auslande*, London, 1889, p. 72; Heinrich Dorgeel, *Die Deutsche Colonie in London*, London, 1881, p. 1; Emil Stargardt, *Handbuch der Deutschen in England mit Wegweiser für London*, Heilbronn, 1889, p. 8. See also Leopold Katscher, 'German Life in London', *Nineteenth Century*, vol. 21, 1887, p. 726, who estimated that 'throughout England there can hardly be fewer than a quarter of a million, if we include the German-speaking Austrians and Swiss.'

7. *Census of England and Wales, 1901: Summary Tables, Area Houses and Populations*, London, 1913, pp. 260–1.

8. *Census of England and Wales, 1911: Birthplaces*, London, 1913, pp. xviii, 166, 167.

German Immigrants in Britain

Table 3.1 Numbers of Germans in England and Wales, 1861–1891

	1861	1871	1881	1891
London	16,082	19,773	21,966	26,920
South East	1,327	1,774	2,187	3,376
South Midlands	489	638	930	2,123
East	482	417	973	2,161
South West	799	632	687	1,029
West Midlands	1,199	1,171	952	1,468
North Midlands	542	664	1,096	817
North West	3,136	3,701	3,972	5,529
Yorkshire	1,946	1,741	2,673	3,685
Northern Counties	2,200	1,816	1,304	2,339
Monmouth and Wales	442	486	561	1,152
England and Wales	28,644	32,823	37,301	50,599

Source: Census of England and Wales for the Year 1861, vol. 2, London, 1863, p. lxxv; Census of England and Wales, 1871, vol. 3, London, 1872, p. li; Census of England and Wales, 1881, vol. 3, pp. xxvi–vii; Census of England and Wales, 1891, vol. 3, London, 1893, p. xxxvi.

nificant change had taken place by 1891, when the Germans constituted just a quarter of all aliens within England and Wales as immigration by Russians and Poles increased; by the turn of the century the latter groups had taken over as the largest non-British group, although Germans remained the second largest minority until the outbreak of the First World War.[9] This pattern ties in to some extent with the pattern of American immigration during the late nineteenth century, whereby the origins of newcomers changed from predominantly northern and western Europe to include the south and east of the continent.[10]

The most striking fact about the geographical distribution of Germans within England and Wales, as outlined in Table 3.1, is the concentration of Germans within London and its immediate environs, the southeastern counties. The only other two areas of the country which contained significant numbers of Germans were Yorkshire and Lancashire. For Scotland census statistics remain uneven; the first record of the number of Germans there exists in the census of 1871. Throughout the nineteenth and early twentieth centuries the number of Germans in Scotland remained miniscule, rising from just 1,531 in 1871

9. *Census of England and Wales for the Year 1861*, vol. 2, London, 1861, p. lxxv; *Board of Trade Memorandum on the Immigration of Foreigners into the United Kingdom*, P.P., vol. LXXXIX, 1887, pp. 4, 8; *Report of the Royal Commission on Alien Immigration*, vol. 3, p. 63, P.P., vol. IX, 1903; *Census of England and Wales 1911: Summary Tables*, London, 1915, pp. 372–3.
10. Maldwyn Jones, *American Immigration*, Chicago, 1960, pp. 178–9.

to over 2,000 in 1891 and reaching a peak of 2,362 in 1911. Not every census report indicated the distribution of Germans within Scottish cities but those which did point to something of a concentration in Glasgow, where 561 lived in 1911, and Edinburgh, whose German population totalled 461 in the same year.[11]

In addition to the lack of Germans in Scotland there was a sparsity of settlement in other parts of the country, as indicated in Table 3.1, notably in Wales but also in the Midlands generally. Even in Birmingham the total number of Germans remained less than 300 as late as 1871, although this small number of Germans in the Midlands ties in with the size of other foreign communities in this part of the country.[12]

Having mentioned areas with small numbers of German immigrants, attention will now focus on those parts of the country where they formed concentrations, using both statistical and other contemporary sources. The largest was London, whose German population increased from 9,566 in 1851 to a peak of 27,290 in 1911,[13] so that throughout the period 1861–1911 about half of the Germans in England and Wales lived in the capital. Within London they were concentrated in particular districts as Table 3.2 indicates. Areas where Germans did not reside in large numbers include south London as a whole; Lambeth was the only metropolitan borough with more than 1,000 Germans. Apart from that exception, Germans did remain fairly well spread through the capital. Nevertheless, two definite concentrations existed by the end of the nineteenth century, consisting of the East End and the West End.

The first of these areas had a German population from at least the eighteenth century involved in the sugar-baking industry, as mentioned in chapter 1. After 1800 this industry continued to be a major employer of Germans in the area and receives more attention below, although the subsequent discussion on employment in this chapter also indicates that other occupations became important. The concentration of Germans in this area led to the establishment of German institutions, including social clubs, churches and schools, which receive attention in chapter 4.

11. *Eighth Decennial Census of the Population of Scotland, 1871*, vol. 2, Edinburgh, 1874, p. 192; *Tenth Decennial Census of the Population of Scotland*, 1891, Edinburgh, 1893, p. 57; *Census of Scotland, 1911*, vol. 3, Edinburgh, 1913, p. x.
12. The figure for Germans in 1871 comes from Zoë Josephs, *Birmingham Jewry 1794–1914*, Birmingham, 1980, p. 8, who states that 'By 1871 the 397 Russians and Poles had far outnumbered the 251 immigrants from Germany and Western Europe.' For details of other immigrant communities in the Midlands during the nineteenth century see Sponza, *Italian Immigrants*, p. 322; and, for the Irish, see Neal, *Sectarian Violence*, p. 10.
13. *Census of Great Britain, 1851, Population Tables*, II, vol. 1, p. 36; *Census of England and Wales, 1911. Birthplaces*, p. xviii.

Table 3.2 indicates that the concentration of Germans in East London focused on Whitechapel, St George's in the East and Mile End. Of the first of these in particular, much information survives. In his autobiographical account of a visit to the area in the 1830s the refugee August Jäger described this area as a slum, although it appealed to him because of the presence of large numbers of refugees. He wrote of visiting 'two big rooms' which contained thirty youths and men, consisting of artisans, artists and scholars. A more favourable series of articles on the Germans in Whitechapel, from a London German newspaper, contrasted the Germans in the area with its ghetto reputation and pointed out the way in which the population remained German by continuing to eat German food and attending German church services and clubs. The articles described the activities of skin-dyers, boot and shoe-makers, cap-makers and tailors.[14]

As well as Whitechapel, Germans also settled in significant numbers in St George's in the East. As early as the 1830s the German community here had attracted the name of 'Little Germany', 'because in one part of the parish people of this nationality most did congregate. Their speech, dress, and habits differed from those around them; the very babies were wrapped up in a strange manner, and many of the shops bore German names.'[15] The reason for German settlement in St George's in the East lay not just in the fact that many sugar refineries lay in the area:

> but also on account of its being surrounded by the various docks, and consequently being the landing place of almost all foreigners. Very frequently they take up their abode in this locality on arriving here, and for many years remain unchanged inhabitants; and it is no rare occurrence to meet with Germans in this district who have lived here for several years without either knowing, or having seen, any other part of the metropolis.[16]

Both the census statistics and studies of other foreign communities in Victorian London would support the above statement. As late as 1901 Stepney contained 54,310 out of the 135,377 aliens in the capital, and served as the focus for the largest communities of, amongst other minorities, Russian and Polish Jews, Scandinavians, Dutch, Germans, Austrians, and Hungarians. In addition, for much of the nineteenth cen-

14. August Jäger, *Der Deutsche in London*, 2 vols., vol. 1, Leipzig, 1839, pp. 156; *Londoner Deutsches Journal*, 22, 29 September, 6, 13, 20 October 1855.
15. *East London Observer*, 30 March 1912.
16. *London City Mission Magazine*, 2 January, 1865; John Weylland, *These Fifty Years: Being the Jubilee Volume of the London City Mission*, London, 1884, p. 201.

Table 3.2 Major Areas of German Settlement in London, 1861–1911.

	1861	1871	1881	1891	1901	1911
Kensington	650	1,378	1,564	1,221	1,286	1,482
Westminster	480	1,327	967	1,070	2,031	2,010
St Marylebone	846	1,054	1,259	1,602	1,764	730
St Pancras	796	1,317	1,517	2,216	2,850	3,250
Paddington[a]	–	–	–	836	877	1,176
Holborn	151	954	921	996	1,008	956
Hampstead	53	211	380	–	984	1,223
Islington	629	1,080	1,543	1,866	1,842	2,092
Hackney	273	574	929	1,272	1,052	1,039
Shoreditch	604	581	708	1,021	1,004	730
Bethnal Green	267	552	451	475	481	386
Whitechapel	2,626	2,045	1,805	1,651	–	–
St George's in the East	2,625	2,058	1,493	1,423	–	–
Stepney[b]	370	367	326	523	3,576	2,095
Mile End Old Town	1,208	1,262	1,212	1,125	–	–
Poplar	603	416	659	780	627	599
Lambeth	363	537	807	1,136	1,270	1,632

(a) Paddington did not exist as a London borough before 1891
(b) From 1901 Whitechapel, St George's in the East and Mile End Old Town became part of Stepney due to boundary changes.

Source: Census of England and Wales for the Year 1861, vol. 2, London, 1863, pp. 42–4; *Census of England and Wales, 1871*, vol. 3, London, 1872, p. 25–6; *Census of England and Wales, 1881*, vol. 3, pp. 23–5; *Census of England and Wales, 1891*, vol. 3, London, 1893, p. 19–21; *Royal Commission on Alien Immigration*, vol. 3, p. 70, P.P., vol ix, 1903; *Census of England and Wales, 1911: Birthplaces*, London, 1913, pp. 136–46.

tury East London acted as a major focus for the Irish, as well as for small numbers of Chinese and Asian sailors to whom the above quotation proves especially apt.[17]

The majority of most immigrant groups did make their way out of East London, although this did not always happen. In the case of Russian and Polish Jews, for instance, 78.5 per cent of the London population, 42,032 out of 53,537, lived in Stepney alone in 1901. In comparison the German community remained far less concentrated, resembling in this sense the Irish, who had several focuses of population

17. *Report of the Royal Commission on Alien Immigration*, vol. 3, pp. 70–1, P.P., vol. IX, 1903; Chaim Bermant, *Point of Arrival: A Study of London's East End*, London, 1975, chapter 10; Lees, *Exiles of Erin*, pp. 57, 67–8; Douglas Jones, 'The Chinese in Britain: Origins and Development of a Community', *New Community*, vol. , 19, p. 399; Joseph Salter, *The Asiatic in England: Sketches of Sixteen Years Work Among Orientals*, London, 1873.

within the capital.[18] In the case of the Germans, their population in the four East End boroughs of Shoreditch, Bethnal Green, Poplar and Stepney in 1911 amounted to just 3,810 out of 27,290, or 14 per cent. Table 3.3 indicates that Germans concentrated in the East End of London to a greater extent during the earlier part of the century. In 1861, for instance, 8,303 from 16,082 lived in the East End boroughs of Shoreditch, Bethnal Green, Whitechapel, St George's, Stepney, Mile End and Poplar.

Twenty years later some movement had taken place out of this area but Charles Booth's survey of London still gave a figure as high as 7,583 for the eight East London boroughs of Whitechapel, St George's in the East, Stepney, Mile End, Poplar, Shoreditch, Bethnal Green, and Hackney. Booth's study asserted that 'There is no district in East London without a large contingent of German inhabitants' and while Germans 'are far more evenly scattered than the Poles in the area', he identified three focuses of concentration. These consisted of, first, the northern part of St George's in the East, which 'was in 1881 the chief centre of German population, then largely engaged in sugar baking and refining, but also in many miscellaneous trades'. In addition, 'There are also a large number of Germans in the western sub-district of Mile End Old Town', while 'Three quarters of the foreigners in Shoreditch are Germans.'[19]

Nevertheless, as Table 3.3 indicates, by the early 1880s, the period which Booth considered, the process of German migration out of East London had started, although between 1881 and 1891 a small increase in the East London population actually took place. But the most striking fact revealed by the table concerns the decline of concentration of London Germans in the East End.

The explanation for this decline is probably similar to that for the Irish. In her study of the London Irish, Lynn Hollen Lees pointed to the movement of the Irish communities out of the central London districts of Westminster, the City, St Giles, Whitechapel and Southwark, which she explained in the context of the general move of populations out of these areas caused by 'the many demolitions and so-called improvements carried on in the metropolis during the century'.[20] Evidence of German migration for similar reasons exists in the change of location of many of the German churches during the course of the nineteenth century, although none of these moved out of the East End; in fact, the

18. Lees, *Exiles of Erin*, pp. 55–87.
19. Charles Booth, *Life and Labour of the People in London*, First Series, vol. 1, London, 1902, pp. 102–3, 112.
20. Lees, *Exiles of Erin*, pp. 59.

Table 3.3   German Settlement in the East End[a] of London, 1861–1911

	1861	*1871*	*1881*	*1891*	*1901*	*1911*
Total German population of London	16,082	19,773	21,966	26,920	27,427	27,290
Total German population of the East End	8,303	7,280	6,654	6,998	5,668	3,810
% of London's German population in the East End	51.6	36.8	30.3	26.0	20.7	15.7
Absolute decline of the East End German population per decade		1,023	626	+344	1,330	1,858
% decline of the East End German population per decade		12.3	8.6	+5.2	19	32.8

(a) 1861–1891, Shoreditch, Bethnal Green, Whitechapel, St George's in the East, Stepney, Mile End Old Town, Poplar; from 1901, Whitechapel, St George's in the East, and Mile End Old Town became incorporated within Stepney.

Source: Census of England and Wales for the Year 1861, vol. 2, London, 1863, pp. 42–4; *Census of England and Wales, 1871*, vol. 3, London, 1872, p. 25–6; *Census of England and Wales, 1881*, vol. 3, pp. 23–5; *Census of England and Wales, 1891*, vol. 3, London, 1893, p. 19–21; *Royal Commission on Alien Immigration*, vol. 3, p. 70, P.P., vol ix, 1903; *Census of England and Wales, 1911: Birthplaces*, London, 1913, pp. 136–46.

Hamburg Lutheran Church actually moved into Hackney from the City of London because of the construction of Mansion House Underground Station. However, this area was outside the core district of the East End, and the move has additional significance because Hackney's German population expanded throughout the course of the nineteenth century.[21]

In her explanation for the movement of the Irish out of the East End, Lees also points to the influx of Eastern European Jews,[22] a point also made by contemporaries explaining the migration of Germans from the area. As early as 1882, for instance, the Mission Among the German Poor in London, pointed to 'an astonishing immigration of Jews, which

21. *Hamburg Lutheran Church, London 1669–1969*, Hamburg and London, 1969, pp. 89–90; Susan Gold, 'The Reredos which Slipped Through the Net', *Transactions of the Ancient Monuments Society*, vol. 27, 1984, pp. 106–8.
22. Lees, *Exiles of Erin*, p. 60.

begins to exercise an unmistakable influence upon the dwelling conditions of the German working class' because they settled 'in localities which have for years been almost exclusively inhabited by our poorer countrymen', which meant that 'whole streets hitherto German have assumed a Jewish aspect'. However, the same report asserted that the main reason for movement out of East London lay in 'the gradual but steady closing of the leading Sugar Refineries' which meant that the 'men were obliged to seek employment elsewhere.' The report claimed that, 'In this way entirely new and large colonies of Germans have sprung up in the neighbourhood of Canning Town and Victoria Docks in the East, and of Fulham and Battersea in the West.'[23]

Nevertheless, while migration of Germans out of the East End took place on a significant scale for a variety of reasons, during the late nineteenth and early twentieth centuries an important German community remained in the area. Count Armfelt's article in 1903 on 'German London' focused upon the East End, together with the West End, as one of the two major areas of German settlement in the capital:

> But let us follow the stream of the poor Germans, the old and the young of both sexes, whom a wayward fate has driven to seek fortune in London. From the Thames wharves and St. Katherine's Docks they wend their way through the Minories eastward to Leman Street, which is the High Street of German London in the east...
>
> As they trudge along their guides point out the numberless German names over the doors of the shops and the brass plates of the German business houses. There are bakers and confectioners, boot makers, butchers, drapers, fruiterers, grocers, hosiers, publicans, tailors, tobacco manufacturers and cigar makers, and wine, beer, and spirit merchants who bear German names; and all along the road, to the right and left, buying, selling, and discussing, there are German-looking people.
>
> In the by-streets off Commercial Road and Leman Street there are numerous tenement houses inhabited by several thousand hard-working men and equally hard-working women and girls, many of whom are engaged in warehouses and factories, for almost every class of German industry is represented.[24]

Other commentators, both English and German, described the poverty among Germans in this area, a feature which had attracted attention

---

23. BA, Potsdam, AA, 38981, 'The Twenty-Third Annual Report of the Mission Among the German Poor in London and the School in Connection with It, 1882'.
24. Count E. Armfelt, 'German London', in George R. Sims (ed.), *Living London*, vol. 3, London, 1903, p. 104.

throughout the course of the nineteenth century, not just with regard to Germans but also to natives and other immigrant groups.[25]

Given that some movement of Germans had taken place out of inner East London, or perhaps more accurately that the German East End did not expand as rapidly as other areas of German population in the capital, it remains to be seen which areas did grow. First, there was German East London outside the older areas of the East End. The above discussion made mention of the fact that Hackney became more of a German area as the century progressed, as evidenced by the census statistics. In addition, Germans also began to live in various parts of the present-day London Borough of Newham. By 1911, West Ham had a German population of 868 and a German Church, while the county of Essex, which included West Ham, had 1,970 Germans. In 1902, the School Board of the Borough of West Ham felt it 'necessary to engage the services of a female teacher, proficient in German', owing 'to the large influx of children from foreign parts to the neighbourhood of the Drew Road School', who 'in many instances did not understand a word of English'.[26] Migration into Essex had taken place from as early as the 1850s with the establishment of the first sugar refinery in Stratford. Further movement on a larger scale occurred during the 1870s out of the East End and into Canning Town and Silvertown, as a result of the collapse of the sugar refining industry of St George's in the East. In addition to these communities just north of the Thames in inner East London, others sprang up just south of the river consisting, in the case of Deptford and Charlton, particularly of butchers and tailors by the early twentieth century; although in north Woolwich a bottle-producing firm, Moore and Nettlefold, imported German workmen in 1899 because of difficulties in finding native labour to work in their factory.[27]

But East London outside the East End remained less important as an area of German settlement during the nineteenth century than the West

25. See for instance William F. Brand, *London Life Seen with German Eyes*, London, 1902.

26. *Census of England Wales, 1911: Birthplaces*, p. xviii; School Board of the Borough of West Ham, *Annual Report of the Board's Schools*, December 1902, London, 1902, p. 49.

27. BA, Potsdam, AA, 38981, 'Jahresbericht über die deutsche evangelische Stadt- und Seemanns-Mission und Armenschule in London für das Jahr 1888'; BA, Potsdam, AA, 38983, 'Jahresbericht über die deutsche evangelische Stadt- und Seemanns-Mission und Armenschule in London für das Jahr 1900'; Howard Bloch 'German Immigrants in Newham', unpublished manuscript. In the area of inner East London the number of Germans had reached, by 1911, 299 in Bermondsey, 225 in Deptford, and 301 in Greenwich. See *Census of England Wales, 1911: Birthplaces*, pp. 136–46. For the importation of bottle makers into Woolwich see *The Times*, 15 December 1901; BA, Potsdam, 30034, extract from *Neue Korrespondenz*, 29 October 1904.

German Immigrants in Britain

End. The principal areas of settlement were Westminster, St Marylebone, St Pancras and Paddington. More specifically, two places which acted as particular focuses were Soho and an area between Goodge Street, Euston Road, and Tottenham Court Road. In 1865 Henry Mayhew had commented on the cosmopolitan nature of Soho, with its 'Restaurants, Cafes, Estaminots, and Deutsche Gasthäuser', and where one could buy 'the impotent and blustering German Broadsheet called *Hermann*'.[28] The area certainly acted as a centre for refugees of both German and other nationalities during the mid-nineteenth century. The German Workers Educational Association established itself in Great Windmill Street in this area, while Karl Marx spent the first six years of his stay in England, 1850–6, in 'two small dark unventilated rooms' in Dean Street, with the five other members of his immediate family. His home lay near the temporary residence of another famous refugee, William Liebknecht, in Church Street and also a short distance from the German Hotel in Leicester Square, which acted as 'a transit camp for the many political refugees who had fled the revolutionary upheavals in France, Italy, Austria and Germany' and 'who arrived in England almost penniless and with no contacts'.[29]

Soho also acted as a centre of attraction for political refugees fleeing Germany after the passage of the Anti-Socialist Laws, partly because of the continued location of the German Workers Educational Association in the area, which 'was flooded with German refugees' in 1878.[30] However, this district also housed non-political immigrants by the turn of the century including waiters, tailors, governesses and 'Austrian and German gymnasts, lion-tamers, and strong-men', for whom German restaurants catered, while German newspapers were still sold in the area. In 1900 a missionary from the Mission Among the German Poor in London paid 1,230 visits to between forty and fifty families in Soho.[31]

28. Henry Mayhew (ed.), *The Shops and Companies of London*, London, 1865, p. 174.
29. Charles Bull, *Soho in Olden Times*, London, 1839; Asa Briggs, *Marx in London: An Illustrated Guide*, London, 1982, pp. 23, 36, 37; Edmund Wilson, *To the Finland Station: A Study in the Writing and Acting of History*, London, 1974 edition, p. 209; Communist Party of Great Britain, *London Landmarks: A Guide with Maps to Places Where Marx, Engels and Lenin Lived and Worked*, London, 1963, pp. 2, 3, 4; Rosemary Ashton, *Little Germany: Exile and Asylum in Victorian England*, Oxford, 1986, p. 154.
30. Hermia Oliver, *The International Anarchist Movement in Late Victorian London*, London, 1983, p. 5.
31. Armfelt, 'Cosmopolitan London', in Sims, *Living London*, vol. 1, pp. 242, 243–5; BA, Potsdam, AA, 38983, 'Jahresbericht über die deutsche evangelische Stadt- und Seemanns-Mission und Armenschule in London für das Jahr 1900'. See also Sims, *Off the Beaten Track in London*, London, 1911, pp. 117, 121, for an indication of the cosmopolitan, including German, nature of Soho.

Slightly north of Soho lay an area of more substantial German settlement centering around Goodge Street and Mortimer Street, 'the south-western corner of St Pancras; that is, the angle bounded by Tottenham Court Road, Cleveland Street, and Euston Road', and the locality of St Mary's Church, which had moved to this area in 1877 from the Savoy because of railway construction. At the turn of the century contemporaries commented on the fact that overcrowding existed in the area, due to recent influxes in the foreign population which had caused pressure for accommodation: 'Often one room will be occupied by two or three people. The tenant has a sub-tenant, who shares the expenses, and another may come in as a boarder.' Some houses in the area 'were originally built for one family, and now are occupied by four, five, and six, and sometimes seven families in one house, and a family in a single room.' As this area lay 'near to the West End houses of business, tailors and kindred tradespeople who bring their work home, of necessity, try and live near the district, because of the difficulty of getting a distance.' The proximity of this part of German London to the West End also meant that it attracted prostitutes.[32]

Attention has so far focused upon the working-class communities of Victorian and Edwardian London. More middle-class communities also existed, particularly by the early twentieth century. 'In the North, especially in Islington, there is a large settlement of small tradespeople and mechanics; while more to the North-west and West, about Hampstead, and more particularly in the South-eastern suburbs, Camberwell and Forest Hill, dwell most of the German merchants who go daily to the city'.[33] Those who lived in Forest Hill included Charles Bayer, a corsetmaker and stay manufacturer who moved to a mansion in the area in 1890.[34]

Having provided introductory details about the distribution of Germans in London, attention will now focus briefly upon the location of Germans outside the capital. We can begin by examining the two most important centres of Manchester and Bradford, whose importance lies not necessarily in the fact that they served as home to the largest numbers of Germans outside the capital, but that they attracted significant numbers of influential merchants and other middle-class professions. Table 3.4 provides an indication of the distribution of Germans in provincial cities in the late nineteenth century.

32. Armfelt, 'German London', p. 62; *Royal Commission on Alien Immigration*, vol. 2, pp. 443, 652, P.P., vol. IX, 1903.

33. Brand, *London Life*, p. 117.

34. Rene Quinault, 'A Note on Charles Bayer, Corset Maker and Stay Manufacturer', unpublished manuscript; A. Rutari, *Londoner Skizzenbuch*, Leipzig, 1906, p. 274. Brand, *London Life*, pp. 117–18.

German Immigrants in Britain

Table 3.4 German Populations in Provincial Cities, 1891

	1891	1911
Bradford	508	553
Manchester	1,321	1,318
Liverpool	1,779	1,326
Hull	906	855
Leeds	581	470
Sheffield	298	390

Source: Census of England and Wales, 1891, vol. 3, London, 1893, p. 300–1, 445; *Census of England and Wales, 1911: Birthplaces,* London, 1913, pp. xviii, 166–7.

The opening chapter of this study, which examined the pre-nineteenth century background to German immigration into Britain, demonstrated that a Jewish community, coming substantially from Germany, had developed in Manchester by the end of the Napoleonic Wars. This Jewish community continued to grow during the first half of the nineteenth century, with a further influx of German Jewish merchants during the 1820s and an entry of poorer Jews from East Prussia and western Russia during the late 1840s. The second influx actually formed the foundation of the major growth of the Eastern European community in the city, which grew apace from the 1870s. But by the 1850s the Jews of German origin, together with those from Holland, had developed a closely knit Ashkenazi community with religious, social and educational activity; a community of Sephardic Jews also developed from 1850.[35]

In addition, non-Jewish Germans also entered Manchester between 1815 and 1914 and developed a lively German community, with social and religious activity, from the middle of the nineteenth century. As well as the entry of well-known figures to nineteenth century Manchester, including the composer Sir Charles Halle and Frederick Engels, large numbers of less well-known German businessmen, together with academics, also made their way to the city. By the late nineteenth century approximately ten per cent of merchants in Manchester were German immigrants or their descen-

35. N. J. Frangopulo, 'Foreign Communities in Victorian Manchester', *Manchester Review,* vol. 10, 1965, p. 195; Bill Williams, *The Making of Manchester Jewry 1740–1875,* Manchester, 1985 reprint, pp. 81–5, 127, 168–9, 170–1, 319–24; Williams, '"East and West": Class and Community in Manchester Jewry, 1850–1914', in David Cesarani (ed.), *The Making of Modern Anglo-Jewry,* Oxford, 1990, pp. 16–17.

dants in the second or third generation, a total of 154 in 1870.[36] Much of the German social activity within Manchester revolved around middle-class clubs right up to the outbreak of the First World War.[37]

Nevertheless, less humble German immigrants also lived in Manchester. Bill Williams has identified 'three "gentlemanly" but penniless adventurers – Felix Bernhard Meyer, Carl Kemper and Frederick William Bagdansky – who in May 1833 were caught in the act of robbing the house of the respected German merchant, Martin Schunck', although Williams describes these as the 'only exceptions on record' to the general composition of German immigrants of the years 1825 who 'were for the most part merchants, professional men and exiled revolutionaries'. Williams claims that this social balance continued to exist throughout the course of the nineteenth century and places the Germans 'with other immigrant groups in Manchester' which 'existed on a higher social level' rather than with those of Irish or East European origin. However, he also recognises the existence of a 'floating population of paupers in northern towns',[38] a picture confirmed by an article of 1871 which points to pauper foreigners moving around Manchester from one charity to another.[39] The existence of these poor Germans is further proved by a study on Germans and their church communities in Manchester, which indicates that 'in 1862 the Society for the Relief of Distressed Foreigners gave active support to 309 German families at the bottom of the social scale.' A German Mission church and school were specifically aimed at assisting the poorer Germans in the city.[40]

Analysis of the German community in Bradford encounters problems similar to those in Manchester, in the sense that the success of German businessmen obscures the possible existence of a humbler community. In Bradford the name of 'Little Germany' actually applied to an area where 'German businessmen established a mercantile centre', in contrast to the normal use of this term to describe a working class ethnic

36. C. C. Aronsfeld, 'German Jews in Manchester', *Association of Jewish Refugees Information*, November, 1954, January 1955, February 1955; and Frangopulo, 'Foreign Communities', pp. 196–202; Hartmut Berghoff, *Englische Unternehmer 1870–1914: Kollektivbiographie führender Wirtschaftsbürger in Birmingham, Bristol und Manchester*, Göttingen, 1991, p. 72.

37. See the pages of *Manchester Nachrichten* which ran between 1910 and 1912, and pp. 187–9 below.

38. Williams, *Manchester Jewry*, pp. 75, 334.

39. Manchester City Archive, M38/4/2/17, William Thorp, 'Poor Foreigners'.

40. Institut für Auslandsbeziehungen, Stuttgart, Curt Friese, 'Some Thoughts on the History of the Germans and Their Church Communities in Manchester'.

community, as in the case of East London or New York.[41] The middle-class Bradford community originated in the 1830s, when individual merchants such as Behrens began to enter the city, and continued to develop during the course of the nineteenth century with a further immigration of people involved in textile production and export.

Like Manchester, Bradford had several middle-class social clubs during the Victorian and Edwardian period, together with a church and a German-Jewish synagogue. Also like Manchester, Bradford attracted Germans of more humble standing including pork butchers, as well as others who worked for both the pork butchers and the textile merchants, although in a community of less than 600, as it stood in 1911, it seems difficult to speak of a German working class. The Germans did not all reside in 'Little Germany', centred on Peckover Street and Vicar Lane, but lived also in Maningham in St Paul's Road, Wylmer Street, Spring Bank and Oak Lane, as well as in the Claremont, Ash Grove, and Trinity Terrace areas.[42] One German commentator, writing in the *Daily Mail* of 29 June 1909, claimed that he had never 'seen so many German names in one community outside Germany', but that 'the German colony is remarkably small. There is no competition at all from German labour, and indeed very little of it in the professional classes.' Referring particularly to the middle-class German immigrants, a more recent commentator has written that 'their influence was out of all proportion to their numbers' as reflected 'in the architecture of parts of central Bradford and the rich cultural heritage they bestowed on the city.'[43]

As well as Bradford, Table 3.4 indicates that several other cities in Yorkshire had small German communities. In Leeds, for example, Jacob Behrens had found a 'colony of Germans' as early as the 1830s, and he initially settled in that city in 1834 before moving to Bradford four years later. The German circle, 'which usually met in his rooms on Sunday

41. Stanley Varo, *A Mercantile Meander*, Bradford, 1989, p. 2; A. R. Rollin, 'The Jewish Contribution to the British Textile Industry: "Builders of Bradford"', *Transactions of the Jewish Historical Society of England*, vol. 17, 1951, p. 45. In East London, the term 'Little Germany' is used by *East London Observer*, 30 March 1912, to describe the area of St George's in the East from the 1840s. For New York see Nadel, *Little Germany*.

42. Michael Pratt, 'The Influence of the Germans in Bradford', (unpublished BA dissertation, Margaret Macmillan College, Bradford, 1971), pp. 31–2; Rollin, 'The Jewish Contribution'; C. C. Aronsfeld, 'German Jews in Nineteenth Century Bradford', *Yorkshire Archaeological Journal*, vol. 53, 1981, pp. 113–14. For a description of the Germans in Bradford using evocative language see the account of J. B. Priestley, *English Journey*, Harmondsworth, 1977 edition, pp. 153–5.

43. Bradford Heritage Recording Unit, *Destination Bradford: A Century of Immigration*, Bradford, 1987, p. 12. A similar assertion is made by Priestley, 'Born and Bred in Bradford', *Listener*, 27 December 1945.

evenings and played whist, was a large and happy one – Jacob himself, Carl Schmidt...two Wurtzburgs, three Liebreichs, Trosdorf, Milsheimer, Reunert, Boyes, Marcy, Boscoviz, Cahn Atterbury, Graves and a few others.'[44]

The German community in Hull had at least two origins. The first was in 'the local residue' of the 'movement destined chiefly for the United States', which Bill Williams has recognised as important for the development of eastern European Jewish communities in several northern cities. As late as 1889 Thomas Forth, a customs officer at Hull, recognised this factor as contributing to the growth of immigrant communities, including those of German origin, in Hull, Bradford, Leeds and even Nottingham and Manchester. However, in the case of Hull and other east coast German communities, visits by German sailors also played a role. In 1844 alone, 2,291 German sailors landed in Hull on 274 different ships. As in Bradford, German pork butchers also established themselves, including Georg Friedrich Hohenrein who came to Hull at age sixteen and worked for two years for another German pork butcher, G. H. Frederick, before opening up his own business in 1850.[45]

The nineteenth-century German community in Sheffield never exceeded 400 people. However, some information survives about this tiny minority. First, with regard to employment, Gerald Newton has drawn up a list of 103 Germans and their trades in 1914. Those which appear most frequently include engineers, 'managers' and 'travellers', while other occupations include language teachers, clerks and tailors. Dr Newton has also identified the existence of German pork butchers' shops in the city; their number grew from just one in 1817 to fourteen in 1883 and eighteen in 1914.[46]

A few Germans became prominent in nineteenth-century Sheffield. Fritz Schölhammer from Württemberg conducted the Sheffield Amateur Musical Society, and also taught German at Firth College, which later formed part of the University of Sheffield. Several Germans played a

44. Sir Jacob Behrens, *Sir Jacob Behrens, 1806–1889*, London, 1925, pp. 32–5.

45. Williams, *Manchester Jewry*, pp. 176, 269–70; *Report of the Select Committee on Emigration and Immigration (Foreigners)*, pp. 25–9, P.P., vol. 10, 1889; James Joseph, Sheahan, *General and Concise Description of the Town and Port of Kingston-Upon-Hull*, London, 1864, p. 439; Deutsches Kirchen Verein, *Bericht der Deutschen Kirchen-Vereins in Hull*, Hull, 1845; Reinhard Münchmeyer (ed.), *Handbuch der deutschen evangelischen Seemansmission*, Stettin, 1912; John Markham, *Keep the Home Fires Burning: The Hull Area in the First World War*, Beverly, 1988, p. 32. For German communities in the North East of England, see, for Sunderland, BA, Potsdam, AA, 38969; and for Middlesbrough, BA, Potsdam, AA, 38976.

46. Gerald Newton, 'Notes on Germans in Sheffield', unpublished document.

part in the steel industry of the city, including Carl Wilhelm Kayser, Paul Kuehnreich and Joseph Jonas, identified in the previous chapter. Two other Germans, Henry Seebohm (1832–95) and George Diecküstahl founded Arthur Balfour & Co. in 1865, another major steel producer in the city. Joseph Jonas (1845–1921) became the most famous German resident of Sheffield, playing a part in local politics and eventually becoming Lord Mayor.[47]

In comparison with other major cities, the German community in Sheffield did not develop a social life to the same extent. A survey of Germans in Britain during 1913 listed just one social body in Sheffield, the *Deutscher Klub*; this was described, however, as one of the oldest in England, having come into existence twenty-five years previously. Evidence also survives of German religious services in Sheffield from as early as 1861.[48]

Table 3.4 indicates that the largest German community outside London during the late nineteenth and early twentieth centuries was in Liverpool. This settlement had begun to develop from the 1820s and, like communities in some east coast cities, sailors formed a significant part in its early growth so that 'at the end of the 1840s, one could expect to meet about 250 German sailors in the port of Liverpool'. By this time regular religious meetings had been organised for them. We have also seen in the previous chapter that large numbers of transmigrants passed through Liverpool, some of whom remained.

In addition, at least three other groups formed fundamental components of the Liverpool community. First, there were merchants from German ports such as Bremen, Danzig and Stettin, who were attracted to Liverpool during the course of the nineteenth century as its trade grew. They included representatives of the Stadterfohrt, Barendt, Hausburg, Blessig, Kundhardt, Lemonius and Prange families. Like German merchants in Bradford and Manchester, many exported cloth. The second important group within the German community of Liverpool consisted of sugar bakers, an occupation which became important from the 1840s and remained so until the First World War. In

---

47. Schölhammer is mentioned by E. D. Mackerness, *Somewhere Further North: A History of Music in Sheffield*, Sheffield, 1974, p.85; and G. Newton, *German Studies at the University of Sheffield: An Historical Perspective, 1880–1988 together with a Graduate List, 1910–1988*, Sheffield, 1988, pp. 44–52. Kayser is mentioned in *Histories of Famous Firms*, vol. 18, 1958, pp. 4–5. For a mention of Dieckstahl and Seebohm, and, particularly, Kühnrich, see Geoffrey Tweedale, 'The Razor Blade King of Sheffield: The Forgotten Career of Paul Kühnrich', *Transactions of the Hunter Society*, vol. 16, 1991, pp. 39–51. The career of Jonas can be traced in *Sheffield Daily Telegraph*, 26, 30 July 1918.
48. *Die Deutsche Kolonie in England*, London, 1913, pp.17–32, 51, 72; Mackerness, *Somewhere Further North*, p.59.

the mid-nineteenth century, the German sugar bakers concentrated in the area around Great Mersey Street which, like the community in east London, was named Little Germany. A third occupational group of Germans consisted of pork butchers, particularly from Württemberg, who began to enter the country from the mid-nineteenth century.[49]

In addition to the major German settlements outlined above, numerous other towns and cities in Britain had small numbers of Germans. These include Nottingham, which had a middle-class Jewish community involved particularly in the manufacture and export of lace and hosiery. Prominent figures included Josef Neuberg, who moved to the city as an agent of a Hamburg firm in the 1820s, as did Jacob Weinberg in 1849. The lace manufacturer Lewis Heymann established the firm of Alexander and Heymann, and became Lord Mayor of the city in 1857.

In Birmingham fifteen per cent of tradesmen in the city were born in Germany, including Theodor W. Peterson who played a role in the opening of the Scandinavian market for Birmingham metal goods and agricultural machinery.[50] In Edinburgh, the city's small German population included a greater social mix; in 1865, for instance, it included sailors, street musicians, foreign correspondence clerks and 'a number of young Germans who had been engaged in the American army' and who 'arrived in Leith on their way back to the "Fatherland".' The other German communities of Scotland in the early twentieth century contained a similar mixture of occupations.[51] We should also briefly mention Ireland which contained a small Jewish community, most of whose members came from Germany during the nineteenth century. As with other provincial German communities, the one in Belfast consisted largely of middle-class cloth merchants; here most were involved in linen.[52]

49. A. E. Rosenkranz, *Geschichte der deutschen evangelischen Kirche zu Liverpool*, Stuttgart, 1921, pp. 15–16, 25–7, 57; *Report of the Select Committee on Emigration and Immigration (Foreigners)*, p. 15, P.P., vol. 10, 1889; Henry Peet, *The German Church in Renshaw Street Liverpool*, Liverpool, 1935, pp. 65, 66.

50. For Nottingham see C. C. Aronsfeld, 'German Jews in Nottingham', *Association of Jewish Refugees Information*, December 1955, p. 8; Aronsfeld, 'Nottingham's Lace Pioneers, 1', *Guardian Journal*, 19 April 1954; Aronsfeld, 'Nottingham's Lace Pioneers, 2', *Guardian Journal*, 20 April 1954. R. A. Church, *Economic and Social Change in a Midlands Town: Victorian Nottingham, 1815–1900*, London, 1966, pp. 76–7. For Manchester see Berghoff, *Englische Unternehmer*, p. 74.

51. BA, Potsdam, AA, 38965, 'Third Annual Report of the German Church and Mission for Edinburgh and Leith, 1865'; *Census of Scotland, 1911*, vol. 8, Edinburgh, 1913, p. x.

52. C. C. Aronsfeld, 'German Jews in Ireland', *Association of Jewish Refugees Information*, December 1953, p. 5; Lewis Hyman, *The Jews of Ireland from Earliest Times to the Year 1919*, London, 1972, pp. 203–9.

Age and Gender Structure

Between 1855 and 1909, 57.4 per cent of German emigrants making their way to all destinations were males and 42.6 per cent were females, while the proportion of children under fifteen years of age totalled 18.3 per cent, as was shown in Table 2.3. The previous chapter asserted that the Germans in Britain consisted of the same kinds of people who made their way to the USA because they originated from the same areas where similar push factors were in force. Table 3.5, when compared with Table 2.3, shows how the age and sex structure of the immigrants to Britain compares with that of immigrants to America.

In comparison with Table 2.3, two factors stand out. First, there is a greater proportion of males to females, a situation which remains stable throughout the period 1861–1911, although it becomes less marked towards the end of the nineteenth century. More striking is the percentage of children, which in comparison with the overall emigration from Germany represents a much smaller percentage. The main conclusion to draw here is that, when compared with the overall movement of people out of Germany, immigration to Britain consisted mainly of individuals.

Nevertheless they did not remain individuals, as Table 3.6, on the marital status of Germans in Britain indicates. Table 3.5 also deals only with first-generation immigrants in Britain and ignores children born to families of Germans who married in Britain. Table 3.6, although not indicating the nationality of the marriage partner of each individual, suggests that Germans married other Germans because the middle column, of married people, ties in closely with the percentage of German males to females indicated in Table 3.6. German males married German

Table 3.5 Age and Sex Structure of the German Population in Britain, 1861–1911

Year	Percentage of Males	Percentage of Females	% under 15 Years of Age
1861	69.0	31.0	6.7
1871	64.7	35.3	5.2
1881	63.6	36.4	4.8
1891	60.0	40.0	4.9
1901	61.8	38.2	7.5
1911	63.1	36.9	2.9

Source: Census of England and Wales for the Year 1861, vol. 2, London, 1863, p. lxxvii; *Census of England and Wales, 1871*, vol. 3, London, 1872, p. liii; *Census of England and Wales, 1881*, vol. 3, p. xviii; *Census of England and Wales, 1891*, vol. 3, London, 1893, p. xl; *Census of England and Wales, 1901: Summary Tables, Area, Housing and Population*, London, 1903, p. 266; *Census of England and Wales, 1911: Summary Tables*, London, 1915, p. 373.

Table 3.6 Marital Status of the German Population of England and Wales, 1891–1911

Year	Single		Married		Widowed	
	Males	*Females*	*Males*	*Females*	*Males*	*Females*
1891	13,422	9,007	15,821	9,354	1,143	1,852
1901	15,484	8,644	16,620	8,287	1,549	2,740
1911	14,511	8,887	14,720	8,125	1,125	1,765

Source: *Census of England and Wales for the Year 1861*, vol. 2, London, 1863, p. lxxvii; *Census of England and Wales, 1871*, vol. 3, London, 1872, p. liii; *Census of England and Wales, 1881*, vol. 3, p. xviii; *Census of England and Wales, 1891*, vol. 3, London, 1893, p. xl; *Census of England and Wales, 1901: Summary Tables, Area, Housing and Population*, London, 1903, p. 266; *Census of England and Wales, 1911: Summary Tables*, London, 1915, p. 373.

females when available, but the shortage would have been made up by marriages to non-German women. A breakdown of unmarried Germans according to age reveals only a small percentage of single people over the age 45.[53]

The above claims receive support from Table 3.7, taken from the marriage register of St George's German Lutheran Church and indicating that of those people married there during the course of the nineteenth century a large percentage chose partners of their own nationality. As the century proceeds the percentage of marriages with non-German spouses increases, although this is partly explained by the fact that non-German also includes people of German parentage born in London, whose number increased during the course of the century.

However, an examination of census returns for Whitechapel and St George's from 1851 and 1891 contradicts this picture. This shows that in the former year about two-thirds of all marriages involved an English and a German partner, whereas in 1891 such unions had declined significantly, with marriages between two German partners making up 60 per cent of the total. By this time unions between German and other non-British partners accounted for almost as many as those between Britons and Germans. The explanations for these figures lie partly in an increase in the number of German females in this area of London; in 1851 the percentage of German males to females was extremely uneven, connected with the overwhelming importance of the sugar baking industry for the German community in this part of

53. The figures are 932 from 30,386 males and 790 from 20,213 females in 1891; 968 from 30,356 males and 873 from 18,777 females in 1901; 1,336 from 32,421 males and 1,326 from 18,742 females in 1911. See *Census of England and Wales, 1891*, vol. 3, London, 1893, p. xl; *Census of England and Wales, 1901: Summary Tables, Area, Housing and Population*, London, 1903, p. 266; *Census of England and Wales, 1911: Summary Tables*, London, 1915, p. 373.

Table 3.7 Marriages in St George's German Lutheran Church, Whitechapel, 1843–96

Years	% Both Partners German	% One Non-German Partner
1843–53	83.3	16.7
1853–6	87.3	12.7
1856–62	91.4	8.6
1862–9	94.0	6.0
1869–82	82.3	17.7
1883–96	75.6	24.4

Source: Tower Hamlets Local History Collection, TH/8371/13, TH/8371/14, TH/8371/15, TH/8371/16, TH/8371/17, TH/8371/18, St George's German Lutheran Church Marriage Registers.

London. In the census sample taken, German males outnumbered females by nine to one in 1851, whereas by 1891 the proportion had changed to 60 per cent males and 40 per cent females.[54]

Socio-Economic Structure

Having outlined the bare essentials of the age and sex composition of Germans in London, we can now move on to examine their economic activities. The discussion on migration in the previous chapter asserted that the Germans who made their way to Britain during the nineteenth century consisted of several different strands, i.e. economic immigrants, political refugees, migrants whose movement had connections with religious persecution, and cultural visitors. The present discussion recognises these divisions but it concentrates, as did the previous chapter, on the activities of those people who made their way to Britain for economic reasons. Within this group of economic immigrants, it further emphasises the difference between middle-class businessmen and more humble immigrants, pushed out of Germany by the economic transformations taking place in the country. The discussion on economic activity proceeds by looking at different groups on a class basis, beginning with the very poor, or sub-proletariat, before moving on to discuss the more stable working class who had fairly secure employment, although

54. The census returns consist of samples from PRO HO107, 1545, 1546, 1547, 1548, for the year 1851. The sample consists of 497 Germans, of whom 447 are males and 50 females. Of 102 marriages, 33 involve 2 German partners, 65 involve one German and one British partner and 4 involve one German and one foreign partner. The sample for 1891, from PRO RG12 273, 280, 281, 282, 284, 287, totals 460 Germans made up of 280 males and 180 females. The marriage patterns are: 89 marriages with two German partners, and 21 marriages consisting of one German and one foreign partner.

they often remained poor. The discussion then considers the middle-class professions, of which there are numerous examples, indicating that a substantial proportion of the German immigrants in nineteenth-century Britain fell into this social category.

To begin with the sub-proletariat, although the census returns of occupations would have missed people who fell into this social category, contemporaries, both English and German, recognised the existence of a German underclass consisting of people without fixed occupations who, in some cases, fell in and out of the lowest level of society. But this level did not consist of an amorphous mass. Instead, it contained at least three components, the destitute, criminals and prostitutes.

The first group, the destitute, consisted of a variety of people including those who had made their way to London and then found difficulty in obtaining employment, individuals who did have steady employment but then faced problems due to a general economic downturn or to a deterioration in the employment prospects in their trade, and the aged. During the 1850s some of the refugees of all nationalities who had made their way to England, as many as two-thirds according to one report, found themselves 'in straitened circumstances'. Some turned to begging while others ended up in debtors' prisons. Rosemary Ashton has pointed out that the German poor of this period resembled 'many of London's native population' but differed 'in being foreigners of more than one class'. In some cases, refugees simply sank down the social scale, as in the case of a 'Prussian military officer' who 'after trying to teach mathematics here, had actually become a workman and even set up a workshop with some of his comrades making brooms and brushes'. [55]

This idea of the German poor of London coming from all sections of society receives stress in contemporary German accounts later in the century. Leopold Katscher writing in the mid-1880s, stated that:

As regards the houseless poor, there is not an evening when we may not see, in the sea of houses called London, a great many persons, chiefly foreigners, who know not where to lay their head, after a day in which they have not known where to find a morsel of food. And it is not only poor workmen who are without shelter; among the numerous homeless Germans in London there are always to be found persons of culture and education, who have seen better days, and now could be thankful to be sure of a bed, a crust and a cup of tea. It is frequently a matter of astonishment on the Continent that men willing and able to work should be left to starve in rich London, and the question is asked whether they cannot find employment. To this we answer decisively: No, in innumerable cases they cannot. Competition is so fierce in all

55. Ashton, *Little Germany*, pp. 225–8; Francesca M. Wilson, *They Came as Strangers: The Story of Refugees to Great Britain*, London, 1959, p. 129.

departments of labour, in all branches of business, that there are constantly many thousands of natives, as well as foreigners, who can find no opportunity of utilising their stalwart arms or acquired skill.[56]

Writing in the same decade Heinrich Dorgeel supports Katscher's assertion, although he placed some blame upon the victims who entered London without finance, knowledge of London or references. The newcomers would spend several days looking for accommodation and for a position which might have five hundred other applicants. If lack of success in obtaining a position continued for any length of time the newcomers would sink lower, perhaps losing their homes, finding their way onto the streets or even committing suicide. The Society of Friends of Foreigners in Distress also pointed to 'the unfortunate state of reduced circumstances amongst educated persons, governesses, teachers, professors of music, &c, who continue to apply for assistance in their distressingly straitened position.' Such a situation existed both in the 1860s and the 1890s.[57]

Some individuals did not fall to such a level, including those who found assistance from one of the many German charities in existence in London and its vicinity. In 1913, for instance, those assisted by the German Farm Colony in Libury Hall included 'a mechanic' who 'arrived in England with £10 in his pocket, but all his efforts to find work were unsuccessful'. He stated that had he not received assistance, 'I should have perished in the morass of London'. Similarly, 'a farm labourer, who, having quarrelled with his parents, left them in a fit of temper, and came to England almost penniless to seek his fortune...soon became utterly destitute, and was admitted to the Colony.' Finally, a clerk, who had spent seven years in America, 'landed in Liverpool in a very wretched condition, having worked his passage home on a cattle-boat. From Liverpool he tramped to London and eventually came to the Colony.'[58]

The German charities in England also dealt with people who had secure employment but had fallen into poverty because of an economic downturn. Such a situation existed in the 1860s and mid-1880s. In 1866 the Society of Friends of Foreigners in Distress in London mentioned that:

56. Leopold Katscher, 'German Life in London', p. 732.
57. Heinrich Dorgeel, *Die Deutsche Colonie in London*, London, 1881, pp. 19–21. Society of Friends of Foreigners in Distress, *An Account of the Society of Friends of Foreigners in Distress for the Year 1866*, London, 1866, p. 23; also, *An Account of the Society of Friends of Foreigners in Distress for the Year 1892*, London, 1892, p. xv.
58. BA, Coblenz, AA, 3100, 'German Farm Colony and Pensioners' Home in England'.

There has been much distress latterly from slackness of work generally, but
particularly among the tailors and sugar-boilers, many of the latter trade
being thrown out of work for weeks together by the partial or total suspen-
sion of business by their employers... Among the causes that at present seriously affect the interests of the poor, may be mentioned the enhanced price
that they have to pay for their humble and frequently most miserable
dwellings. Rents have everywhere so increased, that the poor are not only put
to very serious inconvenience from being turned out of their lodgings to
make way for railways or local improvement, but the heavy extra percentage
on their security earnings for advance in rent is a very serious evil, and adds
another element in the difficulties and struggles of the poor.

Later, the 1880s represented 'a period of exceptional trials for the
German labouring classes, large numbers of whom were stricken down
by poverty and sickness'. The depression also 'reduced to beggary a
considerable number of respectable and hardworking people'.
Consequently, the years 1884 and 1885 saw an increase in the numbers
of people assisted by the Society of Friends of Foreigners in Distress,
from 4,137 in 1883 to 6,489 in 1884 and 6,637 in the following year.
The 1880s also coincided with the largest decennial increase in the
German community within Britain, which swelled the number of the
German poor even further.[59]
Twenty-five years later, 'The struggle for existence' amongst the
Germans in east London, 'in consequence of the scarcity of work owing
to the sugar factories being closed' became very acute, and the suffering
undergone by some of them very great. Those involved in seasonal
employment also sometimes fell into straitened circumstances. In 1911
the German Society of Benevolence reported that during the months of
May to October the young Germans of London could find employment
easily but that November brought an increased number of applicants for
relief, especially from waiters and other victims of the 'seaside season'.[60]
Any attempt to measure the numbers of German poor in Britain
proves difficult because of the lack of information outside the capital.
Nevertheless, within London some information is available thanks to the
survival of selected documents of the three major German charities: the

59. Society of Friends of Foreigners in Distress, *Account for the Year 1866*, pp. 23–4;
BA, Potsdam, AA, 38981, 'The Twenty-Fifth Annual Report of the Mission Among the
German Poor in London and of the School in Connection with It, 1884'; *Report of the
Select Committee on Emigration and Immigration (Foreigners)*, pp. 12–14, P.P., vol. 10,
1889.
60. *The Seventy Fourth Annual Report of the London City Mission*, London, 1909;
BA, Coblenz, R57 neu, 1065/3, 'Jahresbericht der Deutschen Wohltätigsgesellschaft in
London, 1910–11'.

Society of Friends of Foreigners in Distress, the German Society of Benevolence, and the Mission Among the German Poor in London. Again, we have to refer to the mid-1880s because of a coincidence of surviving information from all three groups. For the years 1880–8, the Society of Friends of Foreigners in Distress helped an average of 5,693 people per year although, as the name suggests, not all of these consisted of Germans. Nevertheless, we can guess that about sixty per cent of them were,[61] meaning that the total included about 3,400 Germans. In the same period the German Society of Benevolence, which relieved 'all people who can speak German', assisted an average of 2,568 people per year.[62] The statistics from the Mission Among the German Poor of London prove less reliable as they simply refer to the number of 'domiciliary visits', which seem to have been at least partly for 'spiritual' purposes. Nevertheless, the figures prove interesting, totalling 'upwards of 3,000' in 1882, 2,903 in 1884, 2,839 in 1886, and 1,118 in 1889.[63]

Taken together, these figures suggest a high level of poverty amongst the German community of London during the 1880s, confirming the impressionistic accounts of Katscher and Dorgeel quoted above. But this poverty existed throughout the nineteenth and early twentieth centuries, as the scattered documents of the German charities make clear. In 1874, for instance, the Mission Among the German Poor in London made 4,768 domiciliary visits, a year in which its annual report actually claimed that 'there are no more so many poor Germans coming over to this country as formerly.'[64] Furthermore, as well as relief from German charities, German immigrants in Britain could also receive assistance from the poor law authorities within the country; in 1902, 599 Germans obtained such relief in London, a figure which had risen to 682 by 1904.

---

61. This guess is based on figures from *An Account of the Society of Friends of Foreigners in Distress for the Year 1892*, p. xvii, which states that 'The number of persons relieved since the establishment of the Society independently of their wives and families, amounts to 35,216; but these persons have received relief in 191,722 instances', of whom 114,979 consisted of Germans.

62. *Report of the Select Committee on Emigration and Immigration (Foreigners)*, pp. 12–14, P.P., vol. 10, 1889. The number of Austrians in London reached 6,189 in 1901. See *Royal Commission on Alien Immigration*, vol. 3. p. 71, P.P., vol. 9, 1903.

63. BA, Potsdam, AA, 38981, 'The Twenty-Third Annual Report of the Mission Among the German Poor in London and of the School in Connection with It, 1882'; 'The Twenty-Fifth Annual Report of the Mission Among the German Poor in London and of the School in Connection with It, 1884'; 'Siebenunddreissigsten Jahresbericht über die Deutsche Stadtmission und Armenschule in London, 1886'; 'Jahresbericht über die deutsche evangelische Stadt- und Seemans-Mission und Armenschule in London für das Jahr 1888'. For more general information on 1880s London see W. J. Fishman, *East End 1888: A Year in a London Borough Among the Labouring Poor*, London, 1988.

64. Bremer Staatsarchiv, 2 6 t 4 d, 'The Twenty-Fifth Annual Report of the Mission Among the German Poor in London, and the School in Connection with It, 1874'.

In Birmingham, Cardiff, Leeds, Liverpool, Manchester and Sheffield a combined total of 277 Germans received relief in 1903.[65]

A substantial percentage of the German poor in London consisted of the aged, some of whom had fallen into quite desperate circumstances as the applications for pensions from the Society of Friends of Foreigners in Distress indicate. For example, in 1866 the unsuccessful applicants included George Rendow, aged 57 and a native of Berlin, who had spent twelve years in London. He had worked as a commission agent but had been bed-ridden and paralysed for six years, while his 54-year-old wife occasionally earned money from needlework and obtained a pension of two shillings per week from the Society. Julius Kleinhaus, a successful applicant and a seventy-year-old native of Hesse, had lived in Britain for 42 years; he had served for eleven years in the army of Darmstadt, and had moved to England on the dissolution of his regiment, 'intending to join the German Legion in Spain, in which he had been promised a commission, but the authorities at home detained his passport, and he declined to go.' He had found work making transparent blinds, but had been paralysed for nine months. One of the worst cases, who was actually unsuccessful, was Frederick Schilling, a 71-year-old native of Oldenburg, who had lived in England for 45 years and worked as a sugar baker and light porter. But both he and his wife had become crippled.[66]

After the poor, the second strand of the German underclass consisted of criminals. Information about them is more scarce. Katscher believed that 'an astonishing number of swindlers and impostors exist among the Germans of London. The more the immigration increases numerically, the more it deteriorates in quality.' He pointed to 'the "long firm swindlers", i.e. German clerks, &c., who under various false names obtain samples and even goods from manufacturers, and never pay for them, but pawn them at once – and decamp'. A report on the German Catholics in London from the 1860s made similar assertions, claiming that criminals who had committed crimes in Germany continued with the same activities once they had arrived in London. For the period between 1906 and 1913, Lucio Sponza has drawn up a list of convicted foreigners expelled under the Aliens Act of 1905. Interestingly, according to this list the minority which had committed the most crimes were the Germans, rather than the Russians and Poles, despite the fact that the latter group made up the largest immigrant community in the country

---

65. *Statistical Tables Relating to Emigration and Immigration from and into the United Kingdom in the Year 1904, and Report to the Board of Trade Thereon*, P.P., vol. 98, 1903.

66. Society of Friends of Foreigners in Distress, *Account for the Year 1866*, pp. 130, 136, 141.

during the Edwardian years. Sponza's list shows that the offences which resulted in expulsion orders for Germans consisted of 287 cases of larceny and receiving, 68 of housebreaking and frequenting, 42 of forgery and false pretence, and 30 of crimes against the person.[67]

Sponza's work has also revealed that the Germans had the largest number of expulsion orders issued against them for crimes connected with prostitution. These consisted of 103 cases of soliciting and importuning (47 less than in the case of the French minority), 85 of keeping a brothel, and 64 of living on prostitution or procuring. In this sense the German community resembled other minorities in both Britain and the USA which also had a percentage of their population involved in prostitution. In Victorian and Edwardian Britain, prostitution clearly existed throughout the period under consideration and indeed was widespread throughout Europe. Wide-scale prostitution was 'a by-product of the first, explosive stage in the growth of the modern industrial city'. Sponza says of the Italian community that 'It is doubtful that there were many Italian prostitutes at any time in Victorian and Edwardian London'; but the German situation comes closer to that amongst the Russian and Polish Jewish community outlined by L. P. Gartner, where women deceived in Eastern Europe found themselves in London, often as a staging post on their way to South America, while other women were recruited as prostitutes once they had arrived in London. Both of these practices occurred in the German community.[68]

In the case of the 'White Slave Traffic', cases of abduction of girls from Germany brought to London existed throughout the nineteenth century. For instance, in 1856 a letter received by the Hamburg police dealing with 'a fresh case of abduction' mentioned an eighteen-year-old daughter of a banker who claimed 'she was decoyed away from Hamburgh [*sic*] about two months since and brought to a certain house near Regents Quadrant, where a wealthy nobleman seduced her.' Similarly, nearly thirty years later the Metropolitan Police discovered that 'Lisette Schweighoffer, age $15\frac{1}{2}$, native of Homburg, Germany, had been abducted from her home on 15th June 1895, brought to London and here procured for immoral purposes.'[69]

---

67. Katscher, 'German Life in London', pp. 733–4; F. X. Kärcher, *Bericht über die Mission der deutschen Katholiken in London*, Düsseldorf, 1869, p. 9; Sponza, *Italian Immigrants*, p. 330.

68. Sponza, *Italian Immigrants*, pp. 236, 310–11, 329; Lloyd P. Gartner, 'Anglo-Jewry and the International Traffic in Prostitution, 1885–1914', *Association for Jewish Studies Review*, vol 7–8, pp. 129–31. For the widespread nature of prostitution in nineteenth-century Europe, see, Richard J. Evans, 'Prostitution, State and Society and Imperial Germany', *Past and Present*, no. 70, 1976, p. 106–8.

69. Hamburg Staatsarchiv, 132–6 London, Hanseatischer Generalkonsultat in London, 18; PRO MEPO2 558/6.

Other women entered England after an offer of a position which did not materialise. In 1846, for instance, the Hanseatic Consul in London reported the case of 'a certain number of unfortunate Hamburgh [*sic*] female children' who had 'been abandoned by their parents to Madame Weiss of Vienna'. After 'having exhibited them as a corps de ballet in England and Ireland' Madame Weiss had intended to take them to 'Yankee Land', but they never reached their destination, returning to Liverpool, as 'white slaves'.[70] Hamburg remained important throughout the period under consideration, as a 'constant trade' took place between that city and London.[71]

Many German women found themselves deceived into prostitution upon answering newspaper advertisements. William Sanger's *History of Prostitution*, originally published in 1859, gave the example of 'a scoundrel named Phinn', who advertised for ladies to go to Cologne in order to become governesses abroad but found themselves defrauded of their money at their destination.This process continued into the nineteenth and early twentieth centuries. In the 1890s, one trafficker advertised in a Hamburg newspaper for orphaned girls aged between nine and twelve for a family in Edinburgh.[72] Perhaps the most common way in which German women became prostitutes involved their 'enticing' shortly after landing in London, in a frightened and confused state and without knowledge of the language, where they would turn to the first person who could offer them a helping hand; this often consisted of 'German-speaking touts of a dozen nationalities...inveigling the unwary *mädchen* into questionable lodging houses'. In other cases the 'befriending' had taken place during the journey to England.[73]

Wherever the recruiting of German prostitutes took place, much of their activities and those of German pimps in London occurred in the West End. Kellow Chesney pointed to Kellner's in Leicester Square

70. Hamburg Staatsarchiv, 132–5/7 London, Hanseatische Residentur London, 1 Band 7.
71. William W. Sanger, *The History of Prostitution*, New York, 1910 edition, p. 315; Gartner, 'Anglo-Jewry and Prostitution', pp. 156, 172–4; *Pall Mall Gazette, The Maiden Tribute of Modern Babylon*, London, 1895, p. 14; Evans, 'Prostitution, State and Society'.
72. Sanger, History of Prostitution, p. 314; *Pall Mall Gazette, Maiden Tribute*, p. 14.
73. 'Die Gefahren Londons für junge deutsche Mädchen', *Der Deutsche Auswanderer*, vol. 10, 1912, p. 26; Gartner, 'Anglo-Jewry and Prostitution', pp. 155–6; Armfelt, 'German London', p. 58; *Vigilance Record*, March 1904. For details of individual German women arriving in London who did not fall into prostitution because of the efforts of the Travellers Aid Society, see Travellers Aid Society, *Report for the Year, 1895*, London, 1896, pp. 18–20; *Report for the Year, 1898*, London, 1899, pp. 17–18, 21–2. An article in the *Londoner Courier*, 6 February 1884, also claimed that the Society of Friends of Foreigners in Distress 'rescued yearly a large number of girls from their downfall, who became trapped in a system of importation which it is scarcely possible to differentiate from slavery.'

where 'a naughty continental atmosphere was fostered' with the employment of 'attractive French and German barmaids, and concert turns by artistes whose appearance carefully harmonized with conventional ideas of foreign dress.'[74] In 1895 the *Social Gazette* condemned the activities of two German brothel-keepers, Schmidt and Muller, who managed two houses in an alley branching from Long Acre. In these two houses they carried out such 'a profound and extreme system of immorality' with 'such gigantic success that the men had purchased Mill Hill Island on the Thames, near Windsor, living there in luxurious magnificence on the proceeds of the organised system of prostitution and robbery in Conduit Court.'[75] German observers writing at the end of the nineteenth century also pointed to the presence of German prostitutes soliciting in the area around Oxford Street, Regent Street and Trafalgar Square.[76]

The number of German prostitutes in London is difficult to estimate. Sponza's calculations suggest they, along with French prostitutes, made up the largest component of non-English women involved in this occupation. The proportion of foreign women amongst all prostitutes working in London, or within England more generally, is even more difficult to ascertain. A report by the National Vigilance Association from 1904 estimated that 2,000 foreign prostitutes worked in London,[77] while another study from 1914 noted that 'of 168 girls in a London rescue home, 85 were from abroad'.[78]

Moving on to a consideration of the activities of Germans involved in working- and middle-class occupations, the census statistics allow an accurate picture of the numbers of Germans involved in different employments. Rather than tackling all activities in which Germans played a part, this section will deal with those occupations in which the census identifies Germans as playing an important role, and for which information survives. Before moving on to look at these occupations, a few general observations need to be made about German employment.

In the first place it is difficult to identify an ethnic economy of the sort which existed in nineteenth-century New York, or which exists currently in post-War British Asian communities in, for instance, Bradford, Leicester or Southall, where the immigrants produce goods and supply

---

74. Kellow Chesney, *The Victorian Underworld*, Harmondsworth, 1976 reprint, p. 367. William Acton, *Prostitution*, London, 1857, pp. 93–4, mentions French, but not German, prostitutes in London.
75. PRO HO45 10123 B13517, extract from the *Social Gazette*, 12 October 1895.
76. Rethwisch, *Die Deutschen im Auslande*, p. 76; John Henry Mackay, *The Anarchists: A Picture of Civilization at the Close of the Nineteenth Century*, Boston, Massachusetts, 1891, pp. 12, 14.
77. The report is in PRO MEPO2 558.
78. Abraham Flexner, *Prostitution in Europe*, New York, 1914, p. 73.

services for members of their own community. The main explanation for this is the lack of a market for such goods because of the small size of the German community in London and in Britain, in comparison with the 168,225 German-born citizens of New York in 1880, who made up 14 per cent of the population of the city,[79] or in comparison with Pakistanis in Bradford who made up ten per cent of the population of the city in the early 1970s.[80] Instead, the Germans in nineteenth-century Britain involved themselves in occupations inextricably linked with the British economy. In the case of two of the main 'service' occupations, music and waiting, the Germans catered fundamentally for Britons, while clerks found employment in English concerns. Even in the case of butchers and bakers their clientele would have consisted primarily of the native population, particulary in northern cities. In the case of the sugar bakers, there seems more of a case for thinking in terms of an ethnic economy in that both employees and employers in east London consisted of Germans. However, the end product went to English and international markets. The most important way in which occupation helped to maintain ethnicity was through the existence of employment bodies or trade unions.

A second observation regarding German employment in London concerns the fact that the principal occupations changed during the course of the century, as Tables 3.8 and 3.9 demonstrate. These clearly reveal, for instance, the overall decline of sugar baking and the rise of waiting and retailing, although some occupations such as tailoring and teaching remained constant throughout the nineteenth and early twentieth centuries. The tables also reveal the importance of 'middle class' professions, ranging from 'petty bourgeois' activities such as retailing, which includes occupations such as baker and butcher (although these also include assistants) through to office work and to occupations higher on the social scale including teaching and business activities.

We will look first at working-class occupations before going on to petty bourgeois and middle-class employment. As the opening chapter to this study indicated, sugar baking became an important activity for Germans in Britain from the eighteenth century. This process continued through the early nineteenth century. In fact, as Table 3.9 indicates, German settlement in the East End of London remained tied to the sugar-baking industry. Both Tables 3.8 and 3.9 also show the decline of this industry to the point where it was virtually non-existent by the outbreak of the First World War; certainly it employed virtually no Germans.

79. Nadel, *Little Germany*, p. 42.
80. Verity Saifullah Khan, 'The Pakistanis: Mirpuri Villagers at Home and in Bradford', in James L Watson (ed.), *Between Two Cultures: Immigrants and Minorities in Britain*, Oxford, 1991 reprint, p. 57.

Table 3.8 Major Occupations of Germans in England and Wales, 1861–1911

	1861	1871	1881	1891	1901	1911
Males						
Merchant	736	1,084	969	671	349	318
Agent, Factor	202	287	464	530	623	661
Commercial Clerk	883	1,257	1,781	1,946	2,101	2,513
Commercial Traveller	171	125	296	393	394	457
Teachers	210	333	325	365	242	236
Baker	1,039	1,310	2,020	2,276	2,402	2,134
Butcher	244	375	730	1,251	1,224	1,178
Hairdresser	22	169	375	945	1,481	1,916
Watch- Clockmaker	914	908	883	886	602	447
Seaman	1,813	2,434	1,725	2,829	1,198	1,984
Musician	949	773	786	1,028	568	509
Sugar Refiner	1,345	890	443	275	76	–
Tailor	1,195	1,555	1,484	1,958	1,921	1,557
Shoe and Bootmaker	589	718	578	620	375	282
Servant or Waiter	380	628	1,280	2,008	3,618	4,721
Females						
Teacher, Governess	605	1,291	1,625	1,616	941	1,032
Servant	1,014	1,522	2,581	3,350	4,432	3,478

Source: Census of England and Wales for the Year 1861, vol. 2, London, 1863, pp. lxxxi–lxxxxix; *Census of England and Wales, 1871*, vol. 3, London, 1872, pp. lvii–lxxvi; *Census of England and Wales, 1881*, vol. 3, p. ; *Census of England and Wales, 1891*, vol. 3, London, 1893, pp. li–lviii *Census of England and Wales, 1901: Summary Tables, Area, Houses and Population*, London, 1903, p. 268–80; *Census of England and Wales, 1911: Summary* Tables, London, 1915, p. 376–89.

Further indications of the predominance of Germans in this industry and geographical location include the fact that out of 697 men married in St George's German Lutheran Church and St Paul's Evangelical Reformed Church during the 1860s, 197, or 28 per cent, were sugar bakers. This seems to confirm the view of the 'typical German living in mid-Victorian East London' as 'a sugarbaker from Hanover'.[81] At the same time, an examination of the trade directories of sugar refiners confirms the picture of Germans as employers as well as workers. Of a list of 82 firms in East End Directories of 1823–4, at least 30 appear to be German. The rest are mostly English names, but there are also several French ones. A similar examination of the trade directories of 1875 reveals just twenty-five entries for sugar bakers, of whom eight are

81. Jerome Farrell, 'The German Community in 19th Century East London', *East London Record*, no. 13, 1990, pp. 4–5.

Table 3.9 Major Occupations of German Males and Females in Whitechapel and St George's, 1851 and 1891

	1851	*1891*
Baker	10	33
Butcher	2	10
Hairdresser	1	10
Sugar Refiner	321	14
Tailor	19	76
Slipper, Shoe, Bootmaker	19	18
Skin, Fur Worker	9	33
Waiter	2	28
Servant	5	18
Labourer	22	11

Source: PRO HO107 1545, 1546, 1547, 1548; RG12 273, 280, 282, 284, 287.

German, indicating both the overall decline of the sugar-baking industry and German business interests in the industry.[82]

By this time some movement had begun to take place further east towards present day Newham, with firms locating first in West Ham and then Silvertown. Cord Campe established the first sugar refinery in Essex in Stratford Hight Street, and employed twelve people in 1851. The causes for the decline of the importance of Germans in sugar baking lie in the movement into east London of larger firms such as Henry Tate and Sons and Abraham Lyle and Sons who moved into Silvertown from the 1870s, although sugar refining generally had declined by this time with the increased manufacture of beet sugar in Europe. However, there remained a German presence in the sugar industry in Britain even after its decline, as many sugar brokers in the London sugar market were Germans.[83]

Germans also played a role in the confectionery industry, as evidenced by the factories of Ohlendorff, founded in 1874 in Silvertown, and Volckmann in Stratford High Street, which existed from the 1830s until 1890, employing up to two hundred people.[84] Outside London,

82. Tower Hamlets Local History Collection, Misc 13/5, 'London Sugar Refineries, extracted from Trade Directories'; Tower Hamlets Local History Collection, Alexander Gander, 'The Old Sugar Refineries of St. George's-in-the-East'.
83. *Victoria County History of Essex*, vol. 6, London, 1973, p. 80; Howard Bloch, 'German Immigrants in Newham'; George D. Hodge, *56 Years in the London Sugar Market*, Bristol, 1960, p. 13.
84. *Victoria County History of Essex*, vol. 6, p. 80; Howard Bloch, 'German Immigrants in Newham'; W. Glenny Crory, *East London Industries*, p. 207.

Germans also played a role in sugar refining in Liverpool; as late as the 1880s they made up as many as 25 per cent of unskilled employees involved in the Liverpool sugar-refining industry, although they concentrated in particular refineries. The reason for the involvement of Germans in Liverpool lies at least partly in the fact that they accepted lower wages than English employees did.[85]

One of the major contemporary accounts of sugar refining in the East End also put forward a similar reason for the predominance of Germans in the industry, claiming that not even Irish labourers would involve themselves in sugar baking because of the conditions under which labourers worked.[86] However, the fact that Germans played a role in this industry during the eighteenth century may also have led to their continued involvement, and there may have been a continuance of the importation of German workers, as occurred during the Napoleonic Wars and also as happened with the baking industry in the East End of London during the late nineteenth century.

Virtually all contemporary accounts, as well as confirming the predominance of Germans in the East London sugar-baking industry, point further to the severity of the working conditions.The *London City Mission Magazine* reported that 'a visit to a sugar-house' would leave the visitor astonished at 'how these poor Germans endure their arduous task. The heat is so excessive, that all the men work without clothes, and in order to support their strength, or rather to quench their thirst, they are supplied with beer gratis from their employers', which meant that drunkenness had become 'a very prominent feature in the character of the majority of sugar-bakers.'[87] Another visitor to a sugar bakery confirmed the unlimited supply of beer and further pointed to 'the reek of sugar palling to one's sense of smell'. Of the building, he wrote:

It was a sort of handy outer warehouse, that to which we were first introduced – a low-roofed, dismal place with grated windows, and here and there a foggy little gas-jet burning blear-eyed against the wall. The walls were black – not painted black. As far as one might judge they were bare brick, but 'basted' unceasingly by the luscious steam that enveloped the place, they had become coated with a thick preserve of sugar and grime. The floor was black, and all corrugated and hard, like a public thoroughfare after a shower and then a frost. The roof was black, and pendent from the great supporting posts and balks of timber were sooty, glistening icicles and exuding like those of the gum-tree.

85. *Report of the Select Committee on Emigration and Immigration (Foreigners)*, p. 15, P.P., vol. 10, 1889.
86. James Greenwood, *The Wilds of London*, London, 1874, p. 264.
87. *London City Mission Magazine*, 2 January 1865, p. 2.

The actual boiling of sugar took place in 'a vast cellar underground', where the heat 'was sickening and oppressive, and an unctuous steam, thick and foggy, filled the cellar from end to end.' In these conditions, the sugar bakers worked for twelve hours a day. Even worse, census returns for Whitechapel demonstrate that German labourers actually lived in these conditions. In 1851, 12 Leman Street housed thirty-eight sugar bakers, while 113 and 114 acted as a workplace and residence for sixty.[88]

Other occupations in nineteenth-century Britain also imposed intolerable conditions upon German workmen. One of the most important was clothing manufacture, an occupation which attracted a large number of European immigrants especially from Russia and Poland, at the end of the nineteenth century. In Leeds, for instance, Jews from eastern Europe came to play a major part in tailoring and footwear in the space of just twenty years, after they began to enter the city in large numbers during the 1880s.[89] A similar situation existed in London where in 1900 over sixty per cent of Jewish males found employment in tailoring or in the boot, shoe and slipper trades.[90]

As Tables 3.8 and 3.9 indicate, Germans also played a role in clothing manufacture in the specific trades of skin-dying and dressing, tailoring and shoemaking throughout the course of the nineteenth century. In all cases their numbers in these occupations had declined by the First World War, despite a temporary rise in the number of German tailors just before the turn of the century. The skin and fur trades attracted a significant number of Germans in Whitechapel, although even by the middle of the nineteenth century these trades had begun to decline, despite an upturn in orders due to the requirement of furs for soldiers fighting in the Crimean War. With full orders, a worker in this trade could earn as much as thirty shillings a week; otherwise wages went down to about 18, as the production of furs was a seasonal trade.[91]

By the mid-nineteenth century Germans were also involved in footwear production and tailoring in east London. In the former, conditions and pay remained especially bad for women who worked twelve

88. Greenwood, *Wilds of London*, pp. 264–70; PRO HO107, 1545 587, 1546 166. See also Thomas Fock, 'Über Londoner Zuckersiedereien und deutsche Arbeitskräfte', *Zuckerindustrie*, vol. 3, 1985, pp. 233–5, vol. 5, 1985, pp. 426–32.

89. See Joseph Buckman, *Immigrants and the Class Struggle: The Jewish Immigrant in Leeds*, Manchester, 1983; Ernest Krausz, *Leeds Jewry: Its History and Social Structure*, Cambridge, 1964, pp. 14–16; Anne J. Kershen, 'Trade Unionism amongst the Jewish Tailoring Workers of London and Leeds, 1872–1915', in Cesarani, *Making of Modern Anglo-Jewry*, pp. 34–52.

90. V. D. Lipman, *A History of the Jews in Britain since 1858*, Leicester, 1990, pp. 57–8.

91. *Londoner Deutsches Journal*, 22 September 1855.

hours per day and earned between eight and ten shillings a week, while those who simply finished the goods could earn just six shillings. For men the position was similar as they earned between 20 and 21 shillings a week for working as much as fifteen hours a day; although in many cases, according to one report, this work had rescued many Germans from starving to death.[92]

Henry Mayhew, the social journalist, claimed that German employers actually imported their workmen from their land of origin and that, like the sugar bakers, they represented the only labour available as no other group would carry it out. In this industry the French had previously played a role but their numbers fell with a decline in wages. Mayhew interviewed one German workman who gave a very negative picture of conditions. He stated that 'Ven I came over here I vent to sew at one of my own countrymens, and I have mostly been working for my own countrymens ever since. Most of the Chermans I have worked for have peen vot you call sveaters in dis country, because dey do make a man sveat [sic].' The interviewee gave an example of one particular employer who offered accommodation to his workers and then charged them high rents. The interviewee himself earned fourteen shillings a week, but ten of this went towards rent.[93]

Conditions for German tailors in mid and late nineteenth-century London were similar, with wages paid by piece and amounting to no more than three or four pence for a pair of trousers; again, men worked from twelve to fifteen hours per day. One native worker, interviewed by Mayhew, claimed that 'a great number of German and Polish Jew tailors have been brought over to work in the slop trade'. This influx of German and Russian Jewish tailors continued throughout the century, affecting both the newcomers and native workers, who worked in bad conditions due to a surplus of workers. German tailors did not work 'in a high-class shop' like some Swedish tailors, but their workshops appear to have reached 'a higher standard of comfort' than those with east European workers, as these had 'not attracted the attention of the reformers'.[94]

By the beginning of the twentieth century German tailors, together with Swedes, had also become important in the West End of London. One factory inspector believed that the immigrants, despite the fact that

92. *Londoner Deutsches Journal*, 13 October 1855.
93. Henry Mayhew, *The Morning Chronicle Survey of Labour and the Poor: The Metropolitan Districts*, vol. 3, 1981, pp. 189–92.
94. *Londoner Deutsches Journal*, 20 October 1855; Mayhew, *Morning Chronicle Survey*, vol. 2, p. 108; Booth, *Life and Labour*, First Series, vol. 4, p. 44; *Report of the Board of Trade on the Sweating System at the East End of London by the Labour Correspondent of the Board*, p. 4, P.P., vol. 89, 1887; Shadwell, 'German Colony in London', p. 809.

they controlled about fifty per cent of the trade in the area, did not displace native labour because without them 'there would be no one to do the work at all.'[95] In comparison with other occupations which employed significant numbers of Germans, the tailors did have some sort of union organisation both of their own,[96] and within the Amalgamated Society of Tailors which formed a German branch in 1875, although eleven years later this counted just 68 members.[97]

German waiters also developed trade unions, of a more organised nature. As Table 3.8 indicates, large numbers of Germans went into this occupation at the end of the nineteenth century. In London in 1911, about ten per cent of waiters and waitresses involved in restaurant work were German, and by this time they were also working in cities throughout the country; in Lancashire waiting was the third most common occupation for German workers.[98]

The previous chapter examined the reasons for the entry of waiters into Britain. Within the country, their patterns of work differed from that of natives involved in this trade. But while they worked longer hours than Englishmen, up to fifteen hours per day, they did not suffer the sort of exploitation endured by their fellow countrymen employed in the clothing industry. In contrast to Englishmen, who demanded a fixed wage, Germans and other foreigners relied on tips, from which they could earn as much as £2 per week. Germans also differed from English waiters in that they had undergone formal training, which meant, according to one English observer, that they had 'a higher reputation than our own countrymen for neatness and civility'. At the same time many, especially those who wished to return to Germany, would accept low wages simply to obtain experience, although others remained and rose to become hotel and restaurant managers and went on to employ other foreign waiters in turn.[99]

Every census recorded a significant number of German merchant seamen and, although they formed a temporary element in the German community in Britain, as a group they were significant in the develop-

95. *Report of the Royal Commission on Alien Immigration*, vol. 2, p. 403, P.P., vol. 9, 1903.

96. Ashton, *Little Germany*, pp. 228–44.

97. *The Times*, 24 June 1875; *Report of the Board of Trade on the Sweating System at the East End of London by the Labour Correspondent of the Board*, p. 11, P.P., vol. 89, 1887.

98. *Census of England and Wales, 1911. Birthplaces*, pp. 220–8, 230–4. The two occupations with the largest number of Germans in Lancashire consisted of butchers (225), and clerks, while the total for waiters stood at 203.

99. *London Hotel and Restaurant Employees Gazette*, 14 June 1890; Booth, *Life and Labour*, Second Series, vol. 4, pp. 232–5; BLPES, Booth Collection, Group A, vol. 29, pp. 42–4, 52–3, 72–3; Brand, *London Life Seen with German Eyes*, pp. 121–2.

ment of German settlement in east coast ports and in the growth of German benevolent institutions. Unlike other sailors from minority groups who found themselves in England during the nineteenth and twentieth centuries, the Germans did not obtain employment on British ships but worked instead on those of their own country, although part of the explanation for this lies in the fact that African states, as well as the West Indies had no fleets to speak of in this period because of their political situation.[100] In contrast, at least 800 German ships visited ports in the northeast of England in 1882–3, for instance, 340 of which landed at Middlesbrough, Hartlepool and West Hartlepool, bringing in over 3,000 sailors.[101] This indicates that the number of merchant seamen who visited British ports every year totalled considerably more than the figures on the census, which captured the picture on one particular night of one year. An indication of just how many sailors entered the country comes from the annual reports of the German Evangelical Seaman's Mission, which in the year 1910 counted 38,492 sailors who used its reading rooms; by the outbreak of the First World War, the Mission had establishments at fifty ports.[102]

Nevertheless, the German merchant seamen's community in Britain, while a permanent feature, remained temporary in the sense that it did not result in any large-scale settlement. In contrast, many German musicians did stay in the country, although as we have seen there was also an almost seasonal migration of German bandsmen who only played in Britain during the summer months; a picture confirmed by Kellow Chesney, who described them as 'summer migrants'.[103] The presence of German musicians clearly continues a trend started in the eighteenth century when a significant number of orchestral players, together with composers, made their way to the country and remained permanently. In the nineteenth century these two trends continue, with the addition of a new group, the street musicians. Thus the German musical profession within nineteenth-century Britain does not fall into any particular social

100. For black and Chinese sailors see the following: Martin Daunton, 'Jack Ashore: Seamen in Cardiff Before 1914', *Welsh History Review*, vol. 9, pp. 176–93; Salter, *Asiatic in England*; P. J. Waller, 'The Chinese', *History Today*, vol. 35, September 1985, p. 9; Jacqueline Jenkinson, 'The Glasgow Race Disturbances of 1919', *Immigrants and Minorities*, vol. 4, 1985, pp. 45–6; E. W. McFarland, 'Clyde Opinion on an Old Controversy: Indian and Chinese Seafarers in Glasgow', *Ethnic and Racial Studies*, vol. 14, 1991, pp. 493–515.
101. BA, Potsdam, AA, 38969, 'Report of the German Evangelical Church and Mission in Sunderland and Neighbourhood, 1882–3'; BA, Potsdam, AA, 38976, 'Annual Report of the German Evangelical Church at Middlesbrough and Sailors mission for the Hartlepools and Tees District, 1884'.
102. *Manchester Nachrichten*, December 1911; BA, Coblenz, R57, neu, 1065/2, 'Deutsche Evangelische Seemansmission'.
103. Chesney, *Victorian Underworld*, p. 72.

class but consists of both working-class bandsmen who struggled to make a living and more financially secure orchestral players, conductors and composers who, in the case of the last, would often pay only a temporary visit to the country.

Street musicians are included in Chesney's category of 'Wanderers' in his study of the Victorian underworld, although the present study does not place them within the underclass because of, among other reasons, their appearance on census statistics and church registers, as well as the fact that they could support themselves. Chesney actually identifies German musicians as part of a group of foreigners of various nationalities who 'were to be found among the innumerable strolling exhibitionists, stilt-dancers, owners of performing dogs, mice and fleas, and so on – who wandered about singly or in family groups.'[104] These represent categories identified by Mayhew during the 1850s, amongst both native and immigrant populations; he singled out foreign street musicians, as did other commentators during the mid-nineteenth century, focusing on Italian organ-grinders and other street performers, 'Indian Tom Tom Players' and 'Street Negro Serenaders'.[105]

Despite attempts to control them German brass brands, together with some of the other groups outlined above, remained a feature of metropolitan street life in Britain until the outbreak of the First World War. Information about them survives from various sources. Like other groups of mid-nineteenth-century German immigrants, their working conditions remained difficult. The London City Mission believed that German street musician boys, of between twelve and fourteen years of age and of 'very poor parents' were 'imported' into Britain 'by a speculating master, who very scantily provides for their necessaries of life, and who sends them out in small companies of 4 or 6, and by their earnings reaps a bountiful harvest', while keeping them in a 'petty slavery'. This 'importation' continued into the 1890s, when one bandmaster brought over people 'from the agricultural parts of Germany' and payed for their fares, uniforms and board and lodging.[106]

Mayhew's investigations in the 1850s gave a more optimistic account. His interviewee, from Oberfeld near Hanover, who played in a band of seven, claimed that each member of the band earned from six to eight shillings a day. He stated that:

104. Ibid.
105. Henry Mayhew, *London Labour*, vol. 1, pp. 104–20, vol. 2, pp. 114–35, vol. 3, pp. 171–94, vol. 4, pp. 419–27.
106. *London City Mission Magazine*, 2 January 1865; Gilbert Guerdon, 'Street Musicians', *Strand Magazine*, vol. 3, 1892, p. 71

I have saved money in zis country, but very little of it. I want to save enough to take me back to Hanover. We all live together ze seven of us. We have three rooms to sleep in, and one to eat in. We are all single men but one; and his wife, a German woman, lives wis us, and cooks for us. She and her husband have a bedroom to zemselves. Anysing does for us to eat. We all join in housekeeping and lodging and pay alike. Our lodging costs 2s. a week each; our board costs about 15s. a week each; sometime rather less. [*sic*]

Mayhew's interviewee claimed that five bands with 37 players existed in London.[107]

The interviewee also gave a picture of the highly itinerant nature of the German brass bands who played not just in London but throughout the country. He stated that his band performed 'in ze country about half a year; we do middling, and zen we come to London.' An English musician whom Mayhew interviewed claimed that 'The German bands have now possession of the whole coast of Kent and Sussex, and wherever there are watering places.'[108] The Dover census of 1851 reveals that this statement contains some truth, recording 25 German musicians in the same public house; their ages varied from 17 to 39 and they came from Cassel or Bavaria.[109]

Brass bands travelled as far as Scotland where five or six German bands played in the 1870s and 1880s, although other groups had reached the country earlier in the century including one which travelled from Edinburgh to Inverness in 1842. Another band, which originated in the Palatinate, migrated to America in 1872; it had previously played in Switzerland, Spain, the West Indies, France and Australia, before moving to Edinburgh in 1867, where the bandmaster divided the fifteen men into bands of seven and eight. They and other groups only remained in Scotland during the summer, returning home in the winter together with bands which had travelled to 'all the points on the compass'.[110]

The range of the German bands varied. They often included string players and groups dressed in military uniforms, and in some cases they possessed quite a wide repertoire although in others it remained somewhat limited. Most accounts confirm the average size at around six members. At the same time, contemporaries also commented on the fact that the quality of the music varied.[111]

---

107. Mayhew, *Morning Chronicle Survey*, vol. 5, pp. 2–3.
108. Ibid.
109. 'German Travelling Musicians', *Anglo-German Family History Society Mitteilungsblatt*, no. 17, 1991, p. 33.
110. George B. Gardiner, 'The Home of the German Band', *Blackwood's Magazine*, vol. 172, 1902, pp. 451–65.
111. Ibid.; J. Frederick Crowest, *Phases of Musical England*, London, 1891, p. 115; P. F. William Ryan, 'London's Street Performers', in Sims, *Living London*, vol. 3, p. 65.

As well as street musicians other Germans participated in large-scale orchestral playing and conducting, where they had some influence on musical development. The movement of players and conductors must be placed against the background of both the tradition of migration established during the eighteenth century and the musical relationship of the two countries seen in the admiration of the British for German music, which, however, began to falter during the course of the nineteenth century. At the same time, Germans also had an influence on the manufacture of musical instruments in Britain, especially pianos, although by the end of the nineteenth century the fact that Germany became the leading manufacturer of instruments caused hostility in Britain.[112]

Indications of the presence of German musicians in English orchestras come from the number of German names in the lists of specific bands. For instance, the thirty members of the Philharmonic Society of London, formed in 1813, included Messrs Barlemanm, Berger, Graeff, Knyweth and Webbe, while in 1895–6 the Halle Orchestra's 106 players included 14 possibly German names; Germans had played in the orchestra throughout the nineteenth century. In addition to these two major British orchestras, Germans also played in less famous ones.[113]

The Manchester Halle Orchestra remained fundamentally German, not just because of the origins of its players but also because of its founder, Sir Charles Halle, and its financial backing. Halle made his way to Britain after the 1848 revolutions in Paris, together with numerous other musical figures. After initially teaching and playing in London, he moved to Manchester because of an oversupply of musicians in the capital and began to conduct the 'Gentlemen's Concerts'. These developed into the Halle Concerts in 1858, which the founder conducted until his death in 1895. He had also played an important role in the foundation of the Royal Manchester College of Music. Another German, Hans Richter, conducted the Halle concerts from 1899, leaving his position as principal conductor of the Vienna Philharmonic Orchestra to take up the post.[114]

112. Eric Mackerness, *A Social History of English Music*, London, 1964, pp. 214–22; *Report from the Select Committee on the Laws Affecting Aliens*, pp. iv, 35, P.P., vol 5, 1843.

113. George Hogarth, *The Philharmonic Society of London*, London, 1862, pp. 1, 6–7; Thomas E. Batley (ed.), *Sir Charles Halle's Concerts in Manchester*, Manchester, 1896; Michael Kennedy, *The History of the Royal Manchester College of Music, 1893–1972*, Manchester, 1971, pp. 2–3; Shadwell, 'German Colony in London', p. 809; Brand, *London Life*, p. 123.

114. C. E. and Marie Halle (eds), *Life and Letters of Sir Charles Halle: Being an Autobiography with Correspondence and Diaries*, London, 1896; Frangopulo, 'Foreign Communities in Victorian Manchester', pp. 193–4; Kennedy, *Royal Manchester College*, pp. 1–11; Kennedy, *Halle, 1858–1976: A Brief History of the Orchestra's History, Travels and Achievements*, Manchester, n.d., pp. 3–11.

Halle and Richter represented just two examples of German conductors who took up long-term positions in nineteenth-century Britain. Others included Ignaz Moscheles, born in Prague, who conducted the Philharmonic Society from 1832–41; Wilhelm Ganz, who became joint conductor of the New Philharmonic Society in 1874; Otto Goldschmidt, who led the Bach Choir, which he founded, from 1875–85; and August Manns, who conducted the more popular Crystal Palace Orchestra from 1855–1900.[115] Furthermore, numerous German music teachers resided in London, including some who taught at music academies,[116] while German and Austrian composers, notably Mendelsohn, Wagner, and Richard Strauss, made visits to England throughout the period 1815–1914, often conducting their own works.[117]

Not dissimilar to musicians, in the sense that they included members of both the working and middle classes, or at least the petty bourgeoisie in the form of small shopkeepers, were butchers, bakers and hairdressers. As Table 3.8 demonstrates, these became particularly numerous at the end of the nineteenth century. It is impossible to establish the proportion of employers and employees, but evidence exists for both. Much of the contemporary information points both to the desire of Germans to set themselves up in business at an early stage after their arrival in Britain, and to their employment of their own countrymen. Arthur Shadwell writing in the 1890s, asserted that:

> The German generally comes over as a young man, and takes a situation with the view of setting up for himself as soon as he has acquired sufficient knowledge and a little capital. Then he begins in a very small way, and in order to get on employs his own countrymen, whose services he can obtain for a time exceedingly cheap, either because they are newcomers, ignorant of the language and helpless, or because they have failed to get any other employment. As time goes on many of these in turn set up for themselves, and thus a continuous supply, which tends to get larger and larger, is attracted over into the particular trades affected.[118]

This picture is confirmed by Charles Booth's researches, which point to a situation of exploitation in baking similar to that which existed in the tailoring and shoe trades earlier in the nineteenth century. After import-

115. Hermann Klein, *Thirty Years of Musical Life in London: 1870–1900*, London, 1903. p. 56; Wilhelm Ganz, *Memories of a Musician*, London, 1913, pp. 119–20; *New Grove Dictionary of Music and Musicians*, 1980, vol. 7, pp. 149, 506, vol. 12, p. 598.

116. Kennedy, *Royal Manchester College*, p. 7.

117. Francis Hueffer, *Half a Century of Music in England, 1837–1887*, pp. 29–31, 37, 44–73; Klein, *Thirty Years of Musical Life*, pp. 65–6, 408; Curt von Westerhagen, *Wagner: A Biography*, vol. 1, Cambridge, 1978, pp. 206–10; Ashton, *Little Germany*, pp. 176–8.

118. Shadwell, 'German Colony in London', p. 808.

ing German agricultural labourers, German masters would provide their new employees only with food and lodging for two years; then 'having picked up a few ideas about the trade they would go elsewhere and get a place for about 18/- a week', after which 'their thrift pushes them on to become masters in a small way and so they progress.' German bakers worked far longer hours than English ones, in one case up to 112 hours per week, and in another from 11 pm until 6pm for six days a week; they averaged 76 a week during the 1890s.[119]

From the 1880s contemporaries commented upon the domination of the baking trade by Germans. The Board of Trade Labour Correspondent claimed in 1887 that 'there are 4,000 master bakers in London, 2,000 of whom are Germans. Wherever a bread business is to be disposed of the chances are that it is bought up by a German'. He claimed that this development had taken place particularly in that decade, but it continued until the First World War. An official of a master baker's society, interviewed for Booth's *Life and Labour of the People in London* in the early 1890s, claimed that: 'One half of the London Masters and certainly one half of the operatives are Germans.'[120] In 1910 a fairly hostile article in the *Baker's Times*, reprinted in *The Times*, claimed that 'In the Metropolis the German baker is ubiquitous – he flaunts his name over the palatial shops in the West-end and he is equally in evidence in the slums of the East End.' The article then proceeded to list the names of Germans bakers 'from Tooting to Holloway, from Fulham to Stepney, from Edgeware to Cricklewood.'[121]

Germans also developed an important role in hairdressing in the late nineteenth century, so that by 1896 about 30 per cent of the master hairdressers in the capital were foreigners, including Frenchmen; among their employees the proportion was still higher. Germans were particularly important as barbers. They had 'the reputation of being more industrious, more cleanly, and more sober, and for these reasons even many English masters prefer them. In hairdressing no doubt, they are inferior to the French colonists, but this inferiority they share with our own countrymen.'

While some Germans may have entered Britain as unskilled agricultural labourers,[122] others had already received a full training before they

119. BLPES, Booth Collection, Group A, vol. 22, p. 5; Group B, vol. 127, pp. 45, 63–4; *London City Mission Magazine*, 2 June 1884.

120. *Board of Trade Memorandum on the Immigration of Foreigners into the United Kingdom*, p. 11, P.P., vol. 89, 1887; BLPES, Booth Collection, Group B, vol. 127, p. 44. See also Stephen N. Fox, 'The Invasion of Pauper Foreigners', *Contemporary Review*, vol. 53, 1888, p. 859.

121. *The Times*, 28 February 1910.

122. Booth, *Life and Labour*, Second Series, vol. 4, p. 278; Shadwell, 'German Colony in London', p. 809.

moved to the country. For instance, G. Schlecht had served an apprenticeship in Münster and then worked in Mannheim, Dresden and Munich, followed by employment in various Swiss towns and then in Paris before he made his way to London in 1906. W. Fulst followed a similar path: 'He became apprenticed to the hairdressing profession when 14 years old, and later worked in the principal towns of Germany, France, and Switzerland', moving to Britain in about 1905. Both of these men served as officials of the International Union of Journeymen Hairdressers of London, one of two trade unions for German hairdressers and barbers in London. The other was the Concordia in Houndsditch, to the east of the capital, while the first organisation had its offices in Fitzroy Square in the major focus of Germans in inner West London.[123] Despite the existence of these trade unions, working hours amongst Germans in this occupation, as in others previously discussed, became excessive with some shops staying open after 9 p.m. on weekdays as well as on Sundays.[124]

Little information survives on the working or recruitment practices of butchers in official reports, nineteenth-century social surveys or trade newspapers. Rosenkranz asserts that the first German butcher moved to Liverpool from another part of Britain following a visit to the city; after him followed numerous other pork butchers from his land of origin, Württemberg. Mention was also made above of George Friedrich Hohenrein, whose settlement in Hull resembles that of many of the bakers in the sense that he originally worked as an employee before moving on to open his own shop.[125]

To conclude this discussion of German working-class occupations in Victorian and Edwardian Britain, there is little doubt that German employees suffered from exploitation, both in terms of the pay they received and the hours they worked, especially in the early stages of their residence within Britain. In many cases the exploiters were their own countrymen, a situation common in other immigrant groups in nineteenth-century Britain, particularly Russian and Polish Jews who worked in the clothing industry in East London and Leeds. A similar situation has again existed in Britain since the Second World War, with the exploitation of Cypriot and Asian women again in the clothing industry, a process made possible by the 'petite bourgeoisie's ability to appropri-

123. *Hairdresser*, 15 March 1912; BLPES, Booth Collection, Group B, vol. 160, pp. 66–7.
124. BLPES, Booth Collection, Group B, vol. 160, p. 87; *Stratford Express*, 21 November 1908.
125. A. Rosenkranz, *Geschichte der deutschen evangelischen Kirche zur Liverpool*, p. 57; Markham, *Keep the Home Fires Burning*, p. 32.

ate and manipulate an ideology of ethnic solidarity';[126] a situation which almost certainly also existed amongst the German community in nineteenth century Britain. The ability of German employers to make full use of the labour of their countrymen was helped by the latter's lack of knowledge of the English language, which virtually forced many of the immigrants to work for their own countrymen. In some cases, when they had acquired enough English together with experience of their trade, they could set up in business on their own.

With regard to the position of Germans in the London labour market, the only location where they were concentrated in enough numbers to exert any influence was in the East End, and even then, as we have seen, only in a select number of trades. But for much of the nineteenth century the Germans formed almost the cheapest supply of labour and thus had much in common with other major supplies of cheap labour in this period, East European Jews and the Irish. Some changes took place during the later nineteenth and early twentieth centuries, as Germans moved out of some of the worst-paid occupations, notably footwear and clothing manufacture where newcomers from eastern Europe had taken control; but the position of many of the Germans in baking, hairdressing and waiting occupations still remained poor.

An examination of purely middle-class occupations reveals three areas in which Germans in Britain found a role through most of the nineteenth century: clerical work, teaching, and business, often on a significant scale. In all these cases, in contrast with some of the occupations discussed above, the newcomers had become involved in their professions before they had moved to Britain, although as with the working-class occupations they also represented a cheap supply of labour, particularly in the case of clerks.

As the previous chapter demonstrated, many of the German clerks originally entered the country temporarily as part of an apprenticeship, primarily in order to improve their English. This movement continued throughout the nineteenth century and, by 1871, 1.3 per cent of all commercial clerks in Britain were Germans. More especially, Germans became particularly important as foreign correspondence clerks where, during the period 1900–14, they occupied about fifty per cent of positions[127] because of the lack of language teaching in Britain. A London Chamber of Commerce survey found that 'ninety-nine per cent of the Englishmen who take to commercial life are alleged to have no service-

126. Vic Satzewich, *Racism and the Incorporation of Foreign Labour: Farm Labour in Canada since 1945*, London, 1991, p. 23.

127. Gregory Anderson, 'German Clerks in England, 1870–1914: Another Aspect of the Great Depression Debate', in Kenneth Lunn (ed.), *Hosts, Immigrants and Minorities: Historical Responses to Newcomers in British Society*, Folkestone, 1980, pp. 204–7.

able acquaintance with French or German' which meant that 'employers who have dealings with foreigners are compelled to hire strangers able to write and read the languages of their correspondents.'[128] As well as the superior language skills which German clerks possessed they had also, like their countrymen employed as waiters in Britain, received a more thorough training than their English counterparts as they served a lengthy apprenticeship and attended Commercial Colleges.[129]

Those Germans employed as foreign correspondence clerks seem to have represented something of an elite, although like other German clerks and Germans employed in other occupations within Britain, they displayed a willingness to work for lower wages. In clerical employment, evidence even exists to suggest that Germans would work as volunteers, both because of the support they received from Mercantile Unions and because of the fact that they intended to return to Germany where they hoped to obtain better positions. They consequently displayed a willingness to make short-term sacrifices, including living in cheaper accommodation.[130] In reality, many of those who did make their way to Britain, especially those at the bottom end of the market, decided to remain in the country because of the prospect of earning higher wages. These permanent immigrants probably received no support from any German organisation and intended to remain in Britain from the start. Other German clerks went into business on their own, as in the case of Sir Ernest Cassel, the merchant banker; some German clerks employed by British merchants established firms in South American markets.[131] Although concentrated in London, German clerks also found employment in other parts of the country in significant numbers, including the west Midlands where an exaggerated report claimed that as many as 500 worked in 1889. In Liverpool and Manchester clerks received support from the Manchester Society for the Relief of Distressed Foreigners.[132]

Throughout the nineteenth century a significant number of Germans in Britain found employment as 'teachers'. This occupation proved particularly important for the mainly middle-class German exiles from the 1848 revolutions, although not enough opportunities existed; Johanna Kinkel, wife of the liberal refugee, wrote in 1851 that, 'We are now a

128. W. G. Blackie, *Commercial Education*, London, 1888, p. 8.
129. Ibid., pp. 9–10; *Report on the Early Training of the German Clerk*, P.P., vol. 77, 1889; J. J. Findlay, 'The Genesis of the German Clerk', *Fortnightly Review*, vol. 66, 1899, p. 535.
130. Anderson, 'German Clerks', pp. 207–10; *The Times*, 24 September 1901; *National Review*, March 1910, pp. 85–6; *Clerks Journal*, 2 July 1888.
131. Anderson, 'German Clerks', pp. 208–11. For Cassel see below pp. 140–1.
132. *Clerks Journal*, 1 March 1889; Gregory Anderson, *Victorian Clerks*, Manchester, 1976, pp. 63–4.

whole colony of teachers in search of pupils'.[133] Within the general category of teachers there are at least three sub-groups. First there were women, who served particularly as governesses; second, there were male teachers; and third, there were university lecturers and professors. It is on the first of these that the greatest amount of information has survived.

Governesses made their way to Britain throughout the course of the nineteenth century, and may have done so from the reign of George I during the early eighteenth. The initial reasons for moving to England were similar to those which motivated clerks and waiters to make their way to England, in that they desired to spend one or two years in the country in order to learn English with the aim of returning to Germany to secure a position as a schoolteacher. There was an excess of teachers in Germany and this qualification helped the women to compete for jobs. More general reasons for migration to England included the fact that many women believed they would have little difficulty in obtaining a well-paid position.

Their stay in England sometimes became permanent; H. Adelmann, for example, entered the country in 1866 and did not return home.[134] Amely Bölte, having worked as a governess in Germany from 1828 when she was seventeen, moved to England in 1839 and remained there until 1851 when she became too ill to carry on with governessing and returned to Germany. During her stay in England she had been a governess to a series of families, including that of Charles Buller, a merchant with the East India Company, from 1843–7, and then with that of the Jewish financier and banker Sir Isaac Goldsmid, where she remained until 1850; after that she obtained three other appointments in the same year. Malwida von Meysenbug, a political refugee, fell into governessing after moving to England following the failure of the 1848 revolutions. She found employment with a series of German families. During the 1850s the mother of the artist Hubert von Herkomer taught pupils in her home in Southampton, where the family settled after originally migrating from Germany to the USA. Initially she had difficulty attracting pupils because of 'prejudice against foreigners'.[135]

133. Ashton, *Little Germany*, pp. 20–1.
134. Bremer Staatsarchiv, 2T 6t 4e, extract from the *Weser Zeitung*, 9 December 1886; *Vereinsbote*, August 1891, p. 69; Julius Einsiedel, *Das Gouvernantenwesen in England: Eine Warnung*, Heilbronn, 1884, p. 5; H. Z. König, *Authentisches über die deutsche Erzieherin in England: Eine Entgegnung auf: 'Das Gouvernantenwesen in England', eine Warnung, von Julius Einsiedel*, London, 1884, p. 24; Brand, *London Life*, pp. 130–1.
135. Amely Bölte, *Briefe aus England an Varnhagen von Ense (1844–1858)*, Düsseldorf, 1955, pp. 1–2, 19–20, 23, 29–30; Ashton, *Little Germany*, pp. 202–17. Hubert von Herkomer, *The Herkomers*, London, 1910, p. 36.

German governesses could obtain positions in England in various ways including family connections or the use of agents, although the latter often simply saw the plight of German women in London as a way of securing money and treated them as commodities. In the late nineteenth century many governesses obtained employment through the Association of German Governesses, after its foundation in 1876. During its first thirty years in existence the organisation secured 6,000 positions, averaging about 200 per year during the late 1880s and 1890s but declining to less than two hundred just before the outbreak of the First World War.[136]

A demand existed amongst both German and, more importantly, native families in Britain for German governesses throughout the course of the nineteenth century. While the construction of secondary schools for girls from the late nineteenth century may have lessened the demand for governesses, causing greater difficulty for German women trying to obtain positions, the demand did not disappear altogether; in 1913 as many as 171 German women obtained positions as governesses in Britain, fifty more than in the previous year, as a result of 'the return of more favourable conditions between England and Germany'.[137] The basic demand for governesses of all nationalities came from the fact that middle-class and aristocratic families preferred to use them to educate their daughters and younger children. German, and foreign governesses generally, had advantages over native ones in their command of foreign languages, both French and German, and also in the fact that they often had an ability to offer music tuition. Those with command of these skills, as well as of drawing and painting, could obtain the best positions with the highest salaries.[138]

Nevertheless, most German governesses in England did not lead 'comfortable' lives either from a financial or, more especially, a social point of view. During the first year in a post the salary would not exceed £30–40 for a woman who could not teach music, and those who had no command of music would have to wait three times longer to secure a post from the Association of German Governesses. The organisation

136. Einsiedel, *Gouvernantenwesen*, pp. 13–19; *The Times*, 26 January 1877; Bremer Staatsarchiv, 2T 6t 4e: extract from the *Weser Zeitung*, 9 December 1886; extract from *Wochenblatt der Johanniter-Ordens-Bally Brandenburg*, 26 November 1884; Association of German Governesses in England, 'Seventh Annual Report, 1883', 'Fourteenth Annual Report, 1890', 'Sixteenth Annual Report, 1892', 'Twenty-Second Annual Report, 1898'; Bremer Staatsarchiv, U1a, Nr 135, 'Verein Deutscher Lehrenninen in England, n.d.'; Association of German Governesses in England, 'Thirty-Seventh Annual Report, 1913'.

137. Einsiedel, *Gouvernantenwesen*, pp. 37–8; Bremer Staatsarchiv, U1a, Nr 135, Association of German Governesses in England, 'Thirty-Seventh Annual Report, 1913'.

138. Einsiedel, *Gouvernantenwesen*, p. 12; König, *Authentisches über die deutsche Erzieherin*, pp. 22–3; Brand, *London Life*, p. 132.

also placed German women in schools, but pointed out that these paid about 33 per cent less than families. Any woman much over thirty who made her way to England would have difficulties in obtaining a position at all, and some women of all ages returned home either because they had trouble in securing a post or because they could not manage on the pay they received.[139]

With regard to the position of a governess in the household one German observer, in an essay on German women employed in this occupation in the early twentieth century, claimed that:

> In Germany, the governess is accustomed to an easy-going life; she is like the eldest daughter of the house, and generally welcome everywhere. Here she is relegated to the schoolroom, which is her kingdom indeed, but also her island, where she has to live as it were, in seclusion. Outside the schoolroom she has no rights. Her supper she has to eat in solitude within the same four walls, while she knows that the whole family are dining together comfortably downstairs, and that they will spend a cheerful, sociable evening afterwards in the drawing-room. This seems a heartless custom to be adopted by a people who pride themselves so much on their Christian love and charity.[140]

Other accounts of the life of a German governess confirm this picture, especially the loneliness of the evening.[141]

German males as well as females became teachers in Britain during the course of the nineteenth century. The German Teachers' Association, founded in 1883, filled positions with both families and schools. In addition, it also supplied German staff who worked temporarily in a variety of positions, as examiners or as 'Superior Visiting Tutors in London and twenty miles round, most successful in producing Pupils for examinations'. Furthermore, the organisation also supplied 'Holiday Engagements' whereby 'Masters experienced in accompanying pupils on their holiday trips or in working up backward boys during the vacation', took up short-term positions. Once again, as in the case of German women, there also existed a demand for staff who could teach music and languages.[142]

By the outbreak of the First World War Germans also held positions in universities throughout Britain, continuing a trend which had been

139. *Vereinsbote*, August 1891, pp. 74, 76; Bölte, *Briefe aus England*, p. 1.
140. Brand, *London Life*, p. 135. Einsiedel, *Gouvernantenwesen*, p. 12, compared the position of a governess to that of a 'necessary evil, like a cook or room lackey'.
141. See, for instance, Ashton, *Little Germany*, p. 52; Bölte, *Briefe aus England*, p. 1.
142. BA, Coblenz, R57 neu, 1064/44/1034, 1035, 1036; BA, Potsdam, AA, 38956, 'Prospectus of the School Agency in Connection with the German Teachers' Association', and 'Rules of the German Teachers Association in England'.

developing before 1800 as academics formed a traditional source of migration from Germany to England from the Middle Ages onward.

Many of the immigrants moved to England to take up newly-established positions at recently-founded institutions, which would suggest that the increase in the number of German academics in England took place against the background of British admiration for German learning.

During the first half of the nineteenth century Germans were particularly important as orientalists in Britain. Friedrich Rosen became the first Professor of Oriental Languages at the University of London in 1828; another German, Theodor Goldstücker, succeeded him. In Oxford Max Müller, also an orientalist, took up the Chair of Modern Languages in 1854. Shortly before the outbreak of the First World War German orientalists in Britain included C. F. C. Lehmann-Haupt at Liverpool and H. J. Eggeling at Edinburgh.[143]

Refugees from the 1848 revolutions who obtained university positions included Friedrich Althaus, who became Professor of German at University College London in 1873. German language and literature, as might be expected, was another area which attracted German academics. In Sheffield, for instance, the first two Professors in German from 1901–16 were Karl Wichmann and Julius Freund. Elsewhere during the Edwardian years, German academics who taught German included Max Freund, Professor at Belfast, and lecturers at Reading, St Andrews, Dundee and Nottingham.[144]

The final group of middle-class immigrants in Britain and perhaps the most important, if we wish, in Bill Williams' phrase, 'to evaluate an immigrant group in terms of its "contribution" to British life',[145] consists of what we might broadly describe as, 'businessmen', identified in the census statistics primarily by the term 'merchant'; although the middle-class cultural body for Germans in England, the *Deutscher Verein für Kunst und Wissenschaft*, used the term 'Kaufmann', a German word which counts those involved in both trade and business. The members of this organisation in 1910 included 325 businessmen, by far the most

143. Friedrich Althaus, 'Beiträge zur Geschichte der deutschen in England, 1', *Unsere Zeit*, vol. 9, pp. 436–40; Stuart Wallace, *War and the Image of Germany: British Academics 1914–1918*, Edinburgh, 1988, p. 161.
144. Ashton, *Little Germany*, p. 179; Newton, *German Studies at the University of Sheffield*, pp. 7, 9, 52–7; Wallace, *War and the Image of Germany*, pp. 160–1; Leopold Stahl, 'Erste deutsche Lektorat in England: Ein Rückblick auf Meine Tätigkeit am Nottingham University College, 1906–1909', *Die Neueren Sprachen*, vol. 18, 1911, pp. 25–33.
145. This phrase, from Bill Williams, is quoted by Tony Kushner, 'An Alien Occupation – Jewish Refugees and Domestic Service in Britain, 1933–48', in Werner E. Mosse, et al (eds), *Second Chance: Two Centuries of German-speaking Jews in the United Kingdom*, Tübingen, 1991, p. 554.

numerous profession; the next most important group was musicians, with just 33 members.[146]

As the previous chapter indicated, Germans were involved in a wide variety of business activities. While textiles may have been the major area, other important 'industries' included chemicals, steel and banking. The men involved in these areas had reached a higher social status as well as a wealthier position than the bakers and butchers already described, in many cases because they entered the country as representatives of German companies. Nevertheless, many historians have commented on the success of Germans within their areas of business activity. This question was first tackled by C. C. Aronsfeld, whose descriptive accounts certainly fit into Bill Williams' phrase quoted above; the reasons for the wealth and importance of Germans in British industry have more recently received attention from E. J. Hobsbawm and, more particularly, Stanley Chapman and W. D. Rubinstein, all of whom have viewed the success of Germans in the more general context of the importance of firms of non-British origin.

Hobsbawm wrote that 'the rare dynamic entrepreneurs of Edwardian Britain were, more often than not, foreigners or minority groups', amongst whom he included Germans, German-Jews, Americans and Quakers.[147] Rubinstein has demonstrated that a substantial proportion of the very wealthy in Britain since the eighteenth century have consisted of people of non-British birth, and the most important fields of activity for this group have included banking and chemicals; however, Rubinstein's research proves difficult to use from the point of view of the present study because it deals with 'origins' and therefore covers 'immigrants' of the second generation and beyond. His main criterion in what constitutes a minority consists of religion rather than country of birth.[148]

Chapman's work proves the most valuable, both because of his recognition of different generations of immigrants, and for his particular concern with Germans, both Jewish and Gentile, although he also recognised the importance of Greeks and Americans. Of merchant banking houses with a capital of more than £1 million before 1914, Chapman has identified four founded by German first-generation immigrants and has linked their success with German economic growth which 'not only powered the expansion of the Anglo-German banks' but 'also provided

---

146. Deutscher Verein für Kunst und Wissenschaft, *Jahresbericht und Mitgliederliste, 1910*, London, 1911, pp. 22–37.

147. E. J. Hobsbawm, *Industry and Empire: From 1750 to the Present Day*, Harmondsworth, 1969, edition, p. 169.

148. W. D. Rubinstein, *Men of Property: The Very Wealthy in Britain Since the Industrial Revolution*, London, 1981.

them with vision and commitment'.[149] Chapman's studies of the earlier
nineteenth century have revealed the presence of large numbers of
German 'merchant houses' in cities developing during the industrial
revolution. By 1850 there were 97 of these in Manchester, 38 in
Bradford, 6 in Leeds, 7 in Nottingham and 12 in Birmingham. Chapman
explains this fact and the presence and success of non-British firms
more generally by referring to three factors in particular: first, they
could supply credit to English firms; second, 'their migration brought
valuable reserves of entrepreneurial experience to Britain at a period
when resources of enterprise were extended'; and third, 'because of
their family-centred loyalties', which we may see as an ethnic solidarity,
a factor recognised by Barry E. Supple in his study of German-Jewish
businessmen in nineteenth-century New York.[150]

Banking represented a major area of involvement for Germans in
Britain during the nineteenth century and included both Jews and
Gentiles, family firms and enterprises essentially started by individuals,
as well as both large and small-scale firms. Of the family enterprises, the
largest were the Schröders and the Speyers which both sent members of
an established firm in Germany to Britain, on more than one occasion in
the case of the former, as was described in the last chapter.[151]

Both Alexander Kleinwort and Ernest Cassel entered the country to
take up positions as clerks before moving on to become major financial
figures. Kleinwort formed a partnership called Drake, Kleinwort & Co
in 1858 with £200,000 capital, specialising in dealing with Cuban and
continental business; by 1914, when Kleinwort's sons had taken control
of the business, the capital totalled £4 million and the firm was 'probably the largest private bank in the City apart from the Rothschilds';
which, as we have seen, was also founded by an earlier German Jewish
immigrant, Nathan Meyer Rothschild.[152] Cassel, meanwhile, developed
interests in a wide variety of domestic and international projects, with
involvements in North and South America, Europe and Africa. As well
as acting as a financier he also purchased interests in industrial con-

149. S. D. Chapman, 'Aristocracy and Meritocracy in Merchant Banking', *British Journal of Sociology*, vol. 37, 1986, pp. 181–4. See also his 'Merchants and Bankers', in Mosse *Second Chance*, p. 338.

150. Chapman, 'The International Houses: The Continental Contribution in British Commerce, 1800–1860', *Journal of European Economic History*, vol. 19, 1977, pp. 19, 44–8; Barry E. Supple, 'A Business Elite: German-Jewish Financiers in Nineteenth Century New York', *Business History Review*, vol. 36, 1957, pp. 158–77.

151. For brief details on Sir Edgar Speyer see Paul H. Emden, *Jews of Britain*, London, 1943, pp. 344–5. For the Schröders see above.

152. S. D. Chapman, *The Rise of Merchant Banking*, London, 1984, p. 43; Stefanie Diaper, 'Sir Alexander Drake Kleinwort', in *Dictionary of Business Biography*, London, 1985, pp. 605–6.

cerns, many of which he had helped to finance. He became one of the 'richest lone wolves in European banking' and the range of his activities 'was exceptional'.[153] Together with these highly successful figures there were also other German bankers in London, including Samuel Japhet who had moved from Frankfurt in the 1890s but continued to maintain a branch there as well as in Berlin and Hamburg,[154] and Rüffer and Sons who moved to the City of London at about the same time.[155]

Chapters 1 and 2 noted the immigration of German textile merchants to English cities as the continental fairs declined and the merchants wanted to establish branches of their firms in Britain; in fact the founders of the branches often remained permanently in the country. One striking fact here concerns the range of textile industries in which Germans became active, ranging from linen in Dundee to worsted in Bradford, lace in Nottingham and cotton in Manchester. Germans became particularly important in Bradford and Manchester; in the former city, Jacob Behrens became the most successful merchant and during the course of the nineteenth century his company opened branches in London, Glasgow, Calcutta and Shanghai. The Bradford Chamber of Commerce came into existence in 1851 at his initiative, but with the support of the other German merchants who formed a substantial proportion of the 65 foreign merchants present in the city by 1861, making up forty per cent of all merchants in Bradford.[156] A similar situation existed in Manchester where, in 1837, 101 foreign export firms existed the city, 75 of which originated in Germany; in other cities, the number of German merchants remained considerably smaller.[157]

In the chemical industry there was no community of Germans in particular cities such as the worsted or cotton merchants in Bradford and Manchester. The number of Germans who became involved in the chemical industry was much smaller. The most notable was Ludwig Mond, as successful as any German entrepreneur in Britain within any field of activity. In 1873, Mond went into partnership with John

153. Pat Thane, 'Financiers and the British State: The Case of Sir Ernest Cassel', *Business History*, vol. 17, 1986, pp. 80–9; Kurt Grunwald, '"Windsor-Cassel" – The Last Court Jew: Prolegomena to a Biography of Sir Ernest Cassel', *Leo Baeck Yearbook*, vol. 14, 1969, pp. 119–61.
154. Saemy Japhet, *Recollections from My Business Life*, London, 1931, pp. 62, 67–8, 72.
155. Chapman, *Rise of Merchant Banking*, p. 51. For examples of other German banks in London see *The London Banks*, an annual publication. See also Manfred Pohl, 'Deutsche Bank London Agency Founded 100 Years Ago', in *Studies on Economic and Monetary Problems and on Banking History*, Mainz, n.d., pp. 233–42.
156. Rollin, 'The Jewish Contribution', p. 48; Harold Pollins, *Economic History of the Jews in England*, London, 1982, p. 96; Eric M. Sigsworth, *Black Dyke Mills: A History*, Liverpool, 1958, p. 65. Pratt, 'Influence of the Germans on Bradford', pp. 23–4.
157. Pollins, *Economic History of the Jews*, pp. 94–6.

Brunner, the son of a Swiss pastor, and opened a factory in Winnington Hall in Cheshire which produced alkali; in 1881 the partnership became a limited company with assets of £600,000 and with support from small investors in Lancashire and Chesire. As well as playing a part in this company, Mond continued to practice as a chemist. Karl Emil Markel, the son of a German father and an English mother, moved to England in 1885 at the age of twenty-five, having studied at a series of German universities, and took over the management of a chemical factory, subsequently becoming a manager in several similar concerns.[158]

German involvement in the engineering sector was similar to that in chemicals, in that it involved individuals. Once again, as with banking, these included people who entered the country as individuals and/or as representatives of already-established companies. Those who fall within the former category include Hugo Hirst, who initially worked as a clerk in a shipping office in London from 1880 but who in 1886, together with a fellow Bavarian Gustav Bing, established the General Electric Company.[159] Similarly, the Germans who opened companies in the Sheffield steel industry, Charles Kayser, Sir Joseph Jonas and Paul Kühnrich, entered the country as individuals, as did Henry Simon who moved to Manchester in 1860 after studying in Breslau and Zurich and subsequently going on to Magdeberg. He developed an international farm machinery company.[160] Alexander and William Siemens provide the best example of Germans who moved to Britain as part of a family concern.[161]

The above survey has demonstrated that during the course of the nineteenth century, German economic activity covered a range as wide as that of English society, varying from the destitute to millionaires who made fortunes as first-generation immigrants. Those who did rise to the top of the social scale consisted of individuals who began in the middle classes, rather than those landless labourers who had moved to the country as a result of the economic changes taking place within Germany. But even in the case of these groups opportunities existed for the accu-

158. W. J. Reader, *Imperial Chemical Industries, A History*, vol. 1, London, 1970, pp. 47–56; F. G. Donnan, *Ludwig Mond, FRS: 1839–1909*, London, 1939; Jean Goodman, *The Mond Legacy*, London, 1982, p. 44; Pollins, *Economic History of the Jews*, pp. 96–7; George Haines, *Essays on German Influence upon English Education and Science*, Hamden Connecticut, 1969, p. 123; 'Karl Emil Markel', *Der Ausland Deutsche*, vol. 15, 1932, pp. 317–19.
159. R. P. T. Davenport Hines, 'Lord Hirst', *Dictionary of Business Biography*, vol. 3, pp. 275–8; Hugo Hirst, 'Two Autobiographical Fragments', *Business History*, vol. 28, 1986, p. 124.
160. For Sheffield see above, pp. 105–6 Simon receives attention from Berghoff, *Englische Unternehmer*, p. 73.
161. See William Pole, *The Life of Sir William Siemens*, London, 1888; and J. D. Scott, *Siemens Brothers 1858–1958: An Essay in the History of Industry*, London, 1958.

mulation of a limited amount of wealth, as the example of butchers and bakers illustrates. In other cases, social mobility did not take place or, for a variety of reasons, took place downwards, as the example of some women who fell into prostitution demonstrates.

While the destitute may seem to have little in common with their countrymen higher on the social scale, they both illustrate the variety of people, in terms of occupation and social structure, who emigrated from Germany to Britain, and the richness in diversity of a large immigrant community, a facet of the study of immigrant groups in Britain which does not tend to receive sufficient attention. While the studies of, for instance, Colin Holmes,[162] Stanley Nadel,[163] Bill Williams[164] and, to a lesser extent, L. H. Lees[165] have recognised this diversity, monographs on the Russian and Polish Jews who made their way to Britain in the late nineteenth century tend to focus upon a long-established Anglo-Jewish middle- and upper-class hierarchy confronted by the problem of a mass migration of exclusively poor newcomers.[166] Lucio Sponza's work remains rare in that it consciously focuses upon poor Italians.[167]

The reason for the focus on either rich or poor immigrants may be due to the fact that scholars of immigration history are often either economic and business historians, who tend to focus on wealthier newcomers, or social historians who usually deal with 'ordinary' immigrants and therefore have problems in linking the wealthier and working class members of the same community. The above survey of employment patterns has demonstrated that connections existed through work, while the next chapter will show that the various strands of the German community in nineteenth-century Britain also came together through charitable and religious activities.

Nevertheless, this does not deny that middle-class Germans had more in common with their English counterparts than they did with their destitute countrymen, with whom they would have no contact, especially if they did not live in the same areas of the same cities. The survey of settlement patterns in London demonstrates that different communities of

162. One of the main strengths of Colin Holmes, *John Bull's Island: Immigration and British Society, 1871–1971*, London, 1988, lies in its comprehensiveness, covering all newcomers to Britain whatever the class or country of origin.

163. Nadel, *Little Germany*, p. 90, writes that 'The mature economy of Kleindeutschland included an occupational range that went from street urchins to magnates and included most of the occupations in between'.

164. Williams, *Making of Manchester Jewry*, is similar to Holmes in its comprehensiveness. The author looks at all Jews who settled in Manchester.

165. Lees, *Exiles of Erin*, p. 98, points out that only four per cent of the Irish in London worked in middle-class occupations but does not study them in any detail.

166. See, for instance, *The Jewish Immigrant in England 1870–1914*, Detroit, 1960.

167. Sponza's *Italian Immigrants* is based on his 1984 London Ph.D thesis entitled 'The Italian Poor in Nineteenth Century London'.

Germans existed for different classes in Victorian London which, by the outbreak of the First World War, varied from the still-existing community in Stepney, the focus of not just the immigrant but also the native poor, to Sydenham, which attracted some of the wealthiest of London Germans. In short, the relationship of Germans to their own community and to English society remains complex and forms one of the focuses of the next chapter.

–4–

Ethnic Organisations: Religion, Philanthropy, Culture and Politics

All immigrant groups during the nineteenth and twentieth centuries, from all destinations and in all new locations, have attempted to recreate in some way the conditions of their land of origin, despite the fact that by migrating they have fundamentally cut themselves off from their homeland. The previous chapter demonstrated that German newcomers in nineteenth-century Britain, again as with all immigrant communities, particularly those of working class or peasant origin, focused on particular areas of a city, especially in London where they lived in the largest numbers. It also indicated that many newcomers worked in particular fields of employment, a pattern which encompassed all classes, although this working together also offered an opportunity for exploitation where employees in the baking and clothing industries saw the lack of knowledge and disorientation of newcomers as an opportunity to employ them at cheaper rates, in return for a feeling of ethnic solidarity.

This search for ethnic solidarity, through the creation of religious, philanthropic, cultural, trade union and political activities, forms the basis of the present chapter. Once again, it demonstrates that the German institutions which came into existence were not founded solely on the concept of ethnic solidarity encompassing all groups of Germans from all classes. As with native English society, it would prove difficult to find instances of Germans in Whitechapel having any contact with their richer countrymen in Sydenham, as both geography and class forbade this. The cultural clubs which came into existence catered for people on a class basis. The *Vereine* in central London, Manchester or Bradford remained exclusive, serving the richest members of German society within those cities, just as similar organisations in Whitechapel served the local communities of sugar bakers, tailors or bakers, or as the trade union organisations catered for working class members of a particular occupation. Even in religion, certainly within London, a similar division developed as churches existed on a geographical basis, serving their local communities. In the provinces the situation was different because the size of the German community meant that only one church

could exist in cities such as Hull, Bradford or Middlesbrough, catering
for all classes of the German population. There were also welfare organisations which linked all members of the German community but in a
clearly hierarchical manner, with the wealthy members of the community assisting their poorer countrymen, therefore essentially re-emphasis-
ing class divisions.

But class did not serve as the only division amongst the German
communities in nineteenth-century Britain. Frederick C. Luebke's
assertion that 'few ethnic groups in America have been as varied in religious belief, political persuasion, socioeconomic status, occupation, culture, and social character as the German are',[1] applies equally to their
countrymen in Britain as well as to other immigrant groups there,
including the Irish[2] and Jews.[3] Politically, for instance, there existed
amongst the Germans during the nineteenth century a whole a range of
groups, including left-wing anarchists and communists, liberals, and
right-wing pan-Germanists and supporters of the German Navy League.
In religion, the situation again resembled the United States in that newcomers included Jews, Catholics, Lutherans and Evangelicals, each with
their own places of worship, although the latter two Protestant sects had
close connections and often used the same churches, as well as developing a synod at the end of the nineteenth century.

Different organisations, whatever their nature, came into existence
with new groups of Germans that entered the country. In politics, for
instance, some of the organisations for the newcomers of the 1830s differed from those established by the refugees of 1848 and those of the
late 1870s, although continuities also exist. In religion, as Chapter 1
demonstrated, the foundations of German religion in Britain lay essen-

1. Frederick C. Luebke, 'Introduction', in Luebke (ed.), *Germans in the New World: Essays in the History of Immigration*, Urbana and Chicago, 1990, p. xiii. See also James M. Bergquist, 'German Communities in American Cities: An Interpretation of the Nineteenth Century Experience', *Journal of American Ethnic History*, vol. 4, 1980, p. 13, who points out that, after 1850, 'German communities developed the immense diversity that was to characterize them until the end of the century.'

2. The Irish included both Catholic and Protestant newcomers who formed their own organisations, which came into combat with each other. For a sample of the literature on sectarian rivalry amongst Irish Protestants and Catholics in Britain, see Tom Gallagher, *Glasgow the Uneasy Peace: Religious Tension in Modern Scotland*, Manchester, 1987; Frank Neal, *Sectarian Violence: The Liverpool Experience, 1819–1914*, Manchester, 1988; P. J. Waller, *Democracy and Sectarianism: A Political and Social History of Liverpool 1868–1939*, Liverpool, 1981.

3. Class and religious differences played a fundamental role amongst the Jewish com-munities in nineteenth century Britain, as did different countries of origin, a point stressed previously. The most assertive account of class differences is Joseph Buckman, *Immigrants and the Class Struggle: The Jewish Immigrant in Leeds 1880–1914*, Manchester, 1983. Bill Williams, *The Making of Manchester Jewry, 1740–1875*, Manchester, 1985 reprint, emphasises the other divisions.

tially in the late seventeenth and eighteenth centuries when both Protestant and Jewish places of worship came into existence, the latter catering for more than just Jews of German origin. In the development of religion, the German community of the 1815–1914 period resembles its Irish counterpart in Britain, as this also developed from pre-nineteenth century origins.[4] In both cases developments before 1800 formed the basis from which the newcomers after this period added new churches in their areas of settlement, while those already established moved to the places of new population concentration.

In short, the German organisations of the nineteenth century, as well as reflecting the diversity of the newcomers, also indicate both its continuous and, contrarily, its changing nature. While some organisations existed throughout the course of the nineteenth century and before, others sprang up during this period and in some cases lasted only for short periods of time. Both in terms of its development and in terms of its diversity, the German communities in nineteenth-century Britain have little relationship to any sort of monolithic structure. Stanley Nadel writes that:

> When it came to ethnicity, German New Yorkers did what most people have done – they formed their ethnicity out of the misty regions of their consciousness, and they did so on an ad hoc basis, selecting from a broad range of developed options, they shaped their ethnicity in accordance with whichever set of rules seemed appropriate for the particular culture.[5]

While agreeing with much of the above, we can also suggest that in Britain the choice of which grouping to join was a conscious decision based on the variables of class, religion, occupation and political persuasion outlined above.

German newcomers did not remain tied to any one organisation; they could belong simultaneously to a trade union, club and church. Frederick Engels, as well as participating in political activities, also played an important role in the major middle-class German organisation in nineteenth-century Manchester, the Schiller-Anstallt. The immigrants also had contacts with British society, although little evidence exists about membership in non-German organisations.

Any explanation of the reason for the development of organisations might focus on the disorientation felt by newcomers in their new society. In the classic statement on this subject from the 1950s, Oscar

4. Lynn Hollen Lees, *Exiles of Erin: Irish Immigrants in Victorian London*, Manchester, 1979, pp. 172–3.
5. Stanley Nadel, *Little Germany: Ethnicity, Religion, and Class in New York City, 1845–80*, Urbana and Chicago, 1990, p. 7

Handlin wrote of the 'loneliness' of the immigrants who 'reached for some arm to lean upon'. Therefore, 'the newcomers took pains early to seek out those whom experience made their brothers; and to organize each others' support, they created a great variety of formal and informal institutions.' Handlin focused particularly upon religion as a link with the past.[6] But we also need to place the ethnic organisations which came into existence within the context of their new societies, as these have parallels with similar organisations within the dominant culture. This applies to religion, which continued to play a fundamental role in nineteenth-century life in both Britain and the USA, and to trade unions which, in the case of German unions in Britain, mirrored activities amongst the native populations. The growth of socialism and trade unionism were events which took place throughout Europe during the course of the nineteenth century.

The organisations which perhaps most clearly differentiate the immigrants from their countrymen were the social organisations which seem to have no other purpose than emphasising ethnicity. These contrast with many other bodies which served a dual function of both keeping the members of the new group together and also helping them in other aspects of their lives, occupational, political, or spiritual, although even this is not straightforward because the middle-class German organisations included many Englishmen as members.

Having outlined some of the main characteristics of German organisations in nineteenth-century Britain, we can now move on to consider them under the broad groupings of religious, benevolent, cultural, and trade union and political organisations. If we begin with religious organisations, we can first consider the role of religion in any ethnic community, a subject tackled by many historians of minorities.

Religion

Of these historians, Handlin put forward one of the most extreme views, claiming that 'The very process of adjusting immigrant ideas to the conditions of the United States made religion paramount as a way of life'. This position was supported by Will Herberg, who believed that the 'first concern of the immigrants...was with their churches'.[7] Similarly, Luebke, referring to the Germans in the USA during the nineteenth century, claimed that they 'identified themselves first of all as Catholics,

6. Oscar Handlin, *The Uprooted: The Epic Story of the Great Migration that Made the American People*, 2nd edn, London, 1979, pp. 105–28, 152.
7. Ibid., p. 105; Will Herberg, *Protestant-Catholic-Jew: An Essay in American Religious Sociology*, Chicago, 1983 edition, p. 14.

Lutherans, Evangelicals, Mennonites, or Methodists, and only secondar-
ily (sometimes only incidentally) as Germans.'[8]

This seems an extreme position, which was slightly modified by
Luebke in his subsequent study of Germans in Brazil where, although he
maintains that 'the various churches, individually or collectively, performed social roles that were crucial to the life of the community', he
also admits that, 'This is not to say that every German immigrant was a
practising Christian or that the church was a pervasive influence in
everyone's life'.[9] These last two statements, taken together, would apply
to some extent to the situation of Germans in nineteenth-century Britain.
Here the church played a role in education and welfare organisations,
although it would be difficult to maintain that all Germans felt their religion before their nationality, without denying that, in some cases, this
may have held substantial truth.

The role of German churches in nineteenth-century Britain can also
be placed in the context of declining attendance on the part of the native
population, during a period when secularisation was ongoing.[10] The situation was similar among other immigrant groups in Britain. For the
Irish in London, Lees claims that 'most migrants as well as their
English-born children took part in the major Catholic rituals marking
birth and probably death', but 'far fewer had either the opportunity or
the interest to sustain the pattern of regular parochial devotions recom-
mended to them by their priests.'[11] Perhaps the most accurate statement
on religion and ethnicity comes from Jay P. Dolan, who wrote that
immigrants to the USA reproduced 'the type of religion with which they
were familiar within the old country; for some it was an active spiritual
life centered in the parish; for others it was an indifferent attitude toward
religion, and the immigrant parish was hard-pressed to change these patterns of tradition.'[12]

In order to assess the situation amongst the Germans in Britain, we
need to look at the major developments of their religious life in some
detail. Several introductory comments are in order. First, as previously
indicated, a diversity existed within the spiritual allegiances of Germans

8. Frederick C. Luebke, *Bonds of Loyalty: German Americans and World War I*, De
Kalb, Illinois, 1974, pp. 34–5.
9. Frederick C. Luebke, *Germans in Brazil: A Comparative History of Cultural
Conflict during World War I*, Baton Rouge and London, 1987, pp. 35–6.
10. K. S. Inglis, *Churches and the Working Classes in Victorian England*, London,
1963, pp. 19–20, 322–36; Hugh McLeod, *Religion and the Working Classes in
Nineteenth-Century Britain*, London, 1984, pp. 15–16, 57–66.
11. Lees, *Exiles of Erin*, p. 182. See also John Archer Jackson, *The Irish in Britain*,
London, 1963, p. 141.
12. Jay P. Dolan, *The Immigrant Church: New York's Irish and German Catholics,
1815–1865*, Baltimore and London, 1975, p. 58.

in nineteenth-century Britain, who were divided amongst Lutherans, Evangelicals, Catholics and Jews. Second, the various German religious groups also had a series of benevolent, educational and women's organisations connected to them either directly or indirectly. This excludes organisations such as the Society of Friends of Foreigners in Distress and the German Hospital, because while these may have received support from the German communities of London, financial and otherwise, they remained independent. But most of the German schools in London remained fundamentally dependant upon an individual German church, which paid the salary of the priest and offered free school places to poorer pupils.

It should also be re-emphasised that German religion in Britain had strong roots in the pre-nineteenth century period. As Chapter 1 indicated, by 1815 there existed five Protestant churches, one Catholic church, and at least four Synagogues in London, together with German worshippers in provincial Jewish settlements, in all cases established between the late seventeenth and early nineteenth centuries.

We can begin with the Protestant churches and the institutions directly connected with them, focusing firstly upon those already in existence in London and then moving to consider those newly-founded during the course of the nineteenth century both in the capital and in the provinces. Of the places of worship established during the late seventeenth century, the Court Chapel played the smallest role amongst the Germans in London after 1800, making little adjustment to meet the new influx of the nineteenth century so that in 1901 Edward VII dissolved the Chapel by Royal Decree because it had ceased to have any purpose.[13]

In contrast, the other German churches of London founded at the same time as the Court Chapel increased rather than declined in importance, and resembled many similar ethnic churches in the USA both because of their focus within particular areas of German settlement[14] and because of the educational activities which accompanied them. Much information survives about these and each can be considered in turn.

First, there was the Hamburg Lutheran Church, which possessed one of the largest congregations amongst the German churches of London before the First World War (see Table 4.1). As previously mentioned, it moved its site during the course of the nineteenth century because of the purchase of its site in Trinity Lane by the Metropolitan District Railway

13. Heinrich Dorgeel, *Die Deutsche Colonie in London*, London, 1881, p. 44; John Southernden Burn, *The History of the French, Walloon, Dutch, and Other Foreign Protestant Refugees Settled in England*, London, 1846, pp. 235–7; J. Rieger, 'The British Crown and the German Churches in England', in F. Hildebrandt (ed.), *And Other Pastors of Thy Flock*, Cambridge, 1942, pp. 122–3.

14. Dolan, *Immigrant Church*, pp. 4–6.

Ethnic Organisations

Table 4.1 Attendance at German Church Services in London in 1905

Location	Attendance		
	Morning	Evening	Total
St George's, Stepney	166		166
St Paul's, Stepney	49	126	175
German YMCA, Stepney		29	29
German Seaman's Church, Stepney		11	11
German Sailor's Home, Stepney		34	34
Hamburg Lutheran, Hackney	86	132	218
Great Titchfield Street, Marylebone		34	34
Eccleston Street, Westminster		33	33
Fowler Road, Islington	119	58	177
Dacres Road, Forest Hill	138	58	196
High Street, Deptford		35	35
Windsor Road, Camberwell	57		57
Star Lane, West Ham	10	19	29
St Mary's, St Pancras	120	161	281
Leighton Crescent, St Pancras		47	47
Total	745	777	1,522

Source: Richard Mudie Smith, *Religious Life of the People in London*, London, 1905, pp. 52, 66, 99, 107, 173, 177, 235, 239, 243, 253.

Company for the construction of Mansion House Underground Station. Consequently, the last sermon took place on the old site on 15 January 1871. The new church was consecrated five years later in Dalston near the German Hospital, an area which, as we have seen, had attracted some movement of German population out of inner East London. A former Bavarian General, named Brandt, provided funds for the construction of a church hall which was opened in 1899. Baron Bruno Schröder became treasurer of the church in 1910 and his uncle John Henry Schröder also 'donated' the German orphanage in the area in 1879, the Schröder family playing a major role in much philanthropic activity amongst the Germans in Victorian and Edwardian Britain.[15]

St George's in Whitechapel actually remained the only one of the German churches in London which did not change its location during the course of the nineteenth century because, as we have seen, its situation in Little Alie Street in Whitechapel lay in the heart of the major area of German settlement in nineteenth-century London, and one in which

15. G. Schönberger (ed), *Festschrift zum 70. Geburtstag von Freiherr Baron von Schröder*, London, 1937, pp. 66–8; *Hamburg Lutheran Church London, 1669–1969*, Hamburg and Berlin, 1969, pp. 89–90; Susan Gold, 'The Reredos which Slipped Through the Net', *Transactions of the Ancient Monument Society*, vol. 28, 1984, pp. 106–8.

many of the poorest members of the German community lived. Nevertheless, the church underwent renovation in the late 1850s with the help of contributions from both members of the congregation and friends of the church.[16] The church could accommodate as many as 600 people, and at the beginning of the twentieth century it was 'attended largely by German tradespeople, such as tailors and bakers, coming from various districts as widely apart as Stockwell and Covent Garden, Stamford Hill and Camberwell.'[17] In reality its attendance did not reach 600; Richard Mudie Smith's survey of religion in London in 1903 only counted 175 people who attended the Sunday morning service, less than the number at many of the other London services for Germans, as shown in Table 4.1. But earlier in the nineteenth century, perhaps because of the greater concentration of Germans in Whitechapel, the services attracted greater numbers, when two per day took place. Up to 500 people attended on Sunday, and the number of baptisms totalled between fifty and sixty per year.[18]

As mentioned previously, St George's Church had 'institutions' directly connected with it, in contrast to the Hamburg Lutheran Church in Hackney. These consisted of a Ladies Clothing Society, which provided new clothes annually for about 100 children of poor German families during the whole course of the nineteenth century; a poor fund for the congregation, which provided a weekly payment for older members of the congregation who had fallen into poverty; and a free library for members of the congregation.[19] But St George's School, founded in 1805, became the most important institution connected with St George's Church, providing free education for over 12,000 German children during the succeeding century.[20] The peak of attendance at the school occurred in the year 1874, at a total of 495. By the 1880s the total number of pupils had declined to a yearly average of 350 and ten years later to 250; from 1905 until 1914 the total remained between 200 and 250. The rise and fall in numbers corresponds with the growth and subse-

16. BA, Coblenz, R57 neu, 1065/7, 'Kirchenordnung und Schulordnung für die Deutsche Lutherische St. Georg's-Gemeinde in Little Alie Street, Goodman's Fields, London, 1861'; Anglo-German Publishing Society, *Die Deutsche Kolonie in England*, London, 1913, p. 19; Dorgeel, *Deutsche Colonie in London*, p. 45.

17. F. M. Holmes, 'Some Foreign Places of Worship in London', in George R. Sims (ed.), *Living London*, vol. 3, London, 1906, p. 234.

18. Carl Schöll, *Geschichte der deutschen evangelischen Kirchen in England*, Stuttgart, 1852, p. 47.

19. Ibid.; Dorgeel, *Deutsche Colonie in London*, p. 45; Burn, *History of Protestant Refugees*, p. 240.

20. Tower Hamlets Local History Collection, 'Jubiläums-Bericht der deutschen und englischen St. Georg's Schule, 1. Juli, 1905'; Dorgeel, *Deutsche Colonie in London*, pp. 53–5; BA, Potsdam, AA, 38988, extract from the *Weser Zeitung*, 2 July 1905.

quent shrinkage of the German population of Whitechapel.[21] As well as an expansion in the number of children who attended the school, there also occurred a growth in the numbers of teaching staff, to six in 1905.[22]

The school described its purpose as not simply educating pupils in academic subjects but also in caring for their spiritual needs and showing them the way to God from the age of two until they had become ready to work. But it did offer instruction in a wide variety of subjects by the 1880s.[23] The school received support from a variety of sources including the English and German Royal Families, the German community in London, both prominent and not-so-prominent members, and members of the native population.[24]

The history of St Paul's Evangelical Reformed Church during the nineteenth century has parallels with that of St George's, in that both were located in Whitechapel and both had a school. As Chapter 1 indicated, St Paul's originally began in the Savoy, moving to Hooper Square in the East End in 1819 because of the large concentration of Germans there but, more especially, due to the construction of Waterloo Bridge upon its old location. The Church moved again in the 1880s because of further railway construction, but because of the continued presence of Germans in the area in significant numbers, the new site in Goulston Street was also situated in Whitechapel.[25]

The size of the congregation remained similar in size to that of St George's, as shown in Table 4.1. But the school had less success than St George's in attracting pupils. It originally came into existence shortly after the Church moved to Hooper Square, although the number of its pupils only totalled between twenty and thirty in 1847. However, by the

21. Tower Hamlets Local History Collection, 'Jubiläums-Bericht der deutschen und englischen St. Georg's Schule, 1. Juli, 1905'; BA, Potsdam, AA, 38986, 'Report of the Present State of St George's German and English School', 1894, 1897, 1899; BA, Potsdam, AA, 38987, 'Jahres-Bericht der deutschen und englischen St Georg's Schule', 1901, 1903; BA, Potsdam, AA, 38988, 'Jahres-Bericht der deutschen und englischen St Georg's Schule', 1907, 1909, 1910, 1911.

22. Tower Hamlets Local History Collection, 'Jubiläums-Bericht der deutschen und englischen St. Georg's Schule, 1. Juli, 1905'.

23. BA, Coblenz, R57 neu, 1065/7, 'Kirchenordnung und Schulordnung für die Deutsche Lutherische St. Georg's-Gemeinde in Little Alie Street, Goodman's Fields, London, 1861'; Dorgeel, *Deutsche Colonie in London*, p.54.

24. Rieger, 'British Crown and the German Churches', p. 121; *Report of St George's German and English School*, London, 1827, pp. 6–7; Tower Hamlets Local History Collection, 'Jubiläums-Bericht der deutschen und englischen St. Georg's Schule, 1. Juli, 1905'; BA, Coblenz, R57 neu, 1065/8, 'Jahres-Bericht der deutschen und englischen St. Georg's-Schule, 1906'; BA, Potsdam, 38987, Alwin Schenck, 'Ein Besuch in einer deutschen Gemeinde und deren Schule in London'; BA, Potsdam, 38988, extract from the *Weser Zeitung*, 2 July 1905.

25. Heinrich Deicke, *A Short History of the German Evangelical Reformed St Paul's Church*, London, 1907, p. 4.

late 1870s the number had increased to such an extent as to necessitate the construction of a new building, which opened in November 1880. It accepted children paid for by their parents as well as those received for free.

In the subjects studied and in its aims it resembled St George's, although it did not accept more than 120 children. One former pupil subsequently wrote that 'we had German lessons in the morning and English in the afternoon.' The school closed in 1896, but in order 'to give members an opportunity to have their children taught the German language and to bring them up as good members of the congregation, or at least to enable them to attend confirmation classes and understand the church service sufficiently well', a Saturday evening school replaced the more permanent institution. By the early twentieth century a Women's Union also existed: 'On average 28 ladies meet on the last Tuesday of a month, to work industriously and to prepare Christmas gifts for the needy in our congregation.'[26]

The largest German congregation in London in the early twentieth century attended St Mary's in Cleveland Street, St Pancras, the last of the London churches founded before 1800. As well as possessing the most substantial congregation within the capital, in 1904 it also carried out 51 baptisms and 23 burials in one year. 'German merchants attend here from Hampstead and Regent's Park, Cavendish Square and Bayswater, and German-speaking Swiss would probably be found among them', although the majority of the congregation probably came from the local working-class community.[27]

Like St George's Church, St Mary's also received financial support from the British Royal Family, particularly when it moved from its old site in the Savoy to the new one in Cleveland Street in the centre of the German district in West London in 1877, following the construction of the Victoria Embankment on the location the Church had used from 1768. The German Royal Family also provided backing from the start of the twentieth century, and the Church received visits from Prince William of Prussia in 1848, during a stay in London as a temporary refugee from the 1848 revolution, and from Empress Augusta Victoria, the wife of William II, in 1907. Like St George's, the church also received backing from members of the London

26. Ibid., pp. 4–50. Mrs Streitberger is the pupil who attended the school and the brief account of her experiences survive in Greater London Record Office, German Evangelical Reformed Church, Hooper Square, Acc 1767.
27. BA, Potsdam, AA, 38989, 'Jahres-Bericht der deutschen ev.-luth. St. Marien-Gemeinde, 1905'; Holmes, 'Some Foreign Places of Worship', p.233.

German community through continuing donations and special funds.[28]

St Mary's possessed the oldest German school in London, which resembled St George's rather than St Paul's during the nineteenth century in its success, although it never quite succeeded in attracting as many pupils as St George's. In 1819 forty boys and thirty girls received instruction in both German and English, the poorer ones free of charge, of whom about twenty obtained a new set of clothing at Christmas from a foundation begun in 1817. The school also received support from collections until 1852 when a school committee and board of directors took responsibility for fund-raising.[29]

This institution moved with the church to Cleveland Street in 1877. By the turn of the century the school faced various problems including a fluctuating attendance and a deterioration in the condition of the building. The construction of a new building, opened in 1909 by the German ambassador in London, Count Metternich, solved the problem of accommodation; a sum of £5,000 provided for the move. This came from a variety of sources including collections, interest on school capital and donations, of which Baron Schröder provided the largest.[30]

St Mary's Church also had other organisations connected with it. For educational purposes, for instance, in addition to the school outlined above, there also existed by the start of the twentieth century a Sunday School and a Society for German and Swiss Girls. The Church had also begun to gather books for a library. The Women's Committee, meanwhile, aimed at caring for the poor and old in the parish, and like many of the German organisations in Britain, the Church held an annual fund-raising evening.[31]

Clearly, the old-established churches in London had developed an important range of activities during the course of the nineteenth century of both an educational and philanthropic nature. Likewise some of the newer Protestant places of worship undertook a similar role within their communities. Actually establishing the number of places which held

28. BA, Potsdam, AA, 38989, 'Geschichte der deutschen evangelischen St. Marien-Schule, 1908'; Holmes, ibid.; Anglo-German Publishing Company, *Deutsche Kolonie in England*, p. 20; Rieger, 'British Crown and the German Churches', pp. 121–2; D. C. F. U. Steinkopff, *Predigt, Gehalten am 19ten Sonntage nach Trinitatis, in der Deutschen St. Marien Kirche in der Savoy, Strand*, London, 1819, pp. 15–16.

29. *Londoner Deutsches Wochenblatt*, 3 December 1819; BA, Potsdam, AA, 38989, 'Geschichte der deutschen evangelischen St. Marien-Schule, 1908'.

30. BA Potsdam, 38987, 'Bericht des Geheimen Regierungsrats. Professor Dr W Münch über eine Reise nach England, 1904'; BA, Potsdam, AA, 38989: 'Geschichte der deutschen evangelischen St. Marien-Schule, 1908'; 'Jahres-Bericht der deutschen ev.-luth. St. Marien-Gemeinde, 1905'; *The Times*, 4 November 1909.

31. BA, Potsdam, AA, 38989, 'Jahres-Bericht der deutschen ev.-luth. St. Marien-Gemeinde, 1905'.

German Lutheran or Evangelical services in London proves difficult; the number clearly varied and Mudie-Smith's 1905 list (in Table 4.1) shows the situation only as it existed at the moment. An advertisement in a London German newspaper from 1880 mentioned services in the chapel of the German Hospital, as well as in Dean Street Soho, for German Methodists. Another report from 1902 described eleven 'German Evangelical' places of worship in London, in locations which included Tottenham and Blackheath. In some cases churches existed for just a short period of time, such as the one in Charles Street in Whitechapel during the first half of the nineteenth century, and another in Blenheim Street which lasted for just seven years from 1844 until 1851.[32] Nevertheless, several German churches in London, founded during the nineteenth and early twentieth centuries, in some cases for middle-class congregations, did establish themselves.

The most successful of these, both in terms of the size of its attendance and the activities connected with it, included the German congregation at Forest Hill, established in 1875 to serve the middle-class community in that area. The founding of the church came about through the actions of the German Consul, Victor von Bojanowski, who worked together with several London Germans who wanted to see the establishment of a church in the area, which actually opened in 1883, after fundraising through means such as church bonds and a fundraising concert. Services actually first took place in the Lecture Hall in Sydenham from 1875 under the first pastor, Carl Wagner. In 1878 the congregation founded a Women's Committee to assist poor Germans within the parish, and in the next year there followed the German School in Forest Hill.[33]

Another south London church, in Denmark Hill, came into existence in 1856 to serve the wealthy German community in Camberwell, although by the early twentieth century its numbers had declined. The finance for the construction of this church had come through collections. The church had less of a role in the lives of its parishioners than many of the other London places of worship for Germans.[34]

---

32. *Londoner Zeitung*, 9 January 1880; Pfarrer Urban, 'Statistik der deutschen evangelischen Gemeinden und Pastoren und der mit ihnen in Verbindung stehende Schulen im Auslande', *Deutsch-Evangelisch Zeitschrift*, vol. 2, p. 114. Schöll, *Geschichte der deutschen evangelischen Kirchen in England*, pp. 20, 50, also mentions a chapel at the German Hospital founded in 1845.
   33. Albert Rosenkranz, 'Die Anfänge der Gemeinde in Sydenham' in *Hundert Jahre Deutsche Evangelische Gemeinde Sydenham (London) 1875–1975*, London, 1975, pp. 22–4; BA, Coblenz, R57 neu, 1064/27, 'Chronik der Deutschen Evangelischen Gemeinde zu Sydenham'; Dorgeel, *Deutsche Colonie in London*, pp. 47–9; Anglo-German Publishing Company, *Deutsche Kolonie in England*, pp. 23–4; *The Times*, 14 July 1882.
   34. Anglo-German Publishing Company, *Deutsche Kolonie in England*, pp. 22–3.

Christ's Church in Kensington held its first service in 1904. Its congregation originated in that which had used the Royal Chapel and had found itself 'homeless' following Edward VII's decision to close down the latter in 1901. Christ's Church had connections with St Mark's, a mission church in Fulham, administered through the Women's Church Mission Society which was supported by Baron Schröder, and with the aim of gathering together the Germans of southwest London in order to care for their spiritual needs.[35]

A final London Protestant parish which should be considered is the Evangelical Church in Islington founded in 1857 with an initial congregation of 100, which subsequently expanded. This church aimed at attracting the German community in Islington and North London generally, which by the late 1850s totalled 4,000 and for whom no church existed, meaning that people either had to travel several miles or participate, from 1857, in the 'German Public Service held every Sabbath morning, in the small room underneath Islington Chapel' and 'conducted first by German Students from the Church Missionary College in Islington.' An appeal for funding, which also reached individual German state governments, was required for the construction of a church building, as the petty-bourgeois community of clerks, governesses and artisans could not raise the funds alone.[36]

In 1860 the Church organised a Women's Committee. It also developed one of the major London German Schools, established in 1862 as a Sunday School for bible and hymn instruction, and developing in 1872 into a more independent institution offering instruction in a wider range of subjects. The school began with twenty pupils but by 1881 this figure had risen to 68. By the early-1890s the total number of children had reached 96 but this had fallen back to 71 by 1904. As many as twenty per cent received free tuition. Interestingly, not all the children consisted of Protestants; there were also Jews and Roman Catholics.[37]

35. Ibid., p. 25; Schönberger, *Festschrift*, pp. 61–2; *75 Jahre Deutsche Evangelische Christuskirche zu London*, Hampton Hill, Middlesex, 1980.

36. Bremer Staatsarchiv, 2T 6t 4c, 'Appeal for Contributions towards the fund for the erection of a German Evangelical Church in Hatton Street, Cross Street, Islington, London, 1861'; Dorgeel, *Deutsche Colonie in London*, p. 46; Anglo-German Publishing Company, *Deutsche Kolonie in England*, p. 24.

37. Dorgeel, *Deutsche Colonie in London*, pp. 56–9; Greater London Record Office, P83/PET2/209, German School Islington; BA, Potsdam, AA, 38979, 'Twelfth Annual Report of the German School at Islington, 1884'; 'Twenty-Second Annual Report of the German School at Islington, 1894'; 'Zweiunddreissigster Jahresbericht der Deutschen Schule in Islington, 1904'; BA Potsdam, 38987, 'Bericht des Geheimen Regierungsrats Professor Dr W Münch über eine Reise nach England, 1904'; Bremer Staatsarchiv, 2T 6t 4d, 'Subscription List in Aid of the German School in Islington in Connection with the German Evangelical Church, 1874'.

Also in the capital, mention should be made of the German Mission Among the German Poor in London, originally established in 1849. It described its aims in the following way:

> The object of the Mission is twofold, first with regard to adults, to visit the poor in their houses, especially the sick, to offer them kind christian advice and the comforts of the Word of God, to sell, lend or distribute among them Christian books and Bibles, to gather them also in weekly Bible classes specially suited for the poor, and to induce them, if possible, to attend any of the German Protestant churches, and to lead a Christian life...
>
> The second object of the Mission embraces the education of the German poor, chiefly in the East of London for which a day-school has been established...in Leman-street Whitechapel.[38]

The first activity received some attention in the previous chapter, which indicated that during the years 1874–1900 the number of annual domestic visits totalled several thousand. In 1874 there were 4,768 visits for London as a whole, but in 1900 there were more than 3,000 in the Canning Town and Soho districts alone. In the earlier part of the century most activity had taken place in the East End, but as Germans settled in new parts of London without any churches, the missionaries followed them. In 1900, for instance, in addition to the 'City Mission' in Whitechapel, there also existed 'Mission Stations' in Canning Town, Deptford and Charlton, Soho, Fulham, and Walthamstow, together with a missionary to German sailors.[39]

The committee of the Mission consisted of the pastors of the German churches in London, together with prominent London Germans including the German Consul. Initially, finance came primarily from the churches and from subscriptions, but from the mid-1880s financial support on a substantial scale also arrived directly from German sources in the form of grants from members of German royal families, as well as from collections in German cities, such as the one which took place in Hamburg in 1885.[40]

The school connected with the Mission, located in Whitechapel, resembled the other London German schools in various ways including

38. Bremer Staatsarchiv, 2T 6t 4d, 'The Twenty-Fifth Annual Report of the Mission Among the German Poor in London, and the School in Connection with It, 1874'.

39. Bremer Staatsarchiv, 2T 6t 4d, 'The Twenty-Fifth Annual Report of the Mission Among the German Poor in London, and the School in Connection with It, 1874'; BA Potsdam, AA, 38983, 'Jahresbericht über die Deutsche evangelische Stadt- und Seemansmission und Armenschulen für das Jahr 1900'.

40. BA, Potsdam, AA, 38981, 'The Thirty-Third Annual Report of the Mission Among the German Poor in London and the School in Connection With It, 1882'; 'Jahresbericht über die deutsche evangelische Stadt- und Seemansmission und Armenschule in London für das Jahr 1888'.

Ethnic Organisations

the rise and fall in the number of pupils, which rose from between 60 and 80 in the original Sunday School during the early 1850s to a peak of 206 in 1872, almost the same year in which St George's School reached its greatest number. Subsequently, the figure fluctuated around 150 during the 1880s, despite the attraction of 'the increasing number of Board Schools, which are for many families nearer at hand.' However, 'the parents still give the preference to a school in which their children are instructed in their native tongue and well-grounded in religious subjects, so as to be able to join the preparatory classes for confirmation.' Returning to the Mission School, its numbers also fell at the end of the nineteenth century, to 90 in 1894 and to 60 in 1899, when it closed down. By this time another Mission School had also come into existence in Canning Town, with 50 pupils.[41]

Outside the capital no German churches existed before the middle of the nineteenth century because of a lack of German population. In some cases, such as Liverpool, Hull and Sunderland, the foundation of a congregation occurred partly because of a temporary passage of sailors or transmigrants, but in others, such as Manchester and Bradford, more permanent settlement provided the stimulus, as happened in London.

We can begin with Manchester, which had the most vital religious activity outside London. By the end of the nineteenth century three German churches existed in Manchester, divided on class and geographical lines despite the small size of the German community. The foundation of the first two occurred in the mid-1850s; the more middle class of the two began to hold services in 1855, when 'German business men in Manchester grouped together as prospective elders of a German church.' Services took place in the Dutch Protestant Church in Wright Street, in the city centre, which the congregation purchased in 1871. Until the First World War about eleven christenings and three marriages took place every year, although as the wealthier Germans began to move into the suburbs the size of the congregation declined. Nevertheless, in 1912 the congregation still totalled approximately 200, while the school connected with the Church attracted fifty pupils. A building which acted as a parish centre held activities which attracted as many as 1,000 par-

41. Schöll, *Geschichte der deutschen evangelischen Kirchen in England*, p. 61; BA, Potsdam, AA, 38981, 'The Thirty-Third Annual Report of the Mission Among the German Poor in London and the School in Connection With It, 1882'; 'The Thirty-Fifth Annual Report of the Mission Among the German Poor in London and the School in Connection With It, 1884'; 'Siebenunddreisigsten Jahresbericht über die Deutsche Stadtmission und Armenschule in London, 1886'; 'Jahresbericht über die deutsche evangelische Stadt- und Seemansmission und Armenschule in London fuer das Jahr 1888'; BA, Potsdam, 38982, 'Jahresbericht über die deutsche evangelische Stadt- und Seemansmission und Armenschule in London für das Jahr 1895'; Schönberger, *Festschrift*, p. 84.

ticipants on some evenings, including waiters. The Church also made some provision for the poor Germans of Manchester. As with the London congregations, its funding came through a variety of sources consisting of collections and subscriptions from Britain and Germany.[42]

The German Mission Church also came into existence in Manchester during the 1850s, aimed at people lower down the social scale. Josef Steinthal was its first Pastor, holding the position for thirty-five years. Initially Steinthal faced financial problems, but by 1874 the position had improved mainly due to 'the income from regular pledges by 367 German and English firms and individuals', which amounted to nearly £350. By this time the congregation had moved from its original site, 'a rented room at No. 6 John Dalton Street, near Deansgate', to a new building in Cheetham where it attracted a congregation of three hundred, large by the standards of any other German congregation in nineteenth-century Britain. Steinthal also established a day school for destitute children with the modest aim of bringing the pupils 'to a point where the boys could work as errand boys or in warehouses and the girls could become housemaids in German or English middle-class families.' But by the end of the nineteenth century the Mission School had ceased to exist, like many similar institutions in London.[43]

The third German Church in Manchester came into existence in the north of the city in 1896 through the initiative of T. R. Waltenberg, a Church of England Vicar who allowed German services in his church every Sunday afternoon, although the congregation moved to an Anglican School. By 1912 services attracted an average of 59 people. Despite its small size the church carried out philanthropic activities, including a school with twelve pupils, visits to the sick, and a waiters' mission.[44]

As mentioned previously, the origins of the German church in Liverpool lay in the temporary visits to the city by German sailors at the beginning of the nineteenth century. Their spiritual needs received attention from 1821 through the Liverpool Seaman's Friend Society and

---

42. Institut für Auslandsbeziehungen, Stuttgart, Curt Friese, 'Some Thoughts on the History of the Germans and their Church Communities in Manchester'; BA, Coblenz, R57 neu, 1065/12, 'Bericht der Deutschen Protestantischen Gemeinde zu Manchester über das Jahr vom 1. April 1912 zum 31. Maerz 1913.'

43. Institut für Auslandsbeziehungen, Stuttgart, Curt Friese, 'Some Thoughts on the History of the Germans and their Church Communities in Manchester'; N. J. Frangopulo, 'Foreign Communities in Victorian Manchester', *Manchester Review*, vol. 10, 1965, p. 201.

44. Institut für Auslandsbeziehungen, Stuttgart, Curt Friese, 'Some Thoughts on the History of the Germans and their Church Communities in Manchester'; BA, Coblenz, R57 neu, 1065/14, 'Jahresbericht über die Deutsche Evangelische Gemeindarbeit zu Nord-Manchester, 1912'.

Bethel Union, which held services for them. The organisation also built a guest house and offered instruction to the children of sailors. Services initially took place on a ship in the dock, but by the mid-1840s the need for a more permanent home increased due both to the influx of transmigrants and to the development of a more stable German community. Services began to take place in St Michael's Church in 1846; during the same year another place of worship became vacant, at a cost of £100 rent per year, and the congregation moved here with support from the Bishop of Chester, who ordained a pastor to conduct services. The congregation moved yet again in 1849 when it purchased a Church in St Thomas Building, with money gathered from the usual sources including the Prussian Consul, members of the Royal Family and English and German businessmen, following a tour of the country by the pastor.[45]

In 1849 about 120 people participated in church services, although this figure increased during the following years due to the fact that transmigrants participated, reaching a peak of 4,000 in 1852. The Church remained on the same site until 1871, when it moved to its final home of Newington Chapel in Renshaw Street, formerly used by a mixed nonconformist congregation. The new building, purchased with support from German merchants in Liverpool and other British cities, had a more central location and Evangelical Lutheran Rites could be celebrated in it. In comparison with congregations in other parts of Britain the one in Liverpool remained large, exceeding 300 for much of the late Victorian and Edwardian years, although falling just before the outbreak of the First World War to between 250 and 300. The congregation also came from a wider social mix, as well as including transmigrants.[46]

The church in Liverpool developed a wide range of parish activities in the form of missionary and educational work. The city mission began in the year 1862 with the aim of reaching poorer Germans throughout Liverpool and offering them instruction in the form of, for instance, bible classes. The mission also had contact with sailors and visited homes used by German migrants, including those of German descent who moved from eastern Europe in the late nineteenth and early twentieth centuries. Later in the century a Women's

45. Liverpool Foreigners Mission, *Brief Narrative of the Past Efforts and of the Opening Prospects of the Mission*, Liverpool, 1847, pp. 4–6; 'Geschichte der deutschen evangelischen Kirchgemeinden in Grossbritannien', *Monatschrift für Innere Mission*, vol. 7, 1887, pp. 410–11; A. E. Rosenkranz, *Geschichte der deutschen evangelischen Kirche zu Liverpool*, Stuttgart, 1921, pp. 15, 43.

46. Henry Peet, *The German Church in Renshaw Street Liverpool*, Liverpool, 1935, p. 66; Rosenkranz, *Geschichte der deutschen evangelischen Kirche zu Liverpool*, pp. 49, 57, 105, 137, 155, 180; 'Geschichte der deutschen evangelischen Kirchgemeinden in Grossbritannien', p. 417.

Mission helped in the gathering of clothes for the needy, while by
the 1890s a German Christian Waiters' Society had developed. The
establishment of a genuine school occurred in 1865, which offered
afternoon instruction in bible study, German language and singing to
about seventy pupils, in German only. The school moved with the
church to Renshaw Street but in 1888 another school came into existence, using the same teacher who taught there in the morning. The
total number of pupils reached a peak of 98 in 1885, and then fell
back before reaching another peak of 103 in 1912. Throughout the
course of the nineteenth century finance came from a combination of
yearly subscriptions, especially from wealthy Liverpool Germans,
collections and interest on capital which helped to fund the church
activities.[47]

These activities touched virtually all sections of Liverpool German
society, crossing classes, ages and length of stay. In reality, these groups
would rarely have come together except in church services, although
even here the activities of the mission meant that many poorer Germans
would not attend the main church as they could receive religious
instruction in their locality. Nevertheless, the importance of the church
in the city seems fundamentally clear, acting almost as a central organ
for the maintenance of German culture through the medium of religion
for the different sections of German Liverpool, catering to what it perceived as the needs of each. It remained typical of many of the German
churches in Britain, although the range of its activities and the number
of people it touched singles it out from many of the smaller provincial
and London churches.

The German Lutheran Church in Hull resembles the one in Liverpool
in its foundation during the 1840s, partly to cater for visiting German
sailors and transmigrants. Initially services took place in a lecture hall
belonging to the Sailor's Institute, but these moved to Bethesda Chapel
in 1855 and changed location again to a newly-built church in 1910.
Because of the size of the German community in Hull in comparison
with the one in Liverpool, its congregation remained much smaller than
Liverpool's, averaging no more than 100 throughout the period under
consideration; it pursued a similar range of missionary and educational
activities with, for instance, a Women's Society. At the end of the nineteenth century the church had both a Sunday and daily school attached
to it, attracting 50 and 25 children respectively in 1897, which had
changed to 33 and 32 by 1903. By the 1880s there was more representa-
tion across class lines at the services in the congregation in Hull, which

47. Rosenkranz, *Geschichte der deutschen evangelischen Kirche zu Liverpool*, pp.
59–202; BA, Coblenz, R57 neu, 1064/12, 'Fünfzig Jahre Deutsche Kirche in Liverpool,
1887'.

consisted of businessmen, artisans, pork butchers and refugees, because of the smaller size of the German community.[48]

The number of Germans in the northeast was smaller, but even so German church services began to develop in the second half of the nineteenth century, again partly because of the visits of German sailors. Sunderland acted as something of a starting point, as services began to take place there from the 1860s to cater for pork butchers and travelling musicians. Following more general support from the native community, the Lord Mayor laid the foundation stone for a church in 1872. Although it almost faced closure during the early 1880s, being saved by collections in Sunderland and a grant from Baron Schröder, it survived until 1914. Its first minister, Pastor Harms, initially held responsibility not just for Sunderland but also for services in South Shields, Newcastle, Hartlepool and Middlesbrough. The last two developed into an independent congregation in 1884. The congregation in Newcastle followed a similar path in 1890, and by 1913 had developed a school and Women's Society. An independent German Church also came into existence in South Shields.[49]

Bradford represents something of a unique case amongst the cities with German communities in nineteenth-century Britain, in that it possessed both a German church and a German synagogue. We can deal with the former here, which actually did not come into existence as a congregation until 1877. In 1882 the new congregation purchased a former school in Great Horton Road, which it transformed into a church. Financial support came not just from local Germans but also from the German Kaiser and the King of Bavaria. The mainly middle-class congregation initially totalled between 70 and 80 but increased to 165 by 1889 and declined to 49 in 1913, by which time only 14 pupils attended the church school. The Women's Committee also had a lack of work in comparison with similar bodies in other parts of the country, assisting just twelve children and six women in 1890, which may reflect the pre-

48. James Joseph Sheehan, *General and Concise Description of the Town and Port of Kingston-Upon-Hull*, London, 1864, p. 439; Deutsches Kirchen Verein, *Bericht des Deutschen Kirchen-Vereins in Hull*, Hull, 1845; BA, Potsdam, AA, 38972, 'Jahresbericht der deutschen lutherischen Kirche in Hull über das Jahr 1897'; BA, Potsdam, AA, 38974, 'Jahresbericht der deutschen lutherischen Kirche in Hull über das Jahr 1903'; Bremer Staatsarchiv, 2T 6t 4b, 'Bericht des Deutschen Kirchen-Vereins in Hull, Februar, 1845'; 'Geschichte der deutschen evangelischen Kirchgemeinden in Grossbritannien', pp. 425–31; Anglo-German Publishing Company, *Deutsche Kolonie in England*, pp. 68–9; Schöll, *Geschichte der deutschen evangelischen Kirchen*, pp. 53–4.

49. Anglo-German Publishing Company, *Deutsche Kolonie in England*, pp. 71–3; BA, Potsdam, AA, 38969: 'New-German Evangelical Church and School in Sunderland'; extract from the *North and South Shields Gazette*, 26 November 1872; 'Report of the German Evangelical Church and Mission in Sunderland and Neighbourhood 1882–83'; BA, Potsdam, AA, 38976, 'Annual Report of the German Evangelical Church at Middlesbrough and Sailors Mission for the Hartlepools and District'.

dominantly petty bourgeois and middle-class nature of the German population in Bradford and the lack of poor.[50]

Of other German Protestant congregations in Britain, that in Edinburgh came into existence in 1863 at least partly due to the efforts of John Blumenreich, a converted Jew who became its first minister. Membership of the church stood at just 40 in 1865 but Blumenreich made strenuous efforts to increase this number through missionary work involving visits to the Germans throughout the city as well as to hundreds of ships every year, not just in Edinburgh but also as far away as Dundee. Blumenreich had further 'adopted a plan whereby I reach Germans scattered over Scotland, by sending them useful books and religious periodicals.' He received support from both local and German individuals and companies, including the Royal Family of Hesse. In 1885 the new Pastor of the church, C. Wagner, continued Blumenreich's energetic activities, making 73 journeys to Glasgow and visiting 373 ships in the Firth of Forth as well as seeking out the 'many sick and poor Germans in the infirmaries and throughout Edinburgh'. The church continued into the early twentieth century, by which time it had developed separate societies for men, women and youths, together with a school with an attendance of 33 in 1906. By the start of the twentieth century independent congregations also existed in Glasgow and Dundee.[51]

In Birmingham a congregation did not develop until just before the outbreak of the First World War. Two services in 1912 and 1913 conducted by Pastor Martin Kramer of Manchester attracted as many as 75 people, by which time a committee had received assurances from the *Evangelisches Ober-Kirchenrat* in Berlin that it would pay the salary of Rudolf Hartman as curate. Services took place on a regular basis, with an average attendance of 50 people, from October 1913, although problems existed with the distance involved in travelling to services in the city centre YMCA, while many Germans had married English women and attended the same churches as their wives.[52]

The above survey only reveals part of the picture of German Protestant life in Victorian and Edwardian England, having focused

50. BA, Coblenz, R57 neu, 1064/3, 'Zur Errinerung an die Feier des 50-jährigen Bestehens der Deutschen Gemeinde Bradford, 1927'; *Hundert Jahre Evangelische Kirche Bradford-Huddersfield-Leeds*, 1877–1977 (n.d.); Michael Pratt, 'The Influence of the Germans on Bradford' (unpublished BA thesis, Margaret Macmillan College, Bradford, 1971), p. 60.
51. BA, Potsdam, AA, 38965: 'Third Annual Report of the German Church and Mission for Edinburgh and Leith, 1865'; 'Twenty-third Annual Report of the German Church of Edinburgh and Leith and the Coast Mission Connected with It, 1885'; Anglo-German Publishing Company, *Deutsche Kolonie in England*, pp. 65–7. For Edinburgh specifically see *Deutsch-Evangelisch im Auslande*, vol. 6, 1906, pp. 390–2.
52. Friedeborg L. Müller, *The History of the German Lutheran Congregations in England, 1900–1950*, Frankfurt, 1987, pp. 33–7.

upon the most important congregations. Any attempt to measure the precise number of German Lutheran and Evangelical churches during the whole course of the nineteenth century would prove difficult because of the temporary nature of some of them. Nevertheless, we do have a snapshot from 1913, which lists services in fifteen locations in London and thirteen outside the capital, nearly all of which had missionary or educational activities connected with them and in many cases had both. In some of these cases one minister or priest served more than a single congregation; in 1914, 26 German pastors held positions in Great Britain.[53]

Any consideration of German ethnic organisations in nineteenth-century Britain must clearly recognise the importance of the foundations of the Protestant churches which sprang up on the initiative of either local English clerics or, in many cases, an individual German, as in Manchester and Edinburgh. Finance came from a wide variety of sources both local and national, British and German, which contributed to the fact that such a large number of cities could support German Lutheran congregations. The foundation of a church had almost a symbolic value, indicating that a German community had established itself in a particular location and could raise the necessary funds to support a place of worship. The building of German churches both reinforced German ethnicity and indicated the links between middle-class English and German society through the support by the former for the latter. Participation in many of the churches, especially if we also take into account missionary and educational activities, remained high and it seems unlikely that any other aspect of German culture in Victorian and Edwardian Britain touched so many people.

The growth of German Protestant religion in Britain eventually led to the development of a central organisation. Links had existed between pastors in both the north of England and in London[54] during the second half of the nineteenth century, with the former group meeting from 1878 in Bradford when only three members participated. Subsequently, the location changed every year, but the number who took part did not reach double figures until 1898. By this time the Conference of German Evangelical Pastors in Great Britain had come into existence, founded in 1887. This became the Association of German Evangelical Congregations in Great Britain and Ireland in 1904. It aimed at bringing together the German churches of the British Isles to work collectively

53. BA, Coblenz, R57 neu, *Kirchlicher Anzeiger zum Gemeinde-Boten*, October 1912; ibid., p. 31.

54. The organisation considered by Karl Heinz Voigt, 'Georg Gottfried Triviranus: Mitgründer der Evangelischen Allianz in London', *Hospitum Ecclesiae*, vol. 8, 1973, pp. 66–80, was not concerned with the London churches, but with an international evangelical alliance.

for the purpose of supporting German evangelical religion in Britain. Despite its name, members of Lutheran congregations participated, as did pastors of seamen's missions in Britain, so that its final conference in Sunderland before the outbreak of the First World War attracted over seventy delegates. Nevertheless, it had little real power or influence.[55]

As the introduction to this chapter stressed, a fundamental characteristic of German immigrant life in nineteenth-century Britain concerned its variety, particularly in religion. As well as Catholicism and Judaism, there were also nonconformist congregations in London. Wesleyans formed the major group, similar in size to the eighteenth-century Brethren, counting no more than several hundred adherents but possessing four places of worship by 1914 in Commercial Road, Canning Town, Fulham and Soho with 220 members and three Sunday schools. The development of Wesleyanism owed its origin to the missionary efforts of English adherents of this sect from the 1860s. The first Church opened in Canning Town in 1893.[56]

The German Catholics in London also developed connections with English Catholics during the nineteenth century. For instance, Bishop Poynter played a major role at the opening of St Bonifacius' Church in 1809. Later in the century, Cardinal Edward Manning, who took particular interest in Irish immigrants, played a significant role in the construction of the fourth church used by the St Bonifacius congregation, while Cardinal Herbert Vaughan viewed the German Catholics as a solid part of the Catholic population of London during the 1890s.[57] It seems likely that Catholics constituted the second largest German reli-

55. Müller, *History of German Lutheran Congregations*, pp. 25–31; P. Götz, 'Geschichte der Konferenz deutscher Pastoren in Grossbritannien', *Deutsch-Evangelisch im Auslande*, vol. 8, 1908, pp. 299–303; BA, Potsdam, AA, 38964, 'Satzungen des Verbandes der deutschen evangelischen Gemeinden in Grossbritannien und Irland, festgestellt zu Liverpool, den 11. Oktober 1904'; BA, Coblenz, R57 neu, 'Verband der deutschen evangelischen Gemeinden in Grossbritannien und Irland: Verhandlungen des V. Gemeindetages am 13. und 14. Mai 1914'.

56. *West Ham Guardian*, 19 August 1893; Anglo-German Publishing Company, *Deutsche Kolonie in England*, pp. 25–7; and Dorgeel, *Deutsche Colonie in London*, pp. 49–50.

57. Georg Timpe, *Die Deutsche St Bonifatius-Mission in London, 1809–1909*, London, 1909, pp. 22, 46, 59. F. X. Kärcher, *Bericht über die Mission der deutschen Katholiken in London*, Düsseldorf, 1869, p. 4, claims that Catholics from Baden, Westfalia and the Rhineland made up one quarter of the Germans in London in 1861. 'London und die deutsche Mission: II. Die deutsche Mission', *Katholische Bewegung*, vol. 18, 1881, p. 147, claims that ten per cent of those treated in the German Hospital in London consisted of Catholics. The first part of this two-part article, 'London und die deutsche Mission: I. London', *Katholische Bewegung*, vol. 17, 1880, pp. 546–54, basically describes a journey to London, although the anonymous author mentions a meeting with Cardinal Manning. The efforts of Manning amongst the Irish receive attention in Inglis, *Churches and the Working Classes*, chapter 3; and Lees, *Exiles of Erin*, pp. 173, 210.

gious group in Britain, although the existence of St Bonifacius' Church alone may argue against this. However, Germans may have attended some of the Irish Catholic churches, as nineteenth-century reports on the German Catholics mention the fact that some of them joined Protestant congregations.[58] Furthermore, the congregation at St Bonifacius included non-Germans until 1875.[59]

During the course of the nineteenth century, as mentioned above, St Bonifacius occupied four different buildings. The move from Great St Thomas Apostle Street in the City of London to Union Street in Whitechapel took place in 1859–62, with financial support from wealthy German Catholics in London as well as from the Pope, the King of Bavaria and the Austrian Emperor, together with an annual grant from the Ludwig Missions Verein in Munich. During the period of the move the congregation met in Ludgate Circus, its second home. The fourth church lay on the same site as the third, involving the erection of a new building opened in 1875 at the initiative of Cardinal Manning, who laid the foundation stone and played a large role in the gathering of money from English and Irish sources. Finance also came from Bavaria.[60]

Throughout the course of the nineteenth century the German Catholic priests, like the pastors of the Lutheran and Evangelical churches, made efforts to seek out poor members of their faith throughout the capital, through visits to hospitals as well as to hundreds of individual Germans. The size of the congregation is difficult to establish with accuracy at any one time. In 1836 there were 600 members of the church while in 1867 it carried out 190 baptisms, although only 90 were Germans.[61]

By the start of the nineteenth century St Bonifacius had developed a large number of activities. Its educational activities date from the 1840s, when a school with two classes came into existence. During the 1850s six nuns from a sisterhood in Bavaria took over its educational role, and the same order continued in this role until the First World War. The number of pupils in 1868 totalled 490, but by 1909 the figure had fallen to 180. By this time the church also had seven societies in connection with it, which were aimed at female servants, the support of families, the maintenance of the faith amongst families, and social activities encompassing women, businessmen and young men.[62]

58. Kärcher, Bericht, pp. 12–13; 'London und die deutsche Mission: II', pp. 158–9.
59. 'London und die deutsche Mission: II', p. 150.
60. The changes of location can be traced in Timpe, *Deutsche St Bonifatius Mission.*
61. 'London und die deutsche Mission: II', pp. 150, 153.
62. Timpe, *Deutsche St Bonifatius Mission*, pp. 41, 63–70; BA, Potsdam, AA, 38975, letter of the Generalkonsulat des deutschen Reichs to Reichskanzler Dr von Bethmann Hollweg, 3 February 1910; BA Potsdam, 38987, 'Bericht des Geheimen Regierungsrats. Professor Dr W. Münch über eine Reise nach England, 1904'; P. Beda Kleinschmidt, *Auslanddeutschtum und Kirche*, vol. 1, Münster, 1930, p. 300; Charles Booth, *Life and Labour of the People in London*, 3rd series, vol. 2, London, 1902, pp. 40–1.

In its missionary activities, its connections with the English Catholic Church and the raising of funds through a combination of German and English sources, the German Catholic Church in London strongly resembles the Protestant congregations which existed throughout the country. Most significantly, despite connections with the Archbishopric of London, the German Catholics did remain a distinct entity, as they did in New York.[63]

German Jews in Britain, however, did not maintain the same level of independence as Protestants and Catholics. The process of assimilation, which we have identified in the above two groups, took place to a greater extent among German Jews. We can only identify two synagogues established by German Jews during the course of the nineteenth century. The main reason for this may actually lie in the small number of Jews of German origin who made their way to Britain during the course of the nineteenth century, although in other cases middle class Jews consciously became Unitarians as part of an assimilatory process. We should recognise an additional complicating factor here, in that for devout German Jews a Jewish ethnicity needed to be superimposed upon their German ethnicity so that they had 'allegiances' to both Jewishness and Germaness.

Only two congregations of purely German Jews were established during the course of the nineteenth century. The Dundee congregation, based on middle-class merchants, came into existence in 1874;[64] the Bradford congregation was formed a year earlier. The predominantly middle-class German Jews of Bradford had previously worshipped in private houses, but the growth of the community to between 200 and 300 meant the requirement for a rabbi, who arrived from Germany in March 1873 in the person of Joseph Strauss. Initially the congregation totalled just 40 and a Synagogue did not come into existence until 1881. The Bradford congregation also conducted religious classes, which were attended by the poet Humbert Wolfe, the son of an Italian Sephardic mother and an Ashkenzi German father, as a child. Here, 'The preacher was paid less than the clerk in a warehouse, though he had a large family; and he had always to translate his thoughts from German into English before giving them utterance.' Significantly, Wolfe pointed out that his parents 'attended the synagogue only on the New Year and Atonement Days', and that there was 'plainly no enthu-

63. Dolan, *Immigrant Church*, pp. 68–86.
64. C. C. Aronsfeld, 'German Jews in Dundee', *Jewish Chronicle*, 20 November 1953, p. 15.

siasm for the faith' amongst the Bradford Jewish community more generally.[65]

But despite the fact that German Jewish immigrants may have founded just two synagogues, many prominent Jewish 'functionaries' in nineteenth-century Britain had been born in Germany, most notably Nathan Adler, who became Chief Rabbi in 1845.[66] German Jews played a part in the development of places of worship elsewhere in the country, but only in conjunction with Jews from other parts of Europe, and with English Jews descended from eighteenth-century immigrants. It is difficult to identify a mixed Jewish congregation which maintained German culture because Jewishness in this case became far more important than remaining German, unlike the case with the Churches outlined above where the German and Lutheran or Evangelical aspects remained inextricable, especially as so many of the schools offered instruction at least partially in German.

Examples of mixed congregations in which Germans played a role included the Park Place Synagogue in Manchester, which opened in 1858 and included 29 Germans amongst the founding membership of 46. German Jews in Manchester had also played a part in the formation of the Synagogue in Halliwell Street in 1825.[67] In Birmingham, however, German Jews did not continue to practice their religion, as 'their names appear on no synagogue lists.'[68]

In fact, there was even open hostility during the early nineteenth century between German Jews and those of English origin, linked to the fact that most of the German immigrants fell into the more 'modern' reform Judaism, in comparison with Anglo-Jewry, which practised a

65. M. R. Heilbron, 'Bradford', in Aubrey Newman (ed.), *Provincial Jewry in Victorian England*, London, 1975; C. C. Aronsfeld, 'German Jews in Nineteenth Century Bradford', *Yorkshire Archaeological Journal*, vol. 53, 1981, pp. 114–15; Humbert Wolfe, *Now a Stranger*, London, 1933, p. 128; Norman Bentwich, 'Humbert Wolfe: Poet and Civil Servant', *Menorah Journal*, vol. 36, 1943, pp. 34–6.

66. Todd M. Endelman, *Radical Assimilation in English Jewish History, 1656–1945*, Bloomington and Indianapolis, 1990, pp. 127–8; H. D. Schmidt, 'Chief Rabbi Nathan Marcus Adler (1803–1890): Jewish Educator from Germany', *Leo Baeck Institute Yearbook*, vol. 7, 1962, pp. 289–311; Marcus N. Adler, *The Adler Family*, London, 1909, p. 5.

67. Williams, *The Making of Manchester Jewry*, Manchester, 1985 reprint, pp. 262, 350–1; Frangopulo, 'Foreign Communities in Victorian Manchester', p. 195; Neville J. Laski, 'The History of Manchester Jewry', *Manchester Review*, vol. 7, 1956, p. 374.

68. Zoë Josephs, *Birmingham Jewry 1794–1914*, Birmingham, 1980, p. 24.

'middle-of-the-road' orthodoxy.[69] Significantly, the synagogues in Bradford, Dundee, and Park Place in Manchester catered for reform congregations. But the desire of some middle-class German Jews to assimilate became so strong that they did not wish to continue the religion of their birth, and chose instead Unitarianism, a Christian ideology which attracted many of the newcomers both because it allowed the development of connections with other members of the upper bourgeoisie in provincial cities, notably Manchester and Nottingham, and also because its theology remained relaxed. Other German Jews embraced Anglicanism and even Catholicism, as in the case of Sir Ernest Cassel who adopted his wife's religion.[70]

In short, the role of religion in maintaining a German ethnicity amongst Jews remains small in comparison with its function amongst Catholics and Protestants, because of the variety of complicating factors outlined above. In contrast to other German religious groups in Britain, many Jews preferred to abandon their religion altogether rather than to establish new reform congregations. But this may have as much to do with other factors not considered above, such as the availability of funding from a wide variety of German and British sources for the Protestants and Catholics, because of their closeness to the dominant religions in both Britain and in Germany. A more important factor is the far smaller number of German Jews who made their way to Britain during the nineteenth century and who could consequently not maintain synagogues in the way that the much larger number of Protestants could support churches in cities throughout Britain. However, while German Jews may have been prepared to dispense with their Jewishness, the same was not always true of their German ethnicity which they maintained by joining some of the middle-class cultural bodies discussed below.

69. For discussions about Reform and Orthodox Jewry in nineteenth century Britain see, Julius Carlebach, 'The Impact of German Jews on Anglo-Jewry – Orthodoxy, 1850–1950' and Albert H. Friedlander, 'The German Influence on Progressive Judaism in Great Britain', both in Werner E. Mosse, et al (eds), *Second Chance: Two Centuries of German-speaking Jews in the United Kingdom*, Tübingen, 1991, pp. 405–35; Stephen Sharot, 'Religious Change in Native Orthodoxy in London, 1870–1914: The Synagogue Service', *Jewish Journal of Sociology*, vol. 15, 1973, pp. 57–78; Williams, *Manchester Jewry, passim.*

70. Endelman, *Radical Assimilation*, pp. 119–27; C. C. Aronsfeld, 'German Jews in Victorian England', *Leo Baeck Yearbook*, vol. 7, 1962, pp. 321–4; Aronsfeld, 'German Jews in Nottingham', *Association of Jewish Refugees Information*, December, 1955, p. 8; Pat Thane, 'Sir Ernest Joseph Cassel', *Dictionary of Business Biography*, vol. 1, London, 1984, p. 605.

Philanthropy

Having examined the fundamental role of German religion, particularly Christianity, in maintaining German ethnicity in nineteenth-century Britain, we can now move on to look at philanthropy through the formation of several bodies which cared specifically for the German sick and poor. We have already evidence of philanthropy in the activities of the churches. Philanthropic organisations played a fundamental role in holding German Britain together during the nineteenth century, indicating, as much as the foundation of the churches outlined above, the consciousness of middle-class Germans that their poorer countrymen also lived amongst them. Along with the churches, the purely philanthropic organisations played the most important role in the creation of a German 'community' in Victorian Britain, in the same way that the establishment of similar organisations brought together the different strands of British Jewry during the course of the eighteenth and nineteenth centuries.[71] However, it must again be stressed that these organisations fundamentally maintained class differences, as the rich gave while the poor received.

The first group of institutions to be included is charities. Three major charities existed, the Mission Amongst the German Poor in London, the German Society of Benevolence and the Society of Friends of Foreigners in Distress, each of which had important connections with the Protestant churches and each of which has received some attention in this work, especially the first. At this stage we will look simply at the financing and the activities of the other two, as well as mentioning some of the smaller German charities founded in the late nineteenth and early twentieth centuries.

The German Society of Benevolence originally came into existence in 1817 as an organisation for social meetings amongst German artisans and businessmen in the west of London, but soon afterwards established a fund to assist members who had fallen into distress. In 1848 the organisation decided to make the assistance of needy Germans its only task, and two years later it spent £260 on this task. During the course of the nineteenth century the annual sum dispensed increased significantly, to £2,488 by 1910. The numbers receiving assistance rose from 903 in 1871 to peaks of over 4,000 in the years 1890, 1894, and 1900–9. At the start of the twentieth century a prominent London German, the banker Ernst Schuster, became chairman. The number of friends and patrons rose from 300 in 1855 to 1,100 just before the outbreak of the First

---

71. These are outlined by V. D. Lipman, *A History of the Jews in Britain since 1858*, Leicester, 1990, pp. 31–4.

World War; each paid a sum of £1 per year. In addition the organisation received support from individuals such as Bruno Schröder, who gave £3,000 between 1903 and 1912, as well as from other German firms, cities and royal families. The charity offered assistance in a variety of ways, concerning itself especially with old people who could no longer work, to whom it gave 117 full and 260 provisional pensions in 1910, of at least £2 6s per week. The Society also sometimes sent people to the German Farm Colony in Libury Hall, which will be discussed below, but more often provided sums for short-term relief to individual applicants, totalling £1,574 in 1910. In other cases people received money in order to pay for their return to Germany.[72]

The Society of Friends of Foreigners in Distress was perhaps more important than the German Society of Benevolence because of its larger resources, although, as we have seen, these went towards the assistance of all immigrants in difficulty rather than only those who could speak German. In addition, its list of patrons included the rulers of Austria, Russia, Holland, Norway and Denmark. But its major support came from the usual sources of assistance for the Germans in London, the German princes and city senates, together with Anglo-German philanthropists, the British Royal Family, and senior British figures including the Archbishop of Canterbury, Lord Roseberry and Earl Granville in 1866, all of whom acted as vice-presidents: 'The directors are the pastors of the various German congregations and ten German laymen, while the executive committee are two-thirds Germans.'[73]

In its annual report of 1817 the Society described the type of assistance it offered, including medical and legal aid as well as aid in the search for employment, and donating sums of money for a return back to an immigrant's land of origin. Furthermore, as we have seen, it also provided pensions. The annual reports of the Society reveal the nature and extent of these activities. In 1828, for instance, the organisation supported 60 pensioners, who received £13 per year; this figure increased to 84 in 1866 and, dramatically, to 163 in 1884. In 1892 the Society supported 284 pensioners, including 197 Germans, and in 1866 the organisation had provided 'sick allowances' in 301 instances, while the amount of

72. BA, Coblenz, R57 neu, 'Jahresbericht der Deutschen Wohltätigkeitsgesellschaft in London, 1910–11'; *Londoner Deutsches Journal*, 25 August 1855; Anglo-German Publishing Company, *Deutsche Kolonie in England*, pp. 42–4; Schönberger, *Festschrift*, p. 101; Leopold Katscher, 'German Life in London', *Nineteenth Century*, vol. 21, 1887, p. 735; Schöll, *Geschichte der deutschen evangelischen Kirchen*, p. 56.

73. Society of Friends of Foreigners in Distress, *An Account of the Society of Friends of Foreigners in Distress for the Year 1817*, London, 1817, p. 9; *An Account of the Nature and Present State of the Society of Friends of Foreigners in Distress for the Year 1828*, London, 1828, pp. 11–13; *An Account of the Society of Friends of Foreigners in Distress for the Year 1866*, London, 1866, pp. 3–5; Katscher, 'German London', p. 735.

money it spent on casual relief increased from £1,084 to £1,392 between 1861 and 1866. In 1851 it further granted passage money in 108 cases in order to enable a return to country of origin, a figure which had increased to 172 by 1866. The organisation also provided money to almshouses.[74]

In addition to the London headquarters, branches of the Society of Friends of Foreigners in Distress were also established outside the capital in Hull, Leeds, Bradford, Huddersfield, Manchester and Liverpool. The first five of these appeared in the late 1840s 'as panic spread along the line of transmigration', because of the entry of Germans on their way to America via Hull and Liverpool. The branches cooperated in 'order to detect the worthless, and to confine their relief to really deserving subjects.' In its early years, the Manchester branch particularly concerned itself with assisting people to destinations outside its boundaries, either within Britain or on the continent, but later in the century it offered other forms of assistance.[75] The association in Hull came into existence in April 1847 following a meeting 'at the offices of F. Helmsing and Co', involving 'several foreign merchants'. This body wanted 'to afford timely assistance and support to really unfortunate and deserving foreigners, and to protect the public against the schemes of the worthless.' By 1864 the branch had offered assistance to almost 5,000 people either by providing fares or helping 'with lodgings, clothes, &c.'[76]

The Liverpool association came into existence in 1852. In 1864–5 it received 1,497 applications for relief, most of which came from Germans. For the period 1852–65, the total number of applications amounted to 14,359. Of those it helped in 1864–5, 214 received funding to make their way to destinations outside the city, in Britain, Continental Europe and North America. But the association was concerned not only with transmigrants, as it assisted 113 people with clothing and tools and also received 215 applications in cases of illness. It also helped the families of men who had settled in Liverpool but had then sailed to the USA. The Bradford organisation continued to exist until the early twentieth century, assisting 332 people in 1904, while a similar body for Edinburgh and Leith helped 429 aliens in 1905.[77]

74. Society of Friends of Foreigners in Distress, *Account of 1828*, pp. 14, 17; *Account of 1866*, pp. 20, 22, 24, 25, 27; *An Account of the Society of Friends of Foreigners in Distress for the Year 1892*, London, 1892, pp. xvi, 131; *Londoner Courier*, 6 February 1884; Schöll, *Geschichte der deutschen evangelischen Kirchen*, p. 55.
75. Williams, *Manchester Jewry*, p. 156; Gregory Anderson, *Victorian Clerks*, Manchester, 1976, pp. 63–4; Sheehan, *General and Concise Description of Hull*, p. 609.
76. Sheehan, ibid.
77. Bremer Staatsarchiv, 2T 6t 4c, 'Fourteenth Annual Report of the Liverpool Society of Friends of Foreigners in Distress, November 1865'. For Bradford and Leith see *Tables Relating to Emigrants and Immigrants to and from the United Kingdom in the Year 1904, and Report to the Board of Trade*, P.P., vol. 98, 1905, pp. 73–4.

From as early as 1850 the London branch of the Society of Friends of Foreigners in Distress had launched a fund to establish its own poor-houses. Despite the collection of £3,000, nothing seems to have materialised until the opening of the German Industrial and Farm Colony at Libury Hall in September 1900, with, once again, a substantial grant from the Schröder banking house. Although this institution had some connections with other German charities, in the sense that they offered some financial support and sent people to the colony, it remained independent, with an office in east London.[78]

Libury Hall, situated in Ware in Hertfordshire, thirty miles from London, had three aims. The first was 'To provide, under Christian influence, temporary work, shelter, board and lodging for German-speaking unemployed and destitute men of whatever creed, who are able and willing to work, thus giving them a fresh start in life'. The second was 'To assist those anxious to return to their home to earn sufficient money for that purpose.' The final aim was 'To suppress as far as possible habitual begging with its concomitant moral degradation'. In addition, a Pensioners' Home attached to the institution offered residence to German-speakers over sixty. Those in the Farm Colony had to work between ten and twelve hours per day, for which they obtained a small wage. Their numbers fluctuated between about fifty just after the foundation of the institution, and one hundred and fifty, shortly before the outbreak of the First World War. During the first five years a total of 2,500 men were admitted to the Colony, a figure which had risen further by the end of 1913 to 6,941 men, including 5,073 Germans.[79]

As well as Libury Hall, several other smaller German charities came into existence in the early twentieth century. These included the King Edward VII British-German Foundation, founded in 1911 with a grant of over £100,000 with the aim of assisting individual Germans and German charities in England, as well as enabling Germans to attend educational institutions in England. The Kaiser Wilhelm II Fund was established in 1905 and supported by John Henry and Bruno Schröder, who gave £50,000, and the German Emperor, who provided £250,000 'for the relief of needy and deserving persons of German nationality.'[80]

Libury Hall represented just one German charitable institution established by the German community during the course of the nineteenth

78. Schöll, *Geschichte der deutschen evangelischen Kirchen*, p. 55; Schönberger, *Festschrift*, p. 94; BA, Coblenz, R85 3100, 'Fourteenth Annual Report of the German Industrial and Farm Colony in England, 1913.'

79. *The Times*, 13 July 1906; *Morning Post*, 3 February 1909; BA, Coblenz, R85 3100, 'Fourteenth Annual Report of the German Industrial and Farm Colony in England, 1913'; Bremer Staatsarchiv, 2T 6t 4f, letter from W. Müller, 13 November 1901.

80. Charity Commission, London: File 227637, King Edward VII British-German Foundation; File 214283, Kaiser Wilhelm II Fund.

century. The most famous consisted of the German Hospital, which opened in 1845 in Hackney in order to assist the Germans who 'chiefly belong to the humbler classes of society' and of whom 'there are, at all times, hundreds amongst them in want of hospital relief', but who had difficulties in obtaining hospital care at English institutions.[81]

Consequently, a committee came into existence in 1843 for the purpose of establishing a hospital for the poor Germans of East London. It consisted of German businessmen, doctors and pastors of the German congregations of London, and had the support of the Prussian and British royal families. When a former infant asylum in Dalston was offered for sale in 1845 the committee purchased it, and the hospital opened on 15 October. The hospital originally had three dispensaries in London, one in the East End, one in the West End and the other in the hospital itself. Although the hospital simply took in Germans as in-patients, it also received English patients in cases of accidents. By 1911 it catered for 1,838 in-patients and 28,596 out-patients. Physicians had to have a command of the German language, and the nursing staff were all Germans. In 1864 the hospital expanded its accommodation in Dalston and in 1908 it opened a convalescent home in Hitchin in Hertfordshire, which could cater for forty-two patients. As with other German religious and philanthropic organisations in London, the German Hospital survived on donations on a massive scale obtained from a wide variety of British and German sources and through a range of activities.[82]

As well as the German Hospital two other residential institutions had come into existence by the First World War, the German Old People's Home and the German Orphanage. The first did not open until 1911, again with backing from Bruno Schröder. It lay in Clapton, near the Hamburg Lutheran Church, and admitted eleven people.[83] The German Orphanage had a longer history, founded in 1879 through the Kaiser Wilhelm Foundation, which was established to celebrate the golden wedding anniversary of Wilhelm I. The school was situated in Dalston; during its first year it accepted eight children but after a building exten-

---

81. BA, Coblenz, R57 neu, 1064/23, 'German Hospital, Dalston, NE, 1912'.

82. Maureen Neumann, 'An Account of the German Hospital in London from 1845 to 1948' (unpublished B.Ed thesis, University of London, 1971); Jurgen Pürschel, *Die Geschichte der German Hospital in London (1845 bis 1945)*, Münster, 1980, pp. 22–83; German Hospital London, *Concerning the Early History of the German Hospital, London. Remarks by Dr F. Parkes Weber at the Centenary Commemoration Tea, at the German Hospital, London, October 25th, 1945*, London, 1945; BA, Coblenz, R57 neu, 1064/23, 'German Hospital, Dalston, NE, 1912'; Hamburg Staatsarchiv, Hanseatische Residentur London, 132–1, I, 'German Hospital, Dalston, NE, 1911'.

83. Schönberger, *Festschrift*, pp. 70–1.

sion in 1890 it had forty beds. By the outbreak of the First World War a second home existed for children under six.[84]

At the other end of the educational scale, in social terms, there also existed four independent schools. Although hardly philanthropic themselves, because they catered for the sons and daughters of the German middle classes, we can consider them here because their foundation owed much to private German capital in London, resembling many of the institutions considered above. The first of the independent schools, the German-English Boys School, came into existence in 1878 in Brixton with the support of the wealthy German community in southwest London. For a yearly fee of twelve guineas during the mid-1890s, the pupils received instruction in a wide range of subjects including physics and chemistry, but the essential aim was to prepare pupils for careers in London business houses. The school catered for about seventy pupils from the age of seven and engaged up to ten teachers.[85] A similar institution existed for the instruction of the daughters of the German middle classes in London in the form of the 'German Higher Daughters School', first set up in 1862 and then re-established in 1893. It offered instruction in fifteen subjects in German and sixteen in English, and aimed at providing 'the children of Germans in England a thorough, intellectual, spiritual and character building education.' As this quote suggests the school catered for more than just girls, serving also as a boys preparatory school.[86]

The other two German independent schools in London came into existence shortly before the outbreak of the First World War, although by this time the Anglo-German Boys School no longer seems to have existed, as one account speaks of the foundation of the Deutsche Realschule in 1912 as filling a gap in the education of German secondary-school boys. Finance for this institution came from a collection which raised almost £2,000; it charged £15 a year for instruction, although it offered reductions. During its first session it attracted only six pupils but this had risen to nearly twenty by the following year. Like the Brixton institution it lay in southwest London, in Sydenham. The second German school founded during the early twentieth century, the Deutsches Pädagogium, actually lay outside London in Bexhill, on the

---

84. *Londoner Zeitung*, 3 July 1880; Schönberger, ibid., pp. 73–6; Dorgeel, *Deutsche Colonie in London*, pp. 34–7; Anglo-German Publishing Company, *Deutsche Kolonie in England*, pp. 50–1; Johannes Paul Müller, *Die Deutschen Schulen im Auslande*, Breslau, 1895, pp. 44–5.

85. Müller, ibid., pp. 33–6; Dorgeel, *Deutsche Colonie in London*, pp. 59–61; Emil Stargardt, *Handbuch der Deutschen in England*, Heilbronn, 1889, p. 17.

86. Dorgeel, ibid., p. 62; BA, Coblenz, R57 neu, 1064/45, 'Deutsche Höhere Töchterschule und Vorbereitungschule für Knaben'; Müller, ibid., pp. 45–6.

Kent coast. Most of its students were the sons of German 'officials' and businessmen, although the school also accepted pupils directly from Germany. The 28 students received intensive tuition in a wide range of subjects from religion to natural sciences. The yearly charge of 100 guineas covered not just academic instruction costs but also residence charges. Both the school in Sydenham and the one in Bexhill received support from the Deutscher Mittelschulverein für England, which aimed, as its name suggests, at supporting German secondary school education in England.[87]

Philanthropic support for schools from a wide variety of sources, combined with fees paid by parents, made possible the education of all sections of German society in Britain. The range of instruction available, from that in the institutions of the East End of London to that of the public school in Bexhill, indicates as much as any other aspect of German life in Britain the class divisions within German society. Clearly, education also played a fundamental role in the maintenance of German ethnicity in Victorian and Edwardian London, as thousands of children of German immigrants, born either in Germany or in England, must have passed through these institutions. Any attempt to provide exact numbers proves hazardous, but figures of attendance at the German schools do exist. For instance in 1885, perhaps the peak year of attendance, Johannes Paul Müller gave a figure of 1,331 for London,[88] while another count from 1902 probably underestimated the situation when it gave a national figure of 759 pupils.[89] A final estimate for the national total in 1906, of 1,247 pupils, may come closer to the truth.[90]

Two final topics to be considered in this section on philanthropy are the German Young Men's Christian Association and the German Sailors' Homes. The first of these came into existence in 1860 on the initiative of the English YMCA, and used a room at the Aldersgate branch until 1872 when it acquired a house in Finsbury Square, also in the city of London. The location changed again in 1910, moving to another site at City Road in the City of London. J. H. Schröder provided the largest sum for its establishment. The organisation devoted much attention to missionary work; for instance, in the summer of 1884 it held

87. Anglo-German Publishing Company, *Deutsche Kolonie in England*, pp. 30–2; BA, Coblenz, R57 neu, 1064/50: 'Deutsche Realschule, Prospekt, 1913'; extract from the *Londoner General Anzeiger*, 2 August 1913; BA, Potsdam, 38977, 'Satzungen des Deutschen Mittelschulvereins für England, 1909'; 'Deutsches Pädagogium zu Bexhill-on-Sea'; BA, Potsdam, 38978, 'Aufzeichnung über das Deutsche Pädogogium in Bexhill.'
88. Müller, *Die Deutschen Schulen*, p. 33.
89. Urban, 'Statistik der deutschen evangelischen Gemeinden', p. 114.
90. Allgemeiner Deutscher Schulverein zur Erhaltung des Deutschtums im Auslande, *Handbuch des Deutschtums im Auslande*, Berlin, 1906, pp. 461–2.

open air meetings in Hyde Park preaching the gospel in German. These meetings developed into a Commission for the Evangelisation of the Germans in London. The German YMCA devoted attention to artisans, especially bakers, establishing a home in Whitechapel which lasted from 1887–1904, and more particularly to waiters, beginning with a mission to them in 1887 and in the establishment of a home in Fitzroy Square, which closed in 1904 when the location moved to Charlotte Street. In the following year the YMCA also set up an International Christian Waiters' Society. Much of the work at the City headquarters was aimed at German clerks.[91]

The German Evangelical Seemansmission was one of the largest German philanthropic organisations in Britain. It originated in the various independent missions visiting German sailors which had developed in British ports during the course of the nineteenth century. Those interested in these missions came together at a meeting held in Liverpool in 1885; the organisation they founded had the aim of protecting German sailors visiting England from the dangers they faced and caring for their physical and spiritual well-being. The founders hoped to achieve the latter goal in a variety of ways including visits to ships, the distribution of religious literature, and the establishment of seamen's homes. In 1913 as many as 11,998 sailors attended religious services in the fifty-four stations which existed throughout the country, which were divided into the twelve districts of Sunderland, Tyne, Tees, Humber, London, Firth of Forth, Clyde, Mersey, Firth of Tay, Manchester and Bristol Canal.[92]

In fact, despite the formation of the General Committee in 1885, the individual missions retained considerable independence. For instance in the raising of money, which both the local committees and the national body could carry out,[93] most income came from local activity. In the case of Manchester, only £90 from the £735 raised in 1913 came from the central committee.[94] In London the first Sailors' Home opened in 1889 in East India Dock Road, 'thanks to the generosity of numerous friends both in Germany and England.' This followed the establishment

91. Deutscher Christlicher Verein Junger Männer, *Ein Glaunbenswerk in der Themsestadt: Rückblick auf 50 Jahre Vereinsarbeit des Deutschen Christl. Vereins Junger Männer zu London*, London, 1910; Bernd W. Hildebrandt, *1860–1985: 125 Years German Young Men's Christian Association in London*, Edenbridge, Kent, 1985; *The Times*, 22 April 1901.
92. BA, Coblenz, R57 neu 1065/2: 'General Kommitee für Deutsche-Evangelische Seemansmission in Grossbritannien, 1914'; '50 Jahre Generalkomitee für Deutsche Evangelische Seemansmission in Grossbritannien'; Reinhard Münchmeyer, *Handbuch der deutschen evangelischen Seemansmission*, Stettin, 1912, pp. 90–108, 210–11.
93. Münchmeyer, *Handbuch*, p. 211.
94. BA, Coblenz, R57 neu, 1065/11, 'Zweiter Bericht des Komitees für Deutsche Seemans-Mission in Manchester, 1914'.

in 1886 of 'a preliminary Committee for a Seaman's Mission in London as a branch of the' Mission Among the Poor, which resulted in the change of name by the latter to the German Evangelical City and Seaman's Mission for London. The Committee appealed for donations in various ways, including a letter to *The Times*, and collections from German royal families. Princess Christian of Schleswig-Holstein opened the home, and from 1899 until 1908 more than 15,000 sailors used it. Princess Christian also opened the new home in West India Dock Road in 1908, which came about following the establishment of a charity called the German Sailor's Home in 1907.[95]

Clearly German philanthropy within Britain had become extremely widespread by the outbreak of the First World War, in the sense that it catered for many of the needs of both the short-term and long-term German population of Britain and provided help for the poor and educational and religious services. Its role in maintaining German ethnicity remains fundamental because the German charities established by the end of the nineteenth century, with the exception of the Society of Friends of Foreigners in Distress, catered solely for Germans. The dates of formation and the development of these organisations reveal something of a pattern. In the first half of the nineteenth century those which had come into existence remained small in scale, connected with the smaller number of German immigrants in Britain but also with the lack of sophistication in gathering funds, which by the end of the nineteenth century had encompassed, as we have seen with religion, British and German businessmen and members of royal families in both countries. We should particularly stress the role of individual philanthropists, especially the Schröders, who played a fundamental part in the foundation of numerous bodies at the end of the nineteenth century.

Cultural Organisations

The consideration of religion and philanthropy focused upon German bodies involved in the maintenance of German ethnicity, which organised activities from above. The purely cultural organisations had less influence upon the formation of a higher body in the form of a superior social class or an external religion. The cultural bodies which existed varied from bowling alleys to middle-class clubs which formed inde-

---

95. Schröders Bank Archive, letter from P. M. Novell to G. Mallinchoft entitled 'A Brief Outline of the German Sailors Home, London', 9 May 1966; *The Times*, 15 February, 24 May 1889, 9 April 1908; BA, Potsdam, AA, 38981, 'Jahresbericht über die deutsche evangelische Stadt- und Seemans-Mission und Armenschule in London für das Jahr 1888'.

pendently and remained self-supporting. More than any other activity in German Britain, these organisations emphasised social differences as they excluded members of other classes. There was a wide range of activity which essentially remained purely cultural, with little or no external influence from religion, politics or philanthropy.

We can begin by mentioning some of the German newspapers which existed in Britain during the nineteenth century, and which both contemporaries and historians of German minorities in other parts of the world have seen as fundamental in the maintenance of German ethnicity. Heinrich Dorgeel, for instance, expressed this view in his study of German London from 1881,[96] while Luebke has described the German-language press of Brazil as 'an essential structural element in the immigrant house of culture.'[97] The most thorough examination of German newspapers in the USA, by Carl Wittke, stresses that the 'reasons for the development of a foreign-language press are obvious... The newcomer wants to know what is going on in the strange neighbourhood in which he has decided to make his home, and he can learn about that most easily' in his native language. Wittke also stresses that 'The immigrant press is the most effective instrument for maintaining that contact between the old country and the new which is so important in the early years of residence in a strange land.' Finally, Wittke further recognises that while it 'has been relatively easy to start a foreign-language paper... It has been far more difficult to keep a foreign-language newspaper alive.'[98]

Bearing in mind the last assertion, it is difficult to estimate the exact number of newspapers which existed in nineteenth-century London, but the figure could total more than 100. Significantly, I have discovered only one newspaper which existed outside the capital at any time before the First World War; this was the *Manchester Nachrichten*, which published from 1910–12. The explanation for this lies in the lack of a market in the tiny provincial German communities, which would support a print run of no more than a few hundred copies. The papers identified fall into at least five categories, which we can describe as news; political; trade union; and religious.

Of the press organs which had as their central aim the dissemination of news, a good example is the *Londoner Deutsches Wochenblatt*, which ran for a few issues in November and December 1819. Similarly, the *Londoner Deutsche Chronik* only appeared for a few months in 1913. In its first editorial from 4 August 1855, the *Londoner Deutsches*

96. Dorgeel, *Deutsche Colonie in London*, p. 84.
97. Luebke, *Germans in Brazil*, p. 54.
98. Carl Wittke, *The German-Language Press in America*, Lexington, 1957, pp. 1–3.

Journal, stressed the importance of the German community maintaining its language in Britain, but also spoke of a need for developing ties between England and Germany in order to strengthen the case for German unification. Many of its stories focused on the poor German community of Whitechapel and, in this context, it produced strong anti-semitic remarks against Polish-Jews in the same area whom it viewed as threatening the position of Germans in the labour market of the area.[99] In 1878 the printer C. A. Schweitzer launched the *Londoner Journal*, and followed this six years later with another weekly newspaper, the *Londoner Courier*, a 'German organ for politics, trade, art and literature'. This paper had four aims: publishing German and Austrian news; gathering together information on Germans in London and the provinces; carrying extracts from German and Austrian comic papers; and serialising novels.[100]

In its first edition of November 1910, the *Manchester Nachrichten* pointed out in one of its front page editorials that the German community of the northwest had grown to such an extent that the time had arrived for an organ to represent its interests. It described itself as a 'preserver of love for the Fatherland, bound with sincere loyalty to the new homeland', and, significantly, its other front page editorial carried the title of 'England and Germany: A Word Towards Understanding'.[101] The paper published international news stories as well as local ones covering culture and politics, especially stories concerning the German community and aimed not just at the Manchester German community but also those in northern England and Scotland which had developed in Birmingham, Glasgow, Manchester and Liverpool.

The three longest-running German newspapers in Victorian and Edwardian London, all still in print on the outbreak of the First World War, consisted of first, *Die Finanzchronik*, a financial weekly launched in 1895. Second, the *Londoner General Anzeiger*, a twice weekly journal, which began in 1889 and concentrated upon major British news stories as well as those affecting the British community.[102] The third, the *Londoner Zeitung*, originally began life in 1858 as *Hermann* under the editorship of the liberal refugee, Gottfried Kinkel, and was aimed at the German exile community though it subsequently changed its name and broadened its scope.[103]

99. *Londoner Deutsches Journal*, 29 September, 6 October 1855.

100. Dorgeel, *Deutsche Colonie in London*, p. 87; *Londoner Courier*, 28 January 1884.

101. See also *Manchester Nachrichten*, February 1912, which carries a front page editorial entitled 'Anglo-German Relations'.

102. Allgemeinen Deutschen Schulverein zur Erhaltung des Deutschtums im Auslande, *Handbuch*, p. 127.

103. *Hermann*, 8 January 1859; Dorgeel, *Deutsche Colonie in London*, pp. 88–9.

Two newspapers similar to *Hermann* in its original form, in the sense that they appealed to liberal refugees, were *Kosmos*, launched in 1851, and *Der Deutsche Eidgenosse*, of 1865–7. The first of these, edited by Ernst Haug, a former Austrian officer who had participated in the 1848 revolutions in Austria and then Italy, also had the support of other refugees such as Arnold Ruge, Gustav Struve and Kinkel. It ran to just three editions which appeared on 17 May, and 14 and 21 June 1851.[104] *Der Deutsche Eidgenosse*, under the editorship of Karl Blind, appeared once every two weeks from March 1865 'with the explicit aim of working for the overthrow of tyranny in Germany.' It published articles from other liberal exiles in England, including Schaible. 'The events of 1866 and 1867 killed the *Eidgenosse*: most of its readers were willing to accept the new Bismarckian order as adequately satisfying its national sentiments'.[105]

In addition, more left-wing journals existed, such as the *Deutsche Arbeiter*, which appeared only once in 1868. The anarchist Johann Most edited his own newspaper, *Freiheit*, in London during 1881–2. This had originally begun publication in Germany on 4 January 1879 as a social democratic organ, but by the following year it printed anarchist articles. The majority of its circulation of a few thousand went to Germany, smuggled into the country, but some copies remained in Britain. The newspaper actually faced prosecution twice in Britain because of articles which applauded the assassinations of Tsar Alexander II in 1881 and Lord Frederick Cavendish, the Chief Secretary of Ireland, in 1882. The last London issue of *Freiheit* appeared on 3 June 1882, after which it emigrated first to Switzerland and then to New York with Most, where he published it from December of 1882.[106]

At least three German trade journals appeared in London during the late nineteenth and early twentieth centuries, catering for waiters, hairdressers and governesses. In each case the journals received sponsorship from a trade organisation connected with the occupational group. For instance the *London Hotel and Restaurant Employees Gazette*, which published from 1890–1, served as the organ of the London Hotel and

104. Julius H. Schöps, '"Der Kosmos": Ein Wochenblatt der Bürgerlich-Demokratischen Emigration in London im Frühjahr 1851', *Jahrbuch des Instituts für Deutsche Geschichte*, vol. 5, 1976, pp. 216–18.

105. Melvin Cherno, '*Der Deutsche Eidgenosse* and its Collapse, 1865–1867: An Attempt to Stimulate a German Revolution Through Emigre Propaganda', *German Life and Letters*, vol. 35, 1962, pp. 138, 141, 145.

106. Bernard Porter, 'The Freiheit Prosecutions, 1881–1882', *Historical Journal*, vol. 123, pp. 833–56; Frederic Trautman, *The Voice of Terror: A Biography of Johann Most*, London, 1980, pp. 41–2; Andrew R. Carlson, *Anarchism in Germany*, Metuchen, New Jersey, 1972, pp. 183, 205, 206, 230, 235; John Quail, *The Slow Burning Fuse: The Lost History of British Anarchism*, London, 1978, p. 13.

Restaurant Employees Society. It described its task as helping 'companions' to become accustomed to their new country. Although it claimed to serve no party or nationality, its language of publication clearly demonstrated that it aimed at German waiters.[107] The *Hairdresser*, a monthly published in 1912, was the 'Official Organ of the International Union of Journeymen Hairdressers of London'. Its initial print-run totalled 2,000.[108] The longest running trade journal, *Vereinsbote*, which remained in circulation from 1889 until the outbreak of the First World War, appeared four times a year and acted as the organ of the Association of German Governesses in England.

Finally, we can mention two religious newspapers, *St Georgesbote*, an evangelical monthly which ran from 1895, and the *Londoner St Marien Bote*, which described itself as the journal of the Old Catholic Union of London, with the aim of promoting 'intercommunion and union between the Church of England and Churches in communion with her and the Church of Holland and Churches in her communion.' The Old Catholic Union worshipped in French and German at St Mary's in Soho and the *Londoner St Marien Bote* appeared primarily in German.[109]

Moving away from newspapers, the most important way in which German immigrants maintained their ethnicity through their own efforts involved participation in the activities of clubs, of which hundreds must have existed during the course of the Victorian and Edwardian years catering for both the middle and working classes and for a wide variety of interests. The situation resembled New York where: 'The associations, or Vereine, of Kleindeutschland were legion. The Germans banded together for all kinds of ostensible purposes – or for none at all – and they did so on the basis of almost any shared characteristic.'[110] Similarly in Brazil: 'Societies were created wherever German Brazilians were numerous enough in one place to organize and maintain them.'[111]

Within Britain, little information about the working-class organisations survives, but these existed in large numbers, as contemporary accounts point out. In 1882 the Mission Among the German Poor, for instance, pointed to 'the ever increasing number of German clubs, mostly held under various names in low public houses, and of associations of

107. *London Hotel and Restaurant Employees Gazette*, 31 May 1890.
108. *Hairdresser*, 15 January 1912.
109. Allgemeinen Deutschen Schulverein zur Erhaltung des Deutschtums im Auslande, *Handbuch*, p. 127; *Londoner St Marien Bote*, April, June 1912.
110. Nadel, *Little Germany*, p. 109, who even mentions 'a German Bald-headed Men's Verein'.
111. Luebke, *Germans in Brazil*, p. 47.

openly avowed infidel and socialist tendencies.'[112] Twenty years later Armfelt, writing from a non-religious perspective, painted a more positive picture of the clubs in a passage which covered all the types which existed in London:

> It has been said with truth that wherever a dozen Germans meet there is sure to be a *Verein* of some sort. The *Verein* is not a club, nor is it a union, as we understand these words, but it partakes of both and is something more besides.
>
> Here, for instance, is the *Deutscher Turnverein* (the German Gymnastic Society), which imparts instruction in athletics, fencing, and boxing, and has its special days for signing-on. It is also a club, for it has its restaurant and its wine cellars. The fair sex is not neglected, for its dances are features of the Society. In the centre of London there is the *Deutscher Gewerbe und Theater Verein* (the German Industrial and Theatre Club). It caters also for families. Attached to it are the *Verein* of German Bicyclists and the *Verein* of Typographers and the Chess Club. On Saturdays there is a *Tanzkranzchen* (a dance gathering), a concert, and a dramatic recitation; while on Sundays about half-past five there is a *Schauspiel*, or drama, at the end of which dancing follows. On all occasions there is good eating and drinking at moderate prices. There is also a benefit Society, which provides for the sick, the out-of-work, and the burial of the dead.
>
> A number of these clubs also give facilities for the commercial and industrial training of their members and their instruction in the English language. The *Vereins* in the east and west are all very much alike. They provide for theatrical performances, dramatic recitals, dancing and singing, and all the usual social amusements for both sexes. At Yuletide in particular dances are arranged when the Christmas-tree forms, of course, a very prominent feature. Moreover, there are rooms where billiards, chess, cards, and other games are played in the evening, and where eating and drinking are general at all hours. And each of these clubs, and many German public-houses, have their *Kegel-bahn*, or German skittle alley, which is well patronised...
>
> But no description of German life, be it *Verein* life or home life, can be complete without reference to the *Lied*. Every *Verein* – the German Gymnasium included – has its *Lieder-Tafel*, its social gathering for song...
>
> Besides the *Vereins*, whose membership is counted in thousands, there are all over London very small societies, which meet in rooms reserved for them in the German restaurants. Each society has its one or two evenings in the week, some for chorus singing, others for card-playing.[113]

112. BA, Potsdam, AA, 38981, 'The Twenty-Third Annual Report of the Mission Among the German Poor in London, 1882'.

113. Count E. Armfelt, 'German London', in Sims, *Living London*, vol. 3, 1903, pp. 60–1.

In addition to the clubs which Armfelt identifies, some of which
catered for the middle-class Germans and receive attention below, we
can also identify a few of the countless others which had a primarily
working-class membership. In the East End of London, for instance,
Charles Booth identified the United German, the Sonnenscheine and
Nuremberg's in Whitechapel, two societies called the German Club and
a German Bakers Club in St George's, and a German Social as well as a
German Dramatic club in Shoreditch. In fact the first of those listed
above, with 400 members in 1881, actually catered for middle-class
Germans, despite its location.[114]

We can now move on to examine the more middle-class clubs
which existed during the course of the nineteenth century according to
their geographical location, beginning in London and then moving on
to Manchester, Liverpool and Bradford. In the capital there were the
British Wagner and Goethe societies, although in both these cases the
membership also included natives. The latter, founded in 1886 and
remaining in existence until 1914, reached a peak membership figure
of 260 in 1887. Prominent German members included Ludwig Mond
and Max Müller.[115] The London branch of the German Language
Society, established in 1899, aimed at spreading knowledge of
German literature within England; in 1910 it held over ten meetings in
the capital, some purely social, others for particular occasions such as
the celebration of Kaiser Wilhelm II's birthday on 27 January, and still
others for the purpose of raising funds.[116]

Katscher described the 'German Society for the Encouragement
of Art and Science', or the German Athenaeum, as 'the most select
and exclusive of all German societies' in London. It came into existence in 1869 and, after some struggle, reorganised itself in 1872 and
'soon numbered in its ranks the elite of the German population.' It
aimed at affording 'opportunity for social intercourse' and further
acted as 'a rallying point for German life in a foreign land' as well as
furthering art and science: 'With this latter object it holds periodical
exhibitions of works of art, and has musical and scientific evenings.'
In 1884 it offered eight evenings of scientific lectures. Its member-

114. Charles Booth, *Life and Labour of the People in London*, First Series, vol. 1,
London 1902, pp. 103–5; *Londoner General Anzeiger*, 2 June 1884; Dorgeel, *Deutsche
Colonie in London*, p. 78.
115. Günter Hollenberg, 'Die Englische Goethe Society und die deutsch-englischen
kulturellen Beziehungen im 19. Jahrhundert', *Zeitschrift für Religions und
Geistgeschichte*, vol. 30, 1978, pp. 39–45.
116. BA, Coblenz, R57 neu, 1065/1, 'Zweigverein London des Allgemeinen
Deutschen Sprachvereins, Jahresbericht, 1911'; *Londoner Deutsche Chronik*, 5 April
1913.

ship stood at 387 in 1885, rising to 475 in 1890 and to 575 in 1911.[117]

German music groups in London included the Camberwell Choral Society, the Watchmen's Choral Society, the Liedertafel, the Zither Club and the Liederkranz. The last of these had a membership of 347 in 1881, but this had fallen back to 197 by 1903 when it held just three concerts, as well as its fundraising evening and an excursion to Dorking. It described its aim as bringing its members together to practice and perform in male choirs.[118]

German theatre in London developed to a marked extent in late Victorian and Edwardian London, resembling the situation in London in the 1930s when exiles from Nazism also established their own theatre and cabaret.[119] In 1884 there was a German Dramatic Society which met three times a week, mainly for dancing and music sessions.[120] In 1906 'The German Comedy Company from London Under the Direction of Hans Andersen and Max Behrend' performed 'Der Raub der Sabinerinnen. A Farce in 4 Acts by Franz and Paul von Schönthau' at the Midland Hotel Theatre in Manchester.[121] Two years later the German Volkstheater came into existence 'as a permanent institution' in the capital. It 'will be a club; no money will be taken at the doors, and the subscription will be from 1s to 4s monthly according to the seats, for at least six performances per annum.' The places where it performed included the Queen's Theatre in Shaftesbury Avenue and the Royal Court Theatre.[122]

The foundation of the German Gymnastic Club, or Turnverein, in London 'arose out of the enthusiasm which reigned at the Schiller Festival' in 1859 to celebrate the centenary of the poet's birth: 'The building in St Pancras Road, erected at an expense of 10,000 guineas, and opened in 1861, contains among other things a large gymnasium and a very spacious concert-hall.' Its membership began at 384 in 1862 but reached a steady figure of around 1,000 by the 1880s. Only about

117. Katscher, 'German London', pp. 728–9; William F. Brand, *London Life Seen with German Eyes*, London, 1902, pp. 124–5; BA, Coblenz, R57 neu, 1064/39, 'German Atheaneum, London, Jahresbericht und Mitgliederliste' 1885 and 1890; Deutscher Verein für Kunst und Wissenschaft, *Jahresbericht und Mitgliederliste, 1910*, London, 1911.

118. Dorgeel, *Deutsche Colonie in London*, pp. 70–1; Katscher, ibid., p. 730; BA, Coblenz, R57 neu, 1064/37, 'Liederkranz, London, Jahresbericht, Kassenbericht, Satzungen und Mitglieder-Liste, 1903'.

119. See Günter Berghaus (ed.), *Theatre and Film in Exile: German Artists in Britain, 1933–1945*, Oxford, 1989.

120. *Londoner Courier*, 9 April 1884.

121. BA, Coblenz, R57 neu, 1065, 'Deutscher Dramatischer Verein, Manchester'.

122. London Borough of Holborn Library, Deutsches Volkstheater West-Londons, Programme of a Performance of Jugendfreunde at the Queen's Theatre, 17 November 1912; *The Times*, 1 May, 28 September 1911, 2 October 1911.

one-third were Germans, and the majority of the rest were Englishmen. It described its purpose as giving 'London Germans the opportunity for physical exercise in order to raise their moral fitness, and, through collective co-operation, keep their feeling towards the Fatherland.' Its annual fee of thirty shillings meant that it would have remained a predominantly middle-class body. Its activities in 1886 included gymnastics on Monday, Tuesday, Thursday and Friday; fencing and boxing on Wednesday; women's gymnastics on Tuesday and Friday; a singing group on Wednesday; and a literary meeting on Fridays. The Turnverein also had a pub and a library connected to it, and continued to exist until the outbreak of the First World War.[123]

Outside the capital, Manchester developed a middle-class German culture resembling London's. Its most famous club, and perhaps the best known German society in nineteenth century Britain, was the Schiller-Anstalt, established in 1860, although before this a Liedertafel, a Verein and the Albert Club had also existed, while Germans had gathered together in March 1848 to demonstrate their support for the Frankfurt Assembly. The Albert Club had reached a membership of 96 by 1866.[124] The foundation of the Schiller-Anstalt followed the 1859 Schiller Festival in London, which was attended by large numbers of the German community including refugees of all political persuasions.[125] In Manchester a similar gathering occurred in the Free Trade Hall on 10 November, with Engels among the participants. The 'enthusiasm kindled by this celebration' led to the formation of the committee which founded the society. It described its purpose as acting as a social, literary and scientific gathering point for the Germans in Manchester and contained a library as well as rooms for reading, entertainment, games and eating. Its original location lay in the building of the former Mechanics Institute in Cooper Street, but in 1868 it moved to larger accommodation in Oxford Road where it remained for the rest of its existence.[126]

During its history the Schiller-Anstalt counted many of the most prominent Manchester Germans among its members, including Engels,

123. Katscher, 'German London', pp. 729–30; Anglo-German Publishing Company, *Deutsche Kolonie in England*, pp. 61–3; BA, Coblenz, R57 neu, 1064/43: 'Statueten des Deutschen Turn-Vereins, 1876'; 'Sechsundzwanzigster Jahresbericht des Deutschen Turnvereins in London, 1887'.

124. Williams, *Manchester Jewry*, pp. 168–9; F. P. Schiller, 'Friedrich Engels und die Schiller-Anstalt', in D. Rjazanov (ed.), *Marx-Engels Archiv*, vol. 2, Frankfurt, 1928, p. 488, n. 1.

125. Ashton, *Little Germany*, pp. 170–1; and Katscher, 'German London', p. 728.

126. Institut für Auslandsbeziehungen, Curt Friese, 'Some Thoughts on the History of Germans and their Church Communities in Manchester'; Schiller, 'Friedrich Engels und die Schiller-Anstalt', pp. 485–6; BA, Coblenz, R57 neu, 1065/22, 'Statuten und Ergänzungs-Verordnungen der Schiller-Anstalt in Manchester, 1897'.

his business partner Gottfried Ermen, Louis Behrens and Charles Halle, as well as Englishmen, Danes and Dutchmen. By the mid-1860s it had around 300 members, but by 1908 the membership had declined to 161. Concern about declining membership had begun from the mid-1890s when the club offered a discount membership of £1 1s per year instead of the normal £2 2s 6d.[127]

The Schiller-Anstalt became a focus for music in the city. Apart from the fact that it had a Liedertafel attached to it, it further attracted performers of international standing including Richard Strauss, who made his first Manchester appearance in the club's concert hall.[128] Its activities in 1908–9 included a skat tournament, a Christmas party and a celebration of the Kaiser's birthday, an event which it commemorated every year.[129] In 1909 it also marked its jubilee, an event attended by the German Ambassador Count Wolf-Metternich, held not at the club but at the Manchester Turnverein.[130]

Nevertheless by August 1911 the club had ceased to exist, a development explained by various factors including the movement by the Manchester German colony out of the city centre and the lack of interest of second-generation Germans in the club, although this seems difficult to accept considering the fact that as many German immigrants lived in the city at this time as before although they probably did not come from quite the same social background.[131] Nevertheless, prominent Manchester Germans, particularly the German consul in the city, Theodore Schlagintweit, quickly made efforts to establish a club to replace the Schiller-Anstalt, which they had succeeded in doing by the end of 1911 with the foundation of the Deutscher Verein, which used the same building as its predecessor.[132]

127. Institut für Auslandsbeziehungen, Curt Friese, 'Some Thoughts on the History of Germans and their Church Communities in Manchester'; Schiller, 'Friedrich Engels und die Schiller-Anstalt', p. 488; BA, Coblenz, R57 neu, 1065/22: 'Statuten und Ergänzungs-Verordnungen der Schiller-Anstalt in Manchester, 1897'; 'Manchester Schiller-Anstalt. Neunundvierzigster Jahresbericht. Geschäftsjahr 1908–1909'.
128. *Musical World*, 4 March 1905; BA, Coblenz, R57 neu, 1065/13.
129. BA, Coblenz, R57 neu, 1065/22, 'Manchester Schiller-Anstalt. Neunundvierziger Jahresbericht. Geschäftsjahr 1908–1909'; 'Schiller-Anstalt, Manchester, 66, Nelson Street, Manchester, 9 Januar, 1911'; *Manchester Nachrichten*, March 1911.
130. BA, Coblenz, R57 neu, 1065/22, 'Jubiläums Feier des Fünfzigjährigen Bestehens der Schiller Anstalt, Manchester.'
131. *Manchester Nachrichten*, August 1911; BA, Coblenz, R57 neu, 1065/22, extracts from *Manchester Guardian*, 9 August 1911, and *Manchester City News*, 12 August 1911.
132. *Manchester Nachrichten*, February 1912. See also the contents of two files in BA, R57 neu, 1065, with no sub-numbers but entitled Deutscher Verein, Manchester, and Neuer Deutscher Verein, Manchester.

The Manchester Turnverein came into existence in 1860 and aimed at giving its members an 'opportunity to participate in German gymnastics, and to develop the social life of the members through excursions, parties, and gatherings.' It held gymnastic evenings twice a week and devoted much attention to the organisation of celebrations and excursions. Its original membership of fifteen had risen to 103 by 1913.[133]

In Bradford the German residents had also celebrated the anniversary of Schiller's birth by founding a Schillerverein in 1861, which held a meeting to mark its fiftieth anniversary in 1911 attended by two hundred guests including the German-born Lord Mayor, Sir Jacob Moser.[134] Earlier in the century, in 1846, some of the German residents of the city had formed the Liedertafel.[135] The Bradford Germans also held meetings independent of any clubs, such as that in January 1859 to commemorate the return of one of their number, A. M. Goldschmidt, to Hamburg.[136]

In Liverpool there existed a Deutscher Club and a Deutscher Liederkranz by the end of the nineteenth century. The former, which held its first musical evening in October 1888, had a library, card-room and billiard room and charged a high yearly membership fee of £3. It aimed at 'developing a meeting place for Germans and their German-speaking friends in Liverpool.'[137] The Liederkranz had connections with the Deutscher Club, but charged a lower entrance fee of £1. It held regular meetings, some of them for fundraising purposes.[138]

Any overall assessment of German middle-class social activities in nineteenth-century Britain would point to the existence of similar clubs in the major centres of settlement within the country, London, Manchester, Bradford and Liverpool, consisting of a superior social club, a Turnverein and a song society. Many other cities also had at least

---

133. *Manchester Nachrichten*, November 1910; BA, Coblenz, R57 neu, 1065/15, extract from the *Manchester Guardian*, 7 November 1910; BA, Coblenz, R57 neu, 1065/21, 'Gesetze des Deutschen Turnvereins, Manchester. Genehmigt in der Hauptversammlung vom 15. Mai 1901': 'Deutscher Turnverein, Manchester, Jahresbericht 1886–1887'; 'Deutscher Turnverein, Manchester, Jahresbericht 1898–1899'; 'Deutscher Turnverein, Manchester, Jahresbericht 1913–1914'; 'Deutscher Turnverein, Manchester, Hundertjahrfeier der Völkerschlacht bei Leipzig, 1813–1913'.
134. Aronsfeld, 'German Jews in Nineteenth Century Bradford', p. 113; *Manchester Nachrichten*, December 1911, January 1912.
135. William Cudworth, *Musical Reminiscences of Bradford*, Bradford, 1885, p. 42.
136. *Bradford Observer*, 18 January 1859.
137. BA, Coblenz, R57 neu, 1064/11, 'Deutscher Club. Erster Musikalischer Abend am Samstag dem 13. Oktober, 1888'; BA, Coblenz, R57 neu, 1064/17, 'Statuten des Deutschen Clubs'.
138. BA, Coblenz, R57 neu, 1064/17.

one body.[139] London, with its bigger German population, could support numerous other institutions. In most cases the societies established also contained members of the English and other immigrant populations, although in all cases the main aim focused on the maintenance of German culture in a generally non-political way.

Trade Union and Political Activity

In addition, there also existed more purely patriotic organisations run by German immigrants in Britain by the early twentieth century, whose aim was nationalism, as in most cases, they formed branches of similar organisations which existed in Germany, connected with the country's rising nationalism in the years leading up to the outbreak of the First World War. We can consider these in the discussion on political and trade bodies amongst the Germans in Britain, which consisted of at least three strands. First, trade societies. Second, 'radical' political bodies, which existed throughout the nineteenth century, but which ranged from anarchists and communists through to liberals. And, third, the patriotic bodies of the late Victorian and Edwardian years.

The individual representative organisations for groups of employees, which have already received some attention, remained few in number and do not seem to have existed before the late nineteenth century,[140] mainly because of a lack of numbers but also because of the difficulties of organisation in some of the most exploitative of occupations such as sugar baking and shoe-making. The groups which did have organisations, which were either established independently or with the help of external funding, included female servants, governesses, teachers, barbers and waiters.[141]

For the first of these an organisation called Gordon House existed, funded by English and German philanthropy. This had the purpose of

139. For instance, the Glasgow Deutscher Club 1898 mentioned in the *Londoner General Anzeiger*, 10 July 1901. See also BA, Coblenz, R57 neu. 1064/1, which deals with the Deutsche Gesellschaft at Queens University of Belfast, which actually catered for all Germans in the city and not just students who were either German or studied German.

140. *Londoner Deutsches Journal*, 11 August 1855, mentions a fairly universal body called the Association of German Workers and Trade People, which had the aim of assisting people in the above categories in need, and counted 129 members, including 44 women. However, it appears not to have remained in existence for any length of time.

141. Anglo-German Publishing Company, *Deutsche Kolonie in England*, pp. 92, 95, also mentions a branch of the German Bank Employees Society in London, and a Society of German Musicians, established in 1873 as a branch of the General German Musical Association. See also p. 125 of the present study for mention of union organisation amongst tailors.

finding situations in service for German women in London, as well as providing them with accommodation if needed.[142] Gordon House resembles the Association of German Governesses, both in its aims and in the fact that it received external support from British and German 'royal personages' together with London German philanthropists such as the Schröders. Although initially an independent body within England after its foundation in 1876, in 1890 it developed connections with the General Association of Female Teachers in Germany. Helene Adelmann acted as the main force behind the foundation of the London body; after living in the capital for ten years, she found the practices of the agents who secured positions for German women unacceptable and consequently contacted a circle of 14 members which quickly grew to 145.[143]

The aims of the Association consisted of helping members to obtain situations, assisting those members suffering from ill health or without work, obtaining pupils for its members, and temporarily housing those searching for situations. For the last purpose the German Ambassador opened a home in the West End of London in 1879; in addition, the organisation also possessed a convalescent home in Ealing in west London, which subsequently moved to Harrow in the north of the capital following the launch of a fund for its construction. In return for the advantages which they received from the Association, members had to pay a membership fee of 10s 6d during the 1880s, as well as 'a commission of $2\frac{1}{2}$ per cent on the first year's salary' if they obtained a situation through it. With membership averaging out at more than 700 members for much of the period until the First World War, and its claim in 1905 that over 18,000 women had enjoyed its benefits, the Association represented one of the most important German employees organisations in Victorian and Edwardian England.[144]

The German Teacher's Association was virtually a carbon copy for males of the Association of German Governesses in England. It came into existence in 1883 on the initiative of H. Reichardt, attracting 122

142. Dorgeel, *Deutsche Colonie in London*, pp. 39–40; Katscher, 'German Life in London', p. 737.
143. Brand, *London Life*, p. 134; *The Times*, 26 January 1877; H. Z. König, *Authentisches über die Erzieherin in England: Eine Entgegnung auf: 'Das Gouvernanten in England'*, *eine Warnung, von Julius Einsiedel*, London, 1884, pp. 33–8; Bremer Staatsarchiv, 2T 6t 4e, Association of German Governesses in England, 'Fourteenth Annual Report, 1890'.
144. Bremer Staatsarchiv, 2T 6t 4e, Association of German Governesses in England: 'Third Annual Report, 1879'; 'Seventh Annual Report, 1883'; 'Sixteenth Annual Report, 1892'; 'Twenty-Second Annual Report, 1898'; 'Twenty-Sixth Annual Report, 1902'; Bremer Staatsarchiv, U1a Nr 135, 'Verein deutscher Lehrennen in England, n.d.'; BA, Coblenz, R57 neu, 1064/38, Association of German Governesses in England, 'Nineteenth Annual Report, 1895'.

members within its first year. It received financial support from both British and German royalty, and had connections with several teaching organisations in Germany. Like the Association of German Governesses, it both filled positions and acted as a welfare body. Nevertheless, it seems to have ceased to exist after the 1880s.[145]

The organisations for barbers and hairdressers, as well as those for waiters, had far more of a resemblance to trade unions although they also performed some of the functions of the bodies for governesses and teachers, but without the external financial support. Beginning with the organisations for barbers, we have already seen that two organisations existed, the East London Concordia and the West London International Union of Journeymen Hairdressers of London. The first of these 'is of a much lower character, and is frequented by the German and Polish Jew hairdressers of the East End.' Tuition took place at its headquarters which also acted as a residence for those out of work,[146] as well as providing sickness and burial money for members and their families. By the outbreak of the First World War it had also opened a branch in Charlotte Street; in 1913 its membership totalled 290.[147]

The second organisation, founded in 1893 and based in a building called the Harmony Club, counted 400 members at the time when Charles Booth and his researchers carried out research for *Life and Labour of the People in London*. As with the Concordia, members lived on the premises and it conducted classes; it also contained a bowling alley and a billiard room. It charged a subscription of 10s 6d. In 1911 it opened a branch in north London, at a time when it became active in a campaign to ensure shorter opening hours by appealing to local councils and to hairdressers themselves.[148]

German waiters in Britain developed several trade organisations during the course of the nineteenth and early twentieth centuries. Smaller organisations included the German Waiters Club,[149] which existed as early as 1869, and the London and Provincial Hotel Employees Society, with its headquarters in Tottenham Court Road; the latter acted as an employment agency as well as offering accommodation to its members.[150] A more substantial body consisted of the Ganymede Friendly

145. BA, Potsdam, AA, 38956; BA, Coblenz, R57 neu, 1064/44; *The Times*, 31 December 1883, 23 June 1885.

146. BLPES, Booth Collection, Group B, vol. 160, pp. 66–7.

147. *Hairdresser*, 15 January 1912; Anglo-German Publishing Company, *Deutsche Kolonie in England*, p. 96.

148. *Londoner General Anzeiger*, 2 June 1894; BLPES, Booth Collection, Group B, vol. 160, p. 66; Booth, *Life and Labour*, Second Series, vol. 4, p. 281; *Hairdresser*, February, April 1912.

149. *Hermann*, 2 January 1869.

150. *Londoner General Anzeiger*, 10 July 1901.

Society for Hotel and Restaurant Employees, a branch of an international association established in 1878. The English organisation had headquarters in central London, which moved several times during its existence.[151]

Booth considered the International Hotel Employees Society as 'the premier organization' for 'foreigners engaged in this business'; again this was a branch of an international German body. The London branch counted 1,200 members in the 1890s, and like many of the other employment bodies already discussed, it combined the 'advantages of a benefit society, employment bureau and social club'.[152] Finally, we can mention the London Hotel and Restaurant Employees Society, a London based group, which, despite its ability to publish its own journal for a short time, counted no more than 353 members in 1890, of whom 212 consisted of Germans. Its headquarters in Clipstone Street near Fitzroy Square, offered the same range of social activities as the other bodies in this trade, and it also acted as a benefit organisation.[153]

As for more specifically political groupings, political participation offered just one way, probably the least important, in which German immigrants could spend their leisure time. There follows a discussion of the political organisations in chronological order as they developed in Britain, beginning with the refugees of the 1840s and progressing through those from the 1848 revolutions to the victims of the 1878 repression and, finally, to the nationalistic groupings which developed in the late Victorian and Edwardian years.

The refugees of the 1830s and 1840s developed several organisations, sometimes in connection with political exiles from other countries or with the nascent labour movement within Britain. The purely German organisations include Young Germany, which established itself in London as early as 1834 and was strengthened further after the expulsion of the group from Switzerland two years later. This group continued to exist into the 1840s, and also formed the basis for the development of other organisations in the capital. These included the Society for Mutual Support and Understanding, established in 1837 and counting about one hundred members, only half of them refugees. In fact, as its name suggests, its concerns were not simply political.[154]

151. Anglo-German Publishing Company, *Deutsche Kolonie in England*, pp. 95–6.
152. Booth, *Life and Labour*, Second Series, vol. 4, pp. 242–3.
153. *London Hotel and Restaurant Employees Gazette*, 31 May, 14 June, 1 November 1890. Other waiters clubs also existed, for which see the same journal, 6 September 1890. See also Booth, *Life and Labour*, Second Series, vol. 4, pp. 242–3; and BLPES, Booth Collection, Group A, vol. 150, p. 45.
154. August Jäger, *Der Deutsche in London*, 2 volumes, Leipzig, 1839, vol. 1, pp. 187–94; Werner Brettschneider, *Entwicklung und Bedeutung des deutschen Frühsozialismus in London*, Bottrop, 1936, p. 20; J. Watson, *Young Germany*, London, 1844.

A more important group came into existence in 1840 in the form of the communist German Workers Educational Association, founded by Karl Schapper and a circle of six other refugees with the aim of making workers politically conscious so that they could improve their position. It initially met in public houses, with up to 200 people attending its meetings, and developed a substantial library with most books written in German and many on political activity. By the outbreak of the 1848 revolutions its membership had reached over 300. This body actually continued to exist until the First World War, although it split in the early 1880s. By the 1870s it was based in Soho and its membership included Scandinavians, Dutch and east Europeans, as well as Germans.[155]

During the 1840s the German Workers Educational Association acted as the London branch of the League of the Just, which became the Communist Correspondence Committee in 1847 and the Communist League from 1847–52. This in turn had connections with the Fraternal Democrats, formed in 1845 after a similar organisation, the Fraternal Democrats of All Nations, had failed during just one year of existence in 1844. The Fraternal Democrats included members from the German, French, Italian, Polish and Swiss exile communities in London together with support from the Chartist George Julian Harney. Its aims placed it firmly on the left of the political spectrum. Despite this complexity of organisations, however, it seems unlikely that more than a few hundred Germans in London participated in political activity during the 1840s.[156]

The 1848 revolutions meant the movement of most refugees in London to Germany in order to participate in events taking place there, and consequently the end of the Fraternal Democrats. However, the suppression of the uprisings resulted in their return, together with the entry into Britain of many first-time refugees. These formed both communist

155. Alexander Brandenburg, 'Der Kommunistische Arbeiterbildungsverein in London: Ein Beitrag zu den Anfängen der deutschen Arbeiterbildungsbewegung (1840–47)', *International Review of Social History*, vol. 14, 1979, pp. 341–70; Hermia Oliver, *The International Anarchist Movement in Late Victorian London*, London, 1983, p. 5.
156. B. Nicolaevsky, 'Toward a History of "The Communist League" 1847–1852', *International Review of Social History*, vol. 1, 1956, pp. 233, 242; Carl Wittke, *The Utopian Communist: A Biography of Wilhelm Weitling, Nineteenth Century Reformer*, Baton Rouge, 1950, p. 100; Asa Briggs, *Marx in London: An Illustrated Guide*, London, 1982, p. 23; Uwe Jürgen Zemke, 'A Biography of Georg Weerth (1822–1856)' (unpublished Ph.D thesis, University of Cambridge, 1976), p. 62; A. Müller Lehning, 'The International Association (1855–1859): A Contribution to the Preliminary History of the First International', *International Review for Social History*, vol. 3, 1938, pp. 195–7; Henry Weisser, *British Working Class Movements and Europe, 1815–1848*, Manchester, 1975, pp. 125–6, 134–40; Jacques Grandjonc, 'Die Deutsche Binnenwanderung in Europa 1830 bis 1848', in Otto Büsch, et. al. (ed.), *Die Fruhsozialistischen Bünde in der Geschichte der deutschen Arbeiterbewegung: Vom "Bund der Gerechten" zum "Bund der Kommunisten" 1836–1847*, Berlin, 1975, p. 15.

and liberal organisations. The most important of the latter was the German Agitation Union of London, founded in the summer of 1851 by a circle revolving around Arnold Ruge, a former philosophy tutor at the University of Halle, who had become the representative for Breslau in the Frankfurt Parliament. The body described its aim as 're-establishing the lawful rights of the German people' through 'means of agitation only within the limits of the laws of England.' It included both German and Austrian members. Other organisations include the Emigration Club inspired by Gottfried Kinkel, but none of these bodies lasted beyond 1852, partly because of the rivalry between them.[157] Liberal refugees founded another 'very small' grouping in 1860 called 'German Unity and Freedom', which published pamphlets putting forward what it viewed as German national interests, and reflecting the move of German liberalism more generally to the right. It subsequently published *Der Deutsche Eidgenosse* for a short time. Its members included Karl Heinrich Schaible and Carl Blind.[158]

Together with the liberal organisations which existed amongst the Germans in mid-nineteenth century London, the more left-wing organisations developed further following the pattern established before 1848 of working with other refugees, as well as English organisations. In this sense they differ from many of the bodies already considered as their main concern was not establishing contact with other Germans.

The returning Communist exiles played a major role in the continuance of the Communist League, in which Marx and Engels played a central part. In 1850 the organisation split between their supporters and those of two other German refugees, August Willich and Karl Schapper, and in November 1852 the League faced dissolution. After these events the main centre of left-wing activity in German London consisted of the German Workers Educational Association, although German refugees played a role in organisations such as the International Association, which existed from 1855–9 and brought together German, French, English and Polish exiles, as well as the First International, founded in 1864. At the same time more informal contacts remained, while many of the German exiles pursued their revolutionary activity in other ways

157. Weisser, ibid., p. 164; *Reynolds Newspaper*, 24 August 1851; *Correspondence Respecting the Foreign Refugees in London*, PP, vol. LIV, 1852; Christine Lattek, 'Die Emigration der deutschen Achtundvierziger in England: Eine reine "school of scandal and of meanness"?', in Gottfried Niedhart (ed.), *Grossbritannien als Gast und Exilland für Deutsche im 19 und 20. Jahrhundert*, Bochum, 1985, pp. 42–5; Ashton, *Little Germany*, pp. 140–1.
158. Cherno, 'Der Deutsche Eidgenosse', pp. 140–2; Karl Heinrich Schaible, *Siebenunddreissig Jahre aus dem Leben eines Exilierten: Ein Flüchtlinges Lebensbild*, Stuttgart, 1895, p. 149. For details about Blind see Ashton, ibid., 167–73.

such as journalism, writing for English, American and German newspapers.[159]

The next major developments in the history of specifically German collective political activity in nineteenth-century London occurred following the entry of hundreds of refugees after the passage of the Anti-Socialist Laws in the late 1870s and early 1880s. All contemporary accounts of late nineteenth-century German London point to the fact that numerous anarchist clubs existed, which attracted working-class Germans. Those who put forward these views included Katscher, Rethwisch and the Mission Among the German Poor in London.[160] The clubs were concentrated in the East End and West End, and it is impossible to estimate their number.

The first refugees to arrive in Britain in 1878 made their way to the German Workers Educational Association Club in Rose Street, in Soho. Further individuals followed in 1881, to participate in the International Anarchist Congress, which took place in London between 14–20 July of that year, and in 1884.[161] By this time the German left-wing groups in London had become involved in a 'civil war' revolving around personalities and ideologies. Most 'German-speaking socialists, anarchists, and revolutionaries' belonged to the German Workers Educational Association, but by 1884 it contained three different sections; the anarchist Whitfield Club, with its headquarters in Whitfield Street, near Regents Street; a section consisting primarily of Social Democrats, with headquarters in Tottenham Street; and the Club Morgenröthe, situated near the British Museum, which remained neutral in the civil war. Two years later, in 1886, the first group split further, resulting in another new group called the Gruppe Autonomie, based in Charlotte Street and publishing its own newspaper, *Die Autonomie*, under the editorship of a Swede, R. Gundersen, until 1893.[162]

159. Lehning, 'International Association', pp. 199–238; Nicolaevsky, 'Towards a History of the Communist League'; Edmund Wilson, *To the Finland Station*, London, 1974 reprint, pp. 206–7, 264–8; R. W. Postgate, *The Workers International*, London, 1920; Brettschneider, *Entwicklung und Bedeutung des deutschen Frühsozialismus*, pp. 53–5; Utz Haltern, *Liebknecht und England: Zur Publistik Wilhelm Liebknechts während seines Londoner Exils (1850–1862)*, Trier, 1977, pp. 7–53; W. O. Henderson, *The Life of Friedrich Engels*, vol. 2, London, 1976, pp. pp. 505–9.

160. Katscher, 'German Life in London', pp. 731–2; J. Rethwisch, *Die Deutsche im Auslande*, Berlin, 1889, pp. 76–7; BA, Potsdam, 38981: 'Thirty-Third Annual Report of the Mission Among the German Poor in London, 1882'; 'Thirty-Fifth Annual Report of the Mission Among the German Poor in London, 1884'; 'Siebenunddreissigsten Jahresbericht über die Deutsche Stadtmission und Armenschule in London, 1886'.

161. Oliver, *International Anarchist Movement*, pp. 5, 10–19; Carlson, *Anarchism in Germany*, pp. 249, 321.

162. Carlson, *Anarchism in Germany*, pp. 325, 336–7; Oliver, *International Anarchist Movement*, p. 19; Quail, *Slow Burning Fuse*, pp. 55–6; Rudolf Emil Martin, *Der Anarchismus und seine Träger*, Berlin, 1887, pp. 53–74.

There was also a branch of the German Workers Educational
Association in Aldgate in the East End during 1881,[163] while Katscher
mentions the Communistic Society for the Training of Artisans.[164] Like
their predecessors during the 1840s, the bodies which existed during the
late Victorian period also had connections with English and international organisations such as the Socialist League and the Freedom
League.[165] Rudolf Rocker, who arrived in London in 1895, wrote in his
autobiography: 'The long conflict which had split the German movement in London for years had gradually come to an end; the two hostile
sections got together, and the rest of the old Autonomists joined the
Grafton Hall Club.'[166]

Any attempt to estimate the membership of the late nineteenth century German political groupings is difficult, and there is an additional
complicating factor in the presence of non-Germans amongst the membership. Estimates vary from 300 to 1,000.[167] Whatever the true figure
for those who actively participated in politics, we also need to remember
that the socialist and anarchist groups offered the same opportunities for
social activities also available from the more purely cultural and
employment organisations discussed above. In 1869, for instance, the
German Workers Educational Association provided instruction in
English and French as well as opportunities for political discussion. One
of Most's biographers claims that when he arrived in London, he found
the organisation 'without leadership, insipid, drifting: a card party and a
coffee klatsch.' In 1894, its weekly activities consisted of dances on
Saturday, Sunday and Monday and Wednesday, singing on Tuesday, a
lecture on Thursday, and gymnastics on Friday. It also still had its substantial library, founded during the 1840s. Similar activities continued
to be offered until the outbreak of the First World War,[168] by which time
Russian and Polish Jews had become the most politically active immigrants in London.[169]

By 1914 nationalist German organisations also existed in Britain. As
early as 1883, the anti-semitic Adolf Stöcker, founder of the Christian
Social Workers Party, had travelled to London to celebrate the 400th

163. *Daily News*, 21 March 1881.
164. Katscher, 'German Life in London', p. 731.
165. Carlson, *Anarchism in Germany*, pp. 353–4; Oliver, *International Anarchist
Movement*; E. P. Thompson, *William Morris: Romantic to Revolutionary*, New York,
1976 edition, pp. 366–579.
166. Rudolf Rocker, *The London Years*, London, 1956, p. 67.
167. Ibid., p. 67; Carlson, *Anarchism in Germany*, p. 326; Quail, *Slow Burning Fuse*,
p. 193.
168. *Hermann*, 2 January 1869; *Londoner General Anzeiger*, 2 June 1894; *Londoner
Zeitung*, 9 September 1911; Frederic Trautman, *Voice of Terror*, p. 40.
169. See W. J. Fishman, *East End Jewish Radicals*, London, 1975.

anniversary of Martin Luther's birth at the invitation of the German YMCA.[170] The nationalist organisations existing in London by 1914 included the German Colonial Society, which had over 200 members; the Navy League, which had branches in London and Glasgow, the latter of which counted 140 members and the support of the German Consul in Glasgow; and three military clubs in London, the German Officers Club, founded in 1891 and numbering 125 members by 1913, the German Veterans Club, and the Royal and Imperial Hassia. All of these contained a middle-class membership.[171]

Clearly German society in nineteenth-century Britain developed a complex of both formal and informal institutions divided according to class, religion and political affiliation, all of which proved fundamental in deciding the allegiance of a particular German to an individual organisation. The divisions already existing in Germany remained once the immigrants found themselves in Britain. In virtually every case the fact that the immigrant possessed German nationality had fundamental importance, as all of the bodies examined above catered exclusively, primarily or mainly for Germans. Nevertheless, the newcomers did not remain trapped in purely ethnic institutions with no contact with English society. Many of the groups mentioned above possessed members of the native and other foreign populations.

The most constructive way of viewing German institutions in Britain is as a strand within British society; like British society, the German community possessed both formal and informal institutions. In the former group there were the religious and philanthropic organisations, whose role in the lives of nineteenth-century German immigrants paralleled that of the same bodies in British society. At the same time the informal cultural groups also resemble British social activities, divided primarily along class lines. The political organisations during the whole course of the nineteenth century had the classic modern political divisions of socialist, liberal and nationalist; their size and precise principles varied during the course of the Victorian and Edwardian period according to any number of factors, including the freshness of the influx of political refugees.

In contrast to other groups in nineteenth-century Britain and America, the Germans received assistance from both the sending society

---

170. C. C. Aronsfeld, 'A German Antisemite in England: Adolf Stöcker's London Visit in 1883', *Jewish Social Studies*, vol. 49, 1987, pp. 43–52; Deutscher Christlicher Verein Junger Männer, *Deutsches Glaubenswerk*, pp. 31–6.

171. Anglo-German Publishing Company, *Deutsche Kolonie in England*, pp. 74–8; BA, Coblenz, R57 neu, 1042/2, Hauptverband Deutscher Flottenverein im Ausland, 'Jahresbericht, 1911'; *Londoner Deutsche Chronik*, 5 May 1913; Armfelt, 'German London', p. 58.

and the receiving society. This applies especially in the case of philanthropic organisations and churches, which received large amounts of
financial support from the British royal family as well as from noble
houses in Germany. In fact, the German minority played a role in maintaining positive contacts between British and German upper-class society, although with the approach of the First World War and the rise of
Anglo-German rivalry this relationship came under strain.

British Attitudes Towards Germany, Germans and German Immigrants

The previous chapter, which dealt with German society and culture in nineteenth- and early twentieth-century Britain, indicated that the development of German formal and informal organisations drew much support from British society. This assistance came through either financial means, as in the case of churches and philanthropic organisations, or in other ways, as the development of left-wing German political organisations in London demonstrates. In the latter case, the additional numbers provided by members of native society proved fundamental in the development of political groupings. Any consideration of British attitudes towards Germans should first bear in mind that such connections did exist, suggesting a positive view towards an immigrant group within Britain which few other newcomer groups have enjoyed. At the same time, the relative ease with which some German newcomers, especially businessmen, bankers and industrialists, moved into the higher echelons of British society should be viewed as an indication of the existence of a tolerant attitude towards them.[1]

Nevertheless, any examination of British attitudes towards German immigrants in British society cannot ignore the events of the First World War because, while few groups may have been as positively accepted by British society,[2] equally few have faced the intensity of rejection

---

1. The question of the relative ease with which German Jews moved into British society during the course of the nineteenth century, and what this implies for British tolerance is thoroughly considered by Todd M. Endelman, *Radical Assimilation in English Jewish History 1656–1945*, Bloomington and Indianapolis, 1990, pp. 114–43, 209.

2. Two other groups which enjoyed support from British society consisted of Protestant French Hugenots, who made their way to Britain as a result of Catholic persecution in the late seventeenth century, and Belgians, who entered the country on the outbreak of the First World War, although in the case of the latter, at least, negative feeling also existed. The Huguenots receive brief consideration in W Cunningham, *Alien Immigrants to England*, 2nd edition, London, 1969, pp. 223–49 and Colin Holmes, *John Bull's Island: Immigration and British Society, 1871–1971*, London, 1988, pp. 7–8. For Belgian refugees see P. Cahalan, *Belgian Refugee Relief in England during the Great War*, New York, 1982.

endured by Germans in Britain during the First World War. In this conflict, British official and unofficial opinion became saturated with a Germanophobia that rejected everything German. The Government instituted a series of measures, notably internment, repatriation and confiscation of property, and passed the Aliens Restriction Act, which meant the destruction of the German communities which had developed during the course of the nineteenth century: the number of Germans declined from 57,500 in 1914 to 22,254 in 1919. Public opinion, meanwhile, created an image of underground German power in Britain which prevented British victory in the War. Anti-German organisations developed, while Germans faced widespread boycott. Most seriously, attacks took place upon German property, notably in May 1915, in virtually every British city which had a German population of any size.[3]

One of the aims of this chapter is to trace the development of hostility towards Germans in nineteenth-century Britain which led to the crescendo of intolerance of the First World War. For most of the pre-1914 period there is little indication that Britain would become saturated with Germanophobia during the First World War. However, from the last decade of the nineteenth century, and certainly during the Edwardian period, the situation changed as hostility towards German immigrants developed with the rise of Anglo-German political antagonism; although even during this period, positive attitudes remained.

Prior to the 1890s anti-German feeling was sporadic, while after this time Germanophobia began to take root. For the whole of the period under consideration, attitudes towards German immigrants were complex. There did not exist a hostility which focused simply upon one aspect of German life, or which was driven by any one external factor; instead, there were different strands of hostility, alongside positive attitudes. The complex nature of British views of Germans resembles that of Britons towards Italy and Italians during the course of the nineteenth century, where ideas about the beauty of the Italian countryside and admiration for Italian nationalism (before 1850) conflicted with negative views of Italian Catholicism, the Italian people and poor Italian immigrants within Britain.[4]

3. Panikos Panayi, *The Enemy in Our Midst: Germans in Britain during the First World War*, Oxford, 1991; J. C. Bird, *Control of Enemy Alien Civilians in Great Britain 1914–1918*, New York, 1986; and Stella Yarrow, 'The Impact of Hostility on Germans in Britain during the First World War', in Tony Kushner and Kenneth Lunn (eds), *The Politics of Marginality? Race, the Radical Right and Minorities in Twentieth Century Britain*, London, 1990, pp. 97–112.

4. Lucio Sponza, *Italian Immigrants in Nineteenth Century Britain: Realities and Images*, Leicester, 1988, pp. 119–271; Margaret C. W. Wicks, *The Italian Exiles in London, 1816–1848*, New York, 1968 reprint.

Returning to British attitudes towards Germany and Germans, there existed in the first place an underlying image, created through novels, travel literature, journalism and scholarly research in history. This image did not remain consistent, containing both positive and negative views, but it became steadily more negative with the approach of the First World War. Second, there was a prejudice against poor German immigrants which existed throughout the course of the nineteenth century, although this never became as widespread and intense as that directed against either the Irish in the early and mid-Victorian period, or Russian and Polish Jewish immigrants from the late nineteenth century. Third, there was hostility towards Germans in individual trades, which existed throughout the nineteenth century but became more widespread from the 1880s. However, the most important strand of hostility towards Germans in Victorian and Edwardian Britain was political. During the course of the nineteenth century, the highest peaks of hostility were at times of fear of German power, while the animosity from the 1890s had the background of deteriorating Anglo-German relations as its main motivation.

Underlying Images

Chapter 1 indicated that the pre-nineteenth century image of Germans stressed two elements, consisting of the 'faustian', an admiration of German mysticism and philosophy, and the 'grobianisch', which stressed German barbarism, dullness and drunkenness. Elements of both the 'faustian' and 'grobianisch' attitudes remained into the nineteenth century. In addition, this period saw the growth of racial Anglo-Saxonism, stressing the common history of English and German peoples; this reached a peak of acceptance in the second half of the nineteenth century, but existed both before and afterwards. Furthermore, as with views of Italy, we can also point to an admiration for the German landscape.

The last of these existed throughout the course of the nineteenth century, both in the works of serious literary writers and in the impressions of journalists and travellers. Amongst the former was the poet Thomas Hood, who lived in Germany from 1835–7, settling in Coblenz. His impressions survive in both his letters and poems which stressed the beauty of Coblenz, the Rhine and Moselle rivers and the countryside around, as well as his fondness for Rhineland wine.[5]

5. See Walter Jerrold, *Thomas Hood: His Life and Times*, 1969 reprint, pp. 280–310; Jerrold (ed.), *The Complete Poetical Works of Thomas Hood*, New York, 1980 reprint, pp. 352–62; Kurt Weineck, *Deutschland und der Deutsche im Spiegel der englischen erzählenden Literatur seit 1830*, Jena, 1937, pp. 42–8.

Many Englishmen followed Hood on journeys to the Rhine. By the 1850s Germany 'had been discovered' by 'the growing hordes of English sight-seers, and a trip on a Rhine steamer was included in every tourist's itinerary.' No English university student 'would omit an opportunity to stand on the terrace of the Castle in romantic Heidelberg.' Although many English travellers stuck to the Rhine and Neckar valleys,[6] others made their way to other parts of the country. For instance, an article in *Household Words*, the periodical edited by Charles Dickens, pointed to the 'beautifully wooded walks which encircle' Hamburg, as well as commenting on the attractions in the centre of the city. Henry Mayhew spent years in Saxony, where he also met other Englishmen in the early 1860s.[7] Later in the century, an article in the *Contemporary Review*, entitled 'Notes from a German Village', focused on 'Gross Tabarz', which 'lies on the northern slope of the long ridge of the Thuringian mountains, about ten miles from its northern end.' The author, W. Steadman Aldis, commented on 'the variety of natural scenery', which 'requires to be seen in order to be believed'. Aldis further commented on the economic activity which took place in the forests and fields around the village which he and his family visited.[8]

In 1895, Millicent Sutherland, in an article in the *Nineteenth Century* entitled 'In Germany – A Sketch', did not name the part of Germany to which she referred but again commented on the vegetation, the sunny weather and 'the good Rhine wine', which, however, she felt that Germans had 'deserted for commoner brews'.[9] Other novelists who focused upon the attractiveness of the German countryside included George Meredith, who published his *Pictures of the Rhine* in 1851.[10]

In contrast to the positive comments on the German countryside, however, many visitors to Germany commented on what they viewed as the uncouthness of the native population, a factor which Sponza has emphasised in his study of British attitudes to Italy and Italians.[11] This attitude towards Germans fits firmly into the 'grobianish' tradition of the pre-eighteenth century period. Thomas Hood, for example, commented on a journey from Frankfurt to Eisenach when he shared a coach

6. Myron F. Brightfield, *Victorian England in Its Novels (1840–1870)*, Los Angeles, 1968, pp. 281–2, 288.
7. *Household Words*, 19 April 1856; Henry Mayhew, *German Life and Manners as Seen in Saxony at the Present Day*, London, 2 vols, 1864.
8. W. Steadman Aldis, 'Notes from a German Village', *Contemporary Review*, vol. 40, 1881, pp. 63–73.
9. Millicent Sutherland, 'In Germany – A Sketch', *Nineteenth Century*, vol. 38, 1895, pp. 644–8.
10. Ernst Dick, 'Deutschland und die Deutschen bei George Meredith', *Germanisch-Romanische Monatschrift*, vol. 6, 1914, p. 33.
11. Sponza, *Italian Immigrants*, pp. 121–9.

'with four Germans stinking of the accumulated smoke and odour, stale, flat, and unprofitable, of perhaps *two* years' reeking garlic and what not.' Mayhew stated that Rhinelanders 'have no sense of that unchastity of soul which is offensive to the Almighty, nor of that physical or mental filth that is loathsome both to the senses and understanding of every decently-educated man or woman throughout the really civilised world.'[12] Samuel Laing, writing in 1848–9, produced an even more extreme picture, which perhaps encapsulates the grobianish view of Germany. In his most notorious utterances, he claims that:

> The manners...of all classes in Germany are so nearly the same, that there is no incongruity in their sitting together. All, from the prince to the shoemaker, are what our dainty gentry would call slovenly livers, dirty feeders, and insensible to the disgust they may give by habits confined, among us, to our lowest and most roughly bred classes. Spitting all round a room, picking their teeth at meals with the knife, licking it and thrusting it into the butter or cheese, and such petty abominations, show that there is not that marked difference in those small observances of delicacy, and of regard for the feelings of others, in manners and behaviour, which distinguish the gentleman from the non-gentleman in our population.[13]

Despite the strength of this passage, it is not unique. An article in *Household Words* from 1856 commented on another aspect of perceived German uncouthness, namely 'the sly, obese, rather cruel-humour, which distinguishes the Teutons'.[14] This 'grobianisch' prejudice forms part of the literary view of Germany for much of the nineteenth century.[15] Almost inevitably, it also filtered into impressions of the German population of England. An article in the Edinburgh-based *Blackwood's Magazine* from 1840 on 'Foreigners in London' commented on Germans as 'mute, inglorious stulzes in great numbers', and continued: 'Your German in London resembles your German any where else; heavy, dunder-headed, gross, beer-and-'bacco bemused individual', but more positively, 'dogged and steady at his work, patient, and generally trustworthy.'[16] More than half a century later, Arthur Shadwell made

12. Jerrold, *Thomas Hood*, p. 297; Henry Mayhew, *The Upper Rhine and Its Picturesque Scenery*, London, 1863, p. 32.
13. Simon Laing, *Observations on the Social and Political State of the European People in 1848 and 1849*, London, 1850, p. 378.
14. *Household Words*, 23 February 1856.
15. Albert Ludwig, 'Deutschland und Deutsche im englischen Roman des 19. and 20. Jahrhunderts', *Germanisch-Romanische Monatschrift*, vol. 5, 1913, pp. 32–3; Weineck, *Deutschland und der Deutsche*, pp. 246–7.
16. 'Foreigners in London', *Blackwood's Magazine*, vol. 51, 1842, p. 25.

almost the same mixture of positive and negative points in his own article on 'The German Colony in London', when he wrote that:

> The German will go anywhere and compete with anybody where there are streets and pavements and offices and beershops and newspapers and police, but he is wholly incapable of constructing these things for himself in the wilderness. Once set in a groove he is an unrivalled plodder, but he has no initiative in action. He can bring a prodigious industry, an inexhaustible patience, and a rigid economy to the battle of life, and so make his way without fail in the thickest of throng, but his path must follow a strict routine, he must be doing something that can be learnt out of a book.[17]

This last extract, suggests the existence of a connection between the traditional 'grobianish' and 'faustian' images of Germany, which existed for much of the nineteenth century.[18] The latter view, in particular the British admiration for German learning and culture and the positive view of the German landscape, began to develop in the late eighteenth and early nineteenth centuries, especially under the influence of Samuel Coleridge and Thomas Carlyle, and reached a peak by the second half of the nineteenth century. The admiration for culture focused particularly on German research and music and manifested itself both within a literary image and in the admiration amongst English educational reformers and scholars of the example of Germany. This attitude had declined in importance by the Edwardian years, when British writers focused on what they viewed as German militarism in connection with the growing threat to British power. [19]

Literary admiration for German culture and learning was expressed by numerous British writers throughout the course of the nineteenth century. An article from 1914 described one impression of Germany symbolised by 'a genial wool-gathering professor in a formidable pair of spectacles, untidy of habit and far from athletic in form... We have all laughed at the German Professor in our infancy.'[20] Such figures appear in the works of numerous writers, as do other manifestations of German learning and a more general admiration for German education. An 1856 novel by William John Conybeare commented that 'The Teutonic mind

17. Arthur Shadwell, 'The German Colony in London', *National Review*, vol. 26, 1896, p. 805.
18. Weineck, *Deutschland und der Deutsche*, pp. 245–54.
19. Paul Kennedy, *The Rise of the Anglo-German Antagonism, 1860–1914*, London, 1987 reprint, pp. 109–11; Hermann Levy, *England and Germany: Affinity and Contrast*, Leigh-on-Sea, 1949, pp. 6, 12, 17, 18, 19; Rosemary Ashton, *The German Idea: Four English Writers and the Reception of German Thought 1800–1860*, Cambridge, 1980, pp. 1–2.
20. 'Germany and the Prussian Spirit', *Round Table*, vol. 4, 1914, p. 617.

seems determined to master the subject which it attacks with an honest and laborious perseverance almost unknown in England'.[21] The historian Thomas Carlyle, one of the most important English admirers of Germany during the early- and mid-nineteenth century, commented on the 'valour and meditative depth of Germans' and thought that the foundation of Prussia lay not in any accident, but in arithmetic, geometry and the Lutheran Reformation. Carlyle's admiration further encompassed German literature, especially that of Goethe, and philosophy.[22] Similarly, William Thackeray stated that Germans 'loved music and science'.[23] In George Meredith's novel, *The Adventures of Harry Richmond*, the central character of the book travels through Germany, studies at a university in the country, where one of his professors contrasts learning in Germany with its lack in England. We can also point to the characters in George Eliot's novels, many of whom had studied at German institutions; she herself played a role in the spread of German ideas in England through translations of German philosophers.[24] Matthew Arnold, another influential English thinker, focused on German science; in his *Friendship's Garland*, a work which reprints correspondence published in the *Pall Mall Gazette* between Arnold and a German visitor to England called Baron von Thunder-Ten-Trockh, the latter states, 'I, Sir, as a true Prussian, have a passion for what is *wissenschaftlich*... I love to proceed with the stringency of a philosopher.'[25]

The above literary views found echoes in the utterances of journalists, politicians and academics who looked at the German education system as a way forward for the British equivalent. In *Household Words*, an article from 1850 claimed that all the children in Prussia, Saxony, Bavaria, Bohemia, Württemberg, Baden, Hesse-Darmstadt, Hesse-Cassel, Gotha, Nassau, Hanover and the Austrian Empire attended school. Another piece in the same journal in 1853 believed that 'all Germans' were 'great at philosophical deductions'.[26] During the course of the nineteenth century, several official committees took evidence on

21. Quoted in Brightfield, *Victorian England in Its Novels*, p. 243.

22. Fritz Schultz, *Der Deutsche in der Englischen Literatur vom Beginn der Romantik bis zum Ausbruch des Weltkrieges*, Göttingen, 1939, p. 97; Ashton, *German Idea*, pp. 67–104.

23. Philipp Buttler, 'Die Ausländer in den Romanen Thackerays', *Giessener Beiträge*, vol. 2, 1925, p. 121.

24. Dick, 'Deutschland und die Deutschen bei Georg Meredith', pp. 34–5; Weineck, *Deutschland und der Deutsche*, pp. 79, 83–5; Ashton, *German Idea*, pp. 147–77.

25. Matthew Arnold, *Friendship's Garland: Being the Conversations, Letters, and Opinions of the Late Arminius, Baron von Thunder-Ten-Trockh*, New York, 1883 reprint, pp. 230–1.

26. *Household Words*, 20 April 1850, p. 82, 25 June 1853, p. 402.

the example of Germany as a positive model for the improvement of English education. These included the Royal Commission on Elementary Education, which reported in 1861, the Royal Commission on Scientific Instruction and the Advancement of Science of 1875, and the Royal Commission on Technical Education of 1881–4. The Education Act of 1902 owed much to the German example, as did the foundation of science colleges in industrial cities such as Leeds, Birmingham, Sheffield and Liverpool. Throughout the course of the later nineteenth century a series of publicists, including Carlyle and Thomas and Matthew Arnold, argued for the extension of education within Britain, citing Germany as an example. Academics in a range of subjects pointed to Germany as a model which Britain should follow in the expansion of its higher education system. Academic subjects which owed much to German influence included history, geology, geography and chemistry.[27]

Attitudes towards music remained more complex during the course of the nineteenth century because, in addition to positive views, strands of hostility also existed. One indication of positive views lies in the number of generally well-received orchestral musicians, conductors and composers in Britain. Further, in the early nineteenth century 'many English musicians went to Germany to finish their professional education', and: 'For generations men's conceptions of musical idiom had been based upon their knowledge of German and Austrian (and to a lesser extent French and Italian) music.' Outside the music profession, numerous novelists, authors and poets described German music in a positive fashion.[28]

Nevertheless, strands of hostility existed, and these became more solid and widespread at the end of the nineteenth century, especially amongst those involved in music. The reception afforded to Richard Wagner during his 1855 visit to England is an indication of negative attitudes towards German music, rooted partly in more conservative British tastes. He complained that 'I am compelled to conduct an

27. Kennedy, *Anglo-German Antagonism*, pp. 113–18; W. H. G. Armytage, *The German Influence on English Education*, London, 1969, pp. 26–68; Stuart Wallace, *War and the Image of Germany: British Academics 1914–1918*, Edinburgh, 1988, pp. 5–11; George Haines, *Essays on German Influence upon English Education and Science*, Hamden, Connecticut, 1969; Manfred Messerschmidt, *Deutschland in englischer Sicht: Die Wandlungen des Deutschlandbildes in der englischen Geschichtsschreibung*, Düsseldorf, 1955; Günter Hollenberg, *Englisches Interesse am Kaiserreich: Die Aktivität Preussen-Deutschlands für Konservative und Liberale Kreise in Grossbritannien 1860–1914*, Wiesbaden, 1974, pp. 147–178.
28. E. D. Mackerness, *A Social History of English Music*, London, 1964, pp. 214–15; Weineck, *Deutschland und der Deutsche*, pp. 231–3.

English concert programme right down to the end; that says everything'. He felt as if 'eternal night were closing around me' and even compared London with Dante's *Inferno*. The fact that the English press did not rise to his conducting further exacerbated his impressions. However, Wagner obtained a more enthusiastic reception in 1877 when he returned to London 'in the zenith of his fame', although this had much to do with the efforts of the German community in London, members of which helped to found the Wagner Society in 1884.[29]

At the end of the nineteenth century, there arose a more broadly-based negative feeling against German music, connected perhaps with the more general growth of Germanophobia which questioned 'whether Germany really merited the esteem in which her musicians were held'. In the same period of the late nineteenth century, British piano manufacturers began to complain of the fact that one in six pianos sold in Britain was made in Germany, leading to claims about the importation of inferior goods and German influence at court.[30]

Attitudes towards music, especially positive ones, fitted into more general views of German culture, which also focused on literature and the visual arts.[31] There were also positive views connected with the idea of a common heritage. These focused, for instance, on religion, leading one English traveller to Germany to comment: 'For the Protestant Englishman one name, however, overshadows all other interests – the name of the great Martin Luther.'[32]

One of the strongest manifestations of underlying positive attitudes towards Germany was the concept of Britain and Germany having the same racial origins, a view prevalent throughout the years 1815–1914 but reaching a peak of acceptance in the third quarter of the nineteenth century. The idea of racial affinity became almost ubiquitous, affecting the views of journalists, politicians, historians and what might be

29. Mackerness, *A Social History of English Music*, pp. 220–1; Anne Dzamba Sessa, *Richard Wagner and the English*, London, 1979, pp. 11, 30, 37–8; Hermann Klein, *Thirty Years of Musical Life in London: 1870–1900*, London, 1903, pp. 43, 124; Francis Hüffer (ed.), *Correspondence of Wagner and List*, vol. 2, London, 1881, pp. 84–5; Hüffer, *Half a Century of Music in London 1837–1887*, London, 1889, pp. 44–71; Count von Westerhagen, *Wagner: A Biography*, vol. 1, Cambridge, 1978, pp. 206–10.

30. Mackerness, *A Social History of English Music*, pp. 221–2; Cyril Ehrlich, *The Piano: A History*, London, 1976, pp. 88–9.

31. Weineck, *Deutschland und der Deutsche*, pp. 225–6, 233–5; Armytage, *German Influence on English Education*, pp. 22–3; E. M. Butler, 'Heine in England and Matthew Arnold', *German Life and Letters*, vol. 9, 1956, pp. 157–65.

32. Aldis, 'Notes from a German Village', p. 65. Kennedy, *Anglo-German Antagonism*, pp. 104–9, casts doubt over the importance of religion, while not denying it.

described as racial thinkers, the last two groups of whom developed quite sophisticated ideas which have subsequently been defined as 'Racial Anglo-Saxonism'.[33]

These more sophisticated racial ideas will be examined below, but there are examples of the extent to which more general concepts of racial affinity became accepted. For instance, in a speech delivered after the German victory in 1871 to a mixed German and English audience at the German Athenaeum in London, Professor Max Müller declared of the relationship between England and Germany that:

> There was a brotherhood between the two nations, and by this he referred not to a common descent, a common language, a common religion, and common feat of arms, but to their common allegiance to the majesty of conscience, their common recognition of conscience as the highest authority on earth – higher than crowns and churches, books and articles, blame and praise of the world. He declared that the political guidance of Europe belonged to Germany and England – the guidance of the whole civilized world to England, America and Germany – and that a cordial understanding between these three Germanic nations meant peace.[34]

A different example of 'Racial Anglo-Saxonism' comes from an article in a radical journal, the *Bee-Hive*, from 1 February 1873, entitled 'An Infamous Project', referring to a proposal to introduce Chinese workers as strike-breakers into South Wales. The piece commented:

> Everybody knows that there are the gravest objections against the importation of French or German workmen; that such a course of action is fully of danger, and only calculated to increase the hostility between masters and men. Yet, apart from any industrial struggle that is going on, it is by no means a disadvantage for us to have some French and German workmen among us; they are part of our European civilization; their habits and ideas and feelings render them capable of harmonising with the new position in which they find themselves. They can easily conform to our laws and settle down to our modes of life – they may be a powerful influence for good. But it is not so with people imported from an eastern country. They are too strange; their health and customs are altogether different; they would constitute a foreign element, tending to lower and degrade us and hinder our development; they would constitute a serious cause of disturbance and disorder in our present social and political condition.

---

33. This phrase is used by Reginald Horsman, 'Origins of Racial Anglo-Saxonism in Great Britain Before 1850', *Journal of the History of Ideas*, vol. 37, 1976, pp. 387–410.
34. *The Times*, 2 May 1871.

Anglo-Saxon views also found support among senior political figures, especially in the second half of the nineteenth century and into the twentieth century. For instance Sir Charles Dilke, the radical liberal, in his *Greater Britain*, published after a visit to the USA, spoke positively of people of English, German and Scandinavian origin, and negatively of the Chinese and the Irish.[35] In 1899, Joseph Chamberlain suggested a diplomatic grouping involving Germany, Britain and the USA, a 'triple alliance between the Teutonic race and the two great branches of the Anglo-Saxon race', although the idea received a hostile reception as a result of Anglo-German mistrust against the background of the Boer War.[36] Nevertheless, five years later the Prime Minister, Arthur Balfour, in a speech to the Anthropological Association of the British Association on 'Physical Deterioration', commented: 'The new generation, especially in London, is rather smaller; its "Germanic characteristics" – light hair, for example – begin to disappear'.[37]

The above quotations simply represent popular examples of the more sophisticated 'Anglo-Saxonism' developed during the Victorian Era, when 'a small but influential group of gentlemen, including antiquaries, historians, doctors, barristers, and clergymen took part in the quest for racial origins of the modern inhabitants of the British Isles.'[38] In addition, mention should be made of the influence of ethnographers and anthropologists, whose numbers grew with the founding of organisations such as the Ethnological Society of London in 1843 and a breakaway grouping, the Anthropological Society of London, in the following decade.[39] All of these organisations accepted the idea of the superiority of Europeans to people from other parts of the world as articles by John Crawford in the *Transactions of the Ethnological Society of London* reveal. In an article 'On the Classification of Race', Crawford actually spoke of different species of the human race and continued, 'The union of the highest and the lowest species of the human race yields an intermediate progeny, inferior to the first, and superior to the last. The offspring of a Scandinavian and a Negro is

35. L. P. Curtis, *Anglo-Saxons and Celts*, New York, 1968, pp. 45–6.
36. Wolfgang Mock, 'The Function of "Race" in Imperialist Ideologies: the example of Joseph Chamberlain', in Paul M. Kennedy and Anthony Nicholls (eds), *Nationalist and Racialist Movements in Britain and Germany Before 1914*, London, 1981, pp. 196–7.
37. *Spectator*, 27 August 1904.
38. L. P. Curtis, *Apes and Angels: The Irishman in Victorian Caricature*, Newton Abbot, 1971, p. 16.
39. Christine Bolt, *Victorian Attitudes to Race*, London, 1971, p. 1; Peter Fryer, *Staying Power: The History of Black People in Britain*, London, 1984, p. 176.

inferior to the Scandinavian, and superior to the Negro.' However: 'The union of closely allied species of the human race produces no appreciable change in the offspring.' Consequently, 'The people of Italy have suffered no degradation from a large admixture of Greek and Teutonic blood, nor the inhabitants of France from an admixture of Italian and German blood; nor the people of England from a still larger of the latter.'[40]

Despite Crawford's attitude about the similarity of European 'races', some racial thinkers would not have included all European groups, especially the Irish[41] and 'Semites', which in some cases referred only to Jews but in others meant 'the man of the South', essentially all Middle Eastern peoples.[42] Neither of these fitted into the highest racial stratum consisting of those of German origin. Robert Knox, a doctor of medicine, best known for his racial ideology, was one the most extreme proponents of the superiority of Germans. In his *The Races of Men*, he described 'the German' as 'the most philosophical of all men; the most abstract in reasoning; the most metaphysical; the most original; and, in a word, the most transcendental.' However, his geographical conception of what constituted a German remained limited, confined significantly to 'the Saxon or North German'. He further claimed that 'the modern German bears no resemblance in mind or body to the pure Saxon German of Northern Europe', 'composed', instead, 'partly of Saxons, partly of Slovenians'.[43]

The idea of Germans, and especially Saxons, having unique characteristics was supported by historians throughout the course of the nineteenth century, in books which traced the development of the British Isles from the fall of the Roman Empire and stressed the importance of the Anglo-Saxon invasions. The most notable proponents of such ideas included Thomas Carlyle, Thomas Arnold, Charles Kingsley, J. M.

40. John Crawford, 'On the Classification of the Races of Man', *Transactions of the Ethnological Society of London*, vol. 1, 1861, pp. 356–7.

41. Curtis, *Apes and Angels*, and *Anglo-Saxons and Celts*, convincingly argues in favour of the existence of an English racial ideology which viewed the Irish as a dangerous outgroup.

42. Colin Holmes, *Anti-Semitism in British Society, 1876–1939*, London, 1979, pp. 1–120. For an example of anti-semitism which extends beyond Jews see J. W. Jackson, 'The Aryan and the Semite', *Anthropological Review*, vol. 7, 1869, pp. 333–44.

43. Robert Knox, *The Races of Men: A Philosophical Inquiry into the Influence of Race Over the Destinies of Nations*, 2nd edn, London, 1862, pp. 342–3, 345; M. D. Biddiss, 'The Politics of Anatomy: Dr Robert Knox and Victorian Racism', *Proceedings of the Royal Society of Medicine*, vol. 69, 1976, pp. 15–20.

Kemble, J. R. Green, William Stubbs, John Beddoe and Edward Freeman.[44]

A classic statement on this subject comes from the opening pages of J. R. Green's *Short History of the English People*, in which he asserts that, 'For the fatherland of the English race we must look far away from England itself', to 'the district which we now call Sleswick, a district in the heart of the peninsula which parts the Baltic from the northern seas.' He continues:

> Engle, Saxon, and Jute all belonged to the same Low German branch of the Teutonic family; and at the moment when history discovers them, they were being drawn together by the ties of a common blood, common speech, common social and political institutions. Each of them was destined to share in the conquest of the land in which we live; and it is from the union of all of them when its conquest was complete that the English people has sprung.[45]

Green, together with the other historians mentioned above, stressed certain important characteristics which the Saxons had brought with them. He focused on the concept of 'the free man', as did Freeman in his *Comparative Politics*, even mentioning the importation of a 'Teutonic constitution'. Other concepts which he stressed included the construction of society and religion. Charles Kingsley praised the strength of the 'Teuton' as well as his civilising influence after the fall of the Roman Empire. John Beddoe focused on the appearance, especially the blondness, of the Anglo-Saxons who invaded Britain; he believed that 'the Gaelic and Iberian races of the west, mostly dark-haired, are tending to swamp the blond Teutons of England by a reflux migration.' He even created an 'Index of Nigrescence', which he applied to different regions in Britain to illustrate his assertions.[46]

Nevertheless, while stressing racial connections in the past, historians remained careful about drawing too close connections between the nineteenth-century English and Germans. Freeman, for instance, writing of the 'Teutonic nations' which existed 'on either side of the German

44. Messerschmidt, *Deutschland in englischer Sicht*; Hollenberg, *Englisches Interesse am Kaiserreich*, pp. 114–20; C. J. W. Parker, 'The Failure of Liberal Racialism: The Racial Ideas of E. A. Freeman', *Historical Journal*, vol. 24, 1981, pp. 826–8; Horsman 'Origins of Racial Anglo-Saxonism', pp. 399–403.

45. John Richard Green, *A Short History of the English People*, London, 1888, pp. 1, 2.

46. Curtis, *Anglo-Saxons and Celts*, p. 11; Green, *A Short History*, pp. 2–4; Edward A. Freeman, *Comparative Politics*, London, 1873, p. 122; John Beddoe, *The Races of Britain: A Contribution to the Anthropology of Western Europe*, London, 1971 reprint, originally published 1885; Charles Kingsley, *The Roman and the Teuton*, London, 1891 reprint, originally published 1864.

ocean and either side of the Atlantic', described 'ourselves' as 'the truest representatives'.[47] Subsequently, from the end of the nineteenth century as Anglo-German political rivalry increased, historical scholarship turned against the idea of England and Germany having inherited similar characteristics, although the ideas did not entirely disappear.[48] Even as late as 1912 the anthropologist Sir Harry Johnston asked 'whether the German-Gothic peoples have not been ever and again the regenerators of the civilised world'. In the following year Lady Florence Phillips made even stronger assertions when she stated: 'I am most firmly convinced that the white race is superior to any coloured race.' She spoke of a 'Black Peril brooding over Africa' and a 'Yellow peril brooding over Asia', which meant that 'Christendom should abandon all artificial quarrels and unitedly make ready to cope with the stirrings which threaten its very existence.' She continued: 'Going back to the beginnings of our race we can see that we are very close cousins to the Germans.' Consequently, she believed that Anglo-German antagonism should end. Her book concluded:

> These two great nations must join hands if the true interests of humanity are to be served. Western civilisation will thus form a bulwark against the encroaching hordes. Hand-in-hand Germany and England may lead the world to a realisation of glorious ideals.[49]

The above survey of underlying attitudes towards Germany and Germans in Victorian and Edwardian Britain reveals a complex picture of positive and negative views, which makes it difficult to reach any conclusions. While ideas about a common heritage, combined with admiration for German culture and learning, point to positive attitudes, we cannot dismiss the continuing existence of 'grobianism' colouring British ideas. While the positive outlook may offer one explanation for the social mixing which took place between natives and Germans during the nineteenth century, the image of the uncouth German may equally serve to explain the hostility which existed towards poor German immigrants.

47. Freeman, *Comparative Politics*, p. 44.

48. Hugh A MacDougall, *Racial Myth in English History: Trojans, Teutons, and Anglo-Saxons*, London, 1982, pp. 128–9; Messerschmidt, *Deutschland in englischer Sicht*, pp. 67–85; Hollenberg, *Englisches Interesse am Kaiserreich*, pp. 122–5.

49. Sir Harry Johnston, *Views and Reviews: In the Outlook of an Anthropologist*, London, 1912, p. 90; Lady Florence Phillips, *A Friendly Germany: Why Not*, London, 1913.

Socio-Economic Hostility Towards German Immigrants

Our main concern here is to outline the two strands of animosity towards German immigrants, whose main binding force lies in their non-political nature. We can describe the first of these as more of a social hostility and the second as having a more fundamentally economic base, although the two remain interrelated. Social hostility encompasses a variety of aspects in the life of the immigrant, while the main motivation for economic animosity lies in the threat to the employment of Englishmen.

All immigrant groups in nineteenth-century Britain experienced social hostility, notably the Irish during the 1840s–1870s, Russian Jews from the 1880s and, on a smaller scale, Italians. In the case of the first two groups animosity against them rose to its highest peaks during the years of their largest influx into Britain. For the Irish these are the 1840s, 1850s and even 1860s, after the mass movement following the Irish famine of 1846. Although the animosity manifested itself most potently in the form of street violence between Catholics and Protestants, socio-economic conflict also represented an important driving force. Working class animosity received support from a middle-class fear, manifesting itself in the written word and in policing policies.[50]

Similarly, hostility towards Russian Jews increased during the years of most concentrated immigration from the 1880s onwards, reaching a peak in the first years of the twentieth century which forced the passage of the Aliens Act of 1905. Apart from claiming that the newcomers took control of jobs belonging to Englishmen and depressed the economic conditions in the areas into which they moved, hostility against east European immigrants also focused on the belief that they caused an increase in rents by paying more for their accommodation. Furthermore, the anti-aliens saw the newcomers as insanitary and dishonest. The extent of the hostility towards newcomers led to the development of anti-alien organisations such as the British Brothers League and the

---

50. Frank Neal, *Sectarian Violence: The Liverpool Experience, 1819–1914*, Manchester, 1988, pp. 105–75; Frances Finnegan, *Poverty and Prejudice: A Study of Irish Immigrants in York, 1840–1875*, Cork, 1982, pp. 166–7; Curtis, *Apes and Angels*, p. 97; R. F. Foster, 'Paddy and Mr Punch', *Journal of Newspaper and Periodical History*, vol. 7, 1991, pp. 35–40; Walter L. Arnstein, 'The Murphy Riots: A Victorian Dilemma', *Victorian Studies*, vol. 19, pp. 51–71; Pauline Millward, 'The Stockport Riots of 1852: A Study of Anti-Catholic and Anti-Irish Sentiment', in Roger Swift and Sheridan Gilley (eds), *The Irish in the Victorian City*, London, 1985, pp. 207–24.

Immigration Reform Association in East London, as well as to regular attacks upon the newcomers.[51]

Socio-economic hostility towards Italians never reached the intensity of that towards Irish and Russian Jewish immigrants. In the case of the Italians, animosity focused upon specific aspects, such as their poverty, as well as the noise created by street musicians. Italians also received incidental mention during the campaign for the Aliens Act of 1905.[52]

Socio-economic hostility towards Germans resembled that against Italians in the sense that no nationwide all-encompassing animosity developed against them; in contrast to the political anti-Germanism inspired by the deteriorating condition of Anglo-German diplomacy in the early twentieth century. Even at times of heaviest German immigration, such as 1881–91, anti-German socio-economic hostility remained relatively limited, perhaps because Britain never experienced a German influx comparable to the Irish immigration of 300,000 between 1841 and 1851,[53] or with the increase of 37,704 in the Russian and Polish population of England and Wales in the last decade of the nineteenth century.[54] The relative absence of anti-German hostility inspired by socio-economic causes may also have connections with the positive images of Germans in British society outlined above, of which fewer existed with regard to the Irish and Jews.[55]

Nevertheless, socio-economic hostility to Germans did exist in nineteenth-century Britain. It reached something of a crescendo in the late nineteenth century during the campaign for the Aliens Act of 1905, although even here the Germans were minor targets when compared with Russian Jews. Separate from this campaign, we can point to hostility against German immigrants from the London City Mission, on account of their perceived lack of religion, and animosity towards German musicians.

An examination of the *London City Mission Magazine* reveals a constant belief that German immigrants were irreligious, although this idea

51. Bernard Gainer, *The Alien Invasion: The Origins of the Aliens Act of 1905*, London, 1972; John A. Garrard, *The English and Immigration, 1880–1910*, London, 1971, pp. 3–153; Holmes, *Anti-Semitism*, pp. 89–97; W. J. Fishman, *East End 1888: A Year in a London Borough Among the Labouring Poor*, London, 1988, pp. 60–81; Jill Pellew, 'The Home Office and the Aliens Act, 1905', *Historical Journal*, vol. 32, 1989, pp. 369–72.

52. Sponza, *Italian Immigrants*, pp. 141–265.

53. Colin Holmes, *John Bull's Island: Immigration and British Society, 1871–1971*, London, 1988, p. 20.

54. *Report of the Royal Commission on Alien Immigration*, vol. 3, p. 63, P.P., vol. IX, 1903.

55. Foster, 'Paddy and Mr Punch'; Sheridan Gilley, 'English Attitudes Towards the Irish in England, 1780–1900', in Colin Holmes (ed.), *Immigrants and Minorities in British Society*, London, 1978, pp. 81–110; Holmes, *Anti-Semitism*.

needs to be placed within the context of more general views of nine-teenth-century missionary societies, which stressed the lack of religion of all of those to whom they preached in order to justify their own exis-tence.[56] The reports in the *London City Mission Magazine* stress per-ceived immorality as well as lack of religious adherence amongst the Germans. In September 1864, for instance, we read that 'the Germans are very low and dissipated in their morals and habits'.[57]

In the following year, a long article on 'The Germans in the East of London' provided extensive details of the lives of German immigrants:

> The locality of St George's-in-the-East, better known in the neighbourhood by the common appellation of 'the Highway', may truly be called a sink of iniquity. There is no vice in existence which has not its representative and agency in this locality. Haunts of drunkenness and debauchery are here to be met with in abundance, and every snare is laid to entrap the unguarded stranger. Here may be met from abroad the runaway bankrupt, the degraded politician, the exiled democrat, and every other grade of outlaw and outcast in society, as well as the poor honest artisan, who, blinded by hopes too gold-en to be realised, has left his native land, and by the failure of his anticipa-tions has been reduced to a state of miserable poverty. These deceived hopes do not merely apply to workmen, but also to female servants – needlewomen and such like – who, by false delusions, are enticed to come over here and, alas! too often fall victims to the most ruinous vices.

The same article mentioned the 'rescuing' of 'upwards of fifty couples who lived in sin and iniquity'. It further pointed to 'German coffee and lodging-houses', which it described as 'the very dens of sin and misery', whose 'infecting influence is brought to bear on many hundreds of inno-cent persons'. The 'houses are generally infested with fallen females, some of whom seem so hardened to their miserable fate, that shame has quite forsaken them.'[58] Lodging houses also received attention on other occasions, especially as places in which a 'great deal of gambling goes on'.[59]

Before moving on to consider the London City Mission's views of spiritual poverty amongst the Germans of East London, it should be pointed out that more general hostility to German drinking habits exist-ed, as attacks upon Germans in 1892 and 1895 reveal. The first incident, which took place in August 1892, began as a dispute between a wife and

---

56. See for instance Joseph Salter, *The Asiatic in England: Sketches of Sixteen Years Work Among Orientals*, London, 1873, which contains passages of extreme prejudice.
57. *London City Mission Magazine*, September 1864, p. 191.
58. Ibid., January, 1865, pp. 1–12.
59. Ibid., 2 June 1884, p. 121; 2 March 1885, p. 51.

husband, when the woman, Catherine Brady, went to collect her husband from the German Club in Brunel Street in Canning Town on a
Saturday night, to find him not present. She returned on the following
day, when a crowd gathered outside. A 'great number of panes of glass
were broken', while 'Brady "turned on the beer", and a large quantity
was wasted.' The attitude of the magistrate and police witness who dealt
with the case at the West Ham Police Court prove interesting. While
condemning the 'disgraceful manner' in which Brady had behaved, the
magistrate also described the club as 'an unlicensed drinking hell, and
must be cleared out at once'. Police Constable Bland, meanwhile,
asserted that: 'A lot of loafing men go in there for the purpose of drinking. The place is open up to twelve and one o'clock.' On 10 September,
at an inquest into the death of the child of the proprietor of the club,
whose death had no connection with the incident, the coroner 'said these
clubs were nothing more or less than "dens of iniquity", and he quite
concurred that they should be under restraint.'[60]

Three years after this incident another 'Hostile Demonstration
against Germans' took place in east London, involving a case in which a
mother, Alice Dallman, living with Gustav Kops, made money by using
her fourteen-year-old daughter for the purposes of prostitution. After an
appearance in the West Ham Police Court 'en route for Holloway gaol,
a crowd of about 1,000 persons met' Alice Dallman and her daughter 'in
the Stratford Broadway, and followed them to the railway station, hoot-
ing all the way.'[61]

The above two incidents indicate the existence of a perception of
Germans as drunken and immoral which affected more than just the
workers of the London City Mission, and we can draw connections here
with the underlying 'grobianish' view of Germans. Similarly, the negative views of this religious body about the non-observance of Germans
in London have connections with more widespread anti-Semitism and
anti-Catholicism,[62] as much of the Mission's hostility focused on
German Jews and Catholics. With regard to the former, for instance, a
missionary to the Jewish population of East London in 1885 spoke of
their 'bitter opposition' and 'intense hatred' towards 'the truths of

60. *West Ham Guardian*, 27 August, 3, 10 September 1892; *West Ham Herald and South Essex Gazette*, 3 September 1892.
61. *East Ham Echo*, 3 May 1895; *East Ham Express*, 4 May 1895.
62. For more general hostility towards Catholics in nineteenth century Britain see for instance E. R. Norman, *Anti-Catholicism in Victorian England*, London, 1968; W. L. Arnstein, *Protestant Versus Catholic in Mid Victorian England*, Columbia, Missouri, 1982; and Stuart Wolf, *The Protestant Crusade in Great Britain*, Oxford, 1991.

Christianity', which meant that 'the bitterest curses were freely showered upon me'.[63]

With regard to German Catholics, a missionary described them in 1854 as 'very ignorant of the way of salvation' and 'always destitute of the Holy Scriptures'. He hoped to 'turn their hearts from the darkness of Romish superstition to the marvellous light of the Gospel, and from the power of Satan unto the living God.' Eleven years later, a missionary to the Germans claimed that just after he had established twice weekly meetings, 'the German Jesuits from the Church of Rome were stirred up, and, in order to counteract my efforts among the Germans, they also opened a meeting'.[64] However, the London City Mission also directed hostility towards Germans who had no religious affiliations at all, freely using the term 'infidel'. In 1865 the missionary to the East End Germans claimed: 'The spiritual destitution of the Germans in this locality surpasses the power of description', and asserted that 'It is quite a common occurrence to meet with German families who have resided in London *for several years* and are totally ignorant of the existence of any spiritual agency.'[65]

Another strand of anti-German social hostility existing during the course of the nineteenth century involved opposition to German street bands, which was part of a wider animosity towards street music played by immigrants. The opposition, which combined anti-alienism and class prejudice, reached peaks in the mid-1860s and mid-1890s, resulting in the introduction of bills into Parliament for the suppression of street music.

The first campaign against street music had amongst its supporters Charles Dickens, Thomas Carlyle,[66] the mathematician Charles Babbage and the MP Michael Bass, as well as sections of the press. The main complaints against street musicians focused upon their numbers, the noise which they made, and the hazards which street musicians caused to London traffic. With regard to the first of these, Charles Babbage claimed that 'in the course of a few days he was interrupted 182 times', while George Cavendish Bentinck, the Conservative MP, asserted that 'There was no town in Europe, not even Rome, with so many street beggars as London.'[67]

As to the noise which street bands made, an article in *The Times* asserted that 'a German brass band creates discord upon system', while

63. *London City Mission Magazine*, August 1854, p. 168, 2 March 1885, pp. 52–3.
64. Ibid., August 1854, p. 168; 2 January 1865, p. 5.
65. Ibid., September 1864, p. 192; 2 January 1865, pp. 3, 7.
66. *Hansard*, third series, CLXXVI, 468, 29 June 1864.
67. *Hansard*, third series, CLXXII, 972–3, 975, 17 July 1863.

Charles Babbage particularly complained about the fact that street music prevented him from working, as it 'robs the industrious man of his time' and 'destroys the time and energies of all the intellectual classes of society by its continued interruptions of its pursuits.' On one occasion in June 1860 Babbage actually 'summoned' four German brass band musicians before Mr Secker, the police magistrate of Marylebone, upon a charge of annoying him with their noise.' One MP wanted a 'German crusade, and the prevention of twenty or thirty trumpets blowing a blast into the houses in many streets of the metropolis.'[68]

Several commentators, including Babbage, claimed that street musicians hindered London's traffic, apparently leading to accidents in some cases because they frightened horses. Babbage gave an example of an incident in St Pancras in October 1861. One MP apparently informed Michael Bass that 'he lost a division because his horse refused to pass through a band of German musicians'.[69]

As mentioned above, the first campaign against street musicians combined hostility towards both the working classes and towards immigrants. Babbage believed that 'The great encouragers of street music belong chiefly to the lower class of society.' Press articles contained examples of anti-alienism; for instance, the *Examiner* wrote that 'German vagabonds may form a group, set up their music-stands, and torment a neighbourhood with sounds like those of a pig to which they are so near akin.' An article in the *City Press* from 1864 asserted that 'anywhere in the suburbs' one could find 'filthy Germans – as filthy in speech as in looks', blackmailing householders by refusing to move until they had received a payment.[70]

Not all the hostility against street musicians included the German brass bands, as revealed by debates in Parliament over the suppression of street music. Lord Lyndhurst, for instance, claimed that 'there were in London many German bands of great merit which played in the streets surrounded by crowds of people who were attracted by the beauty of their music', a sentiment shared by Sir John Pakington, who 'should be very sorry to get rid of the German bands, for some of them were well worth listening to'. Some commentators felt German brass bands represented less of an evil than Italian, Swiss and French organ

68. *The Times*, 2 October 1859, 2 July 1860; Charles Babbage, *Passages from the Life of a Philosopher*, London, 1864, p. 337.

69. Babbage, *Passages*, pp. 343–4; *Hansard*, third series, CLXXVI, 471, 29 June 1864.

70. Babbage, *Passages*, p. 338. The extracts from the *Examiner* and the *City Press* are from Michael T Bass, *Street Music in the Metropolis*, London, 1864, pp. 91–2, 108.

grinders.[71] But despite traces of positive feeling, the Street Music (Metropolis) Bill became law in 1864. This allowed London magistrates to fine or imprison musicians who refused to move on.[72]

Despite the passage of this Act of 1864, further campaigns for the suppression of street music developed during the 1890s, leading to the foundation of an Association for the Suppression of Street Noises and unsuccessful attempts to pass tighter legislation. The objections remained similar to those of the 1850s and 1860s, with much emphasis on the disruptive nature of German brass bands as well as Italian organ-grinders. An article in the *Nineteenth Century* claimed that these two groups earned 'execration of a very large majority of people whose work is hindered, whose nerves are shattered, and whose rest is disturbed by the detestable and obnoxious nuisance which is the result of their existence.'[73]

Any consideration of the agitation of the 1890s needs to be placed against the background of more widespread hostility towards aliens of the late nineteenth and early twentieth centuries, directed mainly against Russian and Polish Jews but also affecting other minorities, including Germans. The first point to re-emphasise, however, is the fact that the Germans received relatively little attention in comparison particularly with Russian and Polish Jews. The committees established from the 1880s onwards to look into the affects of immigration dealt with Germans in passing,[74] while some of the strongest anti-aliens devoted no attention to the Germans. These included Arnold White whose *Destitute Alien in Great Britain* simply ignored the poor German immigrant, although as we shall see below, this propagandist displayed concern about Germans higher up on the social scale. The strong anti-alien campaign conducted by the *Evening News* in the summer of 1891 also focused almost exclusively on Russian and Polish Jewish emigrants.

71. *Hansard* (Lords), third series, CXLIX, 1928, 29 April 1858; *Hansard* (Commons), third series, CLXXVI, 29 June 1864; 'Music Grinders in the Metropolis', *Chambers' Edinburgh Journal*, vol. 17, 1852, pp. 199–201.

72. Sponza, *Italian Immigrants*, pp. 177–9; Dave Russell, *Popular Music in England, 1880–1914: A Social History*, Manchester, 1987, p. 65.

73. J. Cuthbert Hadder, 'The Regulation of Street Music', *Nineteenth Century*, vol. 39, 1896, p. 950–56. See also *The Times*, 24, 28 December 1895, 8 April 1896, the latter two references of which contain letters from Charles Fox, Honorary Secretary of the Association for the Suppression of Street Music. Sponza, *Italian Immigrants*, pp. 187–94, gives an account of the campaign of the 1890s.

74. See for instance *Report of the Board of Trade on the Sweating System at the East End of London by the Labour Correspondent of the Board*, P.P., vol. LXXXIX, 1887; *Report of the Select Committee on Emigration and Immigration (Foreigners)*, P.P., vol. X, 1889; *Report of the Royal Commission on Alien Immigration*, P.P., vol. IX, 1903.

The only mention of Germany and Germans concerned the fact that many of the Russian and Polish immigrants sailed from German ports on German ships to England.[75]

Nevertheless, despite a comparative lack of social opposition to German immigrants from the 1880s, opposition still existed. We can begin with one propagandist who did not ignore the Germans, the journalist Joseph Banister, whom Colin Holmes has described as having 'engaged in a savage and unremitting hostility towards Jews'.[76] His most important work in this context, *England Under the Jews*, which originally appeared in 1901, attacked Germans together with other groups only incidentally, but did so with the sort of viciousness which Germans rarely faced before 1914. Banister's main aim was to limit immigration through the introduction of legislation. He claimed that:

> From Germany we receive swarms of gambling-house keepers, hotel-porters, barbers, 'bullies', runaway conscripts, bath-attendants, street musicians, criminals, bakers, socialists, cheap clerks, etc. The large annuities we pay to members of our Royal Family, seem to have filled the minds of a considerable proportion of the Teutonic people with an idea that they, too, may live luxuriously on the British public, and so all the 'War Lord's' subjects who are without an inclination or the ability to make a living in 'Yarmany', or have not enough patriotism to fulfil their military obligations, proceed to inflict themselves on this country.[77]

Milder examples of hostility towards Germans in the late nineteenth and early twentieth centuries also existed. During the 1880s and 1890s, for instance, stories appeared about the apparently insanitary conditions of German bakehouses, where baking took place in 'any cellar', which in some instances held 'pigs, poultry, rabbits, and horses'.[78] The 1880s coincided with more widespread hostility towards Germans and German bakers in the East End, as revealed in the pages of a journal entitled the *Briton*, which ran between April and June 1887. Animosity also existed in the local press; the *East End News* complained that 'Not a few manufacturers which used to employ a large number of persons in the East End are now almost entirely in the hands of the Germans and Jews.'[79]

75. Arnold White, *The Destitute Alien in Great Britain*, London, 1892.
76. Holmes, *Anti-Semitism*, p. 39.
77. Joseph Banister, *England Under the Jews*, London, 1901, pp. 8–9, and passim.
78. See *Tower Hamlets Independent*, 29 April, 26 August 1892; and *East End News*, 1 May 1893.
79. *Briton*, 30 April, 7, 21, 28 May 1887; *East End News*, 19 April, 31 May 1887.

Other press reports focused on the apparent fact that Germans entered Britain in large numbers. For instance, an article in a journal entitled the *Thames Iron Works Gazette* of 31 December 1897, signed 'A German' although almost certainly written by a xenophobic and Germanophobic Englishman, claimed that 'Steamers leave the Elbe twice a week, which never fail to land in London the German immigrant, mit his wife and his family – and mit noddings else – and then just as regularly take back the worn-out horses of London for conversion into the succulent sausages of Germany.' Twelve years later an article in the *Morning Post* claimed that the German Industrial and Farm Colony at Libury Hall housed people who had evaded the Aliens Act of 1905.[80] The Select Committee on Emigration and Immigration, which reported in 1889, displayed concern about the size of the German population of Britain; there was close questioning of Rudolph Frentzel, chairman of the Society of Friends of Foreigners in Distress, and Adolph Dellschaft, Honorary Secretary of the German Society of Benevolence, regarding the precise number of people their organisations assisted.[81]

The Royal Commission on Alien Immigration, which reported in 1903, was concerned about various aspects of the lives of Germans in London. For instance Charles Ensor Walters, a member of St Pancras Borough Council, referring to the area around Fitzroy Square, spoke of the 'great increase of foreign prostitutes, and the utter absence among them of moral sense'. Another witness, W. R. McConnel, KC, believed that the main crime carried out by Germans was burglary, for which they used an advanced tool imported from Germany. He further asserted that 'a good many...German waiters procured employment on false characters in lodging-houses or in restaurants, and there they steal from inhabitants and visitors in the boarding houses, and also steal the property of their employers.'[82] Several years later, in 1909, Judge J. A. Rentoul claimed that seventy-five percent of cases tried before him involved 'the Russian burglar, the Polish thief, the Italian stabber, and the German swindler'. The last referred to 'a man who deserted from the German Army', and was 'sought by the police, escaped, committed embezzlement in his own country, and had undergone a long sentence there. He then came to this country, and began business here, with the result that he swindled several innocent people, and had now gone to prison to be supported by the people of this country.' Rentoul's animosity fits into the context of continuing anti-immigrant hostility after the

80. *Morning Post*, 3 February 1909.
    81. *Report of the Select Committee on Emigration and Immigration (Foreigners)*, pp. 12–17, P.P., vol. X, 1889.
    82. *Report of the Royal Commission on Alien Immigration*, vol. 2, questions 12730–35, 13100, P.P., vol. IX, 1903.

passage of the 1905 Aliens Act; he made equally strong comments with regard to Italians.[83]

Economic Hostility Towards German Immigrants

Having examined the main strands of socio-economic hostility towards Germans in Victorian and Edwardian Britain, we can now move on to consider the more purely economic animosity against them, best explained by Leopold Katscher:

> Many Englishmen who esteem the Germans do not love them because they compete in the labour market with the natives of this country. German bakers, tailors, waiters, hairdressers, watchmakers, clerks, music teachers, schoolmasters, &c., are naturally the horror of all the English who work in these various industries, for the Germans are satisfied with lower salaries, and are therefore preferred, not only by their own countrymen, but frequently also by English employers.[84]

As well as hostility towards Germans within individual occupations, which we can discuss below, there also existed a more widespread animosity against German employees, especially from the late nineteenth century. This was connected with the development of British fear of German economic power, whose growth appeared to threaten the British economy. Hostility towards the German economy reached something of a peak in the mid-1890s with the publication of *Made in Germany* by E. E. Williams, pointing to the increased number of German goods in England. Other publications also expressed concern; the Tariff Reform Campaign, launched in 1902, directed much of its propaganda against Germany, Britain's main economic rival. Producers in individual trades, including cutlery, viewed Germany as a threat to their survival.[85]

Williams made connections between German labour and German goods in England in *Made in Germany*, in which he wrote that: 'Your governesses's *fiance* is a clerk in the City; but he was also made in Germany', like 'your wife's garments', 'the material of your favourite

83. *Expulsion of Aliens: Correspondence between the Secretary of State for the Home Department and His Honour Judge Rentoul, KC, 11 March 1909*, P.P., vol. LXX, 1909.

84. Leopold Katscher, 'German Life in London', *Nineteenth Century*, vol. 21, 1887, p. 740.

85. E. E. Williams, *'Made in Germany'*, London, 1896; B. H. Thwaite, 'The Commercial War Between Germany and England', *Nineteenth Century*, vol. 40, 1896, pp. 925–31; Kennedy, *Anglo-German-Antagonism*, pp. 41–58, 291–305; G. I. H. Lloyd, *The Cutlery Trades*, London, 1913, pp. 345–50.

(patriotic) newspaper', as well as virtually everything in the house. Furthermore, 'you are awakened in the morning by the sonorous brass of a German band'.[86] Other commentators used less restrained language to make a similar point. For instance, in a book published in 1885, Thomas Hay Sweet Escott spoke of 'an invasion of Germans as formidable in its way as that which France experienced in the Great War', and 'which substitutes German clerks and lawyers, German merchants and big and small tradesmen for English'. The author especially focused upon the fact that 'Every grade in English life, from the royal family to the domestic servant, is leavened by the German element.' Escott pointed to tailors in particular, as well as focusing upon the influence of German culture. He further claimed that 'in no city in the world, Berlin alone excepted, are there so many destitute Germans as in London.'[87] But the language used here remains milder than Banister's, which combines hostility towards Germans with anti-semitism. The latter wrote: 'The German waiters and porters who cringe for tips at so many of our principal hotels are brought over by the German Jews who manage these hotels, and the cheap German clerks we hear so much about are imported and nowadays employed almost entirely by Jew firms.'[88]

The extent of this general hostility towards German employees is difficult to estimate, but we can obtain some idea from the probably exaggerated impressions of a German governess who visited London in 1906 in an unsuccessful attempt to find a position. She recorded her impressions in a letter to a German newspaper, in which she claimed that she and her compatriots faced strong hostility which they feared might explode into violence. Because of the 'awful poverty of the English workmen and workwomen', she claimed that, 'No good commercial house now engages Germans, but only English or French workmen and messengers. Only Jews or poor English people now engage Germans.'[89]

Hostility towards Germans in individual occupations existed before the late nineteenth century. As the extract from Katscher suggested, it surfaced whenever native workers faced competition. In the 1850s, for instance, Mayhew interviewed an English bandsman who declared:

> The German bands injure our trade very much. They'll play for half what we ask. They are very mean, feed dirtily, and the best band of them, whom I met

86. Williams, *Made in Germany*, pp. 10–11.
87. Thomas Hay Sweet Escott, *Society in London*, London, 1885, pp. 47–9.
88. Banister, *England Under the Jews*, p. 37.
89. *Anglo-German Courier*, 9 March 1906.

at Dover, I know slept three in a bed in a common lodging-house, one of the lowest. They now block us out of all the country places to which we used to go in the summer.[90]

Half a century later in 1901, hostility of a similar nature still existed, as indicated in an article in a journal entitled *Bandmaster's Help* which declared that 'English bands in our hotels and restaurants are being steadily replaced by foreign ones.'[91]

Hostility towards German tailors, linked with an animosity towards all immigrants engaged in this occupation, existed for as long as did the negative feeling towards German musicians. One of Mayhew's interviewees declared that 'every summer brings a fresh importation' of 'German and Polish Jew tailors'. In 1887, a report into the 'sweating system' in the East End of London pointed to 'an enormous influx of pauper foreigners', especially German and Russian Jews, 'and there can be no doubt that the result has been to flood the labour market of the east end of London with cheap labour as to reduce thousands of native workers to the verge of destitution.'[92]

Two German occupational groups towards whom hostility developed at the end of the nineteenth century were clerks and waiters. In his article on the former, Gregory Anderson has rightly identified an animosity fuelled by both 'the more general and well-known Anglo-German economic and political rivalry', and by the 'particular impact' of German clerks on the labour market.[93] Some of the attention devoted towards German clerks rationalised the reasons why they had succeeded in finding a niche in the British labour market by pointing to the educational system in Germany, while others managed to keep their influence in Britain within perspective.[94] But in some cases we can identify a strong hostility, such as in a speech of W. Field, MP for Dublin, who claimed in 1902 that 14,000 German clerks worked in Manchester, while the figure for London totalled hundreds of thousands.[95] An article in the *National Review* of 1910 used stronger language when it claimed that

90. Henry Mayhew, *The Morning Chronicle Survey of London and the Poor: The Metropolitan Districts*, 5 vols., Horsham, 1981, vol. 5, p. 2.

91. *Bandmasters Help*, September 1901.

92. Mayhew, *Morning Chronicle Survey*, vol. 2, p. 108; *Report of the Board of Trade on the Sweating System at the East End of London by the Labour Correspondent of the Board*, p. 4, P.P., vol. LXXXIX, 1887.

93. Gregory Anderson, 'German Clerks in England, 1870–1914: Another Aspect of the Great Depression Debate', in Kenneth Lunn (ed.), *Hosts, Immigrants and Minorities: Historical Responses to Newcomers in British Society 1870–1914*, Folkestone, 1980, pp. 201, 206.

94. See for instance J J. Findlay, 'The Genesis of the German Clerk', *Fortnightly Review*, vol. 61, pp. 533–6.

95. Anderson, 'German Clerks', p. 204.

German clerks acted as 'spies in the service of the enemy' because, 'not only are our methods of business studied and sometimes improved upon, but the reports furnished to headquarters disclose every weakness in our armour and show where openings offer for the protected wedge of German commerce to enter.'[96]

Hostility towards foreign waiters also became widespread during the late Victorian and Edwardian years amongst both employers and employees in the trade as well as those outside it. In 1890, an article in the *Caterer and Hotel Proprietors' Gazette*, entitled 'English and Foreign Waiters', asserted that 'English hotels are not only open to, but are literally deluged with foreigners'. The author of the piece could 'quite understand the grievance of the English Hotel and Restaurant Union.'[97]

Twenty years later, in 1910, an organisation called the Loyal British Waiters Society had come into existence. At its inception it had 1,625 members and during its first two years it had secured 4,700 jobs, mostly of a temporary nature. It described its first aim as providing 'temporary or permanent employment for British waiters who are reliable and loyal'. In the first issue of its journal, the *Restaurateur*, the organisation drew up a list of 'Reasons why every Britisher should Patronize and Support The Loyal British Waiters' Society and School of Instruction'. These included the fact that 'it is of a Loyal and Patriotic character, and has for its main object the displacement of the foreigner and reinstating the Britisher', and the fact that 'it will greatly reduce the vast amount of foreign labour in this country, thereby strengthening our population and constitution.'

The Society did not solely publish xenophobic propaganda; it also established a School of Instruction to improve the employment prospects of British waiters, realising that immigrants had received a full training. Nevertheless, it remained fundamentally xenophobic in its aims. Its journal carried articles with titles such as 'Foreign Waiters Again', 'English Waiters v Foreign Waiters', 'London Overcrowded with Foreign Waiters', and 'British Waiters for British Hotels'. The last of these claimed that there were just 1,000 British waiters in London, compared with 30,000 immigrants. An article entitled 'To Oust the Foreign Waiter', pointed out that 'A movement has been inaugurated at Llandudno with the object of ousting to some extent the army of foreigners who staff the leading hotels as waiters.'[98]

96. Watchman, 'Some New Facts About German Commercial Tactics', *National Review*, March 1910, pp. 84–6.
97. *Caterer and Hotel Proprietors Gazette*, 15 December 1890.
98. *Restaurateur*, March, June, July 1912, October 1913, February 1914.

The campaign of the Loyal British Waiters Society had support outside its membership, as revealed in a pamphlet published in 1914 and based on lectures delivered in 1909 by Colonel J. E. Porteous, with the title of *Peaceful Invasion of Great Britain*. The author claimed: 'The largest and best hotels in Great Britain are under German management, and the staff of servants is almost entirely German. In the smaller hotels throughout Great Britain, whether at Stronachlachar, or the Isle of Wight, the staff is also frequently all German.' However, the main concern of Porteous lay not in the economic threat of the waiters, but in the fact that he saw them as 'the German Army Reserve', carrying out surveillance work in their spare time in preparation for a German invasion of Britain.[99]

Political Hostility Towards German Immigrants

The above survey of socio-economic attitudes towards Germans in Victorian and Edwardian Britain indicates that hostility existed on a significant scale, focusing on specific issues at different times. However, as mentioned previously, we cannot identify a uniquely anti-German campaign resembling those against the Irish in the mid-nineteenth century, or Russian and Polish Jews in late Victorian and early Edwardian Britain. If we examine political hostility towards Germans in Britain, which was connected with developments on the international scene, we can see there was a specifically anti-German campaign which began during the early twentieth century. But there was another strand of hostility, opposition to political refugees, which does not fit comfortably into either socio-economic or politically-inspired hostility.

Despite the existence of positive feeling towards refugees from the 1848 revolutions,[100] their entry into Britain also led to the development of hostility against them. The views of Bernard Porter on this subject, who claims that the refugees 'were unloved' but 'tolerated', remain perhaps the most accurate.[101] However, we should not ignore the passage of the Alien Act in 1848, which allowed the expulsion of 'any Person'

99. J. E. Porteous, *Peaceful Invasion of Great Britain: The Nation Warned in 1909*, London, 1914.

100. See the reception for the Hungarian leader Louis Kossuth described by Denes A. Janossy, *Great Britain and Kossuth*, Budapest, 1937; and for Gottfried Kinkel, mentioned by Rosemary Ashton, *Little Germany: Exile and Asylum in Victorian England*, Oxford, 1986, pp. 153–5.

101. Bernard Porter, *The Refugee Question in Mid-Victorian Politics*, Cambridge, 1979, p. 124.

regarded as a threat to 'any Part of this Realm', although in reality the Government never used this power and it lapsed in 1850.[102]

But traces of hostility exist into the 1850s and beyond, not only in the experiences of individual refugees[103] but also in images of refugees in publications. During the Great Exhibition of 1851, for instance, which took place at a time when the refugee issue still held public attention,[104] *Household Words* carried an article entitled 'The Foreign Invasion', which attacked every national group which made its way to the event. The piece used phrases such as 'the Teuton', and 'The German, meer-shaumed, *kraut* perfumed, and thumb-ringed'. In the following year, a short piece in *Household Words* caricatured refugees from different European nations. The German representative consisted of 'that valiant republican Spartacus Bursch, erst PHD of the University of Heidelberg, then on no pay, but with brevet rank, behind a barricade formed of an omnibus, two water-carts and six paving-stones at Frankfort.' Following further revolutionary activity, he eventually made his way to London as 'promoter of a patent for extracting vinegar from white lead, keeper of a cigar-shop, professor of fencing, calisthenics, and German literature; and latterly out of any trade or occupation.'[105]

German and other refugees continued to attract attention into the second half of the nineteenth century, for example with the prosecution of Johannes Most in 1881–2. Subsequently, concern about foreign anarchists served as one stimulus to the development of the Metropolitan Police Special Branch.[106] Concern about this subject can be seen in novels, including one entitled *The Anarchist*. The author, Colonel Richard Henry Savage, believed that the 'creed of Destruction' threatened the 'civilized world'. The novel was set mainly in the USA, although Savage stressed the international nature of anarchism, and the main character was Carl Stein, a native of Saxony and failed academic.[107]

As mentioned above, the most important strand of hostility towards Germans in Victorian and Edwardian Britain had its origins in the rise of

102. Ibid., p. 86; Ashton, *Little Germany*, p. 42. For a defence of Britain's right of asylum from British official sources, see *Correspondence Respecting the Foreign Refugees in London*, P.P., vol. LIV, 1852; and *Further Correspondence Respecting the Foreign Refugees in London*, P.P., vol. LIV, 1852.

103. See Ashton, *Little Germany*.

104. Porter, *Refugee Question*, pp. 86–8.

105. *Household Words*, 11 October 1851, pp. 60–4, 29 May 1852, pp. 253–5.

106. Bernard Porter, 'The Freiheit Prosecutions 1881–1882', *Historical Journal*, vol. 23, 1980, pp. 833–56; Porter, *The Origins of the Vigilant State: The London Metropolitan Police Special Branch before the First World War*, London, 1987.

107. Richard Henry Savage, *The Anarchist: A Story of To-Day*, London, 1894.

Anglo-German diplomatic rivalry. The focus of hostility on Germans became most widespread when relations between the two countries became most strained, from the 1890s onwards and especially from the early years of the twentieth century. Even before this period, peaks of hostility towards Germany and Germans developed when diplomatic crises which suggested a growth of German power occurred on the continent. This animosity manifested itself especially in the written word, and also transformed the underlying image of the German so that militarism became the most important aspect of his character. By the end of the period under consideration, hostility towards Germans also manifested itself in small outbreaks of violence and the introduction of legislation for the control of aliens, essentially Germans, in the event of war.

Before 1870, we can only detect weak traces of politically-inspired hostility towards Germany and Germans because, until the Franco-Prussian War, the country did not appear to be a threat. One indication of political anti-Germanism lies in views towards Prince Albert which, on many occasions, broke out into open hostility. The first of these actually occurred just before the marriage of the Prince of Saxe-Coburg-Gotha to Queen Victoria in 1840, when 'an uneasy feeling on the subject of the Prince's creed had got abroad'. At the same time questions also arose about his salary.[108]

An indication of the concern about both Prince Albert's religion and the financial implications of his marriage can be seen in an anonymous poem entitled *The German Bridegroom*. The Prince was described as a 'German pauper' on several occasions, although the attack upon him broadened out to include Germany more generally so that one stanza began, 'Yes, the poor *English* must be squeezed more dry,/ That the poor *Germans* may fare sumptuously.' With regard to Albert's religion, the poem proceeded:

How many doubts and fears we've heard expressed
About the faith this German has professed.
Is he a Protestant in word and deed?
A true believer in old Luther's creed?
One who would doom, with genuine Bloomfield wrath,
His Papist brethren to be Satan's broth?
Or does he worship all the motley crew
Of Saints and Martyrs as the Romans do?[109]

108. Theodore Martin, *The Life of His Royal Highness the Prince Consort*, 5 vols, London, 1875–80, vol. 1, 1875, p. 58; Daphne Bennet, *King Without a Crown: Albert, Prince Consort of England 1819–1861*, London, 1983 edition, pp. 32–42; Robert Rhodes James, *Albert, Prince Consort: A Biography*, London, 1983, p. 91.
109. Anonymous, *The German Bridegroom*, London, 1840.

Although negative feeling against Prince Albert remained latent during the 1840s,[110] it resurfaced again on at least two occasions in a more potent manner during the 1850s, focusing upon the Prince's German, or at least non-English, birth. The first occasion followed the dismissal of the Foreign Secretary, Lord Palmerston, by the Prime Minister of the time, Lord Russell, in December 1851 with backing from the Crown. Palmerston's claim that he was 'a victim of foreign intrigue' found support in 'the journals known to support his views'. One journalist described Prince Albert as the chief agent of an 'Austro-Belgian-Coburg-Orleans clique, the avowed enemies of England'.[111]

Anti-Germanism came to the surface in a more potent manner in December 1853 when Palmerston, who had rejoined the Cabinet, offered his resignation, ostensibly over the parliamentary reform issue but, in the view of sections of the press, because the Government had not acted firmly enough over the sinking of part of the Turkish fleet by Russian ships in Sinope. Pro-Turkish and anti-Russian feeling led to claims that Prince Albert had dismissed Palmerston, resulting in a fierce campaign against the former which certainly stressed his German origins.[112] One of the most extreme expressions of the hostility to Albert came in a pamphlet entitled *Lovely Albert*, which accused him of siding with Russia, Austria and Prussia, as well as reminding readers that 'When Al came home you're all aware,/He brought with him no riches.'[113] But the campaign against the Prince died down quickly as sections of the press, together with pamphleteers, came to his defence.[114]

If we pause to consider the campaign against Prince Albert, we can make two observations. In the first place we might view it against the background of a rising British nationalism which did not exclude Germany from a list of enemies. However, at this stage it is virtually impossible to speak of Germanophobia in Britain. The country's failure to assist the revolutionaries of 1848, for instance, represented an inclina-

110. See James, *Albert*, pp. 106, 136, 137, 152.
111. Martin, *Life of the Prince Consort*, vol. 2, London, 1876, pp. 538–40; Martin Kingsley, *The Triumph of Lord Palmerston: A Study of Public Opinion in England Before the Crimean War*, London, 1963 edition, pp. 65–9; Roger Fulford, *The Prince Consort*, London, 1949, pp. 121–42.
112. Fulford, *The Prince Consort*, pp. 155–65; Martin, *Life of the Prince Consort*, pp. 178–86; Robert Blake, 'Prince Albert and the Crimean War', in Adolf M. Birke and Kurt Kluxen (eds), *Viktorianisches England in deutscher Perspektive*, London, 1983, pp. 23–4; Bennett, *King Without a Crown*, pp. 247–51.
113. *Lovely Albert*, London, 1854[?].
114. For examples of supportive publications, see P. J. Nagle, *Prince Albert's Defence*, London, 1854; Anonymous, *Prince Albert's Defence*, London, 1854; Plain Speech, *Who's to Blame, The Prince, The Press, or The Ministry*, London, n.d.

tion to remain apart from continental affairs.[115] A better way to understand the attacks on Prince Albert is by placing them within the context of the anti-German immigrant conspiracy theories, which became widespread at the start of the twentieth century, claiming that rich Germans worked against the interests of Britain. In the Edwardian period, against the background of widespread hostility towards Germany, these ideas became more persistent.

An important turning point in British political views of Germany arrived following the Prussian victory in the war against France in 1871, although negative comment had begun to appear throughout the course of the 1860s. In 1871 the new attitude found expression in press comment and the birth of the invasion novel;[116] the panic occasioned by the 1871 victory focused on the belief that Britain could become the next victim of Germany, and the writers of various articles and books aimed at alerting the public about the weakness of Britain's army and security. An article in a periodical called *Once A Week*, entitled 'Our National Defences', declared that: 'The results of the campaign on the Continent...have made an impression on the minds of Englishmen which is far from comfortable, to say the least of it.' The piece then suggested the introduction of military service.[117]

The invasion novels published in 1871 followed a similar argument. The most famous of these, *The Battle of Dorking*, by George Chesney, depicting the invasion and defeat of England, declared: 'We English have only ourselves to blame for the humiliation which has been brought on the land', because the country failed to reform its army.[118] *The Battle of Dorking*, along with other publications from that year, reveals the surfacing of a new image of a militaristic Germany, which would become the dominant image by the outbreak of the First World War. William Hunter, for instance, admired the reorganisation of the German Army which had taken place during the course of the nineteenth century, and warned that Britain had to follow a similar path in order to avoid the fate of France.[119]

115. Günther Gillesen, *Lord Palmerston und die Einigung Deutschlands*, Lübeck, 1961; Wolfgang J. Mommsen, *Two Centuries of Anglo-German Relations: A Reappraisal*, London, 1984, pp. 11–12.

116. Raymond James Sontag, *Germany and England: Background of Conflict 1848–1894*, London, 1938, pp. 31–3.

117. *Once a Week*, 4 February 1871, 7 September 1872.

118. George Chesney, *The Battle of Dorking*, Edinburgh and London, 1871, pp. 3–6.

119. William Hunter, *Army Speech Dedicated to Those Who Have Been Frightened by the Battle of Dorking*, London, 1871.

Chesney, meanwhile, describes one of the German soldiers who had taken part in his invasion of England as 'a broad-shouldered brute, stuffing a great hunch of beef into his mouth with a silver fork, an implement I should think he must have been using for the first time in his life'.[120]

The growth of Anglo-German antagonism had few negative effects on the German community in Britain at this stage, and these did not manifest themselves until the late 1890s. The first example of antagonism towards the German community in connection with the German military threat does not occur until 1896, after the sending of the 'Kruger Telgram', when Kaiser Wilhelm II congratulated the President of the Transvaal for resisting British aggression. This led to considerable hostility against Germany[121] and, according to German press reports, attacks upon Germans and their property in London. The 'newspapers in question' claimed that 'tumultuous scenes were provoked by assaults and insults to which German and Dutch sailors were subjected'. Furthermore, 'shop windows of German tradesmen were smashed' and 'several German clubs in the East-end and a Dutch club were closed'. Enquiries by the Press Association revealed the reports in the German newspapers to contain no truth.[122] Nevertheless, *The Times* felt that the Germans in London deserved some attention, and several articles and letters on this subject were published in the first half of January 1896, most of them calling attention to the loyalty of the German community within Britain.[123]

Four years later the situation worsened when attacks upon Germans actually did take place. By this time concern about the German threat had grown, while ideas about the instability of the British Empire had begun to surface. The principal concern was the expansionist German imperial and more especially naval policy, particularly after the passage of a new Naval Bill by the German Reichstag in June 1899, which was intended to double the number of German battleships. By the turn of the century insecurity about Britain's position had already led to the development of nationalistic pressure groups including the Primrose League, established in 1893, the Navy League from 1895, and the National Service League from

120. Chesney, *Battle of Dorking*, p. 57.
121. Kennedy, *Anglo-German Antagonism*, p. 220; Arthur J. Marder, *British Naval Policy 1880–1905: The Anatomy of British Sea Power*, London, 1940, p. 256; Robert K. Massie, *Dreadnought: Britain, Germany, and the Great War*, London, 1992, pp. 213–31.
122. *The Times*, 10 January 1896.
123. Ibid., 9, 11, 14 January 1896.

1901. At the same time articles regularly appeared in the periodical press on the subject of Anglo-German relations.[124] Whereas in 1884 an article in the *Nineteenth Century*, entitled 'The Expansion of Germany' by George Baden-Powell, could assert, that 'there is ample reason for every citizen of the British Empire to welcome this new born expansion of Germany', an essay with the same title in the same journal, fourteen years later, took a different perspective.[125] The author, Henry Birchenough, believed that German commercial, industrial, imperial and naval expansion would inevitably bring the country into conflict with other nations.[126] Another article of the same year, 1898, by Sidney Whitman traced the deterioration of Anglo-German relations, but blamed this state of affairs as much upon Britain as upon Germany because of the former's reluctance to accept the latter's expansion.[127]

Two years later, at the height of the Boer War, fears of invasion became widespread although the potential invaders could be either French or German. With regard to the former as a perceived threat we can point to an article in the *National Review* of 1900 which speculated about the effects of a French attack across the English Channel. The author, W. E. Cairnes, believed that a conflict between the two countries 'would be the most colossal struggle the world has ever seen'.[128] As to the German threat, the *Contemporary Review* carried an article by a German author which tried to play down the threat of Germany, claiming that 'Except for a certain number of fanatic Chauvinists, devoid of all political weight, all Germany holds that a war with England would be a mad enterprise.'[129]

However, this did not prevent the publication of works such as T. W. Offin's fictitious account, *How the Germans Took London*, published in 1900, which takes place against the background of develop-

124. Marder, *British Naval Policy*, pp. 55, 456–7; I. Metz, *Die deutsche Flotte in der Englischen Presse: Der Navy Scare vom Winter 1905/06*, Berlin, 1936, pp. 11–21; John M. Mackenzie, *Propaganda and Empire: The Manipulation of British Public Opinion, 1880–1960*, Manchester, 1988 reprint, pp. 148–51; Anne Summers, 'The Character of Edwardian Nationalism: Three Popular Leagues', in Kennedy and Nicholls, *Nationalist and Racialist Movements*, pp. 68–81; Summers, 'Militarism in Britain before the Great War', *History Workshop*, vol. 2, 1976, pp. 111–17.

125. George Baden Powell, 'The Expansion of Germany', *Nineteenth Century*, vol. 16, 1884, pp. 869–78.

126. Henry Birchenough, 'The Expansion of Germany', *Nineteenth Century*, February 1898, pp. 182–91.

127. Sidney Whitman, 'England and Germany', *Harper's Magazine*, April 1898, pp. 778–91.

128. W. E. Cairnes, 'The Problem of Invasion', *National Review*, vol. 36, pp. 341–60.

129. Theodor Barth, 'England and Germany', *Contemporary Review*, vol. 77, 1900, pp. 620–8.

ments in South Africa. In his opening remarks the author declares: 'Having a good local knowledge of Essex, I have always noted the defenceless state of London, if an invasion took place by a landing on the Essex Coast.' Consequently, the fictional invasion takes place when German troops enter Britain through that part of the country. More interesting from our point of view is the role the author assigns to Germans already within Britain, especially clerks. Initially we hear that 'German clerks have been warned by their Government to hold themselves in readiness to return to their country for Military service', which means that 'the German Authorities' send vessels to Tilbury in Essex to transport them back to Germany. The author comments: 'Naturally great jubilation exists among City clerical circles; higher wages; more employment, and a good time generally are looked forward to.' He further adds: 'It will also be interesting to know how many thousands of Teutons have, year by year, crept into our employ. The total, perhaps, would be alarming.' However, the clerks do not make their way back to Germany but to London instead, which the author asserts has consequently fallen into 'the hands of the Germans'. The fall of London together with the military invasion means that Britain falls to Germany.[130]

Against the background of fear of invasion, public opinion became volatile enough to lead to attacks upon people who either did not support British efforts in the Boer War or were perceived as not doing so. Attacks occurred throughout 1900.[131] One high point of feeling occurred in May 1900 following the Relief of Mafeking, a turning point in British fortunes which led to widespread rejoicing throughout Britain on the day of the announcement of the event, 18 May. 'A remarkable demonstration of popular enthusiasm was witnessed on the streets of London', while outside the capital, 'Enthusiastic crowds collected everywhere, the National Anthem was sung, and church bells pealed.' Two days later in London, 'still the city is gay with colour. The sun shines on a mass of red, white, and blue, with here and there a touch of green, and horses and vehicles still carry their emblems of rejoicing.'[132] This enthusiasm spilled over into acts of violence, admittedly on a small scale. Those to suffer included the Consul General of the Netherlands, 'the Rev Silas Hocking, a gentleman who had taken part in meetings protesting against the war', and whose home in Highgate in north London faced attack,[133]

---

130. T. W. Offin, *How the Germans Took London*, London, 1900.
131. Richard Price, *An Imperial War and the British Working Classes: Working-Class Attitudes and Reactions to the Boer War*, London, 1972, pp. 132–77; *Nation*, 27 March 1909.
132. *The Times*, 19, 21 May 1900.
133. PRO MEPO3 196/60; PRO HO45 10813/330667E/20.

and Henry Bish, a German who owned a barber's shop in another part of north London, St Anne's Road in Tottenham.

The background to this latter incident involved the arousal of 'Tottenham's Patriotism' following the news of the Relief of Mafeking. A Metropolitan Police report described Bish as 'a German of pro Boer sympathies who has recently made his opinions known rather widely among his customers.' On the afternoon of Sunday, 20 May, a crowd gathered outside his shop and took offence to a dark blue advertising flag, which they believed was a Boer flag and which they wanted Bish to pull down. When he refused to do this, one member of the crowd tore it down while another proceeded to burn it. The crowd also 'broke some windows':

> At 9.30 another crowd gathered and stones being thrown the windows in the upper part of the house were broken and a lighted firework thrown through the broken window, set fire to the lace curtain. The police estimate that the crowd numbered about 2,000 persons and they were not withdrawn until 1 a.m. on the following morning.

On the next day 'the place looked like a house about to be pulled down after a fire.' Further incidents occurred on the same afternoon, following the remanding in custody of two of the rioters prosecuted by Bish. When he left the court and boarded a tram car he 'was followed by some of the crowd'. Throughout the events of 20 and 21 May Bish's origins received attention from rioters, who insulted him as a 'German' and suggested he should go home to the 'Vaterland'.[134]

Other violent incidents involving Germans also occurred, as can be seen from an incident in east London in December 1901, which took place against a background of more widespread xenophobia. The incident occurred on a train travelling to Custom House Station, when a group of Englishmen told nine Germans conversing in their native language to '"Speak English!" When they arrived at Custom House one of the Germans was knocked down by two or three Englishmen, and about 40 Englishmen chased the nine Germans out of the station.' In fact, this represented just one example of the 'ill-feeling' which 'existed between the English and Germans in South West Ham', as Germans 'were often assaulted on their way home from work, and were pelted with stones by the English, and they had to get the protection of the police.'[135]

134. PRO MEPO3 196/60; PRO HO45 10813/330667E/20; *Tottenham and Stamford Hill Times and Stoke Newington Chronicle*, 25 May 1900; *The Times*, 22 May 1900.
135. *Borough of West Ham, East Ham and Stratford Express*, 21 December 1901; *West Ham Guardian*, 21 December 1901; *South Essex Mail*, 21 December 1901.

From the early years of the twentieth century attitudes towards Germany and Germans in Britain become overwhelmingly negative as relations between the countries deteriorated further, especially after the signing of the *entente cordiale* between Britain and France in 1904. There developed a Germanophobic atmosphere, in which Germany and its representatives within Britain began to be viewed as both an internal and external enemy. Internally, hostility towards Germans did not surpass that towards Jews before 1914 but, as we shall see, propagandists linked the two together. Animosity remained constant, although it reached peaks during significant diplomatic developments such as the Moroccan crises of 1905 and 1911 and the naval panic of 1908–9. We can best examine the hostility of the Edwardian years by breaking it down into underlying images, 'spy-fever', conspiracy theories and official hostility.

The deterioration of the underlying image meant the transformation of the German professor of the mid-nineteenth century into 'a military figure of imposing build, uniformed and spurred, with upturned moustache, a commanding eye, and a powerful arm encased in mail.' But the idea of Germany, or Prussia, representing militarism did have a long tradition, as Mayhew's observations on the Rhineland reveal.[136] However, in the Edwardian period fear of German militarism replaced admiration for German culture, with German soldiers playing a large role in the literature of England in the decade leading up to the First World War.[137] These themes come through in *Her Husband's Country*, a novel by Sybil Spottiswoode published in 1911, in which Patience Thaile moves to Germany in order to marry a German soldier. Her preconception of Germany revolved around 'the idea of fat untidy men, bearded and spectacled, living upon beer and Sauerkraut – learned, perhaps, but thoroughly unprepossessing and unattractive.' We then view German military society through her eyes: 'To a German officer, his Fatherland, comes first – a woman belongs to her husband's country.'[138]

The change in the underlying image of Germans and Germany in literature followed a similar path in children's books, music hall songs, academic study, journalism (above all) and popular fiction. In the music hall, negative attitudes towards Germany and Germans in Britain had begun to develop from the 1890s and during the Edwardian years each

---

136. 'Germany and the Prussian Spirit', p. 618.

137. Theodor Kornder, *Der Deutsche im Spiegelbild der englische Erzählungsliteratur des 19. Jahrhunderts*, Erlangen-Bruck, 1934, pp. 90–106; Schultz, *Der Deutsche in der englischen Literatur*, pp. 150–4; Weineck, *Deutschland und der Deutsche*, pp. 234–6.

138. Sybil Spottiswoode, *Her Husband's Country*, London, 1911, pp. 36, 255. See also D. H. Lawrence, *The Prussian Officer*, London, 1914, who creates a muscular, 'brutal' infantry captain.

'flashpoint in Anglo-German relations produced an angry snarl from the music-hall bulldogs.'[139] In children's books the proportion of negative portrayals of Germans virtually changes place with positive ones, so that the former had reached over eighty per cent by the First World War.[140] In academic study, we can point to history where the focus upon the early history of England and the invasion of the Angles and Saxons died away as an area of interest, replaced by the history of modern Germany viewed as a threat.[141]

For journalists, both serious and popular, Germany became almost an obsession. In addition to the focus on the German threat in newspapers, there was also a constant stream of articles in periodical publications throughout the Edwardian years. In 1903, for instance, a piece in the *Contemporary Review*, entitled 'Germany and Pan-Germany', began with the lines: 'Looking out at the opening of the twentieth century upon the nations of Europe – the enemies of England as they have been described, and not unfitly – it is impossible not to feel that of all the peoples on the Continent the Germans are the most vital.' The country had 'armed to the teeth' and the article concluded that in Germany's 'existence lies one of the greatest possible securities for the maintenance of the British Empire.'

Five years later an article entitled 'The German Peril' appeared in the *Quarterly Review*, at the height of the controversy over the navy estimates. The essay reviewed nine books on the subject of Anglo-German relations, with titles including *German Ambitions* and *The Pan-Germanic Doctrine*.[142] The *National Review*, edited by Leopold J. Maxse, represented one of the most Germanophobic journals, having adopted an anti-German stance from the 1890s and, during the Edwardian period, publishing a constant stream of attacks on Germany.[143] A book issued by the *Daily Mail* in 1909, with the ironic title of *Our German Cousins*, indicates how previous admiration for German learning had now become an object of jealousy within Britain.[144]

139. Russell, *Popular Music in England*, pp. 119–21.
140. Emer O'Sullivan, *Friend and Foe: The Image of Germany and the Germans in British Children's Fiction from 1870 to the Present*, Tübingen, 1990, p. 78.
141. Messerschmidt, *Deutschland in englischer Sicht*, pp. 67–97.
142. 'Germany and Pan-Germany', *Contemporary Review*, vol. 84, 1903, pp. 173–88; 'The German Peril', *Quarterly Review*, vol. 209, pp. 264–98.
143. John A. Hutcheson, *Leopold Maxse and the National Review, 1893–1914: Right-Wing Politics and Journalism in the Edwardian Era*, New York, 1989; Leopold James Maxse, *'Germany on the Brain' or the Obsession of a 'Crank': Gleanings from the National Review, 1899–1914*, London, 1915.
144. *Daily Mail, Our German Cousins*, London, 1909.

The changing journalistic attitude of these years essentially reflects domestic political views of Germany, leading to the development of the 'Radical Right' in Britain in which Leopold Maxse was a pivotal figure, although political historians who have identified this group have pointed to the influence of other figures, notably the aristocratic Willoughby de Broke. The Radical Right, which did not develop into a political party, consisted mainly of Conservative Unionists, but also included people from other parts of the political spectrum including the former liberal journalist Arnold White and the 'rogue socialist' Robert Blatchford. The ideology of the group revolved around nationalism, Germanophobia and a more general xenophobia, especially against immigrants within Britain, both rich and poor. We can point to the nationalistic pressure groups previously outlined above as forming part of the Radical Right. While the group may not have held power its views, supported by substantial sections of the press, played a large role in influencing attitudes towards Germany and Germans within Edwardian Britain.[145]

With the growth of the Radical Right and the Germanaphobia which it reflected during the Edwardian years came the development of a fear of a German surprise invasion, reflected in journalism and the views of politicians[146] but also in the growth of the previously mentioned invasion novel. After Chesney's *The Battle of Dorking* from 1871 there followed a series of other publications in the same year, all influenced by it, and further invasion novels appeared in the 1880s and 1890s. In many cases the conquerors, or at least the opponents, of Britain were not Germans. For instance, in William Le Queux's *The Great War in England in 1897*, originally published in serial form in 1893, an Anglo-German alliance fights against France and Russia. The same author continued to depict the French as the main threat until 1904, in novels with titles such as *In England's Peril*, *Of Royal Blood*, *His Majesty's Minister*, and *The Man From Downing Street*. But 1903, the year in which *The Riddle of the Sands*, by Erskine Childers, appeared, marks something of a turning point because from then on the invaders consist almost exclusively of Germans. *The Riddle of the Sands* con-

---

145. G. R. Searle, 'Critics of Edwardian Society: The Case of the Radical Right', in Alan O'Day (ed.), *The Edwardian Age: Conflict and Stability 1900–1914*, London, 1979, pp. 79–96; Alan Sykes, 'The Radical Right and the Crisis of Conservatism Before the First World War', *Historical Journal*, vol. 26, 1983, pp. 661–76; Gregory D. Phillips, 'Lord Willoughby de Broke and the Politics of Radical Toryism', *Journal of British Studies*, vol. 20, 1980, pp. 205–24; Arnd Bauerkämper, *Die 'radikale Recht' in Grossbritannien: Nationalistische, antisemitistische und faschistische Bewegungen vom späten 19. Jahrhundert bis 1945*, Göttingen, 1991, pp. 11–103.

146. A. J. A. Morris, *The Scaremongerers*, London, 1984, pp. 98–110.

cerns a plot to invade England discovered by two Englishmen who travel to East Friesland.[147]

During 1904–6, against the diplomatic background of the first Moroccan Crisis and growing concern about the growth of the German fleet, a large number of new invasion stories appeared, especially in 1906, 'a bumper year which saw the appearance of several notorious books' with titles such as *The Shock of Battle*, *The North Sea Bubble* and *The Writing on the Wall*.[148]

The most famous book of all from 1906, and perhaps the best known of all pre-war novels which focused on an Anglo-German War was William Le Queux's *The Invasion of 1910*, which first appeared in serial form in the *Daily Mail*. The novel describes a German invasion of the East Anglian coast on a 'quiet September Sunday morning', after which the invading armies proceed to overrun the entire country. Le Queux aimed at alerting Britain to the danger of a surprise invasion, and also at supporting the views of Earl Roberts and the National Service League, of which Roberts was President, for the introduction of conscription. Le Queux actually approached Roberts in 1905, asking him if 'I may send you the outline scheme of the enemy's operations, as sketched out by W. H. W. Wilson [naval specialist of the *Daily Mail*] + myself, + whether you will read it and point out any of its defects.' Le Queux was 'very desirous of having the opinion of the highest authority'. Roberts offered his advice as well as writing a preface for the book, in which he stated: 'The catastrophe that may happen if we still remain in our present state of unpreparedness is vividly and forcibly illustrated by Mr Le Queux's new book.'[149]

As well as focusing on the external threat in the form of the invading army, Le Queux's novel, like Offin's in 1900 and others which followed, also devoted attention to an internal enemy in the form of a 'hundred or so spies' who cut railway lines and blew up bridges following

147. Bernard Bergonzi, 'Before 1914: Writers and the Threat of War', *Critical Quarterly*, vol. 6, 1964, pp. 129–30; Harald Husemann, 'When William Came; If Adolf Had Come: English Speculative Novels on the German Conquest of Britain', *Anglistik und Englischunterricht*, vols. 29–30, 1986, pp. 60–6; David A. T. Stafford, 'Spies and Gentlemen: the Birth of the British Spy Novel, 1893–1914', *Victorian Studies*, vol. 24, 1981, pp. 495–500; Esme Wingfield Stratford, *Before the Lamps Went Out*, London, 1945, p. 10.
148. I. F. Clarke, *Voices Prophesying War 1763–1984*, London, 1966, p. 144; Metz, *Die deutsche Flotte*; Massie, *Dreadnought*, pp. 351–543.
149. William Le Queux, *The Invasion of 1910*, London, 1906; National Army Museum, Lord Roberts Papers, letters from William Le Queux, R47/41, 28 July 1905, R47/48, 27 January 1906, R47/89, 27 October 1912; Clarke, ibid., pp. 144–68.

previous reconnaissance work. Le Queux subsequently claimed that spies in Britain had stolen his manuscript.[150]

Also in 1906 there appeared another novel which focused heavily on the threat of Germans within Britain, under the title of *The Enemy in Our Midst*, by Walter Wood. This combined 'spy fever', born from the fear of German power, with socio-economic hostility against Germans. One of the main characters, Steel, describes himself to his wife as 'a strong, British working-man, but trained to no special trade, because I've been a soldier, a decent labourer, in fact; and here are you, a bonny English lass starving – an' for what? Because we've given a welcome to every bit of foreign scum that's too filthy to be kept in its own country!' They live in a house rented out by Rudolf Schonn, a Berliner, in which they are the only English people. A policeman says of the area in which Steel lives: 'It isn't fit for a Christian Englishman to live in, an' you're about the only one of 'em left. I can't give it a name but it ought to be called either Young Germany or the New Jerusalem.' The novel then moves on to describe the invasion of England, in which German spies play a large part. The most important of these include 'Captain Mahler, nominally an officer in the German Army, but actually a spy long resident in England on behalf of his country.' He has under his control hundreds of thousands of Germans spies. Ultimately, the invasion fails because of English resistance.[151]

The year after the publication of *The Enemy in Our Midst* there appeared another volume of a similar nature, *The Secret* by E. Phillips Oppenheim, which again focused on an internal German threat. As well as singling out individual senior German spies, it also focused upon waiters, and other employees. A 'Captain X' states that 'there are in this country to-day, 290,000 young' Germans who 'have served their time, and who can shoot'. Each had his own task to perform in the takeover of England. However, this never materialises, because of the activities of Englishmen who foil them, one of whom declares: 'At last! The tocsin has sounded, and the rats have come out of their holes! Half a million of scum eating their way into the entrails of this great city of ours.'[152]

Large numbers of invasion stories also appeared in 1908 and 1909 with titles such as *The Swoop of the Vulture*, *The Great Raid* and *When England Slept*. *An Englishman's Home*, a play by an Army Officer, Guy du Maurier, which depicted Britain under an invading army, appeared in

150. Le Queux, *The Invasion of 1910*, pp. 28–9; Le Queux, *Things I Know About Kings, Celebrities and Crooks*, London, 1923, pp. 235–46.

151. Walter Wood, *The Enemy in Our Midst: The Story of A Raid on England*, London, 1906.

152. E. Phillips Oppenheim, *The Secret*, London, 1907.

Wyndham's Theatre in London.[153] Of the novels mentioned above, *When England Slept*, by the popular writer Henry Curties, involved the takeover of London on a Saturday night by German soldiers without warning against the background of concern about Dreadnoughts. The first half of the novel concerns itself with discovering how this happened, and we eventually learn that the 200,000 troops who seized London consisted of: 'German soldiers in civilian dress' who had 'been dribbling into the United Kingdom through every available port', and Germans who had sailed through various British ports and 'distributed themselves' throughout the country. The second half of the novel, as with Le Queux's *Invasion of 1910*, involved a British fight-back and eventual victory.[154]

The year 1908 saw the publication of a new novel by William Le Queux, *Spies of the Kaiser*. The preface to this novel, entitled 'If England Knew', reveals the extent of the author's conviction about the activities of German spies within Britain. Le Queux asserted that 'No sane English person can deny that England is in grave danger of invasion by Germany at a date not far distant.' He continued: 'What I have written in this present volume in the form of fiction is based upon serious facts within my own personal knowledge.' He further stated that 'The number of agents of the German Secret Police at this moment working in our midst on behalf of the Intelligence Department in Berlin is believed to be over five thousand.' Each had a particular task in peacetime and each awaited '"the Day' – as it is known in Germany – the Day of the Invasion of England.' The actual novel involves the foiling of German spying activities, which take place in virtually every strategically important site in Britain by two Englishmen, Jack Jacox and Ray Raymond, who, we learn, will continue their activities.[155]

Le Queux did not publish any more invasion stories before the outbreak of the First World War, but other authors did, notably Hector Hugh Munro (Saki), who wrote *When William Came*. As suggested by its subtitle, *A Story of England Under the Hohenzollern*, the novel actually depicts England after an invasion has taken place, with the country

---

153. Clarke, *Voices*, p. 153; Morris, *Scaremongerers*, p. 157. *The Great Raid*, by Lloyd Williams, appeared in serial form in a weekly periodical entitled *Black and White* from 13 February to 15 May 1909. In this case the enemy consisted not only of Germans but also of Italians, French and Russians, who take over London, before facing expulsion at the end of the novel.

154. Henry Curties, *When England Slept*, London 1909; Massie, *Dreadnought*, p. 638.

155. William Le Queux, *Spies of the Kaiser: Plotting the Downfall of England*, London, 1909.

under military rule and with London street names having become German, while all public notices appear in English and German: 'The British Isles came under the German Crown as a *Reichsland*, a sort of Alsace-Lorraine washed by the North Sea instead of the Rhine.' The novel contains no references to spies but attacks the activities of pre-War German Jews, who did not experience disappointment at the invasion because 'London had suddenly lost its place among the political capitals of the world, and become a cosmopolitan city'. The novel also carries hostile descriptions of German characters, such as Herr von Kwarl, 'a heavily built man of mature middle-age, of the blond North-German type, with a facial aspect that suggested stupidity and brutality'. Elsewhere, an English fisherman declares that 'a highly civilized race like ours, with the record we've had for leading the whole world, is not going to be held under for long by a lot of damned sausage-eating Germans.'[156]

The publication of invasion and spy stories reflected a deeper concern within Edwardian Britain about the threat of Germany and her representatives within the country, especially as potential spies. Part of the motivation for the production of the novels lay in a more widespread desire to highlight the threat of potential spies in order to deal with them. The newspaper and periodical press played a major role in the development of spy fever, especially in the years 1907–10.

In April and May of 1907, for instance, the *Globe*, a Unionist newspaper, carried numerous letters on the subject. On 25 April, for example, a communication signed 'Dum Spiro Spero' claimed: 'There are at present close upon 90,000 German reserve soldiers in Great Britain.' On 2 May another correspondent claimed the total stood at 180,000. The same writer also displayed strong socio-economic hostility, asserting that 'the scum of Europe is pouring into the British Isles'. Lieutenant J. M. Heath, in another letter, asserted:

The streets of London, as anyone must observe, swarm with Germans. Where do they go? What do they do? They appear in no hurry. They are comfortably dressed and well nourished. Undoubtedly soldiers. I have noted them with interest for years. They are unusually numerous now. We shall awake one morning to find all important commanding points in London held by armed Germans. The railways cut, bridges blown up, and points destroyed.[157]

156. *When Wiliam Came*, originally published in 1913, is reprinted in *The Complete Works of Saki*, London, 1989. See also the discussion of the novel in Husemann, 'When William Came', pp. 69–70; and Bergonzi, 'Before 1914', pp. 130–1.

157. For a sample of the letters published see *Globe*, 25, 29 April, 2, 3, 6, 9, 13 May 1907. See also the reaction of the *Army and Navy Gazette*, 11, 18 May 1907.

Attention to the issue of German spies increased further in the following year, reaching the pages of, amongst other publications, *The Times*, *John Bull*, the *National Review*, and the *Contemporary Review*. In a letter to the first of these, a correspondent wondered whether his former German barber, who had left London, had recorded in a notebook 'memoranda as to the telegraph wires outside the shop, the sidings at Camberley Railway Station, or the bridges over the Blackwater.'[158] This quote indicates the main area of concern in 1908, the belief that Germans had an intricate knowledge of the British military landscape. They had partly obtained this information through the activities of the '50,000 German waiters in Britain', many of whom held positions in hotels near railway stations, as well as through the many Germans who owned public houses 'near our forts'. However, German officers, who intended to establish a Service Club in Piccadilly, had also obtained details of military establishments through their own efforts: 'They have examined, as it were, every inch of our surface through a military microscope.'

Colonel Lockwood, Unionist MP for West Essex, put forward the most extraordinary claim of all, which became widely accepted, when he spoke of 'a staff ride through England organised by a foreign power.' H. A. Gwynne, the editor of the *Standard*, believed that between twenty and forty Germans had taken part, 'wandering about Essex' and 'making very pertinent enquiries about everybody', although another claim pointed to as many as 25,000 Germans in Essex.[159]

The spy scare continued into 1909 and 1910. In the House of Commons, for instance, Sir John Barlow asked the War Secretary if he knew that 'there are 66,000 trained German soldiers in England, or that there are, in a cellar within a quarter of a mile of Charing Cross, 50,000 stands of Mauser rifles and 7 millions of Mauser cartridges.' In the following year the *Daily Mail* claimed that 'in the last four years there has been a very marked increase in the number of secret service agents in England' who 'come and go as they like'.[160] Attention also focused on the idea that German workmen played a part in the construction of dreadnoughts for the Royal Navy, which meant that they could steal naval secrets.[161] By this time something of

158. *The Times*, 17 July 1908.
159. 'German Peril', pp. 295–6; Maxse, *Germany on the Brain*, pp. 243–4; *John Bull*, 8 August, 5 September 1908; *Hansard*, fourth series, CXCI, 1230–2, 6 July 1908, CXCII, 392–3, 13 July 1908; House of Lords Record Office, Bonar Law Papers, letters from H. A. Gwynne to Bonar Law, 11 February 1908, 24 May 1909.
160. *Hansard*, fifth series, V, 812, 24 May 1909; *Daily Mail*, 8 September 1910.
161. *Daily Chronicle*, 14 April 1910; *East Ham Echo*, 25 March 1910.

a reaction had taken place against 'spy-fever', as revealed in articles in the *Nation* and *Contemporary Review*, which, however, while dismissing the most extreme claims, admitted that spying almost certainly took place in Britain though not on the scale claimed by some Germanophobes.[162]

As well as 'spy-fever', which remained a fairly primitive form of hostility with a specific aim of alerting the Liberal government to the danger of a German invasion and the role which an internal enemy could play, there also existed a more sophisticated animosity, combining anti-Semitism and Germanophobia to develop the idea of a conspiracy which influenced, if not actually controlled, Britain. Although these ideas were prominent in Edwardian England, put forward mainly by people with Radical Right views, they have a longer history and also obtained backing from other parts of the political spectrum.

In the 1860s and 1870s, for instance, a series of novels attacked both the national and spiritual origins of German Jews in London society, notably Anthony Trollope's *The Way We Live Now* which created the character of Melmotte, 'a grotesque and nauseating monstrosity'. By the early twentieth century popular novelists including Marie Corelli and Guy Thorne adopted similar stereotypes.[163]

At the turn of the century anti-Semitism combined with anti-Germanism in attacks from various sections of the left who believed that the Boer War was being fought in the interests of Jews of German origin, who controlled business interests in South Africa. A pamphlet signed by 83 executive officers of trade unions claimed that 'The capitalists who brought up or hire the Press both in South Africa and in England to clamour for War are largely Jews and foreigners.' J. A. Hobson, the liberal journalist, played a major role in propagating similar ideas. He claimed that the economic resources of the Transvaal had fallen 'into the hands of a small group of international financiers, chiefly German in origin and Jewish in race', who would establish 'an oligarchy of German Jews at Pretoria.' He further claimed that 'We are

---

162. C. Lowe, 'About German Spies', *Contemporary Review*, vol. 108, 1910, pp. 42–56; *Nation*, 10 September 1910.

163. Frank Montagu Modder, *The Jew in the Literature of England to the End of the 19th Century*, New York, 1960, pp. 275–7, 329–30; Pauline Paucker, 'The Image of the German Jew in English Fiction', in W. E. Mosse, et al (eds), *Second Chance: Two Centuries of German-speaking Jews in the United Kingdom*, Tübingen, 1991, pp. 318–19; Bryan Cheyette, 'Jewish Stereotyping and English Literature, 1875–1920: Towards a Political Analysis', in Tony Kushner and Kenneth Lunn (eds), *Traditions of Intolerance: Historical Perspectives on Fascism and Race Discourse in Britain*, Manchester, 1989, pp. 14–15, 25–7.

fighting to place a small international oligarchy of mine owners and speculators in power at Pretoria.'[164]

Agitation during the Boer War against rich German Jews also stemmed from people with radical right views, including the novelist Hilaire Belloc and the journalist Arnold White. The former combined anti-Germanism and anti-Semitism with Catholic anti-Protestantism, originating in his experiences in Paris during the Franco-Prussian War and his opposition to Dreyfus in the 1890s. In England, where he played a role in Radical Right circles, he wrote the novel *Emmanuel Burden*, which originally appeared anonymously in instalments in 1900, and featured I. Z. Barnett, a German Jew whose influence increases in three subsequent novels by Belloc, *Mr Clutterbuck's Election* (1908), *A Change in the Cabinet* (1909), and *Pongo and the Bull* (1910).[165]

In *Efficiency and Empire,* published in 1901, Arnold White attacked all Jews and what he viewed as their international influence, but he focused particularly on those of German origin. In one passage, he wrote:

> In numbers, in wealth, in power, and in subtle influence over the whole community, foreigners, both poor and rich, are increasing by leaps and bounds. Material success is as truly the god of the smart foreign Jew as it was in the days when his ancestors worshipped the calf of gold. Material success has never yet become the British ideal. These German Jews, who have already captured rather than earned so large a part of the good things in England, despise the smart society they use as instruments for advancement. They will not intermarry with them. The island of aliens in the sea of English life is small to-day. It is growing. Rule by foreign Jews is being set up. The best forms of our national life are already in jeopardy.[166]

These themes also received attention from Banister, whose main concern remained Jewish power rather than German power. J. W. Cross, in an article in the *Nineteenth Century* in 1899, using milder language,

164. John S. Galbraith, 'The Pamphlet Campaign in the Boer War', *Journal of Modern History*, vol. 24, 1952, pp. 120–1; J. A. Hobson, *The War in South Africa: Its Causes and Effects*, London, 1900, pp. 189, 196, 197; Holmes, *Antisemitism*, pp. 66–70; Holmes, 'J. A. Hobson and the Jews', in *idem* (ed.), *Immigrants and Minorities in British Society*, London, 1978, pp. 125–57.
165. Bryan Cheyette, 'Hilaire Belloc and the "Marconi Scandal" 1913–1914: A Reassessment of the Interactionist Model of Racial Hatred', in Kushner and Lunn, *Politics of Marginality*, pp. 135–7; Holmes, *Anti-Semitism*, p. 76; Paucker, 'Image of the German Jew', pp. 323–4; Jay P. Corrin, *G. K. Chesterton and Hillaire Belloc: The Battle Against Modernity*, London, 1981, pp. 13–62.
166. Arnold White, *Efficiency and Empire*, Brighton, 1973 reprint (originally, 1901), p. 80.

stated simply that 'in the City of London to-day there is not a single English firm among what may be called "haute finance"'. He pointed particularly to the number of German Jewish bankers.[167]

Leopold Maxse made little distinction between Germans and Jews; in fact, he went as far as to claim that Germans and Jews worked together with the Liberal government, therefore displaying the Radical Right concern for corruption in Government.[168] He even identified the existence of a 'Potsdam Party' which carried out '"good work for the Fatherland'. The Potsdam Party consisted of 'ex-Ambassadors on the stump, Cocoa Quakers, Hebrew journalists at the beck and call of German diplomats, soft-headed Sentimentalists, hypnotised by Hohenzollern blandishments, cranks convinced that their own country is always in the wrong, [and] cosmopolitan financiers domiciled in London.' In one passage in his *National Review* Maxse attacked 'gentlemen of German extraction, who, for one reason or another, are sojourning in our midst' and 'posing as patriotic Englishmen when they are actually animated by one single purpose, "What can I do to please the German Emperor?"'[169] Maxse did not name any individuals in his journalism, but other people did; Viscount Esher, for instance, cited Sir Ernest Cassel, especially in connection with his attempts to reach an Anglo-German agreement in the years 1908–12, when Cassel travelled to Berlin.[170]

Against the Germanophobic background of Edwardian Britain, especially the development of 'spy-fever', the Government took action against the perceived threat of an internal enemy through the introduc-

167. J. W. Cross, 'British Trade in 1898: A Warning Note', *Nineteenth Century*, vol. 45, 1899, p. 854. For Bannister see National Maritime Museum, Arnold White Papers, WHI 112, and WHI 113. The former file contains an antisemitic pamphlet entitled 'The Loyalty and Desirability of Our Jewish Citizens', from January 1914, while the latter has a leaflet called 'Why the London Press Favours Alien Immigration and English Emigration', published in January 1913. See also Banister who focuses upon foreign control of the press in *England Under the Jews*, p. 138.

168. This concern receives more attention in G. R. Searle, *Corruption in British Politics 1895–1930*, Oxford, 1987; and Hutcheson, *Leopold Maxse*, pp. 396–463.

169. *National Review*, March 1912, pp. 10–11, April 1912, p. 189.

170. Kurt Grunwald, '"Windsor-Cassel" – The Last Court Jew: Prologomena to a Biography of Sir Ernest Cassel', *Leo Baeck Yearbook*, vol. 14, 1969, pp. 149–60; Alfred Vogts, 'Die Juden im englisch-deutschen imperialistischen Konflikt vor 1914', in Joachim Radkau and Immanuel Geiss (eds), *Imperialismus im 20. Jahrhundert: Gedankschrift für George W F Hallgarten*, Munich, 1976, pp. 111–43; Jamie Camplin, *The Rise of the Plutocrats: Wealth and Power in Edwardian England*, London, 1978, pp. 209–11; C. C. Aronsfeld, 'German Jews in Victorian England', *Leo Baeck Yearbook*, vol. 7, 1962, pp. 313, 326–7.

tion of a series of measures designed to guard Britain's internal security. The whipping up of spy-fever during the years 1905–10 can be seen as part of a campaign to improve Britain's internal security, and we can compare this campaign with that which led to the passage of the Aliens Act of 1905. In the former case the target group was poor Jewish immigrants from eastern Europe, and in the latter case it was Germans resident in Britain. As we have seen through the statements of journalists and novelists, while the campaign for the introduction of security measures was focused primarily on the political threat posed by Germans, propagandists did not hesitate to use socio-economic arguments of a similar nature to those deployed against Russian and Polish Jews. The reality of German espionage in Britain remained completely different from the hundreds of thousands of spies claimed by some propagandists.[171] By the outbreak of the First World War only a handful of people had faced trial on charges of espionage, not all of them Germans; Gustav Steinhauer, responsible for pre-war German espionage in Britain, 'ran only an inefficient network of poorly-paid and clumsy part-time agents.'[172]

However, the propagandists had created enough embarrassment to force the Government to act, and in March 1909[173] it established a sub-committee of the Committee of Imperial Defence under the chairmanship of Lord Haldane to 'Consider the Question of Foreign Espionage in the United Kingdom'. This examined dubious evidence gathered together by Colonel John Edmonds who, in October 1906, had become head of MO5, the military intelligence counter-intelligence section. We can obtain an indication of the unreliability of the evidence if we consider that he had partly obtained it from Le Queux, as well as from F. T. Jane, founder of the *Naval Annual*, both of whom gave Edmonds copies of letters which they had received from members of the public. The sub-committee had evidence on 76 cases consisting of 'alleged reconnaissance', 'Individual Germans who have come under suspicion', and 'Houses occupied by a succession of Germans who have

171. Lowe, 'About German Spies', p. 53, lists estimates which range between 6,500 and 350,000.
172. Sidney Theodore Felstead, *German Spies At Bay*, London, 1920, pp. 3–9; Nicholas Hiley, 'Spying for the Kaiser', *History Today*, vol. 38, June 1988, pp. 37–43; Christopher Andrew, *Secret Service: The Making of the British Intelligence Community*, London, 1985, pp. 54–73; David French, 'Spy Fever in Britain, 1900–1915', *Historical Journal*, vol. 21, 1978, pp. 361–2; Porter, *Vigilant State*, p. 171.
173. Nicholas Hiley, 'The Failure of British Counter-Espionage Against Germany, 1907–1914', *Historical Journal*, vol. 28, 1985, p. 835, points to a meeting which took place in April 1907 to consider 'the Powers Possessed by the executive in Time of Emergency'.

come under suspicion'. The flimsiness of some of the evidence is extra-ordinary. For instance, 'Engineer clerk Q. M. S. Hurwitz, employed in the office of the Secretary RE Institute, is of German birth. He writes regularly to his relatives in Prussia'.[174]

Nevertheless, in the Germanophobic atmosphere of the pre-First World War years, the sub-committee accepted the information gathered by Edmonds which, its members agreed, indicated that 'a great deal of German espionage was being undertaken in Great Britain, with a view to making a detailed study of our resources and the topography of the country.' Consequently, the sub-committee drew up four recommenda-tions. These included the establishment of a Secret Service Bureau, which quickly happened in 1909 when MI5 came into existence. The sub-committee also wished to see a change in the Official Secrets Act of 1889, which took place in 1911 with the passage of a new Act.[175]

Haldane's group also called for controls on aliens which led to the establishment of another sub-committee of the Committee of Imperial Defence under the Home Secretary, Winston Churchill, to examine the 'treatment of Aliens in Time of War'. This sub-committee reached two decisions: first, the establishment of an unofficial register of aliens kept by provincial police forces which by July 1913 contained 28,830 names of whom 11,100 consisted of Germans and Austrians; and second, the establishment of a 'Standing Sub-Committee of the Committee of Imperial Defence on the Treatment of Aliens in Time of War'. This drew up the draft Aliens Restriction Act,[176] which formed a fundamental plank in Government policy against German immigrants during the First World War.[177]

Despite the rampant Germanophobia which had developed during the Edwardian years, traces of nineteenth-century positive attitudes towards Germans still remained. In the first place, not everybody believed that Germany would, or even could, invade Britain. H. B. Hanna, for instance, in a book entitled *Can Germany Invade England?*, claimed that 'an invasion on even the modest scale of 70,000 men is

174. French, 'Spy-Fever', p. 356; Liddel Hart Centre for Military Archives, King's College London, Edmonds Papers, III/5, memoirs, Ch. 20, pp. 1–5; PRO CAB 16/8, 'Report and Proceedings of A Sub-Committee of the Committee of Imperial Defence Appointed to Consider the Question of Foreign Espionage in the United Kingdom'.

175. French, 'Spy-Fever', p. 358, 360–1; Andrew, *Secret Service*, p. 59; Rosamund Thomas, *Espionage and Official Secrecy: The Official Secrets Acts 1911–1989 of the United Kingdom*, London, 1991, pp. 1–10.

176. PRO CAB 17/90, 'Report and Proceedings of the Standing Sub-Committee of the Committee of Imperial Defence on the Treatment of Aliens in Times of War'; PRO WO32/8875.

177. See Panayi, *Enemy*, 46–61; Bird, *Control of Enemy Alien Civilians*, pp. 200–34.

practically impossible'.[178] Other writers recognised the level of panic into which Britain had descended. An article entitled 'Teutophobia', by Lord Eversley, written during the navy scare of 1908–9, attacked 'Panic-mongers' in both Britain and Germany. This theme appeared in the previous year in articles by Sidney Low and Percy William Bunting in the *Contemporary Review*, after both of these authors had participated in a journalistic tour of Germany. Bunting claimed that 'the great mass of the German people, as well as the German Government, are very wishful and even anxious to be on good terms with England.'[179] Hobson, meanwhile, attacked those whom he saw as responsible for the rise of Germanophobia, including the military and naval authorities and arms manufacturers. He viewed the German threat as far less real than depicted by Teutophobes.[180]

Organisations also came into existence in Britain which had the aim of improving relations with Germany. In 1905, for instance, the foundation of the Anglo-German Friendship Committee took place, a body supported mainly by Liberals but whose membership also included Unionist MPs and Peers. This organisation had connections with the *Anglo-German Courier* which, however, only ran during 1906. In 1911, the Anglo-German Friendship Society succeeded the Anglo-German Friendship Committee, with the aim of removing 'all existing misunderstandings with Germany'. The organisation launched the *Anglo-German Friendship Gazette* but this ran to just one edition. A new body followed in 1912, the British-German Friendship Society, which organised an Anglo-German Understanding Conference attended both by prominent London Germans and senior British figures. The aims of the above bodies included the organisation of exchanges of students between Britain and Germany.[181]

The existence of these groups indicates the survival of goodwill into the Edwardian years between the Germans in Britain and native English society. While hostility towards Germans reached its highest pre-war

178. H. B. Hanna, *Can Germany Invade England?*, 3rd edition, London, 1914.

179. Lord Eversley, 'Teutophobia', *Nineteenth Century*, vol. 62, 1908, pp. 187–97; Sidney Low and Percy William Bunting, 'The Journalistic Tour of Germany', *Contemporary Review*, vol. 92, 1907, pp. 1–15.

180. J. A. Hobson, *The German Panic*, London, 1913.

181. Hollenberg, *Englisches Interesse am Kaiserreich*, pp. 60–113; Anglo-German Friendship Society, *Report of a Meeting Held at the Mansion House, on November 2nd 1911*, London, 1911; *Anglo-German Understanding Conference, London, 1912*, London, 1912; *Anglo-German Friendship Gazette*, 2 May 1911. Karl Breul, 'A British Institute in Berlin and a German Institute in London', *Contemporary Review*, May 1911, pp. 587–93; *The Times*, 5 June, 1909, 15 June, 4, 11 August 1910; *Alldeutsche Blätter*, 18 July 1914.

peak during these years, it had not yet saturated British society in the way that it would do during the First World War. Even after 1905 and the passage of the Aliens Act, Germans represented just one group of immigrants attacked by British racists; anti-Semitism, directed against both rich financiers and poor east European immigrants,[182] retained its potency although, as has been seen, the former strand could also combine with anti-German hostility.

Any explanation for the levels of anti-German immigrant hostility reached during the Edwardian years would have to take into account the increasing diplomatic rivalry, as animosity towards Germany and its representatives in Britain remain inextricably interlinked. During much of the nineteenth century, when Germany appeared to pose no threat to Britain, its representatives did not receive hostile attention of a political nature. This did not prevent the development of socio-economic hostility, which, as we have seen, focused on numerous aspects of the lives of German immigrants and received support from many quarters. In many cases the nationality of the Germans mattered less than other aspects of their lives, although we cannot dismiss the fact that they did possess non-British nationality in the hostility which developed against them. However, due to both the underlying perceptions of Germany within Britain and the relatively small number of Germans who made their way to the country, attention focused not on them but on the more numerous Irish and Jewish immigrants, towards whom potent traditional hostility existed.

182. Gainer, *Alien Invasion*, pp. 199–211; Holmes, *Anti-Semitism*. See also Holmes, 'The German Gypsy Question in Britain, 1904–1906', in Lunn, *Hosts, Immigrants and Minorities*, pp. 134–69, indicating the blending together of a wide range of xenophobic sentiments.

Conclusion

The history of the Germans in nineteenth-century Britain contains both continuity and change, although the latter proves more important than the former in each of the aspects discussed in the present volume. In terms of continuity we can point to the churches which existed throughout the course of the nineteenth century and even before, and acted as focal points for the maintenance of an ethnic life and culture. Settlement patterns also maintained continuities, with a focus on the East End of London. Occupations changed only gradually, but they did change. The same assertion can be made with regard to the image of the German in nineteenth-century Britain.

Elements of change seem more obvious than those of continuity in any history of nineteenth-century Europe. With regard to Germans in nineteenth-century Britain, in the first place migration patterns altered so that by the Edwardian years the mass migration caused by population growth had stopped, with only small-scale movement remaining. At the same time, the nature of political immigration also differed in the 1870s from that of the 1840s, reflecting wider developments in German left-wing politics. However, even in the migration process elements of stability existed, notably in the movement of middle-class businessmen who made their way to Britain, not just during the years 1815–1914 but from as far back as the Middle Ages. Trading connections proved fundamental throughout the history of Anglo-German relations.

An examination of the socio-economic life of the immigrants reveals many elements of change. Their areas of residence in London, for instance, expanded from the traditional East End to encompass new parts of the capital. This expansion reflects a wide variety of factors, including the changing face of the East London landscape, the immigration of eastern European Jews into that area, and the changing occupations of the Germans themselves. One stable factor with regard to residence patterns, however, was the lack of concentration outside London, and in this sense the German community resembles the Italian grouping in nineteenth century Britain.[1]

1. Lucio Sponza, *Italian Immigrants in Nineteenth Century Britain: Realities and Images*, Leicester, 1988, p. 322.

Conclusion

Employment patterns also changed during the course of the nineteenth century so that by the outbreak of the First World War the number of Germans involved in occupations at the bottom of the social scale had decreased, while the numbers of those participating in shop-keeping had increased from the late Victorian period. The reasons for the first development are connected with the changing residence patterns of the immigrants, as well as the availability of a cheaper source of labour in the form of large numbers of east European Jews.

An examination of cultural life demonstrates an expansion of activities from the late 1850s onwards, connected with the growth in the size of the German community in London and in Britain as whole, so that by the outbreak of the First World War countless religious, philanthropic and cultural activities took place amongst the German communities of Britain. In the case of religion especially, these developments built on earlier foundations. Other activities, notably those of a political nature, lasted for shorter periods of time.

The image of the German immigrant also altered, and perhaps this reflected the most drastic transformation during the course of the nineteenth century. While socio-economic hostility focused on Germans in the same way in which it has focused on all immigrant groups in modern British history,[2] before the late Victorian period Germans had not experienced the same intensity of hostility faced by other nineteenth-century groups such as the Irish and Jews. We can explain this both by the smaller numbers of Germans and by the differing underlying images of these ethnic groups. When views of the German nation deteriorated from the 1890s, as Britain began to regard Germany as a threat, its representatives in Britain started to face an animosity similar to that endured by Irish and Jewish minorities, although admittedly not quite as ferocious until the First World War. This indicates that the history of any form of hostility towards immigrants has fundamental connections with more widespread ideologies within a nation. The German immigrants themselves were only partially important; just as important were images of Germany. Similarly, we can only fully understand reactions towards the Irish in the mid-nineteenth century and east European Jews in the late Victorian period if we place them against the British traditions of anti-Catholic and anti-Irish hostility[3] in the case of the former and anti-Semitism with regard to the latter.[4]

---

2. See Panikos Panayi, *Immigration, Ethnicity and Racism in Britain, 1815–1945*, Manchester, 1994, pp. 102–25.

3. See L. P. Curtis, *Anglo-Saxons and Celts*, New York, 1968.

4. For traditions of anti-semitism see Tony Kushner (ed.), *Jewish Heritage in British History: Englishness and Jewishness*, London, 1992.

This last point indicates a second observation which needs to be made, namely that minorities cannot permanently live in a vacuum, cut off from the dominant society and maintaining their ethnicity in its original form. This is simply a physical impossibility; the minority community has to have some contact with the dominant one. Some economic activity has to take place, for instance. Eventually second- and third-generation offspring integrate or even assimilate, although the extent of this process depends substantially upon the level of hostility from the dominant society. However, for large numbers of first-generation immigrants, including the Germans, during the course of the nineteenth century a strong ethnicity remained, indicated by the wide range of organisations which had developed by the end of the nineteenth century.

Yet we cannot view these developments in isolation, as they reflected British society as well as the German immigrant community. As this study has constantly stressed, we cannot speak of a single German ethnicity. Germans maintained a consciousness with regard to their religious roots, while the organisations which they decided to join relied fundamentally upon their occupations, political affiliations and, above all, class. The German immigrants lived in the nineteenth-century British class-stratified society; they could not escape from it. To have maintained their ethnic allegiances above their class ones would have been contrary not only to the economic development of nineteenth-century Britain but also to the economic situation in nineteenth-century Germany. They moved from one class-structured society into another, and they decided which organisations to join on ethnic and class grounds. Each was important.

The Germans remained a society stratified according to religion, politics, occupation and residence patterns. In this sense they resembled other immigrant groups, not least Germans in the USA during the nineteenth century[5] and the major minorities in Britain, notably Jews, who divided even further along class lines as well as according to their countries of origin.[6] The Germans in nineteenth-century Britain consequently represent one typical example of an immigrant minority and its development.

Some comparisons can be made between the nineteenth-century German community and the other major immigrant groups in Britain in the same period, notably the Irish, Jews and Italians. All three resemble the Germans in that they have long traditions of settlement, dating back

5. Stanley Nadel, *Little Germany: Ethnicity, Religion and Class in New York City, 1845–80*, Urbana and Chicago, 1990.
6. See David Cesarani (ed.), *The Making of Anglo-Jewry*, Oxford, 1990.

to the Middle Ages.[7] In the case of both the Irish and the Jews, they, like the Germans, also faced expulsion.[8] The Jewish community began to grow in the late seventeenth century and, as with the Germans, clear connections exist in terms of the foundations of religious life during this period.[9]

A similar pattern of causes to that of the Germans, can be applied to the immigration of all communities during the nineteenth century, involving the existence of underlying, medium-term and personal push and pull factors. During the Victorian period Britain attracted over a million newcomers, although its own population loss was far greater. In the cases of Ireland and Italy we can detect a similar pattern of population growth to that of Germany. In Ireland the short-term crisis of the famine of the late 1840s played a fundamental role, as did the proximity of Britain. The Jewish immigration of the late nineteenth century was extremely complex, revolving around both political and economic push factors. For both the Irish and the Jews enabling factors, in the form of the development of shipping lines, proved fundamental.[10]

All immigrant groups of any size in nineteenth-century Britain had a clearly-defined occupational structure. This observation applies as much to the Jewish community as it does to the Germans. By the end of the nineteenth century, following the influx of newcomers from eastern Europe, Jews could be found working in occupations ranging from prostitution to merchant banking.[11] As with the Germans and, particularly, the Irish,[12] there was a concentration at the lower end of the social scale, a situation more marked for smaller and purely working class non-European minorities, notably the Chinese.[13] As with the Germans, all these immigrant groups conformed with the class society of nineteenth-century Britain.

Ethnic organisations divided along the lines of those formed by the Germans. In most cases religion played a fundamental role, even more important than for the German immigrants in the case of the Irish and

7. Kevin O'Connor, *The Irish in Britain*, Dublin, 1974 edition, pp. 13–15; Terri Colpi, *The Italian Factor: The Italian Community in Great Britain*, Edinburgh, 1991, pp. 25–7; Cecil Roth, *A History of the Jews in England*, Oxford, 1964.

8. O'Connor, *The Irish in Britain*, p. 13; Roth, *A History of the Jews in England*, pp. 68–80.

9. Roth, *A History of the Jews in England*, pp. 149–266.

10. Graham Davis, *The Irish in Britain 1815–1914*, Dublin, 1991, pp. 10–50; Harold Pollins, *Hopeful Travellers: Jewish Immigrants and Settlers in Nineteenth Century Britain*, London, 1991 reprint.

11. Lloyd P. Gartner, *The Jewish Immigrant in England, 1870–1914*, London, 1960.

12. Lynn H. Lees, *Exiles of Erin: Irish Immigrants in Victorian London*, Manchester, 1979, p. 33.

13. K. C. Ng, *The Chinese in London*, London, 1968, p. 10.

Jews. For the former, ethnic adherence revolved around religion rather than national origin, although we should recognise fundamental differences between established Anglo-Jewry and the late nineteenth-century east European immigrants. As with the Germans, religion formed a focus for both the Jews and the Irish, around which revolved a wide range of philanthropic and educational activity.[14] Cultural organisations, independent of religion, were less important for the Jews and the Irish but played a role in the Italian community.[15] Politics, meanwhile, were significant in the ethnic solidarity of all groups, especially those consisting primarily of political refugees such as the Poles.[16]

Finally, the hostility towards Germans in nineteenth-century Britain remained mild compared with that endured by other minorities. The Irish, for instance, faced a constant stream of abuse during the 1850s and 1860s, while east European Jews were the victims of the campaign for the Aliens Act of 1905. In both cases long-term traditions of anti-Catholicism and anti-Semitism acted as a driving force behind this hostility, although the influx of large numbers proved just as important. During the mid-nineteenth century the Irish acted as the main focus of xenophobia, to be replaced by the Jews in the late Victorian and Edwardian years and followed by Germans in the First World War.[17]

In the context of the history of the major ethnic groups in Britain during the nineteenth century, the Germans form a typical example, fitting well into the same patterns as the Irish and Jews in terms of reasons for immigration, social structure, and ethnic organisations. Because they were not perceived as a major threat before the First World War, the Germans did not endure intense hostility, a situation which changed drastically in 1914–18.

14. Steven Fielding, *Class and Ethnicity: Irish Catholics in England 1880–1939*, Buckingham, 1993, pp. 38–78; Gartner, *Jewish Immigrant*, pp. 187–219.

15. Colpi, *Italian Factor*, pp. 65–7.

16. Peter Brock, 'The Polish Revolutionary Commune in London', *Slavonic and East European Review*, vol. 35, 1956, pp. 116–28.

17. Alan O'Day, 'Varieties of Anti-Irish Behaviour in Britain, 1846–1922', in Panikos Panayi (ed.), *Racial Violence in Britain, 1840–1950*, Leicester, 1993, pp. 26–43; Colin Holmes, *Anti-Semitism in British Society, 1876–1939*, London, 1979, pp. 1–120; Panikos Panayi, *The Enemy in Our Midst: Germans in Britain during the First World War*, Oxford, 1991.

Bibliography

A. *PRIMARY SOURCES*

(1) *Archival Material*

Bremer Staastarchiv
Ratsarchiv: 2 P, 2 T
Senatsregistratur: 3 U 1
Miscellaneous Documents: C 4 h 1

Bundesarchiv, Coblenz
Documents of Auswärtiges Amt, R85
Documents of Auslands Institut, R57 (neu)

Bundesarchiv, Potsdam
Auswärtiges Amt, Abteilung III, Auswanderung, Länder Europa,
    England

British Library of Political and Economic Science
Charles Booth Papers

Charity Commission, London
King Edward VII British German Foundation,
    File 227637
Kaiser Wilhelm II Fund, File 214283

Greater London Record Office
German Evangelical Reformed Church, Hooper Square, Acc 1767
    'A Short History of the German Evangelical
    Reformed Church', Acc 1767.
German School, Islington, P83/PET2

Hamburg Staatsarchiv
Hamburgischer Konsulat in Liverpool
Hanseatischer Generalkonsulat in London
Hanseatische Residentur in London

Holborn Library, London
Deutsches Volkstheater West London, Programme

Bibliography

House of Lords Record Office
Andrew Bonar Law Papers

Institut für Auslandsbeziehungen, Stuttgart
Curt Friese, 'Some Thoughts on the History of the Germans and their Church Communities in Manchester'.

Kings College, London, Liddel Hart Centre for Military Archives
J. Edmonds Papers.

Manchester Archives Department
William Thorp, 'Poor Foreigners', MS 38/4/2/17

National Army Museum
Earl Roberts Papers.

National Maritime Museum
Arnold White Papers.

Niedersächsisches Staatsarchiv Osnabrück
Verzeichnis der Auswanderungskonsensen

Public Record Office, Chancery Lane
Census Returns for Whitechapel and St George's, 1851, HO107
Census Returns for Whitechapel and St George's, 1891, RG12

Public Record Office, Kew
Cabinet Papers, CAB16, CAB17.
Home Office Papers, HO45.
Metropolitan Police Papers, MEPO2, MEP03, MEPO5.
War Office Papers, WO32.

Ruhr Universität Bochum
Arbeitsgruppe Geschichte Nordamerikas, Archive, Letter of Karl Uterhart to his mother, 31 December 1862.

Schröders Archive
P.M. Novell, 'German Sailors Home'.

Tower Hamlets Local History Collection
Alexander Gander, 'The Old Sugar Refineries of St George's in the East.'
'Jubiläums-Bericht der deutschen und englischen St. Georg's Schule, 1. Juli 1905'.
London Sugar Refineries extracted from Trade Directories, Misc 13/5
St George's German Lutheran Church, Whitechapel, Marriage Registers, 1843–96, TH 8371 13–18

(2) **Printed Works**

(a) Government Publications

(i) British Parliamentary Debates
Hansard, Lords, Commons, third, fourth and fifth series, 1850–1914.

(ii) British Parliamentary Papers
Board of Trade Memorandum on the Immigration of Foreigners into the United Kingdom, LXXIX, 1887.
Correspondence Respecting the Foreign Refugees in London, LIV, 1852.
Expulsion of Aliens: Correspondence Between the Secretary of State for the Home Department and His Honour Judge Rentoul, K C, 11 March 1909, LXX, 1909.
Further Correspondence Respecting the Foreign Refugees in London, LIV, 1852.
Report from the Select Committee on the Laws Affecting Aliens, V, 1843.
Report on the Early Training of the German Clerk, LXXVII, 1889.
Report to the Board of Trade on the Sweating System at the East End of London, by the Labour Correspondent of the Board, LXXXIX, 1887.
Royal Commission on Alien Immigration, IX, 1903.
Select Committee on Emigration and Immigration, X, 1889.
Tables Relating to Emigrants and Immigrants from and into the United Kingdom in the Year 1904, and Report to the Board of Trade Thereon, XCVIII, 1905.
Dr Theodore Thomson's Report to the Local Government Board on the Methods Adopted at Certain Ports for Dealing with Alien Immigrants, LXVII, 1896.

(iii) British Census Statistics
Census of Great Britain, 1851, Population Tables, II, vol. 1, London, 1854.
Census of England and Wales for the Year 1861, vol. 2, London, 1863.
Census of England and Wales, 1871, vol. 3, London, 1873.
Eighth Annual Census of the Population of Scotland, vol. 2, Edinburgh, 1874.
Census of England and Wales, 1881, vol. 3, London, 1883.
Ninth Decennial Census of the Population of Scotland, 1881, vol. 2, 1883.
Census of England and Wales, 1891, vols. 3, 4, London, 1893.
Tenth Decennial Census of the Population of Scotland, 1891, Edinburgh, 1893.
Census of England and Wales, 1901, County of Lancaster, London, 1902.

Census of England and Wales, 1901, County of London, London, 1902.
Census of England and Wales, 1901, County of York, London, 1902.
Census of England and Wales, 1901, General Report, London, 1904.
Census of England and Wales, 1901, Summary Tables, Area, Houses and Population, London, 1903.
Eleventh Decennial Census of the Population of Scotland, Edinburgh, 1903.
Census of England and Wales, 1911, Birthplaces, London, 1913.
Census of England and Wales, 1911: Summary Tables, London, 1915.
Census of Scotland, 1911, vol. 3, Edinburgh, 1913.

(iv) *British Local Government Sources*
School Board of the Borough of West Ham, *Annual Report of the Board's School*, December, 1902, London, 1902.

(iv) *German State Papers*
Jahrbuch für Volkwirtschaft und Statistik, Berlin, 1852.
Jahrbuch für Volkwirtschaft und Statistik, Berlin, 1861.
Monatshefte zur Statistik des Deutschen Reichs, August 1884.
Preussische Statistik, vol. 26, Berlin, 1874.
Statistisches Jahrbuch für das Deutsche Reich, Berlin, 1913.
Statistik der Zollverein und Nördlichen Deutschlands, vol. 2, Berlin, 1862.

(b) *Publications of Non-Governmental Organisations*

(i) *Allgemein Deutschen Schulverein zur Erhaltung des Deutschtums in Ausland*
Handbuch des Deutschtums im Auslande, Berlin, 1906.

(ii) *Anglo-German Friendship Society*
Report of A Meeting Held at the Mansion House, on November 2nd, 1911, London, 1911.

(iii)*Communist Party of Great Britain*
London Landmarks: A Guide with Maps to Places Where Marx, Engels and Lenin Lived and Worked, London, 1963.

(iv) *Deutscher Christlicher Verein Junger Männer zu London*
Ein Deutsches Glaubenswerk in der Themsestadt: Rückblick auf 50 Jahre Vereinsarbeit, London, 1910.

(v) *Deutscher Verein für Kunst und Wissenschaft*
Jahresbericht und Mitgliederliste, 1910, London, 1911.

(vi) *Deutsches Kirchen Verein*
Bericht des deutschen Kirchen-Vereins in Hull, Hull, 1845.

(vii) *German Hospital London*
Concerning the Early History of the German Hospital, London.
Remarks by Dr F. Parkes Weber at the Centenary Commemoration Tea,
at the German Hospital, London, October 25th, 1945, London, 1945.

(viii) *Liverpool Foreigners Mission*
Brief Narrative of the Past Efforts And of the Opening Prospects of the
Mission, Liverpool, 1847.

(ix) *London City Mission*
Annual Reports

(x) *St George's German and English School*
Report of the St George's German and English School, London, 1827.

(xi) *Society of Friends of Foreigners in Distress*
An Account of the Society of Friends of Foreigners in Distress for the
Year 1817, London, 1817.
An Account of the Nature and Present State of the Society of Friends of
Foreigners in Distress for the Year 1828, London, 1828.
An Account of the Society of Friends of Foreigners in Distress for the
Year 1866, London, 1866.
An Account of the Society of Friends of Foreigners in Distress for the
Year 1892, London, 1892.
Songs, Duets, &c. in the Grand Miscellaneous Concert at the King's
Theatre, on Friday, June 3rd, 1814, for the Benefit of the Society of
Friends of Foreigners in Distress, London, 1814.

(xii) *Travellers Aid Society*
Report for the Year, 1895, London, 1896.
Report for the Year, 1898, London, 1899.

(c) *Newspapers and Periodicals*

(i) *German Publications in England*
Anglo-German Courier; *Anglo-German Friendship Gazette*;
Hairdresser; *Hermann*; *London Hotel and Restaurant Employees*
Gazette; *Londoner Courier*; *Londoner Deutsche Chronik*; *Londoner*
Deutsches Journal; *Londoner Deutsches Wochenblatt*; *Londoner*
General Anzeiger; *Londoner St Marien Bote*; *Londoner Zeitung*;
Manchester Nachrichten; *Vereinsbote*.

(ii) *British Publications*
Anthropological Review; *Bandmaster's Help*; *Bee-Hive*; *Black and*
White; *Borough of West Ham, East Ham and Stratford Express*;
Bradford Observer; *Briton*; *Caterer and Hotel Proprietors Gazette*;

Chamber of Commerce Journal; City Press; Clerks Journal; Cobbett's Weekly Political Register; Daily Chronicle; Daily Mail; Daily News; East End News; East Ham Echo; East Ham Express; East London Advertiser; East London Observer; Evening News; Financial Reformer; Globe; Household Words; John Bull; London Banks; London City Mission Magazine; Manchester Guardian; Morning Post; Musical Herald; Musical World; Nation; National Review; Once A Week; Pall Mall Gazette; Restaurateur; Reynold's Newspaper; Sheffield Daily Independent; South Essex Mail; Spectator; Standard; Stratford Express; Thames Iron Works Gazette; The Times; Tottenham and Stamford Hill Times and Stoke Newington Chronicle; Tower Hamlets Independent; Transactions of the Ethnological Society of London; Vigilance Record; West Ham Guardian; West Ham Herald and South Essex Gazette; World.

(iii) *German Newspapers*
Alldeutsche Blätter; Auslandsdeutsche; Bremer Handelsblatt; Deutsche Allgemeine Zeitung; Der Deutsche Auswanderer; Deutsch Evangelisch im Auslande; Deutsch-Evangelisch Zeitschrift; Deutschtum im Ausland.

(d) *Contemporary Books, Articles and Memoirs*

Acton, William, *Prostitution*, London, 1857.

Adler, N. M., *The Adler Family*, London, 1909.

Aldis, W. S., 'Notes from a German Village', *Contemporary Review*, vol. 49, 1881.

Althaus, Friedrich, 'Beiträge zur Geschichte der deutschen Colonie in England. II', *Unsere Zeit*, vol. 9, 1873.

Anglo-German Publishing Company (ed.), *Die Deutsche Colonie In London*, London, 1913.

Anglo-German Understanding Conference, London, 1912, London, 1912.

Anonymous, *The German Bridegroom*, London, 1840.

Anonymous, *Prince Albert's Defence*, London, 1854.

Armfelt, Count E., 'Cosmopolitan London', in George R. Sims (ed.), *Living London*, vol. 1, London, 1903.

Armfelt, Count E., 'German London', in George R. Sims (ed.), *Living London*, vol. 3, London, 1903.

Archenholtz, Johann Wilhelm von, *A Picture of England*, London, 1797.

Arnold, Matthew, *Friendship's Garland*, London, 1871.

Auer, I., *Nach Zehn Jahren*, Nuremberg, 1913.

Babbage, Charles, *Passages from the Life of a Philosopher*, London, 1864.

Baden-Powell, George, 'The Expansion of Germany', *Nineteenth Century*, vol. 16, 1884.

Baedeker, Karl, *London und Seine Umgebung*, Coblenz, 1862.

Baines, Thomas, *Liverpool in 1859*, London, 1859.

Banister, Joseph, *England Under the Jews*, London, 1901.

Barth, Theodor, 'England and Germany', *Contemporary Review*, vol. 77, 1900.

Bass, M. T., *Street Music in the Metropolis*, London, 1864.

Batley, Thomas (ed.), *Sir Charles Halle's Concerts in Manchester...Also the Whole of the Programmes of Concerts from...1858 to...1895*, Manchester, 1896.

Beddoe, John, *The Races of Britain: A Contribution to the Anthropology of Western Europe*, London, 1971 edition, originally published 1885.

Behrens, Sir Jacob, *Sir Jacob Behrens, 1806–1889*, London, 1925.

Bernstein, Eduard, *My Years of Exile: Reminiscences of a Socialist*, London, 1921.

Besant, Sir Walter, *East London*, London, 1903.

Birchenough, H., 'The Expansion of Germany', *Nineteenth Century*, February 1898.

Blackie, W. G., *Commercial Education*, London, 1888.

Booth, Charles, 'The Inhabitants of Tower Hamlets (School Board Division), their Condition and Occupations', *Journal of the Royal Statistical Society*, vol. 50, 1887.

Booth, Charles, *Life and Labour of the People in London*, Second Series, vols. 3, 4, London, 1902.

Brand, William F., *London Life Seen with German Eyes*, London, 1902.

Breul, Karl, 'A British Institute in Berlin and a German Institute in London', *Contemporary Review*, May 1911.

Bull, Charles, *Soho in Olden Times*, London, 1859.

Burn, John Southernden, *The History of the French, Walloon, Dutch, and Other Foreign Protestant Refugees Settled in England*, London, 1846.

Cairnes, W. E., 'The Problem of Invasion', *National Review*, vol. 36, 1909.

Campbell, R., *The London Tradesman*, Newton Abbot, 1969 edition.

Chesney, George, *The Battle of Dorking*, Edinburgh and London, 1871.

Childers, Erskine, *The Riddle of the Sands*, Harmondsworth, 1984 edition.

Coningham, W., *Lord Palmerston and Prince Albert*, London, 1854.

Cross, J. W., 'British Trade in 1898: A Warning Note', *Nineteenth Century*, vol. 45, 1899.

Crory, W. Glenny, *East London Industries*, London, 1876.

Crowest, F., *Phases of Musical England*, London, 1881.

Cudworth, William, *Historical Notes on the Bradford Corporation*, Bradford, 1881.

Cudworth, William, *Musical Reminiscences of Bradford*, Bradford, 1885.

Curties, H., *When England Slept*, London, 1909.

Daily Mail, *Our German Cousins*, London, 1909.

Defoe, Daniel, *Reasons Against the Succession of the House of Hanover*, London, 1713.

Defoe, Daniel, *The True Born Englishman: A Satyr*, Philadelphia, 1778 edition.

Deicke, Heinrich, *A Short History of the German Evangelical Reformed St Paul's Church*, London, 1907.

Dietz, A., *Stammbuch der Frankfurter Juden*, Frankfurt, 1907.

Dorgeel, Heinrich, *Die Deutsche Kolonie in London*, London, 1881.

Eheberg, K. T., *Die Deutsche Auswanderung*, Heidelberg, 1885.

Einsiedel, Julius, *Das Gouvernantenwesen in England: Eine Warnung*, Heilbronn, 1884.

Escott, Thomas Hay Sweet, *Society in London*, London, 1885.

Eversley, Lord, 'Teutophobia', *Nineteenth Century*, vol. 62, 1908.

Felstead, S. T., *German Spies at Bay*, London, 1920.

Findlay, J. J., 'The Genesis of the German Clerk', *Fortnightly Review*, vol. 66, 1899.

Fischer, W. and A. Behrens, *Amely Bolte: Briefe aus England an Varnhagen von Ense (1844–1858)*, Düsseldorf, 1955.

Flexner, Abraham, *Prostitution in Europe*, New York, 1914.

'Foreigners in London', *Blackwood's Edinburgh Magazine*, vol. 51, 1842.

Freeman, Edward A., *Comparative Politics*, London, 1873.

Ganz, Wilhelm, *Memories of a Musician*, London, 1913.

Gardiner, George B., 'The Home of the German Band', *Blackwood's Magazine*, vol. 172, 1902.

'German Peril', *Quarterly Review*, vol. 209, 1908.

'Germany and Pan-Germany', *Contemporary Review*, vol. 84, 1903.

'Germany and the Prussian Spirit', *Round Table*, vol. 4, 1914.

'Geschichte der deutschen evangelischen Kirchgemeinden in Grossbritannien', *Monatsschrift für Innere Mission*, vol. 7, 1887.

Green, John Richard, *A Short History of the English People*, London, 1902.

Greenwood, James, *The Wilds of London*, London, 1874.

Halle, C. E. and Marie, *Life and Letters of Sir Charles Halle: Being an Autobiography with Correspondence and Diaries*, London, 1896.

Guerdon, Gilbert, 'Street Musicians', *Strand Magazine*, vol. 3, 1892.

Hanna, H. B., *Can Germany Invade England?*, London, 1912.

Herkommer, Sir Hubert von, *The Herkommers*, London, 1910.

Hobson, J. A., *The German Panic*, London, 1913.

Hobson, J. A., *The War in South Africa: Its Causes and Effects*, London, 1900.

Hodge, George D., *56 Years in the London Sugar Market*, London, 1960.

Hogarth, George, *The Philharmonic Society of London*, London, 1862.

Holmes, F. M., 'Some Foreign Places of Worship in London', in George R. Sims (ed.), *Living London*, vol. 3, 1906.

Hueffer, Francis (ed.), *Correspondence of Wagner and Liszt*, vol. 2, London, 1881.

Hueffer, Francis, *Half a Century of Music in England 1837–1887*, London, 1889.

Hunter, William, *Army Speech Dedicated to Those Who Have Been Frightened by the Battle of Dorking*, London, 1878.

Jackson, J. W., 'On the Racial Aspects of the Franco-Prussian War', *Journal of the Anthropological Institute of Great Britain*, vol. 1, 1872.

Jäger, August, *Der Deutsche in London*, 2 vols, London, 1839.

Japhet, Saemy, *Recollections of My Business Life*, London, 1931.

Johnston, Sir Harry Hamilton, *Views and Reviews from the Outlook of an Anthropologist*, London, 1912.

Joseephy, Fritz, *Die deutsche überseeische Auswanderung seit 1871*, Berlin, 1912.

Kärcher, F. X., *Bericht über die Mission der deutschen Katholischen in London*, Dusseldorf, 1869.

Katscher, Leopold, 'German Life in London', *Nineteenth Century*, vol.21, 1887.

Kingsley, Charles, *The Roman and the Teuton*, Cambridge, 1864.

Klein, Hermann, *Thirty Years of Musical Life in London*, 1870–1900, London, 1903.

Knox, Robert, *The Races of Men: A Philosophical Enquiry into the Influence of Race over the Destinies of Men*, 2nd edn, London, 1862.

König, H. Z., *Authentisches über die deutsche Erzieherin in England: Eine Entgegung auf: 'Das Gouvernantenwesen in England', eine Warnung, von Julius Einsiedel*, London, 1884.

Kron, R., *The Little Londoner*, Freiburg, 1908.

Kuhe, Wilhelm, *My Musical Recollections*, London, 1896.

Laing, Samuel, *Observations on the Social and Political State of the European People in 1848 and 1849*, London, 1850.

Lawrence, D. H., *The Prussian Officer*, London, 1914.

Le Queux, William, *The Invasion of 1910*, London, 1906.

Le Queux, William, *Spies of the Kaiser: Plotting the Downfall of England*, London, 1909.

Bibliography

Le Queux, William, *Things I Know About Kings, Celebrities and Crooks*, London, 1923.

Lloyd, G. I. H., *The Cutlery Trades*, London, 1913.

'London und die deutsche Mission', *Katholische Bewegung*, vol. 17, 1880.

'London und die deutsche Mission: II, Die Deutsche Mission', *Katholische Bewegung*, vol. 18, 1881.

Low, Sidney, and Bunting, William, 'The Journalistic Tour of Germany', *Contemporary Review*, vol. 92, 1907.

Lovely Albert, London, n.d.

Lowe, C., 'About German Spies', *Contemporary Review*, vol.18, 1910.

Mackay, John Henry, *The Anarchists: A Picture of Civilization at the Close of the Nineteenth Century*, Boston, 1891.

Margoliouth, Moses, *A History of the Jews in Great Britain*, 3 vols, London, 1851.

Martin, Rudolf Emil, *Der Anarchismus und Seine Traeger*, Berlin, 1887.

Mayhew, Henry, *German Life and Manners as Seen in Saxony at the Present day*, 2 vols, London, 1864.

Mayhew, Henry, *The Morning Chronicle Survey of Labour and the Poor: The Metropolitan Districts*, 6 vols, Horsham, 1981.

Mayhew, Henry, *The Shops and Companies of London*, London, 1865.

Mayhew, Henry, *The Upper Rhine: The Scenery of Its Banks and the Manners of Its People*, London, 1858.

Mills, J., *The British Jews*, London, 1853.

Mönckmeier, Wilhelm, *Die deutsche überseeische Auswanderung*, Jena, 1912.

Moritz, Carl Philip, *Travels, Chiefly on Foot, Through Part of England in 1782*, London, 1793.

Mudie-Smith, Richard, *Religious Life of the People in London*, London, 1905.

Müller, Johannes Paul, *Die Deutschen Schulen im Auslande*, Breslau, 1885.

Münchmeyer, Reinhard (ed.), *Handbuch der deutschen evangelischen Seemansmission*, Stettin, 1912.

Nagle, P. J., *Prince Albert and the Press: A Letter Addressed to the Right Hon. Viscount Palmerston*, London, 1854.

Offin, T. W., *How the Germans Took London*, Chelmsford, 1900.

Oppenheim, E. P., *The Secret*, London, 1907.

Oven, Joshua van, *Letters on the Present State of the Jewish Poor in the Metropolis*, London, 1802.

Pall Mall Gazette, *The Maiden Tribute of Modern Babylon*, London, 1885.

Philippovich, Eugen von (ed.), *Auswanderung und Auswanderungs Politik in Deutschland*, Leipzig, 1892.

Phillips, Florence, *A Friendly Germany: Why Not?*, London, 1913.

Plain Speech, *Who's to Blame, the Prince, the Press or the Ministry?*, London, n.d.

Porteous, J.E., *Peaceful Invasion of Great Britain*, London, 1914.

Rethwisch, I., *Die Deutschen im Auslande*, Berlin, 1889.

Reusch, A., *Ein Studienaufenthalt in England: Ein Führer für Studierende, Lehrer und Lehrerinnen*, Marburg, 1902.

Rules and Orders for a Charitable Society Set Up by Some Germans at London in the Year MDCCXII, London, 1713.

Rutari, A., *Londoner Skizzenbuch*, 2nd edn, Leipzig, 1906.

Ryan, P. F. William, 'London's Street Performers', in George R. Sims (ed.), *Living London*, vol. 3, London, 1906.

Sanger, William, *A History of Prostitution*, New York, 1859.

Savage, R. H., *The Anarchist*, London, 1894.

Schulte, J. F. (ed.), *Johanna Kinkel: Nach ihren Briefen und Erinnerungs-Blättern*, Münster, 1908.

Schneider, Karl, 'Deutsche Soldaten in englischem Dienst', *Deutsche Erde*, vol. 6, 1908.

Schöll, Carl, *Geschichte der Deutschen Evangelischen Kirchen in England*, Stuttgart, 1852.

Shadwell, Arthur, 'The German Colony in London', *National Review*, vol.26, 1896.

Sheahan, J. J., *General and Concise Description of the Town and Port of Kingston-upon-Hull*, London, 1864.

Spottiswoode, S., *Her Husband's Country*, London, 1910.

Stallard, J. H., *London Pauperism Amongst Jews and Christians*, London, 1867.

Stargardt, Emil, *Handbuch der Deutschen in England*, Heilbronn, 1889.

Steinkopf, D. C. F. A., *Predigt Gehalten am 19ten Sonntage nach Trinitatis, in der Deutschen St. Marien Kirche in der Savoy, Strand*, London, 1819.

Sutherland, Millicent, 'In Germany: A Sketch', *Nineteenth Century*, vol. 38, 1895.

Thwaite, B. H., 'The Commercial War between Germany and England', *Nineteenth Century*, vol. 40, 1896.

Timpe, Georg, *Die Deutsche St. Bonifacius-Mission in London 1809–1909*, London, 1909.

Tribbeko, John and Georg Ruperti, *Lists of Germans from the Palatine Who Came to England in 1709*, Baltimore, 1965 edition.

Watson, J., *Young Germany*, London, 1844.

Weisl, Ernst Franz, *Die Auswanderungsfrage*, Berlin, 1905.

Wenderborn, F. A., *A View of England Towards the Close of the Eighteenth Century*, 2 vols, London, 1791.

White, Arnold (ed.), *The Destitute Alien in Great Britain*, London, 1892.

White, Alien, *Efficiency and Empire*, Brighton, 1973 edition, originally London, 1901.

Whitman, Sidney, 'England and Germany', *Harper's Magazine*, April 1898.

Williams, Ernest Edwin, *Made in Germany*, London, 1896.

Wolfe, Humbert, *Now A Stranger*, London, 1933.

Wood, Walter, *The Enemy in Our Midst*, London, 1906.

Wright, Thomas, *The Celt, The Roman, and the Saxon*, London, 1852.

B. *SECONDARY SOURCES*

(1) *Published Works*

Aldcroft, D. H., 'The Entrepreneur and the British Economy, 1870–1914', *Economic History Review*, vol. 17, 1964.

Anderson, Gregory, 'German Clerks in England, 1870–1914: Another Aspect of the Great Depression Debate', in Kenneth Lunn (ed.), *Hosts, Immigrants and Minorities*, Folkestone, 1980.

Anderson, Gregory, *Victorian Clerks*, Manchester, 1976.

Andrew, Christopher, *Secret Service: The Making of the British Intelligence Community*, London, 1985.

Archer, J. W., 'The Steelyard', *Once A Week*, vol. 5, 1861.

Armytage, W. H. G., *The German Influence on English Education*, London, 1969.

Aronsfeld, C. C., 'A German Anti-Semite in England: Adolf Stöcker's London Visit in 1883', *Jewish Social Studies*, vol. 44, 1987.

Aronsfeld, C. C., 'German Jews in Dundee', *Jewish Chronicle*, 20 November 1953.

Aronsfeld, C. C., 'German Jews in Ireland', *Association of Jewish Refugees Information*, December 1953.

Aronsfeld, C. C., 'German Jews in Manchester', *Association of Jewish Refugees Information*, November 1954, January, February 1955.

Aronsfeld, C. C., 'German Jews in Nineteenth Century Bradford', *Yorkshire Archaeological Journal*, vol. 53, 1981.

Aronsfeld, C. C., 'German Jews in Nottingham', *Association of Jewish Refugees Information*, December, 1955.

Aronsfeld, C.C., 'German Jews in Victorian England', *Leo Baeck Yearbook*, vol.7, 1962.

Aronsfeld, C.C., 'Immigration Into Britain: The Germans', *History Today*, vol.35, August 1985.

Aronsfeld, C. C., 'Nottingham's Lace Pioneers: Part 2', *Guardian Journal*, 20 April 1954.

Aronsfeld, C.C., 'They settled in England: German Jewish Immigrants in the 19th Century', *Association of Jewish Refugees Information*, vol.9, 1954.

Ashton, Rosemary, *The German Idea: Four English Writers and the Reception of German Thought 1800–1860*, Cambridge, 1980.

Ashton, Rosemary, *Little Germany: Exile and Asylum in Victorian England*, Oxford, 1986.

Assion, P. (ed.), *Von Hessen in die neue Welt: Eine Sozial und Kulturgeschichte der Hessischen Amerikaauswanderung*, Frankfurt, 1987.

Bade, Klaus J., 'Altes Handwerk, Wanderzwang und Gute Policy: Gesellenwanderung zwischen Zunfökonomie und Gewerbereform', *Vierteljahrschrift für Sozial und Wirtschaftsgeschichte*, vol. 69, 1982.

Bade, Klaus J. (ed.), *Deutsche im Ausland Fremde in Deutschland: Migration in Geschichte und Gegenwart*, Munich, 1992.

Bade, Klaus J., 'German Emigration to the United States and Continental Immigration to Germany in the Late Nineteenth and Early Twentieth Centuries', *Central European History*, vol. 13, 1980.

Bade, Klaus J. (ed.), *Population, Labour and Migration in 19th and 20th Century Germany*, Leamington Spa, 1987.

Bade, Klaus J., *Vom Auswanderungsland zum Einwanderungsland? Deutschland 1880–1980*, Berlin, 1983.

Baines, Dudley, *Emigration from Europe 1815–1930*, London, 1991.

Baines, Dudley, *Migration in a Mature Economy: Emigration and International Migration in England and Wales*, Cambridge, 1985.

Barkai, Avraham, 'German-Jewish Migrations in the Nineteenth Century', *Leo Baeck Institute Year Book*, vol. 30, 1985.

Berghoff, Hartmut, *Englische Unternehmer 1870–1914: Eine Kollektivbiographie führender Wirtschaftsbürger in Birmingham, Bristol und Manchester*, Göttingen, 1991.

Bennet, Daphne, *King Without A Crown: Albert, Prince Consort of England 1819–1861*, London, 1983.

Bentwich, Norman, 'Humbert Wolfe: Poet and Civil Servant', *Menorah Journal*, vol. 31, 1943.

Bergonzi, Bernard, 'Before 1914: Writers and the Threat of War', *Critical Quarterly*, vol. 6, 1964.

Bermant, C., *Point of Arrival: A Study of London's East End*, London, 1975.

Bernard, Roy, *My German Family in England*, Cookham, 1991.

Berquist, James, 'German Communities in American Cities: An Interpretation of the Nineteenth Century Experience', *Journal of American Ethnic History*, vol. 4, 1984.

Bibliography

Besser, Gustav Adolf, *Geschichte der Frankfurter Flüchtlings-gemein-den 1554–1558*, Halle, 1906.

Biddis, M. D., 'The Politics of Anatomy: Dr Robert Knox and Victorian Racism', *Proceedings of the Royal Society of Medicine*, vol. 69, 1976.

Bird, J.C., *Control of Enemy Alien Civilians in Great Britain 1914–1918*, New York, 1986.

Birke, Adolf M. and Kurt Kluxen (eds), *England and Hanover*, Munich 1986.

Birke, Adolf M. and Kurt Kluxen (eds), *Viktorianisches England in deutscher Perspektive*, Munich, 1983.

Bölsker-Schlicht, Franz, 'Von Schledehausen in die Neue Welt: Die Nordamerika Auswanderung im 19. Jahrhundert', in Klaus J. Bade, Horst-Rüdiger Jarck and Anton Schindling (eds), *Schelenberg-Kirchspiel-Landgemeinde: 900 Jahre Schledehausen*, Bissendorf, 1990.

Bolitho, Hector, *Alfred Mond*, London, 1933.

Bradford Heritage Recording Unit, *Destination Bradford: A Century of Immigration*, Bradford, 1987.

Brancaforte, Charlotte L. (ed.), *The German Forty-Eighters in the United States*, New York, 1989.

Brandenburg, Alexander, 'Der Kommunistische Arbeiterbildungsverein in London: Ein Beitrag zu den Anfängen der Deutscher Arbeiterbildungsbewegung (1840–47)', *International Review of Social History*, vol. 14, 1979.

Brettschneider, Werner, *Entwicklung und Bedeutung des deutschen Frühsozialismus in London*, Bottrop, 1936.

Briggs, Asa, *Marx in London: An Illustrated Guide*, London, 1982.

Brightfield, Myron F., *Victorian England in Its Novels*, Los Angeles, 1968.

Brockel, M., 'Auswandererverzeichnis in Staatsarchiv Osnabrück', *Archive in Niedersachsen*, vol. 9, 1990.

Buckman, Joseph, *Immigrants and the Class Struggle: The Jewish Immigrant in Leeds 1880–1914*, Manchester, 1983.

Butler, E. M., 'Heine in England and Matthew Arnold', *German Life and Letters*, vol. 9, 1956.

Buttler, Philipp, 'Die Ausländer in den Romanen Thackeray's', *Giessener Beiträge*, vol. 2, 1925.

Camplin, Jamie, *The Rise of the Plutocrats: Wealth and Power in Victorian England*, London, 1978.

Carley, Lionel, *Delius: A Life in Letters*, vol. 1, London, 1983.

Carlson, A., *German Anarchism*, Metuchen, New Jersey, 1972.

Carr, William, *A History of Germany 1815–1945*, London, 1981 reprint.

Carrothers, W. A., *Emigration from the British Isles: With Special*

Reference to the Development of the Overseas Dominions, London, 1965.

Chapman, Stanley D., 'Aristocracy and Meritocracy in Merchant Banking', *British Journal of Sociology*, vol. 37, 1986.

Chapman, Stanley D., 'The Foundation of the English Rothschilds: N. M. Rothschild as a Textile Merchant', *Textile History*, vol. 8, 1977.

Chapman, Stanley D., 'The International Houses: The Continental Contribution to British Commerce, 1800–1860', *Journal of European Economic History*, vol. 6, 1977.

Chapman, Stanley D., 'The Migration of Merchant Enterprise: German Houses in Britain in the Eighteenth and Nineteenth Centuries', *Bankhistorisches Archiv*, vol. 6, 1980.

Chapman, Stanley D., *The Rise of Merchant Banking*, London, 1984.

Charles, A., *International Business in the Nineteenth Century: The Rise and Fall of a Cosmopolitan Bourgeoisie*, Brighton, 1987.

Cherno, M., '*Der Deutsche Eidgenosse* and its Collpase, 1865–1867', *German Life and Letters*, vol. 35, 1982.

Chesney, K., *The Victorian Underworld*, Harmondsworth, 1972.

Chitty, C. W., 'Aliens in England during the Sixteenth Century', *Race*, vol. 8, 1966.

Church, R. A., *Economic and Social Change in a Midland Town: Victorian Nottingham, 1815–1900*, London, 1966.

Clarke, I. F., *Voices Prophesying War 1763–1984*, Oxford, 1966.

Coad, Roy, *A History of the Brethren Movement*, Exeter, 1968.

Conzen, Kathleen M., *Immigrant Milwaukee, 1836–1860: Accommodation and Community in A Frontier City*, Cambridge, Massachusetts, 1976.

Corrin, Jay P., *G. K. Chesterton and Hilaire Belloc: The Battle Against Modernity*, London, 1981.

Craig, Gordon A., *Germany 1866–1945*, Oxford, 1981.

Cunningham, W., *Alien Immigration to England*, London, 1969, 2nd edn.

Curtis, L. P., *Anglo-Saxons and Celts*, New York, 1968.

Dänell, E., *Die Blütezeit der Deutschen Hanse: Hansische Geschichte von der Zweiten Hälfte des XIV. Jahrhunderts bis zum Letzten Viertel des XV. Jahrhunderts*, 2 vols, Berlin, 1905–6, 1973.

Dictionary of Business Biography, 5 vols, London, 1984–6.

Dick, Ernst, 'Deutschland und die Deutschen bei Meredith', *Germanische Romanische Monatschrift*, vol. 6, 1914.

Dickinson, H. T., 'The Poor Palatines and the Parties', *English Historical Review*, vol. 82, 1967.

Dolan, Jay P., *The Immigrant Church*, Baltimore, 1975.

Dollinger, Phillipe, *The German Hansa*, London, 1970.

Donnan, F. G., *Ludwig Mond: 1839–1909*, London, 1939.

Ehrlich, Cyril, *The Music Profession in Britain Since the Eighteenth Century: A Social History*, Oxford, 1985.

Elasasser, Robert, *Über die politische Bildungsreisen der Deutschen nach England*, Heidelberg, 1917.

Emden, Paul H., 'Baron Paul Julius de Reuter', *Transactions of the Jewish Historical Society of England*, vol. 17, 1953.

Emden, Paul H., *Jews of Britain*, London, 1943.

Endelman, Todd M., *The Jews of Georgian England: Tradition and Change in a Liberal Society, 1714–1830*, Philadelphia, 1979.

Endelman, Todd M., *Radical Assimilation in English-Jewish History 1656–1945*, Bloomington, 1990.

Engelsing, Rolf, *Bremen als Auswandererhafen 1683–1880*, Bremen, 1961.

Erickson, Charlotte, *American Industry and the European Immigrant*, Cambridge, Massachusets, 1957.

Erickson, Charlotte (ed.), *Emigration from Europe 1815–1914*, London, 1976.

Evans, Richard J., 'Prostitution and Society in Imperial Germany', *Past and Present*, vol. 70, 1976.

Farrell, Jerome, 'The German Community in Nineteenth Century East London', *East London Record*, vol. 13, 1990.

Fenske, Hans, 'Die deutsche Auswanderung in der Mitte des 19. Jahrhunderts', *Geschichte in Wissenschaft und Unterricht*, vol. 24, 1973.

Fenske, Hans, 'International Migration in the Eighteenth Century', *Central European History*, vol. 13, 1980.

Fiedler, Herma, 'German Musicians in England and their Influence to the End of the Eighteenth Century', *German Life and Letters*, vol. 6, 1939.

Finestein, Israel, *A Short History of Anglo-Jewry*, London, 1957.

Fishman, William J., *East End, 1888*, London, 1988.

Fishman, William J., *East End Jewish Radicals 1875–1914*, London, 1975.

Fock, Thomas, 'Über Londoner Zuckersiederein und deutsche Arbeitskräfte', *Zuckerindustrie*, vols. 3, 5, 1985.

Frangopulo, N. J., 'Foreign Communities in Victorian Manchester', *Manchester Review*, vol. 10, 1965.

Frangopulo, N.J., *Rich Inheritance: A Guide to the History of Manchester*, Wakefield, 1962.

Freeden, Hermann von, and Smolka, Georg (eds), *Auswanderer: Bilder und Skizzen aus der Geschichte der deutschen Auswanderung*, Leipzig, 1937.

French, David, 'Spy Fever in Great Britain 1910–15', *Historical Journal*, vol.21, 1978.

Fryer, Peter, *Staying Power: The History of Black People in Britain*, London, 1984.

Gainer, Bernard, *The Alien Invasion*, London, 1972.

Galbraith, John S., 'The Pamphlet Campaign on the Boer War', *Journal of Modern History*, vol. 24, 1952.

Gartner, Lloyd P., 'Anglo-Jewry and the International Traffic in Prostitution, 1885–1914', *Association of Jewish Studies Review*, vol. 7–8, 1982–3, pp. 129–78.

Gartner, Lloyd P., *The Jewish Immigrant in England 1870–1914*, London, 1960.

Gelberg, Brigit, *Auswanderung nach Übersee: Soziale Probleme der Auswandererbeförderung in Hamburg und Bremen von der Mite des 19. Jahrhunderts bis zum Ersten Weltkrieg*, Hamburg, 1973.

George, M. Dorothy, *London Life in the Eighteenth Century*, Harmondsworth, 1966 edition.

Gerdes, Heinrich, 'Ein Sohn Harsefelds als Grosskaufmann in London', *Stader Archiv*, vol. 14, 1924.

Gillesen, Günter, *Lord Palmerston und die Einigung Deutschlands: Die Englische Politik von der Paulskirche bis zu den Dresdner Konferenzen (1848- 1851)*, Lubeck 1961.

Glanz, Rudolph, 'The German Jewish Mass Emigration: 1820–1880', *American Jewish Archives*, vol. 22, 1970.

Goodman, Jean, *The Mond Legacy*, London, 1982.

Grandjonc, Jacques, 'Die deutsche Binnenwanderung in Europa 1830 bis 1848', in Otto Büsch, et. al, (eds), *Die frühsozialistischen Bünde in der Geschichte der deutschen Arbeiterbewegung*, Berlin, 1975.

Green, David, *Great Cobbett: The Noblest Agitator*, London, 1983.

Grunwald, Kurt, '"Windsor Cassel" – The Last Court Jew', *Leo Baeck Yearbook*, vol.14, 1969.

Haines, George, *Essays on the German Influence upon English Education and Science, 1850–1919*, Hamden, Connecticut, 1969.

Halsam, Jeremy (ed.), *Anglo-Saxon Towns in Southern England*, Chichester, 1984.

Handlin, Oscar, *The Uprooted*, London, 1990 reprint.

Hanse in Europa: Brücke zwischen den Märkten 12.- 17. Jahrhundert, Cologne, 1973.

Hansen, Marcus Lee, *The Atlantic Migration 1607–1860*, Cambridge, Massachusetts, 1941.

Hansen, Marcus Lee, 'The Revolutions of 1848 and German Emigration', *Journal of Economic and Business History*, vol. 2, 1929.

Hayes, Richard, 'The German Colony in County Limerick', *North Munster Antiquarian Journal*, vol. 1, 1937.

Hayward, John F., 'English Swords 1600–1650', in Robert Held (ed.), *Arms and Armour Annual*, vol. 1, Northfield, Illinois, 1973.

Helbich, Wolfgang, Kamphoefner, W. D., and Sommer, Ulrike, *Briefe aus Amerika: Deutsche Schreiben aus der Neuen Welt, 1830–1930*, Munich, 1988.

Henderson, W. O., 'Friedrich Engels in Manchester', *Memoirs and Proceedings of the Manchester Literary and Philosophical Society*, vol. 98, 1956–7.

Henderson, W. O., *The Life of Friedrich Engels*, 2 vols, London, 1976.

Hennings, C.R., *Deutsche in England*, Stuttgart, 1923.

Herberg, Will, *Protestant-Catholic-Jew*, Chicago, 1983 edition.

Heufer, E., *Pennsylvanien im 17. Jahrhundert und die Ausgewanderten Pfälzer in England*, Neustadt an der Hardt, 1910.

Hildebrandt, Bernd W., *1860–1985: 125 Years German Young Men's Christian Association in London*, Edenbridge, Kent, 1985.

Hiley, Nicholas, 'The Failure of British Counter-Espionage against Germany 1907–14', *Historical Journal*, vol. 28, 1905.

Hiley, Nicholas, 'Spying for the Kaiser', *History Today*, vol. 38, June 1988.

Hippel, Wolfgang von, *Auswanderung aus Südwestdeutschland: Studien zur Württembergischen Auswanderung und Auswanderungspolitik im 18. und 19. Jahrhundert*, Stuttgart, 1984.

Hirschfeld, Gerhard, *Exile in Great Britain: Refugees from Hitler's Germany*, Leamington Spa, 1984.

Hirst, Hugo, 'Two Autobiographical Fragments', *Business History*, vol. 28, 1986.

Hobsbawm, E. J., *Europäische Revolutionen, 1789 bis 1848*, Zurich, 1962.

Hobsbawm, E. J., *Industry and Empire: From 1750 to the Present Day*, Harmondsworth, 1969 edition.

Hobson, J. A., *The German Panic*, London, 1913.

Hogwood, Christopher, *Handel*, London, 1984.

Hollenberg, Günter, 'Die Englische Goethe Society und die deutsch-englischen kulturellen Beziehungen im 19. Jahrhundert', *Zeitschrift für Religions- und Geistgeschichte*, vol. 30, 1978.

Hollenberg, Günter, *Englisches Interesse Am Kaiserreich: Die Aktivität Preussen-Deutschlands für Konservative und Liberale Kreise in Grossbritannien 1860–1914*, Wiesbaden, 1974.

Holmes, Colin, *Anti-Semitism in British Society 1876–1939*, London, 1979.

Holmes, Colin, 'The German Gypsy Question in Britain 1904–6', in

Kenneth Lunn (ed.), *Hosts, Immigrants and Minorities*, Folkestone, 1980.

Holmes, Colin, 'Germans in Britain 1870–1914', *Beiträge Zur Wirtschaftsgeschichte, Band 6: Wirtschaftskräfte und Wirtschaftswege, 3*, Bamberg, 1978.

Holmes, Colin, 'J. A. Hobson and the Jews', in Holmes (ed.), *Immigrants and Minorities in British Society*, London, 1978.

Holmes, Colin, *John Bull's Island: Immigration and British Society 1871–1971*, London, 1988.

Dirk Hoerder (ed.), *Labor Migration in the Atlantic Economies: The European and North American Working Classes During the Period of Industrialization*, London, 1985.

Horsman, Reginald, 'Origins of Racial Anglo-Saxonism in Great Britain Before 1850', *Journal of the History of Ideas*, vol. 37, 1976.

Hundert Jahre Deutsch-Evangelische Kirche Bradford-Huddersfield-Leeds, 1877–1977, n.d.

Husemann, Harald, 'When Wiliam Came; If Adolf Had Come: English Speculative Novels on the German Conquest of Britain', *Anglistik und Englischunterricht*, vols 29–30, 1986.

Hyam, L., *The Jews of Ireland: From Earliest Times to the Year 1910*, London, 1972.

Inglis, Kenneth Stanley, *Churches and the Working Classes in Victorian England*, London, 1963.

Jackson, J. A., *The Irish in Britain*, London, 1963.

James Robert Rhodes, *Albert, Prince Consort: A Biography*, London, 1983.

Janossy, Denes A., *Great Britain and Kossuth*, Budapest, 1937.

Jenkins, D. T., and Ponting, K. G., *The British Wool and Textile Industry 1770–1914*, London, 1982.

Jenkins, Mick, *Frederick Engels in Manchester*, Manchester, 1951.

Jones, Ernest, *The Life of Work of Sigmund Freud*, vol. 1, London, 1953.

Jones, M. A., *American Immigration*, Chicago, 1960.

Josephs, Zoë, *Birmingham Jewry 1794–1914*, Birmingham, 1980.

Kamphoefner, Walter D., 'At the Crossroads of Economic Development: Background Factors Affecting Emigration from Nineteenth Century Germany', in Ira D. Glazier and Luigi D. Roza (eds), *Migration Across Time and Nations: Population Mobility in Historical Contexts*, New York, 1986.

Kamphoefner, Walter D., *The Westfalians: From Germany to Missouri*, Princeton, 1987.

Kargon, Robert H., *Science in Victorian Manchester: Enterprise and Culture*, Manchester, 1977.

Katz, David S., *Philo-Semitism and the Readmission of the Jews to England 1603–1655*, Oxford, 1982.

'Kayser, Ellison & Co. Ltd., Makers of High Grade Special Steels', *Histories of Famous Firms*, vol. 18, no. 6, 1958.

Kellenbenz, Hermann, 'German Immigrants in England', in Colin Holmes (ed.), *Immigrants and Minorities in British Society*, London, 1978.

Kennedy, Michael, *Halle, 1858–1976: A Brief Survey of the Orchestra's History, Travels and Achievements*, Manchester, n.d.

Kennedy, Michael, *The History of the Royal Manchester College of Music*, Manchester, 1971.

Kennedy, Paul M., *The Rise of the Anglo-German Antagonism 1860–1914*, London, 1980.

Kennedy, Paul M. and Anthony Nicholls (eds), *Nationalist and Racialist Movements in Britain and Germany Before 1914*, London, 1981.

Kiel, Karl, 'Gründe und Folgen der Auswanderung aus dem Osnabrücker Regierungsbezirk, insbesondere nach den Vereinigten Staaten, in Lichte der Hannoverischen Auswanderungspolitik betrachtet (1823–1866)', *Mitteilungen des Vereins für Geschichte und Landeskunde von Osnabrück*, vol. 61, 1941.

Kleeberg, Wilhelm, 'Hollandgänger und Heringfänger', *Neues Archiv für Landes- und Volkskunde von Niedersachsen*, vol. 2, 1948.

Kleinschmidt, P. Beda, *Auslanddeutschtum und Kirche: Ein Nachschlagwerk auf Geschichtlich Statistischer Grundlage*, vol. 1, Münster, 1930.

Knittle, Walter Allen, *Early Eighteenth Century Palatine Emigration*, Baltimore, 1979 reprint.

Knodel, John E., *The Decline of Fertility in Germany, 1871–1939*, Princeton, 1974.

Koditschek, Theodore, *Class Formation and Urban Industrial Society: Bradford 1750–1850*, Cambridge, 1990.

Köllmann, Wolfgang and Peter Marschalk, 'German Emigration to the United States', *Perspectives in American History*, vol. 7, 1973.

Kornder, Theodor, *Der Deutsche im Spiegelbild der englischen Erzählungsliteratur des 19. Jahrhunderts*, Erlangen-Bruck, 1934.

Kroker, Werner, *Wege zur Verbreitung technologischer Kenntnisse zwischen England und Deutschland in der zweiten Hälfte des 18. Jahrhunderts*, Berlin, 1971.

Kushner, Tony and Kenneth Lunn (eds), *The Politics of Marginality? Race, the Radical Right and Minorities in Twentieth Century Britain*, London, 1990.

Kushner, Tony and Kenneth Lunn (eds), *Traditions of Intolerance: Historical Perspectives on Fascism and Race Discourse in British Society*, Manchester, 1989.

Laski, N. J., 'The History of Manchester Jewry', *Manchester Review*, vol. 7, 1956.

Lees, L. H., *Exiles of Erin: Irish Migrants in Victorian London*, Manchester, 1979.

Lenin, W. I., 'Kapitalismus und Arbeiterimmigration', in *Werke*, vol. 19, Berlin, 1971, pp. 447–50.

Levy, Hermann, *England and Germany: Affinity and Contrast*, Leigh-on-Sea, 1949.

Lidtke, Vernon L., *The Outlawed Party: Social Democracy in Germany, 1878–1890*, Princeton, 1966.

Linde, Hans, 'Das Königreich Hanover an der Schwelle des Industriezeitalters', *Neues Archiv für Niedersachsen*, vol. 5, 1951.

Lingelbach, W. E., *The Merchant Adventurers of England: Their Laws and Ordinances with Other Documents*, Philadelphia, 1902.

Lipman, V. D., *A History of the Jews in Britain since 1858*, Leicester, 1990.

Lipman, V. D., 'The Plymouth Aliens List 1798 and 1803', *Miscellanies of the Jewish Historical Society of England*, part. 6, 1962.

Lloyd, T. H., *Alien Merchants in England in the High Middle Ages*, Brighton, 1982.

Lloyd, T. H., *England and the German Hansa, 1157–1611: A Study of their Trade and Commercial Diplomacy*, Cambridge, 1991.

Ludwig, Albert, 'Deutschland und Deutsche im englischen Roman', *Germanisch-Romanische Monatschrift*, vol. 5, 1913.

Luebke, David, 'German Exodus: Historical Perspectives on the Nineteenth-Century German Emigration', *Yearbook of German-American Studies*, vol. 20, 1985.

Luebke, Frederick C., *Germans in Brazil: A Comparative History of Cultural Conflict*, Baton Rouge, 1987.

Luebke, Frederick C. (ed.), *Germans in the New World: Essays in the History of Immigration*, Urbana and Chicago, 1990.

Lührs, Wilhelm, *Die Freie Hansestadt Bremen und England in der Zeit des Deutschen Bundes (1815–1867)*, Bremen, 1958.

MacDougall, H. A., *Racial Myth in English History: Trojans, Teutons and Anglo-Saxons*, London, 1982.

MacKenzie, John M., *Propaganda and Empire*, Manchester, 1984.

Mackerness, E. D., *A Social History of English Music*, London, 1964.

Mackerness, Eric, *Somewhere Further North: Music in Sheffield*, Sheffield, 1974.

McLellan, David, *Karl Marx: His Life and Thought*, London, 1973.

McLeod, Hugh, *Religion and the Working Classes in Nineteenth Century Britain*, London, 1989.

Marder, A. J., *British Naval Policy, 1880–1905: The Anatomy of British Sea Power*, London, 1940.

Mare, Margaret L., and Quarrel, W. H. (eds), *Lichtenberg's Visits to England*, Oxford, 1938.

Markham, John, *Keep the Home Fires Burning: The Hull Area in the First World War*, Beverly, 1988.

Marschalck, Peter, *Deutsche Überseewanderung im 19. Jahrhundert*, Stuttgart, 1973.

Marschalk, Peter, 'Zur Geschichte der Auswanderung über Bremen: Entwicklungslinien und Forschungsprobleme', *Bremer Archiven*, vol. 53, 1986.

Marschalck, Peter, 'Social and Economic Conditions of European Emigration to South America in the 19th and 20th Centuries', in Richard Konetzke and Hermann Kellenbenz (eds), *Jahrbuch für Geschichte von Staat, Wirtschaft und Gesellschaft Lateinamerikas*, 1976.

Marschalck, Peter, and Wolfgang Köllman, 'German Overseas Migration since 1815', in Commission Internationale d'Histoire des Mouvements Sociaux et des Structures Sociales, *Les Migrations Internationales de la Fin du XVIIIe Siecle a Nos Jours*.

Martin, Kingsley, *The Triumph of Lord Palmerston: A Study of Public Opinion in England before the Crimean War*, London, 1963.

Martin, Theodore, *The Life of His Royal Highness, The Prince Consort*, 5 vols, London, 1875–80.

Massie, R. K., *Dreadnought: Britain, Germany and the Coming of the Great War*, London, 1992.

Matheson, P. E., *German Visitors to England 1770–1795 and their Impressions*, Oxford, 1930.

Messerschmidt, M., *Deutschland in englischer Sicht*, Düsseldorf, 1955.

Metz, I., *Die deutsche Flotte in der Englischen Presse: Der Navy Scare vom Winter 1904/5*, Berlin, 1936.

Modder, Montagu Frank, *The Jew in the Literature of England*, New York, 1960.

Moltmann, Günter, 'American-German Return Migration in the Nineteenth and Early Twentieth Centuries', *Central European History*, vol. 13, 1980.

Moltmann, Günter (ed.), *Aufbruch nach Amerika. Friedrich List und die Auswanderung aus Baden und Württemberg 1816/17: Dokumentation einer Sozialen Bewegung*, Tübingen, 1979.

Moltmann, Günter (ed.), *Deutsche Amerikaauswanderung im 19. Jahrhundert*, Stuttgart, 1976.

Moltmann, Günter (ed.), *Germans in American: 300 Years of Immigration, 1683–1983*, Stuttgart, 1982.

Mommsen, Wolfgang J., *Two Centuries of Anglo-German Relations: A Reappraisal*, London, 1984.

Morris, A.J.A., *The Scaremongerers*, London, 1984.

Mosse, W. E., et al (eds), *Second Chance: Two Centuries of German-speaking Jews in the United Kingdom*, Tübingen, 1991.

Müller, Friedeborg L., *The History of the German Lutheran Congregations in England*, Frankfurt, 1987.

Müller-Lehning, A., 'The International Association (1855–9)', *International Review for Social History*, vol. 3, 1938.

Nadel, Stanley, *Little Germany: Ethnicity, Religion, and Class in New York City*, Urbana and Chicago, 1990.

Nettel, Reginald, *Music in the Five Towns 1840–1914: A Study of the Social Influence of Music in an Industrial District*, Oxford, 1944.

Nettel, Reginald, *The Orchestra in England*, London, 1946.

Nettlau, M., *Anarchisten und Sozial Revolutionaire*, Berlin, 1931.

New Grove Dictionary of Music, 20 vols., London, 1980.

Newman, Aubrey (ed.), *Provincial Jewry in Victorian England*, London, 1975.

Newton, Gerald, *German Studies at the University of Sheffield: An Historical Perspective, 1880–1988 together with a Graduate List, 1910–1988*, Sheffield, 1988.

Nicolaevsky, B., 'Towards a History of "The Communist League" 1847–1852', *International Review of Social History*, vol. 1, 1956.

Niedhart, Gottfried (ed.), *Grossbritannien als Gast und Exilland für Deutsche im 19. und 20. Jahrhundert*, Bochum, 1985.

Nomad, Max, *Dreamers, Dynamiters and Demagogues*, New York, 1964.

Oakley, Robin, *Changing Patterns of Distribution of Cypriot Settlement*, Coventry, 1987.

Oliver, H., *The International Anarchist Movement in Late Victorian London*, London, 1983.

O'Sullivan, Emer, *Friend and Foe: The Image of Germany and Germans in British Children's Fiction from 1870 to the Present*, Tübingen, 1990.

Panayi, Panikos, 'Dominant Societies and Minorities in the Two World Wars', in Panayi (ed.), *Minorities in Wartime: National and Racial Groupings in Europe, North America and Australia during the Two World Wars*, Oxford, 1993.

Panayi, Panikos, *The Enemy in Our Midst: Germans in Britain During the First World War*, Oxford, 1991.

Panayi, Panikos, *Immigration, Ethnicity and Racism in Britain, 1815–1945*, Manchester, 1994.

Panayi, Panikos, 'Refugees in Twentieth Century Britain: A Brief

History', in Vaughan Bevan (ed.), *The International Refugee Crisis in the Twentieth Century: British and Canadian Responses*, London, 1993.

Parker, C. J. W., 'The Failure of Liberal Racialism: The Racial Ideas of E. A. Freeman', *Historical Journal*, vol. 24, 1981.

Peet, Henry, *The German Church in Renshaw Street, Liverpool*, Liverpool, 1935.

Perks, Robert B., 'A Feeling of Not Belonging', *Oral History*, vol. 12, 1984.

Perry, Thomas W., *Public Opinion, Propaganda and Politics in Eighteenth Century England: A Study of the Jewish Naturalization Act of 1753*, London, 1962.

Peters, Inge-Maren, *Hansekaufleute als Gläubiger der Englischen Krone (1294–1350)*, Cologne, 1978.

Pohl, Manfred, 'Deutsche Bank London Agency Founded 100 Years Ago', in Deutsche Bank (ed.), *Studies on Economic and Monetary Problems and on Banking History*, Mainz, 1988.

Pole, William, *The Life of Sir William Siemens*, London, 1888.

Pollins, Harold, *Economic History of the Jews in England*, London, 1982.

Pollins, Harold, *Hopeful Travellers: Jewish Migrants and Settlers in Nineteenth Century Britain*, London, 1991 reprint.

Porter, Bernard, 'The Freiheit Prosecutions, 1881–1882', *Historical Journal*, vol. 23, 1980.

Porter, Bernard, *The Origins of the Vigilant State: The London Metropolitan Police Special Branch Before the First World War*, London, 1987.

Porter, Bernard, *The Refugee Question in Mid-Victorian Politics*, Cambridge, 1979.

Porter, Roy, *English Society in the Eighteenth Century*, Harmondsworth, 1982.

Postgate, Raymond, *The Workers' International*, London, 1920.

Prawer, S. S., *Frankenstein's Island: England and the English in the Writing of Heinrich Heine*, Cambridge, 1986.

Price, Richard, *An Imperial War and the British Working Classes: Working-Class Attitudes and Reactions to the Boer War 1899–1902*, London, 1972.

Priestley, J. B., 'Born and Bred in Bradford', *Listener*, vol. 34, 1945.

Priestley, J.B., *English Journey*, Harmondsworth, 1977 reprint.

Pürschel, Jürgen, *Die Geschichte des German Hospitals in London (1845 bis 1948)*, Münster, 1980.

Quail, John, *The Slow Burning Fuse: The Lost History of British Anarchists*, London, 1978.

Ramge, Walter, 'Focal Points in the History of the Hamburg Lutheran Church', in *Hamburg Lutheran Church, London 1669–1969*, Hamburg and Berlin, 1969.

Reader, W. J., *Imperial Chemical Industries, A History*, 2 vols, London, 1970.

Renzig, Rüdiger, *Pfälzer in Irland: Studien zur Geschichte deutschen Auswandererkolonien des frühen 18. Jahrhunderts*, Karlsruhe, 1989.

Richter, Robert, *Studien zur London Emigration von 1850–1860*, Berlin, 1966.

Rieger, J., 'The British Crown and the German Churches in England', in F. Hildebrandt (ed.), *And Other Pastors of thy Flock*, Cambridge, 1942.

Rieger, J., 'Der Erste Deutsche Hofprediger in London', *Evangelische Diaspora*, vol. 31.

Roberts, Richard, *Schroders: Merchants and Bankers*, London, 1992.

Robson-Scott, W. D., *German Travellers in England*, Oxford, 1953.

Rocker, Rudolf, *Johann Most: Das Leben eines Rebellen*, Glashütten im Taunus, 1973.

Rocker, Rudolf, *The London Years*, London, 1956.

Rogers, N., 'Popular Protest in Early Hanoverian London', *Past and Present*, vol. 79, 1978.

Rollin, A. R., 'The Jewish Contribution to the British Textile Industry: "Builders of Bradford"', *Transactions of the Jewish Historical Society of England*, vol. 17, 1951.

Rose, Millicent, *The East End of London*, London, 1951.

Rosenkranz, Albert Edward, 'Die Anfänge der Gemeinde in Sydenham', in *Hundert Jahre Deutsche Evangelische Gemeinde Sydenham (London) 1875–1975*, London, 1975.

Rosenkranz, Albert Edward, *Geschichte der deutschen evangelischen Kirche zu Liverpool*, Stuttgart, 1921.

Roth, Cecil, *The Great London Synagogue 1690–1940*, London, 1950.

Roth, Cecil, *A History of the Jews in England*, Oxford, 1941.

Roth, Cecil, *The Rise of Provincial Jewry*, London, 1950.

Rubinstein, W. D., *Men of Property: The Very Wealthy in Britain since the Industrial Revolution*, London, 1981.

Rude, George, *Hanoverian London*, London, 1971.

Russel, Dave, *Popular Music in England: A Social History*, Manchester, 1989.

Schaible, Karl Heinrich, *Geschichte der Deutschen in England*, Strasbourg, 1885.

Schiller, F. P., 'Friedrich Engels und die Schiller Anstalt in Manchester', in D. Rjazanov (ed.), *Marx-Engels Archiv*, vol. 2, 1928.

Schmidt, H. D., 'Chief Rabbi Nathan Marcus Adler (1803–1890): Jewish Educator from Germany', *Leo Baeck Yearbook*, vol. 7, 1962.

Schmitt, Bernadotte E., *England and Germany, 1740–1914*, Princeton, 1916.

Schmitdgall, Harry, *Friedrich Engels Manchester Aufenthalt 1842–1844*, Trier, 1981.

Schönberger, G., (ed.), *Festschrift zum 70. Geburtstag von Freiherr Baron von Schröder*, London, 1937.

Schoeps, Julius H., '"Der Kosmos": Ein Wochenblatt der Bürgerlich-Demokratischen Emigration in London im Frühjahr 1851', *Jahrbuch des Instituts für Deutsche Geschichte*, vol. 5, 1976.

Schramm, Percy Ernst, 'Die deutsche Wirtschaft und England um 1840', *Mitteilungen des Instituts für Österreichische Geschichtsforschung*, vol. 62, 1954, pp. 517–30.

Schramm, Percy Ernest, 'Die deutschen Überseekaufleute in Rahmen der Sozialgeschichte', *Bremisches Jahrbuch*, vol. 49, 1964.

Schultz, Fritz, *Der Deutsche in der englischen Literatur vom Beginn der Romantik bis zum Ausbruch des Weltkrieges*, Göttingen, 1939.

Schulze, Friedrich, *Die Hanse und England: Von Eduards III. bis auf Heinrichs VIII. Zeit*, Berlin, 1911, Stuttgart, 1978.

Schumacher, Martin, *Auslandreisen Deutscher Unternehmer 1750–1851 unter Besonderer Berücksichtigung von Rheinland und Westfalen*, Cologne, 1968.

Searle, G.R., *Corruption in British Politics 1895–1930*, Oxford, 1987.

Sessa, Anna Dzamba, *Richard Wagner and the English*, London, 1979.

Sigsworth, E. M., *Black Dyke Mills: A History*, Liverpool, 1958.

Simpson, G. C., 'Sir Arthur Schuster 1851–1934', *Obituary Notices of Fellows of the Royal Society*, vol. 1, 1932.

Sontag, Raymond James, *Germany and England, 1848–1894*, New York, 1958.

Sparrow, Elizabeth, 'The Aliens Office 1792–1806', *Historical Journal*, vol. 33, 1990.

Sponza, Lucio, *Italian Immigrants in Nineteenth Century Britain*, Leicester, 1988.

Stafford, David, 'Conspiracy and Xenophobia: The Popular Spy Novels of William Le Queux', *Europa*, Tone 4, 1981.

Stafford, David, 'Spies and Gentlemen: The Birth of the British Spy Novel, 1893–1914', *Victorian Studies*, vol.24, 1981.

Stahl, Ernst Leopold, 'Das erste deutsche Lektorat in England', *Die Neueren Sprachen*, vol. 18, 1911.

Stern, W. M., 'The London Sugar Refiners around 1800', *Guildhall Miscellany*, no. 3, 1954.

Stern-Rubarth, Edgar, 'Ihnen wurde England zur Heimat', *Europa*, vol. 13, 1962.

Storey, Graham, *Reuters Century 1851–1951*, London, 1951.

Summers, Anne, 'Militarism in Britain before the Great War', *History Workshop*, vol. 2, 1976.

Supple, Barry E., 'A Business Elite', *Business History Review*, vol. 31, 1957.

Syamken, Georg, 'Englandfahrer und Merchant Adventurers', *Hamburger-Wirtschafts-Chronik*, vol. 5, 1975.

Sykes, Alan, 'The Radical Right and the Crisis of Conservatism Before the First World War', *Historical Journal*, vol.26, 1983.

Taylor, Philip, *The Distant Magnet: European Emigration to the USA*, London, 1971.

Thane, Pat, 'Financiers and the British State: The Case of Sir Ernest Cassel', *Business History*, vol. 27, 1986.

Thomas, Brindley, *Migration and Economic Growth*, London, 1954.

Thomas, R. W., *Espionage and Secrecy: The Official Secrets Acts 1911–1989 of the United Kingdom*, London, 1991.

Thompson, E. P., *William Morris*, London, 1955.

Thompstone, Stuart, 'The Arkwright of Russia', *Textile History*, vol. 15, 1984.

Thümmler, Heinzpeter, 'Zum Problem der Auswanderung aus dem Deutschen Reich zwischen 1871 und 1900', *Jahrbuch für Wirtschaftsgeschichte*, 1975, part 3.

Towey, Peter, 'German Sugar Bakers in the East End', *Anglo-German Family History Society Mitteilungsblatt*, vol. 5, 1988.

Trautmann, Frederic, *The Voice of Terror: A Biography of Johann Most*, Westport, Conneticut, 1980.

Vagts, Alfred, 'Die Juden im englisch-deutschen imperialistischen Konflikt vor 1914', in Joachim Radkau und Immanuel Geiss (eds), *Imperialismus im 20. Jahrhundert: Gedenkschrift für George W F Hallgarten*, Munich, 1976.

Vallance, Margaret, 'Rudolf Rocker: A Biographical Sketch', *Journal of Contemporary History*, vol. 8, 1973.

Varo, Stanley, *A Mercantile Meander*, Bradford, 1989.

Victoria County History of Essex, vol. 6, London, 1973.

Visram, Rosina, *Ayahs, Lascars and Princes: Indians in Britain 1700–1947*, London, 1986.

Wander, Hilde, 'Migration and the German Economy', in Thomas Brindley (ed.), *Economics of International Migration*, London, 1958.

Wauer, G. A., *The Beginnings of the Brethren's Church ("Moravians")
in England*, Baildon, 1901.

Walker, Mack, *Germany and the Emigration 1816–1885*, Cambridge, Massachusetts, 1964.

Waller, P.J., *Democracy and Sectarianism: A Political and Social History of Liverpool 1868–1939*, Liverpool, 1981.

Wallace, Stuart, *War and the Image of Germany: British Academics 1914–1918*, Edinburgh, 1988.

Ward, Adolphus William, *Great Britain and Hanover: Some Aspects of the Personal Union*, Oxford, 1899.

Weineck, Kurt, *Deutschland und der Deutsche im Spiegel der englischen erzählenden Literatur seit 1860*, Halle, 1939.

Weiss, Gerhard, 'Heines Englandaufenthalt (1827)', *Heine Jahrbuch*, vol. 2, 1963.

Weisser, Henry, *British Working Class Movements and Europe 1815–48*, Manchester, 1975.

Westerhagen, Curt von, *Wagner: A Biography*, vol. 1, Cambridge, 1981.

Widemann, Conrad (ed.), *Rom-Paris-London: Erfahrung und Selbsterfahrung deutscher Schriftsteller und Künstler in den Fremden Metropolen*, Stuttgart, 1988.

Willcox, Walter F., *International Migrations*, 2 vols, London, 1969 edition.

Williams, Bill, *The Making of Manchester Jewry*, Manchester, 1985 edition.

Wilson, Edmund, *To the Finland Station*, London, 1974 edition.

Wilson, Francesca M., *They Came as Strangers: The Story of Refugees to Great Britain*, London, 1959.

Wingfield-Stratford, Esme, *Before the Lamps Went Out*, London, 1945.

Wittke, Carl, *The German-Language Press of the USA*, Lexington, 1957.

Wittke, Carl, *The Utopian Communist: A Biography of Wilhelm Weitling, Nineteenth Century Reformer*, Baton Rouge, 1950.

Woodcock, George, *Anarchism*, London, 1963.

Worman, E. J., *Alien Members of the Book-Trade during the Tudor Period*, London, 1906.

Zemke, Uwe, 'Georg Weerth in Bradford', in Bernd Füllner (ed.), *Georg Weerth: Neue Studien*, Bielefeld, 1988.

Ziegler, Philip, *The Sixth Great Power: A History of One of the Greatest of All Banking Families, the House of Barings, 1762–1929*, New York, 1988.

(2) *Theses*

Jones, M. A., 'The Role of the United Kingdom in the Transatlantic Emigrant Trade, 1815–1875', D. Phil, University of Oxford, 1955.

Neumann, Maureen, 'An Account of the German Hospital in London from 1845–1948', B.Ed., University of London, 1971.

Pratt, M., 'The Influence of the Germans in Bradford', BA, Margaret Macmillan College, 1971.

Zemke, Uwe, 'A Biography of George Weerth (1822–1856)', Ph.D, University of Cambridge, 1976.

(3) *Unpublished Papers*

Bloch, Howard, 'German Immigrants in Newham'.

Newton, G., 'Notes on Germans in Sheffield'.

Quinault, Rene, 'A Note on Charles Bayer, Corset Manufacturer'.

Tweedale, Geoffrey, 'The Razor Blade King of Sheffield: The Forgotten Career of Paul Kuehnreich'.

Index

Index

Canada, 43
Canterbury, 5, 7
Cardiff, 115
Carlyle, Thomas, 206, 207, 208,
  212, 219
Carolina, 13, 14
Carus-Wilson, Eleonora M., 5
Cassel, 55, 75, 128, 207
Cassel, Sir Ernest, 74, 134, 140–1, 170,
  247
Caterer and Hotel Proprietors' Gazette,
  227
Cavendish, Lord Frederick, 182
Ceasar, Johann Jacob, 11
Cesarani, David, xiii
chain migration, xv
Chamberlain, Joseph, 211
Chapman, Stanley, 71–2, 139–40
Charles II, 9, 10
Chartism, 194
Chesney, George, 232, 233, 239
Chesney, Kellow, 117–18, 126, 127
Childers, Erskine, 239–40
Chile, 43, 54
Chinese in Britain, 95, 210, 256
Chitty, C. W., 8–9
Christian Social Workers party, 197
churches, German in Britain, 15, 22–3,
  25–7, 85, 93, 94, 99, 145–6,
  149–68, 170, 199, 201
  Birmingham, 164
  Bradford, 163–4
  Dundee, 164
  Edinburgh, 164, 165
  Glasgow, 164
  Hartlepool, 163
  Hull, 162–3
  Liverpool, 56, 160–2
  London,
    Austin Friars, 8
    Camberwell, 151, 156
    Christ's Church,
      Kensington, 157
    Deptford, 151
    Forest Hill, 151, 156
    Hamburg Lutheran, 10, 97, 150–1
    Islington, 151, 157
    Royal Chapel, 11, 19, 150, 157
    St Bonifacius, 23, 166–8
    St George's, 23, 26, 53, 57–9, 60,
      109–10, 120, 151–3, 154
    St John's, 23
    St Mark's, 157
    St Mary's, 10, 26, 100, 151,
      154–5

    St Paul's Evangelical Reformed
      Church, 10, 26, 54, 120,
      151, 153–4
    West Ham, 151
    Manchester, 103, 159–60, 165
    Middlesbrough, 163
    Newcastle, 163
    South Shields, 163
    Sunderland, 163
    Women's Church Mission
      Society, 157
    see also religion
Churchill, Winston, 249
City Press, 220
Clapham, Thomas, 73
Cobbett, William, 30–1
  Weekly Political Register, 30–1
Coblenz, 12, 55, 203
Cock, Edmund, 18
Cohen, Abner
Cohen, David, 28
Cohen, J. E. A., 28
Cohen, L. B., 18
Coleridge, Samuel, 206
Cologne, 3, 4, 5, 7, 54, 55, 117
Colpi, Terri, xiii
Colvin, Ian, xiv
Conference of German Evangelical
  Pastors in Great Britain, 165
Conservative Unionist Party, 239
Contemporary Review, 204, 234, 238,
  244, 245, 250
Conybeare, William John, 206–7
Corelli, Marie, 245
Crawford, John, 211–12
criminal activity amongst Germans in
  Britain, 76, 111, 115–16, 218, 223
Cross, J. W., 246–7
Crusius, Frenaus, 10
Crystal Palace Orchestra, 130
Culver, Robert, 76
Cumberland, 7
Cypriots in Britain, xvii, 1, 132
Cyprus, 1

Daily Mail, 104, 238, 240, 244
Dallman, Alice, 218
Danes in Britain, 10, 188
Danzig, 55, 106
Darmstadt, 115, 207
Dartford, 9
Davis, Graham, xiii
de Broke, Willoughby, 239
Defoe, Daniel, 29, 30
Deicke, Heinrich, 54

Index

Index

Index

Index

International Anarchist Congress, 196
International Association, 195
liberalism, 81, 146, 190, 195, 198
nationalism, 146, 190, 197–8
Royal and Imperial Hassia, 198
Socialist League, 197
Society for Mutual Support and
Understanding, 193
Whitfield Club, 196
Young Germany, 79
see also refugees
Pollins, Harold, 61
Pomerania, 48, 49, 57, 59
Porteous, J. E., 228
Porter, Bernard, 78–9, 228
Portugal, 21
Posen, 47, 48, 49, 54, 55, 64
Potsdam, 55
poverty amongst Germans in Britain,
98–9, 101, 103, 110, 111–15
Prague, 130
Primrose League, 233
prostitution, xvii, 76, 101, 102, 111,
116–18, 143, 217, 218
Prussia, 44, 47, 48, 49, 55, 58, 59, 60, 73,
207, 231, 232, 249

Quakers, 139
Quarterly Review, 238

Radical Right, 239, 245, 247
Recklinghausen, 5
refugees, xv, xvi, 33, 77–83, 87, 94, 100,
103, 110, 111, 134–5, 163, 181–2,
193–7, 253
British attitudes towards, 228–9
religious, 2, 7–8, 33
from Nazism, xiv, 84, 186
see also political activity
Reichardt, H., 191
religion amongst Germans in Britain,
xviii, 7–8, 22, 25–7, 53, 102, 143,
145–7, 148–70, 171, 178–9, 183,
254
Brethren, 14, 83, 167
Methodist, 156
Old Catholic Union, 183
Protestant, 7–8, 9–11, 25–7, 146,
150–66, 167, 168, 169, 170,
171
Roman Catholic, 115, 146, 150, 157,
166–8, 170
British attitudes towards, 219
Wesleyans, 166
see also churches

Rendow, George, 115
Rentoul, J. A., 223–4
Restaurateur, 227
Rethwisch, J., 90, 196
Revolutions of 1848, 37, 43, 44, 73, 80,
81, 85, 134–5, 193–4, 231
Rhineland, 40, 48, 49, 54, 57, 59, 62,
203, 237
Richard I, King, 3
Richter, Hans, 129, 130
Roberts, Earl, 240
Rocker, Rudolf, 82–3, 197
Roman Empire, 2–3, 212
Rome, 16
Roseberry, Lord, 172
Rosenkranz, A. E., 56, 57, 132
Rostock, 5
Roth, Cecil, 21, 23
Rothschild, Nathan Meyer, 18, 23, 140
Rotterdam, 28, 44, 67
Royal Academy of Music, 86
Royal Manchester College of Music, 129
Royal Military Academy, 19
Royal Society, 9, 17
Rubinsten, W.D., 139
Rüffer and Sons, 141
Ruge, Arnold, 81, 182, 195
Ruperti, Goerg, 10
Russell, Lord, 231
Russia, 14, 43, 66, 68, 83, 172, 231, 239

Sabell, Frederick, 63
Saint Andrews, 138
Salford, 90
Salomans, Levi, 18
Sanger, William, 117
Saxony, 3, 44, 48, 49, 58, 59, 60, 204
Savage, Richard Henry, 229
Scandinavians in Britain, 94, 194
Schaible, Karl Heinrich, xiv, 8, 22, 81,
182, 195
Schapper, Karl, 80, 194, 195
Schiller Festival, 187
Schilling, Frederick, 115
Schlagintweit, Theodore, 188
Schlect, G, 132
Schleswig-Holstein, 45, 48, 49, 55, 59
Schöll, Carl, 8, 9, 10
Schöllhammer, Fritz, 105
Schorlemmer, Carl, 76
Schröder, Anton Friedrich, 67
Schröders banking house, 19, 72, 140,
151, 155, 157, 163, 172, 174, 175,
177, 179, 191
Schunk, Martin, 103

Index

Index

Lightning Source UK Ltd.
Milton Keynes UK
UKOW01n0714210117
292579UK00010B/195/P